THE
BOOK
OF
LOVE

RETURN TO ONENESS

THE BOOK OF LOVE

RETURN TO ONENESS

SACHA RONDEAU

INDEPENDENT BOOK PUBLISHING

Duluth, MN

How It All Works

———————— • ————————

Before anything else, congratulations on taking this step towards helping yourself achieve a better life! Regardless of your personal, specific reasons for being drawn to this book, it indicates that you are choosing to improve your relationship with *yourself* and, thus, with the world and how you experience and choose to live in it. By unlocking your potential, you will see that life truly is ours to do with as best serves us, and consequently, find our purpose for being here on Earth. Life is a beautiful gift, and it is time to allow ourselves to see it and live it as such.

The purpose of this book is to help you realize that you have the power to shape your life however you wish, and figure out *how* to do just that. Some obstacles are in the way of these realizations, and the following chapters will help bring them to your awareness so that you may learn, shift, and evolve from them. The guidance offered within these pages will help clear those mindsets and challenges so that you can begin to see your true Soul Journey and pursue it earnestly.

Knowledge is power, and understanding is the key to unlocking our own power. These lessons will guide you into the depths of your existence to clear what no longer serves you and reshape your conscious mind so that it may shed its fears and unconscious beliefs, in order to be able to best serve you.

The goal of this book is to help you step out of victim mentality, own your personal power, live authentically as your true Self, allow in the energy of your Soul, step into your Soul Purpose, and live the most blissful life possible, as you will be flowing perfectly with the Universe and your own Truth. To achieve all of this, you will be required to have an open mind, accept hard truths about yourself and your own shortcomings, face yourself completely, and be willing to heal, shift, and change as required to evolve into your Soul self. The results you will get out of this book depend entirely on the time, effort, and commitment you invest in it and in yourself. The effects of these chapters are directly proportionate to the amount of energy you invest in them. This is true simply because you are the ONLY being capable of changing your Self and your perspective, and consequently raising your vibration to flow through life with ease *because* of the new choices you will be inclined to make.

The concepts found within these pages revolve around the unity, abundance, and benevolence of the Universe we live in, the power of self-love and acceptance, the true power you have in shaping your own reality, self-accountabili ty, inner strength, along with other spiritual concepts, such as the Law of Attraction, the Emerald Tablet, and more in what I call the Return to Oneness. One of the goals is to step out of the Egoic mindset and to adopt the "bigger picture" ideology and consequently have a more mindful understanding of existence.

What I bring forth through these chapters is a culmination of personal experiences and learned concepts from my own teachers and self-learning, amplified by direct Source channeled writing. The value of what is gathered here will continue to serve you throughout your growth and lifetime and inspire others around you to do the same in their own lives, simply by their witnessing of the changes happening in yours. I invite you to cycle through these chapters as they call to you once you have fully completed reading the book. Stay in each chapter as long as you need to fully comprehend the contents in your current vibration and/or state of mind, and do not hesitate to re-explore them as you move through the book and evolve in your personal journey.

As your perceptions shift, you will understand the material differently in a way that will always best serve you in your current reality. Certain concepts can only become clear when you are ready to learn them, which is perfect. Everyone's journey is different. Individual experiences and needs are different, pertaining to our personal Soul evolution. Therefore, there is no need to ever compare yourself to others and their progress, which is always done in a state of wounded Ego. Whenever you want to quantify your personal growth and progress, simply look back at where *you* were a year, month, or week ago. And always allow yourself to recognize and *be proud of* that progress, even knowing you still have more to do. We can always become better, so release now the idea that perfection is attainable. If we were perfect, we would have nothing more to learn; therefore, we would not need to stay within this existence. To be alive is always to be growing.

From this page forward, I ask that you shed the impulse of thinking ill of yourself, being hard on yourself, being unforgiving towards who you currently are, and especially towards who you *were*. Allow yourself to have been where you have been, be grateful for where you are now, and start getting excited about where you are headed. You have already recognized your own shortcomings and need for change by choosing to Master your Self, which is an amazing feat by its very nature of self-accountability and introspection. Now, we focus on uncovering your greatness and living up to your true potential, one step at a time!

Quick Reference Guide (QRG)

·

This guide will serve as a means to get us on the same page about varying concepts. Whenever you come across a word or theme you are unfamiliar with or are curious about, it likely can be found here. If not, a simple internet search will likely yield the answers you are looking for. Never hesitate to be curious and double-check your sources and the information given on the internet. Part of what we will be learning in this book is to uncover and learn to trust our intuition, to feel out the energetic Truth of things from a vibrational standpoint, unbiased by personal opinion, preference, or other Egoic aspects of Self.

This guide can also serve as a refresher, reminder, learning tool, or for the broadening of your personal understanding throughout the course. You will find them separated into two categories: requested reading before starting the course and extra material that might pique your curiosity or interest. It is perfectly fine if you do not adhere to or comprehend these subjects in depth; you do not need to. Either their understanding will come naturally in due time, or they simply are not part of your journey. Both are valid, and neither affects your potential learning and growth through these pages.

These are my understandings, from Source channeling, self-learning, reading, and experiencing. Take in only what resonates with you right now, meaning what touches something inside you and holds your attention or simply feels right. Resonating with something simply means that, right here and right now—in your current reality and state of being—it applies to you specifically or to your life in general. As we evolve, so does what we resonate with, and more importantly, *why* they do or do not resonate anymore. You will feel pulled to learn different things at different times. This is normal and part of evolving as an individual.

The Universe

Also known as Source, God, Allah, etc., it is the benevolent force of creation, the higher power that shapes reality as we understand it. It is as much a part of us as we are of it. Sentient energy that wishes to experience itself. Unconditional love energy that communicates with vibrations, signs, "angels," and energy. It is too vast for complete human comprehension; we translate it and access it through intermediaries until we can find and access the link to Source energy within ourselves on our own. It always conspires to prove you right in your beliefs and always gives you what you ask for and need, based on the vibrations you put out, not solely through conscious thought and spoken word. Gives us more of what we focus on based on our highest good needs.

3D reality perception vs. 5D reality perception

Whenever we speak of 3rd and 5th-dimensional energies, we are speaking about a shift in the perception of reality. In a radical sense, 3D is actively seen in our physical environment by our physical senses, taken at face value, whereas 5D is about the underlying energetic and vibrational layers. Truthfully, they are both states of *being*, 3D being limited to physical perception, while 5D accesses that which is not necessarily tangible nor visible as we know it to be in 3D. It is a higher state of comprehension, spatial awareness, and, ultimately, inherent well-being and support. Accessing the shift of perception from 3D to 5D means that we transcend the illusion of time (4th dimension) and see through repeating energetic cycles for what they are instead of repeating them mindlessly and endlessly.

Earth as we currently know it is in 3D energy, but we are seeing pockets of individuals rising everywhere on Earth who are creating awareness and cultivating the required sensitivity and healing to be able to return to a higher state of perception we currently label 5D; this is an evolution of the species we were always meant to attain as the human race. Individual healing and raising of personal vibration has the effect of raising the vibration of Earth itself, allowing for more and more people to wake up to the truth of ascension. We are collectively creating a great, worldwide grid of healing, unconditional love, and communal support to that effect.

3D energy is mainly about being stuck in what is perceived as negative emotions, such as anger, fear, judgment, etc., which are lower vibrational or denser energies to live through. In summary, it is what feels restrictive, heavy, and cramped, where there is no flowing with Life, only struggling against it. 3D is associated with Ego living, or being constantly in survival mode, whereas 5D is the Soul living, constant abundance, and unlimited possibilities. 5D is equivalent to thriving and being free to achieve what our Soul is calling for us to do, by breaking through the limitations of 3D perceptions of life.

Past Lives

Our Souls have lived through multiple lifetimes to learn what it is they were meant to learn overall about the potential of Life. We can understand a lifetime as a series of events preordained to happen (based on our vibration and Soul choices), which offers us the possibility of learning the lessons offered or not. This is also where wounds and false beliefs are created, either from trauma experienced to keep ourselves alive or having learned the wrong lessons (Ego understanding instead of Soul understanding) from specific situations, which ultimately affects us in our current lives negatively (again through our vibration). These wounds and false beliefs are part of what is keeping us from experiencing the abundant bliss of living. They are all meant to make us learn *different* lessons as we unravel them to heal.

It is all part of a greater, complex process to make us experience extremes and understand what we genuinely want for ourselves and our Soul evolution moving forward. The different epochs of Earth all served a purpose in understanding humanity and the greatest contrast possible in life, to know how to appreciate, grow, and want better things for our existence, both on an individual and collective level.

We must understand that time is a human construct and, therefore, does not exist for the Universe, though it serves its purpose here on Earth as a cyclical pattern to help us see the Truth of our own cyclical patterns. Our Souls are infinite and timeless, meaning all past, current, and future lives happen simultaneously with the express purpose of serving the Soul's personal evolution. The purpose of incarnation is to experience a lifetime where we want to face certain challenges in order to grow and evolve on a Soul level while also transcending the illusion of individual separation.

Past Life Bleeding

As a Soul, we have experienced lessons, wounds, and traumas that have "scarred" our Souls. It was important to learn these lessons then, but they now follow us into this existence and warp our experience in this life through false, deeply held convictions. Past life bleeding is what happens when we have a subconscious belief we hold onto, like an unexplained phobia or an unexplainable trauma response for a trauma that we have not encountered in this lifetime. It comes from an anterior lifetime, but our Soul essence still holds those experiences to be 100% true and relevant in our current life because they are happening simultaneously on a Soul level. We dig into past lives to uncover these false beliefs and traumas/wounds to heal them so that we may release their hold on our current life subconscious mind. We have to understand that what has happened in a past life is no longer accurate or relevant now in order to be able to release its vibrational hold on us. We do not experience future lives, as we are not "there" yet in our current incarnation, but they are also learning and growing from "us" as a "past life". The work we choose to do now helps us in future timelines and lifetimes as well as in this one.

Core Wounds/Wounding

In direct correlation with past lives, a core wound is the initial trauma or event that has scarred our Soul into holding a specific belief to be true 100% without question, which is repeated through all subsequent lifetimes until healed. As long as the Soul holds onto it, the belief will appear in every lifetime needed to be identified and healed. Hence, it is "bleeding through" from the initial core wound lifetime. The core wound itself must be identified and released for the Soul to heal; otherwise, it will keep bleeding throughout this lifetime and in future ones. These are necessary for Soul evolution to occur, as we cannot learn from experiences we have never had. We also could not process a singular lifetime containing all there is to experience in Life, as there is simply too much contrast required to go through all the different levels of Soul expansion and growth.

Soul Contracts

Souls come into existence with specific purposes, and to achieve these purposes, they often need outside help. Having a Soul contract with another Soul simply means that you and that other Soul have agreed upon an energy exchange of whatever sort for both of your benefits, regardless of whether we perceive it as a "positive" or "negative" event in our physical interactions. A contract can be as big as a lifetime partner or as small as a stranger giving you a random, much-needed smile. Every single interaction you have ever had with any living being is a Soul contract. The web of all contracts is so massive, intricate, and infinitely detailed on a gargantuan scale that it is impossible for the human mind to comprehend, much like the concept of the Universe itself.

Think of every single one of your random encounters, along with people who have been around you your whole life. Imagine threads branching from you onto every single person you have been around and encountered—from passing people on a random walk, to going to class, to having pets, to every single situation that has ever happened in your life—every minute of every day. Every event and interaction was all pre-ordained as needing to happen due to Soul contracts. Imagine every single past, present, and future interaction being a string between you and the person or animal involved, brief interactions with strangers included. This is already massive. Now imagine every single other human being, alive and dead, along with every single animal, all having that same scale of rich and varied encounters, if not more! These threads all interweave perfectly together in the grand masterpiece called Life on a global scale. Billions of people have trillions of connections worldwide spanning throughout ages, all serving the purpose of individual growth and evolution on a collective scale.

This intricate web of connection is our tether to the Universe. This tether stems from us, as a separate being, into the interconnected web of the Universe, experiencing itself through our physical bodies. Returning to Oneness means connecting fully with this energy and understanding life from a higher Soul perspective of infinite, intricate, mutual connection with everything, everywhere, all at once, always.

The Ego

It is simply our mind's self-awareness protection system. In essence, it is a tool meant to help our Soul understand its human living experience by being its interpreter/translator. However, it has become extremely unbalanced through current and past life traumas, along with the current state of societal conditioning. It is in full-blown survival mode, which means it is extremely reactive and fully controls all other internal systems, as it believes it is currently unsafe, threatened, and needs to survive at all costs (to Self and others). It is the equivalent of a system being in overload and overdrive, and desperately trying to recalibrate itself. This book seeks to show you how to rebalance and retake control of it (instead of it being in control of you), that the Ego may once again be what it was meant to be: a tool to help process the human experience instead of being the sole driving force behind all of our interactions, choices, and decisions.

Awakening, Ascension, and Raising our Vibration

I've grouped these together because they are similar terms describing different parts of the same process. Put simply, awakening is our "waking up" from the imposed 3D normality that we all experience in today's life, of going around as machines with a checklist of things to accomplish, of pre-programmed thinking and the inflexible vision of what life is portrayed to be, along with what it means to live. Ascension is the process of understanding the underlying Truth and current of existence, namely energy and vibration. It happens when we start to hold ourselves accountable for our perceived reality and work on our inner wounds to release all the energetic baggage we have brought into this lifetime. That release allows our vibration to "rise," become clearer and lighter, and helps us be more attuned to the Universe itself.

We are energetic beings, and the Universe always seeks to communicate with us through energy. When we declutter ourselves through the ascension process, it becomes easier for that communication to reach us, as we are more alert, in tune, and open to receive. The more we release the hold of the lower vibrations we allow to overcome us, the better we feel, and the higher our vibration can rise until peace and bliss are all we know of our current existence. This contrast is necessary for us as human beings to truly understand what we want and what we do not want in our reality. What we choose to allow and what we choose not to. It is all part of the process of our evolution as a species.

The image below shows a rough scale to help with understanding this concept. Alpha here represents 3D consciousness/state of living, while Omega represents 5D. Evidently, the scale keeps going up from there, but for the purpose of this introductory book to mastering the Self, it is not necessary to go further. Ascension is the process of shifting our current living reality from the lower, constricted feelings to the higher, expansive vibrations, as we were always meant to. To be clear, this is not about never feeling these "lower" emotions. It is simply the choice between carrying their weight internally or choosing to free ourselves from them. Ascension focuses on moving through Life as a matter of perspective, or mindset, while freeing ourselves from the emotional baggage and weight we otherwise never shed. The end goal then becomes to be able to live through a perspective of unconditional love and connection with all, of mastering our emotions instead of being slaves to them. This will be further expanded upon in the book.

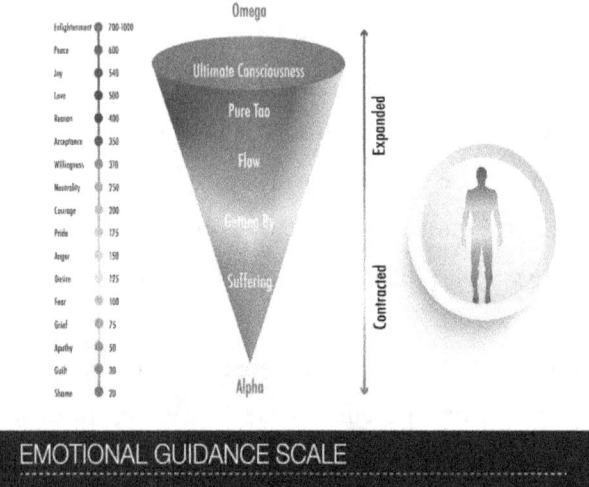

EMOTIONAL GUIDANCE SCALE

Being Centered

This means finding the place of perfect balance within. It means focusing on the core of our physical vessel, the true neutral point within ourselves. It is the default way of being, of existing in peace without external or internal influence and imbalance. It is the point within where we allow ourselves to simply *be*. We are not lost in thought, not feeling anything, not anticipating what is to come, but are completely in the here and now: the present moment. This is where we will find the most clarity, where higher guidance can reach us. It is a state of passive contemplation, where we allow the answers to come to us. We do not seek, we do not reach, we simply are and naturally attract what we need, including answers on how best to proceed. It is an essential step to master if we ever want to reach ascension.

The Human Soul

Your Soul is a piece of the Universe experiencing itself on a mission of learning, teaching, and experiencing human life in all its capacities. Each Soul created is unique and has its own personal purpose and frequency of vibration, which is called its Soul Song. Each Soul Song is unique to a pair of Masculine and Feminine polarities that are contained within One Soul (Twin Flames) and has vibrations similar to those of the Soul Cluster (or family) of creation. The creation of Souls happens when a branch of the Universe breaks apart from the whole into smaller portions over and over and over again until it is "small" enough to fit one vessel. Lightning imagery helps to envision this concept, where the end of the branches would be the creation point of an individual Soul.

Picture it being like a big piece that separates from the whole into a group of clusters, which separate into individual clusters, which separate further into a group of Souls, who separate again into smaller groups of Souls until they do one last separation, which is when all of the pieces produce a singular Soul that contains both Masculine and Feminine (perfect mirror imagery of the other) of complementary Oneness. Incarnation implies choosing one of these polarities as a point of entry to Earth since human bodies are not yet capable of accepting both polarities simultaneously within the same body.

Soulmate

A Soul created in the same Cluster, whom you recognize instantly vibrationally, without necessarily understanding why they feel so familiar to you. Generally, these will be close friends, pets, lovers, or anyone you have a strong, unexplainable connection or attraction to. Soulmates are people who will feel familiar and safe to be around. Note that it does not need to be a romantic attraction, though it can be.

Twin Flame

The two opposing, complementary Masculine and Feminine essences that compose One Soul. They have the same Soul Song because they are the absolute counterpart of balanced energies of the same Soul. In these times, we refer to these as the Divine Masculine and Divine Feminine Souls. They are essentially the Yin and Yang of the same Soul, split apart through incarnation (not both have to be incarnated at the same time; many do not), although both maintain their own equilibrium of masculine and feminine energies within themselves. Being in the vicinity of your Twin Soul is meant to trigger your own wounding and force you to evolve, as neither can hide anything from the other. This is like looking directly at yourself in another body (no need for physical resemblance), and there is this undeniable Soul recognition that is so strong that it can be felt physically by others (not sexual in nature, though there may be desire present). You are witnessing your exact Soul Self in another being, living through a different consciousness.

Because it is such a direct external link for us to Source, it feels incomparably amazing to be around this person. Romance is not necessary, though it is often the tool used to trigger the counterparts in their personal evolution. If romance is part of their Soul Contract, then it can happen if both sides fulfill their parts, but it is not necessary, nor does it mean that your Twin Flame will be the greatest love story in your life; that is simply not its purpose unless it is in the Contract. A Twin Flame can never be deliberately hurtful to its counterpart, as it is one of the purest, most unconditional connections of mutual love and devotion. Twin Flames, as human beings, do not engage in any kind of outright hurtful or destructive behaviour towards the other; they simply cannot even bear the thought of hurting you, intentionally or not. This bond is of the highest vibration of purity and cannot be tainted as it comes straight from Source.

Please do not mistake a Twin Flame connection with being infatuated, experiencing lust and desire, refusing to learn your karmic lessons, being stuck in toxic patterns and behaviours, reacting badly to not getting what you want, being rejected, and so on. Very few Twin Flames actually incarnate simultaneously, despite the current trend of everyone seemingly having one. Most humans are not healed enough to sustain this type of connection, nor have they even done enough personal healing to unlock meeting their actual Twin Flame, much less being one themselves. Only the most ancient and advanced Souls can handle being incarnated twice simultaneously as two separate, complementarily-the-same individuals, as it represents the last journey into Earth and the mastery of all the lessons that can be learnt here as the last fusion of True Return to Oneness.

Soul Purpose

The reason(s) why a Soul has chosen to incarnate. It can be not only to learn, but to teach, experience human reality, help shift the world's vibration, bring about more joy, experience contrast with previous lifetimes, etc. It can really be anything, but it is unique to each Soul. Some will have grand purposes, others smaller, but that scale is not something to compare. It is simply different, yet just as important. Some Souls incarnate on Earth as a vacation, to assist, or to do self-work. When all purposes have been achieved and all contracts held up, the Soul no longer has a reason to stay on Earth in this particular vessel. It can now enter the next phase of reality through death. And yes, someone's death can be part of a Contract they have with other Souls. Nothing is accidental or coincidental. All are parts of the web of Soul Contracts on Earth.

Karma

The spiritual principle of cause and effect. Attributing "good" and "bad" to karma is based on the duality fabrication of humans, when the Truth is that it is an equivalent return of vibrational and energetic output. Karma is not rooted solely in the choices we make in this lifetime; it mostly comes from energetic bonds created between Souls to become aware of internal struggles and triggers. We as Souls have all done both great and terrible things throughout our lifetimes with the higher purpose of acquiring experience. Now, we are entering a timeline where our karma needs to be balanced to create our own personal Heaven on Earth. Reaping what we have sown is the best way to understand the concept of karma. The energy you give out will always return to you, sometimes in this lifetime, sometimes in others. It depends on what your Soul has chosen for itself.

Duality

Duality, or separation consciousness, is human beings' default black-and-white mindset, where everything has to fit into a category. If it is one thing, then it cannot be another. Examples are good vs. evil, us vs. them, black vs. white, love vs. hate, etc.

In Truth, things are never one or the other. They are both. They are everything. Your perception of it, how zoomed in or out it is of the big picture, influences how you choose to react to it or let it affect you.

The truth is that everything and everyone simply are, and we are all one and the same. Everything is deliberately the way that it is and does not need categorisation. Humans categorize because it makes them feel in control. Our life experience is also our choice of how we choose to experience things. We can either categorize it to suit our whims to manage an experience, or we can simply allow it to be what it is without trying to stuff it in the box we want it to be in to explain something away. Forcing separation through categorisation with often hidden assigned worth is an Ego construct that keeps us from fully experiencing Oneness.

The Akashic Records

Energetic "library" where all Soul experiences are stored: the whole of your Soul experience, meaning past, present, and future. This can be understood as a database of everything that makes our Souls what they are: a compendium of all experiences we have had as a Soul throughout space and time. Each evolutionary planet and its incarnation experience has its own separate Akashic Records. It can be understood as an energetic space holding every "save file" of every "playthrough" we have experienced as our Soul.

Starseeds

Most people on Earth are Earth seeds or human Souls. They originate from Earth and are directly linked with the Soul of the planet. Starseeds are Souls originating from other planets, in other constellations, that have come to Earth to help in its current ascension process. There are also human Soul Starseeds and "mythical creatures" Soul Starseeds. Some people have Souls that are originally unicorns, mermaids, fairies, and even dragons (though these last ones are quite rare) from their own "home planet," where these creatures exist. What we know as mythical creatures here on Earth are living beings on other planets, which we have gained an awareness of through the existence of Starseeds throughout the ages. Some of these creatures even exist on Earth in different dimensional realities, and we can feel them when we are attuned to feeling energies beyond the 3D.

Lightworkers

These are Souls that have an advanced capacity for energetic healing. More often than not, they are "advanced" or "old" Souls in the sense that they have leveled up in their own healing and evolutionary Soul journey beyond that of the current human norm. This is what allows them to perform energetic healing. The term lightworker infers a connection with the Light of Source, with the Universe itself, and its healing energies of unconditional love. The strength of a lightworker is based on how little their Ego is in control of their current life persona and how aware and attuned they are to their innate abilities and direct link to Source they are. This can also depend on the specific Journey a Soul wishes to live through in this lifetime.

Ikigai

The Japanese concept of finding our personal path of bliss through living from our strengths and capabilities that best serve the world, along with ourselves. The word itself translates roughly to "reason for being," and it explains how a person can find their way to living their most fulfilling life. Finding our Ikigai can be understood as finding our purpose for being incarnated at this time by expanding upon how our uniqueness can be best utilized to help the world at large.

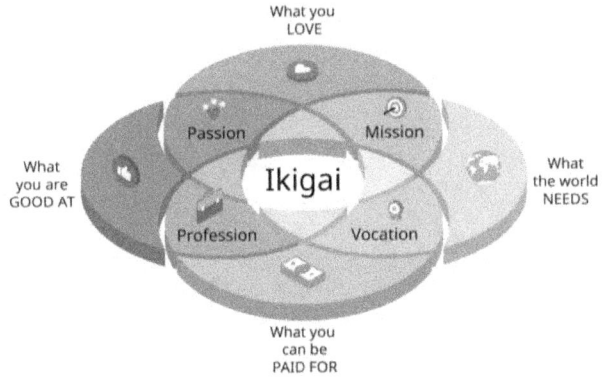

TABLE OF CONTENTS

———— • ————

PART I

DISCOVERING THE SELF

Before we can start changing anything in our lives, we have to understand exactly what it is we are working with. The person who is truly authentic to who they are will know exactly what works for them and what does not. There can be no hesitation because being authentic means knowing yourself for exactly who you are *and* not being afraid to always be free to exist as yourself. Authenticity to Self brings us to a place of deep inner knowing. In this state of being, a person becomes capable of living a very happy life effortlessly because they are not constantly sabotaging or betraying themselves due to various (often subconscious) reasons.

When we are not being our true, authentic selves, life feels like a hard, uninviting, inhospitable, scary place full of danger; living becomes a chore instead of the blessing it truly is. If you are reading these words, it means you have come to acknowledge that you want something better for yourself. You figure that maybe life is meant to be more than what it currently seems. And you are 100% right in that thinking. Life is meant to be easy and flowing. We are meant to have everything we want and need. This does not mean we never experience anything negative, only that it is not our main purpose in being. Through your personal evolution in these pages, you will slowly start awakening from the deep slumber humanity has been put under when it comes to the true possibilities of this world and our own power to shape what happens.

Congratulations on taking the very first steps on your personal Divine Healing Journey, where you will come to understand that life is a blessing, miracles happen every day, that you can (and do) create your own experience, and that everything can be fun and inspiring all the time, if you so choose. Life is not happening *to* you but *for* you. We will reach a point in the following chapters where that last sentence will not only make sense but also become a new default perspective on life.

The first step in this book is self-discovery. In the following chapters, we will dive into everything that makes the current you, you. We will dig into your mind, thoughts, heart, emotions, fears, and how your self-imposed prison is operating to find out how to unlock it and free yourself from a cage you may never have been aware of operating from within your entire life. This journey will guide you toward understanding every aspect of your current-day Self.

Understanding that this book is a safe space is required to get you started. These writings intend to hold a loving, nurturing space for you to face your own demons, hold yourself accountable, accept hard truths, and evolve from them. This is a judgment-free zone of self-discovery, a pillar for you to lean on, a refuge to shelter you, and a home to help you heal, rest, recover, and start over again. This book holds unconditional love for—and faith in—you. We know that you are so much more than you are allowing yourself to be, and we are here to help you morph from the earthly caterpillar to the divine butterfly that you are. This is your cocoon, your safe haven, your tool of transformation. Be at ease and be open to exploring.

Throughout this whole process of personal transformation, be kind and patient with yourself. Change does not happen in one day. It takes dedication, consistency, showing up for yourself, but also knowing when to take a break to recharge, heal, and get back on your feet, ready to work again. Healing comes in cycles: we dive in deep, we resurface with a bunch of stuff, we go through it all, we clean up the mess, we're exhausted and need to rest, then we get at it again when we can. Some breaks will be longer than others, and that is okay. It depends on the level of healing you have unlocked. Give yourself time and love, honour your progress, regardless of its pace, and give yourself a chance to learn and grow. It is all happening perfectly, and you are already amazing for consciously choosing to go for it. This is to be the process of a lifetime; a marathon, not a sprint. Consistency is key.

Lastly, keep in mind that this is to become a fresh new start for you, a new beginning full of amazing discoveries that bring about the freedom to just *be*. To exist without condition. We will be letting go of all the old energies, patterns, and experiences that are not supporting our growth. We will be shedding the illusions of being small and worthless. We will reclaim our personal power and understand our purpose. What you will have to face and accept about yourself may be challenging, but it will be totally worthwhile. We have to acknowledge where we currently stand to make any kind of forward progress.

You are precious and unique. It is time for you to rediscover that Truth and live accordingly.

I strongly recommend having a Journal with you as you read through these pages. You will be encouraged to write down all of your introspection in various ways. Writing down your experiences—your thoughts, feelings, and reflections—helps you process what's coming up and creates a valuable reference when we look back on where we've been. We will track our progress and revisit past states of mind often through this Journal. There are also numerous exercises offered within this book that will yield better results when writing is used for them. Your Journal will become a very valuable tool for you and your healing journey, the more you allow yourself to use it. Any blank notebook can do the trick. You will get to use it as you see fit for your own understanding of Self.

One last note before we get going: read these chapters as slowly as you need. Read one chapter once, then re-read it again before moving on if that feels right for you. Read the whole book in one go, then revisit the chapters one by one while taking time to process all of the information within. Read this book however you feel you need to. Revisit the parts that speak to you the most. Read it again weeks, months, even years later to see if there is more you can get out of it. There will be a lot to unpack and understand within these pages. Do so at your own rhythm, however you feel called to do it. This book contains both psychological and spiritual aspects. Use what works for you at this present moment in time and keep an open mind for the rest.

Without further ado, let's begin!

Chapter 1
Your Thoughts

——————— • ———————

The biggest challenge you will face while reading this book will be the interference of your own thoughts and programming. Therefore, they must be the first things that we start familiarizing ourselves with in order to work on them. Our mind is very powerful. When we let it run rampant, in control of our thoughts, actions, and reactions, we are essentially giving our power away to it. The first thing to understand here is that we are not our minds. We are not our thoughts. Both of these are essential tools we have been given to help us understand the human experience. We are the ones who control them, not the other way around. Unfortunately, we are currently living in a society that believes the mind is all there is to existence and that the brain is the driving force of the body. It is not. The perfect analogy would be that the brain is the engine of the car. YOU are still the driver.

Today's society also believes in absolutes, that one thing can only be one thing, nothing more or less. People stop themselves at face value instead of looking within, into the depths of the Truth held there. There is a lot more to people and things than we can physically see with our eyes, and this is part of the guidance we wish to impart to you in this book. We have been conditioned to never look deeper into things, that what you see is what you get. This is not true. A big part of this chapter will be to look within at what we have learned from an early age and unlearn what is false and detrimental to us and our well-being. As well-intentioned as our care providers might have been, very few people actually know how to properly care for their internal world, much less teach children how to do the same. We have to identify and let go of what we internally believe to be true (which ultimately does not serve us), to grow past these self-imposed limitations into the best possible version of Self.

We have to start digging deeper into things, regardless of how uncomfortable this can make us feel, and accept the Truth for what it really is, even when it is hard or unpleasant. We have to jump off the mindless "follow the masses" bandwagon and into our own independent learning system. We already know what we want and need from this lifetime experience deep down inside, and we also know how to get it, even when we are not consciously aware that we possess this knowledge. This is part of what we are going to uncover together.

This first chapter will help you think for yourself, draw your own truthful conclusions, dissociate from automatic responses, and become aware of your thought patterns and pre-programming, as well as your deeply held beliefs. It will also show you how to make your thoughts work *for* you and how to consciously move through the world in an authentic, genuine state of being.

The first thing we want to become aware of is the flow of our thoughts. What does that look and/or sound like? How does your mind work? What has become so automatic that it is now a thoughtless response? What are the predominant absolutes in your train of thought? How are your thoughts different and separate from your Ego? The Ego is strictly a tool for your Soul to navigate human life. Consequently, thoughts and emotions are also tools that the Ego interprets to understand what is going on in its physical reality. The Ego is *a part* of your Self. You are not your

Ego, and your Ego is not your true Self, as it is simply a built-in defense/survival mechanism.

This must first be understood and accepted before we can access and reshape our thoughts. We have to breach the mind's Ego barrier before change can occur. What is happening is that our Ego is forced into survival mode by our "modern" societies. It does not feel safe to exist in this world, and the Ego cannot cope with the never-ending, 24/7, always need to hustle/grind and be on the go, go, go, we are taught is life. It has been conditioned to believe that it must always be on high alert for threats, and therefore has been in overdrive for most—if not all—of our lives, overriding all other systems in an attempt to guarantee safety. The Ego is explosive, temperamental, arrogant, judgmental, quick to react, and believes itself to be beyond others; that it knows everything better than anyone, and is more important than anyone else. It is very much self-obsessed in an attempt at self-preservation.

Your reflex here will be to believe that you are not like that; therefore, this does not apply to you. The Truth is that you are. You simply are not aware of it yet. The Ego is never aware of itself to begin with. As long as it keeps itself in a triggered state, it cannot become self-aware. Confronting you like this through these written words will likely produce "negative" feelings within yourself, such as anger, denial, irritation, discomfort, disbelief, rebellion, self-righteousness, etc. This is normal. It is, in fact, your Ego responding to a direct confrontation of its existence. It is important at this time to identify this feeling of repulsion and anger at being challenged, as it will make the process of separating the True Self from the Ego that much easier to accomplish as we move through this book.

Your Ego will have the irrepressible need to defend itself whenever it feels attacked. It uses techniques such as deflecting, ignoring, blocking, attacking back, or whichever other tactic it feels gives it a feeling of righteousness, capable of pushing away any scrutiny that may be directed toward it. The Ego cannot contemplate being in the wrong as a possibility and does not tolerate any form of reproach or accountability. It has been inflated by a false sense of self-importance. It believes that it alone runs the show of who you are, simply because it is trying to keep you alive in a perceived threatening environment.

In most cases, the unchecked Ego manifests as excessive pride and arrogance, believing that it inherently *is* and *knows* better than anyone and everyone else. Or, it will go to the other end of this spectrum and act as the ultimate victim of its circumstances, which translates to a belief that everyone owes them everything and that things are never fair, that they are never given what they ought to be receiving, that others get everything easily while they always struggle, etc. This extreme, however, will never appreciate and be satisfied with what they do have because they feel they are always entitled to more.

The Ego also loves to stew in the belief that their personal pain is the absolute worst in the entire world and that no one could ever possibly understand them and what they are going through. Being in triggered Ego energy like this makes it impossible for a person to be empathetic or to think of others first, if at all. The more far-gone ones will not even consider that other people can be living a life just as rich, varied, and complex as their own. They will trivialize everyone else's opinions and treat others' experiences as inferior to their own, regardless of whether they have had a similar experience to begin with.

Evidently, there is a whole plethora of actions and behaviours between these two extremes of the same spectrum, but whenever you are in these energies, you are in Ego. Your position on that spectrum can and will shift as you evolve; you might freely go from one end to the other and even have traits of both at the same time, although there generally is a more dominant side. From my experience, the aspects we reject outright are most likely the ones we are in, albeit unconsciously. As stated previously, the Ego violently rejects scrutiny; therefore, if you touch something pertaining to it, it will immediately push you away from investigating further and try to force your attention elsewhere. This is the self-preservation side of the Ego. When you are analyzing your own behaviour, be on the lookout for immediate, absolute denial and/or rejection of the possibility that something could apply to you, especially when no time is given for actual self-reflection, nor to be open to the idea that "maybe" this could apply to me. The Ego cannot fathom being a bad person or doing hurtful things, and immediate denial and dismissal are used against accountability.

From now on, I want you to pay very close attention to what you reject outright about yourself, what you immediately disbelieve or overlook as absurd concerning who you believe you are; we are speaking here of everything that you believe is so far removed from who you are, things that you refuse to even entertain the thought that you could be, or possess certain traits of. Things that trigger you into feeling angry and/or annoyed, which you dismiss and believe are irrelevant to you before even giving it an introspective chance, are usually strong indicators of avoiding Truth.

I want you to make a list of those triggers, sit down, and actively consider what they have to say about you and what their very existence implies. This exercise will likely trigger you further. That is good. Whenever we are triggered, it means that a sensitive mark has been hit. It made your Ego uncomfortable, and it sought to protect itself. This means that whatever was a trigger is excessively relevant to healing your Ego, and there is a definite need to dig deeper into those specific areas.

When we are working on healing the Ego, we have to understand that it is impossible to do so if you do not choose to have an open mind about yourself. You have to entertain the thought that you might have been wrong, that you have flaws, that you are internally wounded by past experiences, and more than anything, that your Ego does NOT want to work on itself. It does NOT want to face itself. It is like a wounded animal that is pressed into a corner, attempting to defend itself by lashing out. It is terrified of what it believes will be a painful process, something that threatens its well-being. The Ego is entirely driven by fear and the need to survive. It does not understand—and is much less open to the idea—that this healing process is actually a good thing that will benefit it in the long run. It will ALWAYS prefer to avoid confrontation and run away. And it will ALWAYS see itself as a victim, never as the bad guy in any life circumstances, regardless of where the fault actually lies.

I want you to revisit your life and actively look for the moments YOU WERE the bad guy. I guarantee you that there are. Your Ego might have chosen to play the scene differently because it cannot stand to be seen in a bad light. Shifting blame onto the other party to present itself as the victim, justifying its actions through bullshit excuses, and otherwise trying to escape accountability are some tactics the Ego uses to defend itself. But we are all human, and we have all hurt others at some point or another, intentionally or not. We all know how kids can be assholes without meaning to. Some are assholes and mean to be assholes, likely because of what they learned from their own caretakers as acceptable behaviour growing up. Children mimic what they see and seldom listen to what they are told.

That is why YOU have to commit to your own self-healing. No one can do it for you, and the Ego will resist you for as long as it can. Dissuade you, cajole you into believing nothing is wrong, tell you it is pointless, that there is nothing to work on, that things cannot change, etc. The Ego is driven by self-preservation. We cannot villainize the Ego or believe it to be evil to excuse it away. It is simply a part of ourselves that was made for self-preservation, which is currently in over-drive and has taken over control of our human vessel and experience by making us go through life automatically on cruise control, instead of being asleep in the backseat where it belongs and where it is meant to wait for an emergency to awaken and its actual usefulness to be required. It has been warped from the Soul-serving tool that it is, by the need for survival, created and ingrained within us by this "unsafe" world of constant competition and comparison, lack mentality, and duality.

This explains why Ego-driven people are selfish and inconsiderate of others: it is the crab-in-the-bucket syndrome. It is the dog-eat-dog world. It is the everyone-for-themselves mentality that we are raised to believe is our only real choice because there is the widespread false belief that there is not enough of everything for everyone, that we must get to it first before it is all gone forever, and that we can never access any of it again once it is gone. The belief that we must make our own selfish needs come first because not everyone's needs *can* be met also exists predominantly in our society, but these are all lies. They are all limiting beliefs. None of this is true or real. We live in a loving, caring world, nurtured and guided by the Universe, and we ALL have access to unlimited abundance in every aspect of this life. We have simply cut ourselves off from it by disconnecting from the Truth of Self and the Truth of Oneness. This book seeks to help you heal and reconnect to that Truth, to Source energy.

Society today, as we know it to be, encourages that stressed, irrational behaviour from the Ego by running ads of "it's now or never," "one of a kind," "don't miss out," "hurry," "don't think, just do as you are told", which all reinforce that lack mentality. "If you don't get it now, you will lose it forever." It forces consumerism, with the "new and improved" exact same things in a different shell. There is no substance, no satisfaction to be maintained. It is always more, more, more, now, now, now. This gives us a momentary high and leaves us wanting more, so when the high runs out, we feel this pressing need to move on to the next best thing. This all triggers the preservation state of the Ego by making it believe that if it falls behind, it will be left to die.

This can be found in more than just the material aspect of life. Consider relationships. I have often heard that romantic relationships end because the partner becomes boring or routine. This indicates Ego because, since it is not experiencing a high or a rush of adrenaline anymore, the relationship becomes "unsatisfactory." A person in Ego will always want to chase the butterflies and have the feeling of "it has to be now." A stable relationship will be seen as a dangerous thing for the Ego because taking things easy means dying. The Ego in survival mode constantly needs stimulation to keep it going; therefore, being in a peaceful, non-triggering, long-term relationship is a threat to its existence. Cue self-sabotage. It is also why some people are addicted to creating drama and chaos in their lives, consciously or not.

We live in a fear-based conditioning and lack mentality society. Fear keeps us from being rational and stops us from feeling our innate connection to the Universe. From understanding that we are always abundant, loved, and supported. The Universe ALWAYS provides, but it is up to us to allow that abundance to flow into our lives. We are meant to have a thriving experience as human beings, but our fears and doubts always get in the way. We get in our own way of seeing, feeling, believing, and receiving the blessings from the Universe, yet they are always there, all around us. Often, all we need is a change in mindset and/or perspective, but sometimes, we have deep wounds hidden within us that limit our capabilities until they are uncovered and dealt with.

The Ego disbelieves this and chooses to sabotage itself just to prove itself right, while the Soul simply knows Truth. The Ego focuses on what is lacking. The Soul knows the Universe will come through, some way or another, and does not wait around for the delivery to be proven by wasting energy being impatient for their blessings to come in. The Soul just knows the blessings are always coming and keeps the door open. The Ego stands in the doorway, opening and closing that door constantly, and gets angry that there is nothing there yet when they open the door. Impatience is the Ego, believing it deserves everything right NOW. Patience is the Soul that knows things come when they are ready or meant to happen; it knows time is not what it appears to be and that, therefore, things cannot be forced into existence by Egoic desires.

We tend to believe only that which we can see and ignore the *potential* in situations because it needs to be imagined. We forget to appreciate where we are, which stunts our potential growth for the future. There is only ever the present moment and how we choose to be, act, and feel within it. Every argument that comes up about how we cannot achieve certain things, cannot have certain things (every time you decide something is impossible), you close the door not only to Universal abundance but to allowing it into your future reality. All of your perceived limitations are bars you are putting up on your own prison walls. You are the only one holding yourself back. Always. <u>No outside circumstance holds you back.</u> <u>Ever.</u> It is how you choose to perceive and work with those circumstances that determines what happens next. Blame is one of the biggest tools the Ego uses to prove to itself that it is a victim and cannot change things. Self-empowerment is knowing what is and is not within our control; therefore, what should (and should not) be our main focus and how we can operate despite perceived limitations.

As triggering as this may be to read, it is only an indication of how strong the hold of your Ego is. Take note in your Journal of your reactions and triggers to statements like these whenever they happen, how you are feeling, and what the event/trigger was, and keep a portion of your Journal specifically for this. Analyze what is going on within yourself, and do not be afraid to expand on it. What are you refusing outright instead of being open to the possibility that it could apply to you? Remember that you are never judging yourself: you must become a quiet observer of your internal workings and simply write down what you see/feel/hear yourself doing and saying, both internally and externally.

The more thorough you allow yourself to be in your journaling, the easier it will be to produce ease of flow and better results when you come back to it later on. Simply be honest. Also, use your Journal whenever you have something that "clicks" from these teachings, and expand on what you are discovering. There are no wrong answers, only possibilities, and we should allow ourselves to explore all of them to see what sticks and what does not (and what we reject outright). Push your thoughts further on paper, regardless of how "crazy" or "useless" you think it will be in the long run. Also, keep track of the emotions that come up for you on any given day, especially *why*. Were they triggered by a person, a thought, or an event? What exactly is the feeling, and why did it come up? Keeping track of your emotions and their triggers will be an excellent way to further the work done on yourself later on.

The key here is to always become a back-seat observer of how your Ego is driving your vessel, to become aware of it, to detect patterns, and to become impartial and detached within so you can find the Truth of things for yourself. We are spiritual beings, pieces of the Universe experiencing itself through the interim of human life. As Souls, we are infinite, limitless, abundant, and blissful in all ways. As Souls within human bodies, this is all still true, but the vessel is finite. Death is simply release from the vessel, not the end of life itself. It is simply a return to true Oneness, to share and integrate what was learned. The body acts as the vessel to the Soul, yet as long as the Ego is in overdrive and has taken over control of the body, the Soul has no room to operate. If the Soul cannot operate, we cannot access the 5D bliss of living. Therefore, we have to step out of that continuous panic mode by stopping ourselves long enough to understand that we are not in danger and that what we subconsciously hold to be true (survival mode) simply is not the Truth of our current reality, nor our purpose for existing.

If it is not yet clear, this is where you must realize that your self-healing journey cannot be done by anyone other than yourself. This book is here to guide you. It cannot do the work for you. You will find tips and tricks that will assist you greatly if you use them to their full potential. There will be examples of my personal journey to help you understand that you are not alone, that there is more than meets the physical eye, and that your intuition is the best possible guide for you to follow and experience the life you want to experience as a Soul; one that is benevolent and good for you.

This book also holds space for you to grow and heal, to realize and achieve your greatness. Only you can do the work required. All you have to do is want and desire the change, then follow through with resolve. It will not always be easy. It will get down and dirty; you will face your fears and demons, and you will have to own up to and accept harsh realities about yourself, but it is all with the intention of healing the Self for you to greet your Soul. We have conditioned to be ashamed of all the mistakes made in our lives. I am giving you permission to accept these mistakes for what they truly are: lessons for us to learn and grow from. We need to release the guilt we have associated with not being perfect at all times.

You will have to clear out all internal energies that no longer serve you, release patterns and learned behaviours, hold yourself accountable for your own shit and refuse to listen to your own bullshit justifications. You will only be able to evolve if you truly desire to. This may take time, but if you are here, it means that *you do want that for yourself.* Not only do you want a better life, but you also want to become a better person. For that, I commend you, I am proud of you, and I truly, genuinely believe in you. Change is why you are here now. You will be successful, regardless of how long it takes. Your own pace is the perfect pace. I also know that you will find immense amounts of gratitude for having gone through this book, even if it is just one read-through with none of the exercises used or applied. Because you owe it to yourself to want better for yourself, your Soul will always be your biggest supporter in your growth and evolution.

So, with that being reaffirmed, if we take into perspective that the Ego is a tool for the Soul's understanding of its human experience, and both the mind and the heart are tools for the Ego to interpret the flow of this life, then we must reason that the "how" of achieving 5D bliss of living is to start out by healing and balancing the mind (thoughts) and the heart (emotions). Like everything else, we have to dive into the deepest layers and work our way down; otherwise, the surface work we do will continue to be affected by the "corrupted" inner workings, the source of the pain. We have to take out the root cause of the problem to keep it from appearing again, just like ripping out the roots of weeds to ensure no more regrowth of the plant itself.

The mind and the heart are complementary opposites. If you only follow the mind's logic, you will live an extremely ordered, boring life, where everything is always the same over and over and over again. It will be sustainable, and you will lack nothing, but it will not excite you, and there will never be anything to look forward to, always just more of the same. Your Soul would be dying inside, and you would be ignoring it because it is easier to face the Truth of personal dissatisfaction and unfulfillment despite visually apparent "success" markers. On the flip side, if you only follow your heart, you will live an extremely exciting and fulfilling life, full of adventure and creativity, but there will never be any consistency or any kind of stability, especially financially. Though your Soul would feel better, the instability and lack of security in the physical world would eventually wear you down.

When they are healed and balanced individually, the heart and mind can then balance together in perfect harmony, where life can be exciting and fun but also safe and ordered. When they are in perfect balance together, there is no possible way of being unhappy, as they both cancel out each other's negative side effects. When this happens, the Soul can then step into being the driving force of our existence—as it was meant to be—because the Ego no longer panics at the inner turmoil that those two aspects of the Self caused by being at war with each other. The Ego can go back to its intended place in the backseat, where it can keep an eye on what is acceptable and what is not, and help deal with life in a helpful manner, the way it was intended to.

Let's start the whole healing process with the mind. How do we heal and balance that? We have to uncover what dictates our thought processes, as well as find the limitations we have imposed on ourselves and our own capabilities. These limiting beliefs can be rooted both in the conscious mind ("I've previously decided I don't like this, or that I can't do this, or it's impossible for me," etc.) and in the unconscious mind (you were told you were too dumb, unlovable, could never achieve anything on your own, past life trauma, etc.) and choose to never revisit the truth of these things. So, how do we identify and either release or change those beliefs?

First, we have to become aware of our own Self: figure out *why* we act the way we do, think the way we think, and perform the actions that we do every day, in every moment. We have to uncover our own conditioning and patterns that have grown to become our "normal," our autopilot, and to see what they truly reveal about our Self and our inner workings. We need to turn off cruise control and start paying attention to how we move through life every day, and the thoughts that run rampant in our minds at all times. Prepare yourself: we are going to be doing some heavy digging into our own psyche.

Our first objective is to practice becoming our own silent witness 100% of the time. For this to be effective, we have to be completely judgment-free of ourselves in any given situation. We have to start looking at how we react, how we choose to think, what we choose to run away from, if we seek out confrontation, how we view struggle, how we perceive challenges, and any and all seemingly unimportant or uninteresting moments of our lives. How do we view others? How do we view ourselves? What do we choose to focus on? Take a step back within your own mind and simply see what your autopilot looks and feels like. What is our inner monologue, and what does it show us about what we hold to be true? We need to understand where we actually stand regarding our Self and our place in the world, along with what we perceive the world to be, before we can know where to begin.

Next, when we become able to be in that silent witness state and become aware within ourselves, we will identify what we believe, see, or feel to be the driving force behind all of our choices, actions, and responses. The concrete *why* of these aspects and their reasons for being. This is especially important, as it will lead you on your road to understanding your inner wounds and unprocessed pain. We are not yet following that thread to its deepest hiding place, but it is proactive to start identifying it for now so that we may uncover patterns later on. These patterns hold the keys to how to best heal ourselves.

Observe yourself objectively for a week. Every circumstance you encounter—where you gain some form of clarity or understanding about your inner workings—every thread you uncover, regardless of how much or how little, every situation that triggers you and allows you to observe your own autopilot, whether you recognize it in the moment or only after you have come down from being triggered—is part of your healing. I strongly recommend you write everything down in your Journal as you reflect more upon the circumstances, especially when you revisit things you held in certainty.

Write down what happened, what you witnessed of yourself, how you felt, why you believe you reacted the way you did, what you believe it *could* mean, everything that comes to mind. Do not doubt yourself, and do not hold back. Write down all ideas or feelings that you immediately push away as improbable, unlikely, irrelevant, or impossible. Consciously choose to expand your thoughts on what feels uncomfortable or what is hitting too close to home. We do not need to attach any emotions to this process, choosing instead to focus on exploring the possibilities of potential. You do not need to get to "the right answer." We are practicing opening up to the possibilities of Truth. What is written may not be the Truth of Self once we do get to the bottom of things, but this will expand our open-mindedness, which we will need much more of before we reach the end of this book.

Write all your perceived observations regardless of how you feel about them. We are simply collecting data at the moment, so everything helps to identify personal bias. It is perfectly okay if you do not understand what you are uncovering. Eventually, with more data and cross-referencing, you will. Just remember to be in a judgment-free zone at all times, which will allow you to "watch the movie" of what is going on so you can dig into it for possible answers. Whenever you experience shame, guilt, or any other negative emotion towards this process, take note as well. This is likely your Ego showing up and sabotaging, but it could also be indicative of deeper wounding. The paper trail we are creating here will be like puzzle pieces showing us the true image of our actual Self in the present moment. And when you *do* catch yourself judging yourself, write it down and analyze the why.

This digging and observing will bring up a lot of potentially unpleasant and repressed emotions and memories, along with associations of things you did not understand how to deal with at a younger age, which you may have shoved far away in your subconscious mind because you did not know how to deal with them. This is why it is important to be in an energy of self-love and kindness as we uncover everything we were incapable of coping with or understanding as our younger selves. We must understand that those feelings are valid, but that they no longer serve our best interests. Do not fight against feeling them, do not fear what needs to come up, or the potential pain you may experience by revisiting them. Do not push them away any longer. Remember that these are all in the past and can no longer hurt you. What we are doing now is shedding light on why this all happened in the first place and how we can make peace within, as well as ensuring we learn and grow to avoid having to repeat these (or similar) experiences.

Whenever old memories, events, people, triggers, etc., come to our conscious minds, it is because *the associated emotions need to be processed*. We have been taught to repress uncomfortable emotions, shove them away, and ignore what is happening inside of us. Here, we are learning to let them express themselves without losing ourselves in them. You can free them and be free of them by allowing them into your conscious mind and observing them as a silent witness. Give yourself forgiveness for not knowing how to handle all of these previously, as you were not yet capable of doing that.

There is no need to blame anyone or anything, as blame is simply another form of judgment and refusal of Truth, or being stuck in Ego. This remembering is happening for *your* healing. We need to learn to keep all the focus on ourselves, especially when it becomes uncomfortable, because there can be no healing if there is no acknowledgment of what is.

The Ego will resist this process because it will feel completely out of control here. Just let it go, push it away, reclaim your true Self. Do not let it win by taking over and redirecting your focus elsewhere. Choose instead to forgive yourself for whatever happened, for not knowing any better, for trusting the wrong people, for not having valued yourself enough or held yourself in high enough esteem, for ignoring your own judgment, for not finding within yourself the strength to care. Whatever the case may be for you, always forgive yourself. Acknowledge your Ego, then put it aside and write all of this internal process down in your Journal. Write down every obstacle, every ambush, every little fight, in victory or loss. Because the Ego *will* win sometimes. It is so strong at present that it is impossible that it will not overtake you at first. Do not let this discourage you from doing the inner work.

Accept it for what it is (being human in this world), and keep going at it.

I also want you to start noticing (and writing in your Journal) when you are being harsh, strict, unyielding, unforgiving, and hard on yourself. This, too, will start showing patterns of inner wounds in need of healing. Choose consciously to rephrase and reformat those moments into ones that are kind, compassionate, encouraging, and anything else that you would want someone else to be telling you. We often seek absolution for our perceived shortcomings through others and their approval. Take what happened to you and flip it into the situation happening to a dear friend or family member. What would you say to them? How would you comfort and encourage them? How would you want to help them? Turn that advice, love, and support onto yourself.

Tell yourself that you are intelligent, brave, worthy, important, and worthwhile. Use whatever harsh thought you were aiming at yourself, find its opposite, and choose to give and receive that instead. True healing comes from loving and forgiving ourselves 100%. **You have to give yourself the love you wish to receive.** For no other reason than you are inherently worthy of receiving it. Because you are. We all are, and we all need to find our way back to that Truth. Just because we perceive ourselves to be flawed does not take away the Truth that we are worthy of receiving pure, unconditional love, especially from ourselves.

Next, we are going to explore the topic of shame and blame. As with everything else, the roots of our misgivings are *internal*. Never external. The reason why is that it serves our Soul Purpose of evolution and betterment. It is our Egos that always seek to put the focus anywhere other than on themselves. It cannot see the underlying truths and, therefore, cannot dissociate itself from the outside circumstances. It refuses any responsibility for its own state of being. This automatically puts the Ego in a state of pointing fingers, preferring to believe that things happen *to* it instead of *because* of it, much less *for* its greater good. This does not mean turning the blame towards ourselves. It simply calls for acceptance of what happened and letting go of the idea that fault needs to lie somewhere. This does not excuse unacceptable behaviour, neither our own nor someone else's. It does prevent us from *holding onto* what happened and forcing ourselves into the energy of being a victim. By focusing on blame, we give our personal power away and take our attention away from healing, which causes us to remain stuck in a looping cycle of misery.

It is essential to understand that every encounter and situation we experience is always happening for our highest good, as impossible as this may seem. They are never random and always seek to show us the truth of *something* resonating within to help us grow and heal. Therefore, when we refuse to acknowledge that we (our Soul) have called in this experience or encounter for the very purpose of raising our vibration by liberating ourselves from old, heavy, stagnant energies, we cannot subsequently release, heal, grow, and evolve from it. If this situation is not permitted to serve its purpose of furthering our evolution, it will either happen again (cycles), or new players will bring about the same situation to try to trigger the healing we are asking for vibrationally. Even the most horrific experiences hold a truth for us to uncover and heal. This being said, it is very important to understand that although we are not responsible for some events that take place in our lives, which can have deep repercussions on our state of being, we as Souls signed up to *have* those experiences to eventually be free from them on a Soul level. To shift from being limited to being limitless.

In my current life, I have been raped on multiple occasions. In no way were these experiences okay. I am not ignoring that fact, but I am also not holding onto the victim mentality of "I can't do anything with myself until these people come forward and make amends." Seeking external validation NEVER fixes internal problems. Was I asking for it? Absolutely not. But my vibrational energy WAS trying to rid itself of a past life trauma that was bleeding through. In a healing session, I saw a life where I became a prostitute at a very young age to take care of my younger brother and sister. Our parents had both died, and we were left with nothing. In that life, I had learned that my misery kept my loved ones safe; therefore, my happiness was unimportant. I did what I had to do to keep those I loved from experiencing the same terrible things, yet I felt such shame and disgust towards myself that I wholeheartedly believed I would never be worthy of love, not even my own self-love. These deeply held beliefs continued to affect me in this life in many ways—until I cleared them within that session. Being used for others' satisfaction—not only in a sexual manner—while ignoring my own well-being was a constant in my life as a means of self-preservation. I could never be disappointed if I never expected to be treated decently, and it did not matter what happened to me as long as others were safe. I was constantly self-sacrificing for others while receiving nothing in return.

After dealing with and healing this core wound, my entire energy shifted, and I was no longer randomly disrespected by men and women alike for any reason under the moon. Because I had healed and removed the root cause of this vibrational attraction point within me, not only have I been able to start loving myself, but all of my relationships have significantly improved. Today, I can recognize and completely shut off any and all forms of abuse targeted at me, although the more I have continued healing, the less these situations have presented themselves, simply because there is no more need for healing in that department. I no longer have wounded vibrations attracting situations to help me choose to heal. Not only do I now feel safe within myself, but I also tolerate zero disrespect from others because I now love and respect myself. By identifying, healing, and subsequently removing the belief that I was not worthy of being loved and respected, I have finally been able to entirely allow myself to *embody* my True Self.

Going back to the topic at hand, the Ego will refuse the need for growth, healing, change, and anything that it deems uncertain or unsafe (what it cannot control), so it will deflect anything thrown at it. It refuses responsibility and accountability for who it is presenting as and how it behaves and acts. That is why it uses blame to put the responsibility and focus elsewhere. This is often rooted in a deep sense of shame towards a hidden aspect of the Self. Whenever a situation comes too close to exposing this aspect, that is when the Ego becomes explosive in its need to hide from the ugly truth. It wants to keep its head buried in the sand and deny its own shortcomings. There is such great shame anticipated or felt by having its possible failures come to light that the Ego will reject the responsibility onto anyone or anything else. There is often a sense of guilt also attached to this.

We see people placing outside blame every day in so many different ways. People always come up with excuses or reasons why they could not do certain things, be at a certain place on time, or explain their mistakes (which seem to always happen due to external circumstances). This is not about proving their worth to an outside party. It is always about trying to prove their worth to themselves by believing that they never do anything wrong. This is a type of victim mentality as well, playing at being the victim of outside circumstances by choosing to place the blame there. It is often just not true and is a strong form of self-deceit, which can easily be recognized as being the easy way out of personal accountability. We are always responsible (directly or indirectly) for what we attract in our reality, and it becomes our responsibility to grow aware of the <u>why</u>, choose to heal, and make peace within so that we may be freed from these energetic tethers.

Whenever we blame others, either people or situations, we are automatically in the wrong mindset for growth because we refuse to be accountable for our own shit. The driving force of blame is, more often than not, shame; it shows up as an inability to accept our own shortcomings. This means that the Ego not only refuses responsibility for its actions AND inactions but also the repercussions of those choices. Placing blame outside of Self can be blatant and obvious and can look like: "This person never gave me what I needed to do this," "I was waiting for *this* to happen first," "They started it," "I was going to do it, but this thing happened," "it wasn't the right time," "I can't do anything without this thing that this person was supposed to bring me," "I can't control what this thing or person does," etc.

Whenever blame is placed outside of ourselves, we are denying our own truth and throwing away our personal power. We are affirming that unless certain things outside of our control happen first, we cannot possibly do anything about whatever it is that requires our attention. When we feel powerless, we have to become aware that we are choosing to feel that way by focusing on what we do not have the power to control instead of what is within our power to control. The Truth is that we are never powerless; we simply stop ourselves from taking the appropriate actions necessary to be in our power. You can always provide yourself with everything you need. Always. To believe otherwise is both a great disservice to yourself and your personal power. This does not mean that you should never ask for or accept help. It simply means that you cannot constantly depend on needing others. There is a big difference between being able to take care of yourself and allowing others to do you favors, versus not being capable of taking care of yourself and being dependent on others taking care of you.

If you believe that being able to see to every single one of your needs is impossible, realize that this is your Ego choosing to remain stuck in a victim mentality. Not only is it possible, but it is also how we reach 5D living by understanding that we are the creators of our own reality and can manifest anything we need into our lives. We will shed every learned toxic codependency trait that we were taught was necessary or "the right way" of doing things. This book will help you on your journey to becoming independent, powerful, self-sufficient, and naturally abundant on your own first, that your energy and vibration may be stable enough to attract a life partner that can help and share with you in an equal yet complementary fashion (if this is something you are interested in). The point is that we have to be able to stand on our own two feet and take proper care of ourselves before being able to sustain a healthy, dependable relationship of any kind with anyone.

When we speak of shame, its presence always indicates a deep need for healing. Shame is also a response to wanting to deny our reality because we cannot accept our truth or the truth of what is in our present circumstances. It is an instance of our Ego dissociating itself from whatever renders it uncomfortable and makes it feel utterly out of control. Shame often goes hand in hand with guilt, and our response is to push away and ignore (deny) what we perceive as what we cannot control, hoping it will simply go away if we pretend it is not there and ignore it long enough.

Obviously, this does not work, and we just repress things internally into our energetic system. It will still be there, in our vibration, but invisible to our physical eyes; therefore, the Ego will be content with that. What happens afterward is that more situations and encounters will be brought in vibrationally due to the previous cycle being pushed away and left unprocessed, as this unhealed energy is still present vibrationally and must be made visible once more *so that it can be* acknowledged and healed. Ignoring and refusing—or denying—anything will only serve to make it come back in a stronger manner. This is what creates cycles that repeat themselves continuously until the lesson is learned or the wound is healed. Anyone who is obsessed with control is, in fact, immensely insecure and wounded and has chosen not to face themselves.

What shame really needs is to be acknowledged and understood. Sit with yourself and seek to understand what causes the feeling of shame. Where is it that you put so much pressure on yourself that it becomes unbearable if not met with success? What expectation do you have of yourself that causes you to shrink and betray your true self if it is not attained? Have standards been imposed upon you? Were you taught that to be of value, you had to be and act a certain way? Does your behaviour have to reflect something you are not to be deemed satisfactory in the eyes of another? Dive deep into yourself to find these answers, as they are all contained within you. What you believe you must be is not who you are. Chasing after an idea of who we should be instead of accepting and loving the Truth of Self as we currently are is one of the leading causes of self-betrayal and shame.

Shame is also something we feel when we believe we have betrayed either ourselves or someone we look up to. It is a wonderful tool for self-understanding. Never be ashamed of feeling shame. See it for the gift of self-analysis that it is, and let go of what has caused you to feel that way. Realize that *nothing* in life is actually a Big Deal. Allow yourself to be human and be who you are without any kind of pressure to be other than yourself. When we can be grateful for what the initial feeling of shame brought us and thank it for the learning experience, that is when we know we have grown and evolved, as we understand that the expectations and weight others place upon us are not our problem, and are also none of our business. It is not up to us to be what others would want us to be.

Our job is to uncover and be faithful to our True Self and be who *we* are, as ourselves.

As stated previously, every experience in our life is brought on by our vibrational pull. Therefore, whenever we catch ourselves trying to blame someone or something external to us, we will stop and consciously choose to let go of controlling how we perceive things (Ego). Then, we will look at what this situation or person is trying to show us. What am I meant to learn in this encounter? What is being brought into focus within me in this instance? The answer can always be found in what is being triggered within us, which may be reflected back to us by our external reality. Witness what is happening within yourself because of this encounter, the effects happening prior to, during, and after the event, and Journal.

It becomes really important to use your Journal whenever you are practicing this internal observation method so you can write down what you are observing impartially. This will help you realize common themes or threads. To help you out, try to look at what is happening with the eye of an outsider, as though the situation or interaction were happening to people you do not know. When you revisit your writings about them, use this tool again so that it may become easier to recognize what needs healing if you do not associate it with being your own wound.

More often than not, simply becoming aware of our own patterns allows us, in turn, to work towards healing them and changing them to our benefit. There are some, however, that might be too deep-seated (or that come from past lives bleeding through) for us to be able to identify on our own. To heal them fully, we have to access the memory stored in our DNA. These will require you to seek the help of a healer, as we cannot navigate our own subconscious mind as of yet. Before we get into the topic of finding and choosing a healer, I strongly recommend doing more inner work first. In my personal experience, going to a healer when you do not know what needs to be worked on yields fewer results than when you have already done the digging and identified as much as you could on your own. Of course, sessions can bring up completely unforeseen wounds as well, but we cannot rely on others to do all the work for us. No genuine healing can occur if we do not understand the root cause and choose to liberate ourselves from it. It is our human experience, and it is up to us to choose healing and do the necessary work.

You have to bring something tangible to be worked on to a healing session for it to truly be worthwhile. This stems from the core truth that no one can do your healing for you. Healers *assist* in your own healing process. If one claims that they can do all the healing for you, it is likely a scam because no one can change another person, as we only control ourselves. These healers might improve things temporarily, but the clearing will ultimately be superficial. The wound will come back as unhealed because the cause itself is not addressed. If you are not made aware of your wounds, you cannot liberate yourself from your own deeply held beliefs. The "you don't have to do a thing" approach from certain healers may bring about short-term relief, but is mostly band-aids thrown over the actual problem, which means the core wounds are not identified and healed, and remain in your vibrational energy. Surface healers who "do it for you" compare to washing away the blood of an open wound and claiming it is healed. Meanwhile, new blood keeps appearing, and it is clear that the wound needs stitches to heal properly.

The next step we will start working on in regaining control of our own mental space is to develop the awareness to stop ourselves from becoming overwhelmed by anything happening in our external reality, along with controlling our responses to these stimuli. No matter what comes up, we have to always be able to keep a clear mind. This includes not losing ourselves to our fears, rage, anxiety, depression, anger, and panic; however, the feeling of being overwhelmed expresses itself within us. Emotions are tools to help us understand what is going on within us. Like the Ego, they are not who we are and should not be allowed to be in control.

The trick here is to start becoming aware of the initial feelings of those moments coming on so we can put a stop to them immediately. We can stop ourselves from having those experiences and episodes if we choose to. It is entirely our choice to give in to those feelings and let them overwhelm us or not. Before you try to claim that this is impossible, let me inform you that this comes from my own experience in dealing with severe depression, crippling anxiety, suicidal thoughts and tendencies, massive amounts of trauma, CPTSD, ADHD, and being on the autism spectrum. I know what these episodes are, how they feel, and how impossible it seems to be to surmount them when they hit. But they are surmountable. And you absolutely *can* do it. It will take time, practice, patience, and consistency, but when you start feeling like something will overwhelm you, you can choose to give in to it and let it run rampant, or you can distance yourself mentally as the impartial observer and watch it unfold without staying stuck in its cycle. From this place, you can choose not to let your emotions overwhelm you. You can learn from the experience and its trigger to learn how to resist being sucked into it the next time they happen.

It all comes down to what you consciously choose to believe is possible. Whatever it is that you choose to believe, you will be proven right about. That is how the Universe works. It gives you what you ask for both consciously and unconsciously, always (although seldom in a straightforward manner). So why not choose to believe that you, yourself, are capable of putting a stop to whatever you do not want more of in your life? You are capable, and you are already perfect, exactly as you are. You just have to find that truth within yourself, where it is already waiting and eager for you to find it. As perfect as you are, you are simply hurt. We are working on identifying and healing these hurts, so you can feel and be better in your life. It is a process, but it can be done.

Deep breathing is one of the best tools to use anytime we feel as though we will be overwhelmed by something. Practice taking deep breaths in through the nose and letting them fill up your lungs all the way down to the bottom of your stomach. When you think you cannot breathe in anymore, give it that little extra inhale, hold your breath there a few seconds, then release it all through the mouth in a noisy rush until your lungs are completely empty. The key is to focus on nothing other than the intake and outtake of breath, and to bring in as deeply as possible. Repeat this as many times as necessary for you to start feeling that the tension is evaporating from within you and that you start feeling yourself grounded again, feeling at peace within.

Grounding simply means that you can feel the energy flowing through your whole body, all the way to the soles of your feet, and through them into the earth beneath you. It helps to have your feet firmly pressed upon the ground to help you feel just how solid and secure you are within and without. Direct contact with the Earth, if you are able, always helps with this. The more you practice this, the easier it becomes for you to grow aware of what is happening inside of you. You may also start feeling as though "you" are floating within yourself, or a sensation of tingling moving throughout your body; you are feeling and tapping into your energy body.

Feel free to make a list in your Journal of your triggers and what overwhelms you. Write about what comes up when you observe things impartially, along with any other information that you gather. The more you write down, the more you will have to work with when you revisit your notes. From there, you can really look into the driving force and the root cause behind them all. Write down what you believe explains all of your outbursts. Why do you react so strongly to certain things? What is the root of the triggers? Explore and never worry about potentially being wrong. The idea is to be curious and allow for multiple answers to come through so that the Truth may eventually appear.

Write down everything that comes to mind, especially those you hesitate to include or flat-out disregard. Nothing is too silly or too out there. Learn to listen to how your body can communicate with you. These will become your biggest clues into what is really going on deep down. Remember the concept of shame and blame for this, as it will show you where you choose to place blame outside of yourself and, therefore, disown that part of yourself. What do these reveal about you? We can use everything we observe as tools to further our own understanding of Self.

This can look like: "My ex abandoned me," "I feel like my friends and family never contact me," "I feel like my father controls me," "I'm incapable of working if this person is around," etc. In all these instances, we are giving away our personal power by choosing to create an obstacle for ourselves. These are instances where we choose to take something personally instead of accepting things for what they are and establishing healthy boundaries for ourselves when we decide what we will not tolerate anymore. One of the biggest illusions we have to face is the idea that anyone has any power over us. We always decide how much by allowing certain people to get away with things. Often, we tolerate terrible behaviour for the sake of family or friendship, to preserve a bond, but all this does is show how we accept external disrespect. If you wish for things to change, never wait for someone to do it for you. If you do not like someone's behaviour towards you, then do not allow or tolerate it. Stand up for yourself or remove yourself entirely. Always choose yourself when faced with disrespect or abuse, and recognize when you are the one doing it to another.

Good intentions are meaningless when faced with results and consequences.

Additionally, what we choose to believe about others is a direct reflection of what we believe to be true for ourselves. Using the previous examples, when we feel abandoned, it is usually because we are not showing up for ourselves or believe we are not enough or capable on our own. We have to show up for ourselves first, always, before someone else can show up for us, often unexpectedly. Neediness is an extremely repulsive energy to be in. We need to become authentic to who we truly are and examine ourselves thoroughly to see where we fall short of being able to care for ourselves. Whatever we take personally is something that has triggered an inner wound of ours, so use those instances to learn about yourself and uncover subconscious beliefs and patterns.

Sit in absolute silence and stillness with yourself and your experiences. Go over them bit by bit, analyzing your behaviour and responses as you go. If you need to pause and rewind, go ahead; make sure you are extracting as much inner knowledge as possible. Details are important. Since this is all being reprocessed in your mind, you can play it over and over again as you need to understand yourself. When you start drifting into justification and analyzing others' behaviours and responses, you forget that **you** have to always be the focus of your self-analysis. Otherwise, it defeats the purpose, and it becomes blaming. Seeking to understand another through this process is the next step of this exercise, but it will never be accurate if self-understanding is not mastered first. Do not fall prey to the belief that you can read others well if you are unaware of your own True Self.

We have to deeply understand that we cannot change another person, no matter how much or how hard we try; it is simply impossible. We can only ever change ourselves. Even if we do all the work for them and lay it all out in a perfectly crafted, in-depth, explanatory essay, they will not get it and not change simply because it does not come from their own personal desire to grow and evolve. The odds are that they will not even bother reading it. So, do not waste your time wanting others to change and be different. This is controlling behaviour and serves no one. Look at what this behaviour truthfully says about you. Keep the focus on you and your own journey of inner transformation, and give others the grace of choosing that for themselves by seeing the results play out with you in your own life.

It is extremely important for us to sit with ourselves in silence as often as possible to truly be able to hear, feel, and process our emotions, situations, encounters, and triggers. Whatever makes us uncomfortable is something that needs our attention. We process things to understand and release the hold they have on us otherwise. Sweeping anything under the rug is pointless, as even if you are not seeing it or feeling it directly, it is still present and now affects you subconsciously. You only changed your own awareness of how it affects you. Some situations will hit you stronger than others, and that is okay. Do not fight these things. Let them show you what they want to show you, accept them for exactly what they are, and then consciously choose to let them go and move on.

This exercise is something to do a few times a day consciously, with repeating scenarios (for as long as they are still in your vibration) and new ones, but *always* honour what wants to come up. It is coming up for a reason. You also do not need to wait for an event to happen or a trigger to pop things up; you can do this when you are completely calm and relaxed. Continuously revisiting and becoming aware of what wants to come up is a practice of self-care and self-healing. One that should be done regularly without obsessing over it. We are talking here of memories, emotions, and events that are always in the back of our minds, wanting to be witnessed.

If a certain memory keeps revisiting you, it is because there is something there that requires your attention. Suppose it is a memory you thought you had already dealt with, and you are not sure why it keeps coming back to your awareness. In that case, it may mean that you are now capable of seeing what happened in a whole new light, which will grant a different perspective, which will allow for deeper uncovering of hidden wounds. One given situation can be the carrier of multiple wounds, but there may be layers that need to be uncovered in their own turn, layers that are hiding underneath other layers of wounding, which can only be accessed through multiple rounds of revisiting and healing.

It may be a good idea for you to go over this chapter and revisit every concept and tool a few times before we move on to the next one. Take time to practice doing this inner investigation work, get comfortable with the process, and grant yourself the grace to be curious about your own inner workings. These are the foundational healing roots we will be growing for our self-healing journey, and you should make sure that they are growing healthy and strong. Just like a tree, we need strong roots and a strong foundation to support us as we elevate and rebuild ourselves in order to grow and expand upwards into our true potential in life.

I know how scary it can be to face ourselves, as we do not necessarily know what is going to come up, and we might not like what we discover. That is why it is so important to do the work judgment-free and to identify our Ego when it tries to stop us. The Ego needs to feel in control, whereas the Soul knows that whatever happens is always for our highest good. We have to identify both our Ego and its survival mechanisms to be able to surrender the need for control and the perceived amount of safety they both require from us to function. Know that you are always safe in the Universe, *especially* when you are undertaking self-healing. Healing is a major part of why we are all here now as human beings. It is not always an easy or pleasant journey, but it will help you build resilience and help you learn how to be comfortable within your own body. Healing allows us to become our true selves, and being our true selves is when we understand how magical life truly is. Until then, life may look very bleak, scary, or unsafe. The good news is that we all have the power to make this shift happen. We just have to choose it.

Thank you so much for choosing to be brave and to confront yourself and your own bullshit. You are exactly where you need to be. Go through this book at your own pace and take the necessary time to adjust to the guidance offered, even if you do not comprehend everything right off the bat. Understanding will come in time when your Soul has enough room within you to start coming in strongly. All is perfect. You are perfect and worthwhile. Choose to keep at it. Keep choosing You.

Chapter 2
Your Emotions

———————— • ————————

In the previous chapter, we touched on emotions a bit already. Triggers tend to result in emotional discharges that can overwhelm us if we do not stop them. The best way to deal with overwhelm is to distance ourselves mentally and consciously choose to pull out of the emotion. We can help the mental process by physically removing ourselves from the situation to cool off and regain control internally.

The first thing to understand about our emotions is that they are a response to a trigger in our environment, regardless of whether that trigger is positive or negative. This means that *we* are *not* our emotions. Just like the mind and thoughts, emotions are a tool for us to comprehend our human experience. In this day and age, we have a tendency to want to lose ourselves completely in what we are experiencing emotionally because we believe that we will never again experience the same thing once this moment is gone.

This is not true. We can consciously choose to place ourselves in any given emotion at any time, just as we can choose not to forget ourselves in our experience of an emotion.

This creates the effect of us going through life experiencing monstrous highs and destructive lows. The true essence of a human being is to be neutral, content, and at peace in the present moment. This means that we cannot stay in constant energy of a high (or feeling really good) unless our balanced, centered point is already raised that high in our own internal vibrational levels, which would make the "high" our default point of being, our neutral point of inner stability. This means that when our natural center is in low vibrational energy, we chase after highs to feel better. However, since our centered point is so low, we come back down to our natural vibrational state energy by default. Like an elastic band, this means we often experience coming back to our center as a deep plunge, bringing us down deeper than our center point until it comes back again and stabilizes.

Healing the Self is the key to raising our vibrational frequency so we can stay naturally in the higher vibrational "good" feelings of love, joy, and peace as our neutral, centered point of being. **Please refer to the**

QRG image in the Awakening, Ascension, and Raising our Vibration section to help you grasp this concept. Imagine your center point to be at the fear level. Now imagine how high you need to go to reach joy and how big of a drop it is to come back to your centered energy point. We then constantly chase highs because returning to our neutral state of being feels terrible when we are stuck in low vibrational energies.

We have to understand that there is nothing inherently wrong with having highs and lows. They both serve their purpose in our existence to help us understand what we want and what we do not want more of. We just have to learn to accept things as they come, for exactly what they are, and strive to understand what they are trying to teach us. When we try to fight against our circumstances and control either other people or outcomes, we are completely in Ego. Since we know that our Ego is currently in survival mode, we also know its (and by default, our) center point is rooted in fear. We heal ourselves so that our center point can be higher vibrationally, so that we can feel better overall in our natural state of being.

The need to control and make things happen the way we want—without allowing space for anything else—is a defense mechanism of the Ego, which assumes that if things don't happen exactly as it wants, then only much worse outcomes can follow. The Ego always believes it has to safeguard itself. Our goal in this chapter is to stop fighting our emotions when they arise and simply accept them for exactly what they are. Our emotions are always valid. Imposing them onto others because of a lack of self-control, however, is not.

Since we already know that we cannot change others, regardless of how hard we try, and that, therefore, the only way to change our outside reality is to focus on changing our inside reality, we also cannot manipulate the outside perception of Self into being what we would want it to be. People will see you only as deeply as they can see themselves. The same is true for how you view others. With this being said, wanting to change yourself to please outside perception will never bring you happiness. Any change that is not authentic to Self-Truth in its desire to exist will not be sustainable because its foundation is not solid enough to endure. It will have no substance, no permanent drive to keep it going, and this desire for change will ultimately fade or be content to revert to its original state.

People pleasing to get outside approval will only ever end up being a lie we tell ourselves and others about who we truly are, to please others, to feel accepted. This lie automatically creates a false perception of us that requires work and energy to maintain, and will also engineer certain expectations about how we are meant to be and behave. These expectations will be fueled not only by the people around us but especially by ourselves as we try to keep up with all of the personas that have been invented like this so far in our lives in order to fit in and be accepted. This adds more stress and wastes more energy towards creating and maintaining a false Self, which we must remember to be, instead of living the ease of being our true Self authentically. Lack of authenticity creates a strain within us that becomes heavier and heavier the more we try to sustain it. This leads to feeling resentment towards life not being what we truly want it to be, but how could it be what we actually want when we reject our own Truth? Forcing ourselves through the motions of an existence that does not satisfy our Soul, our very being, will always bring about internal conflict and misery. The key to living a worthwhile life really is to live authentically in every possible way.

Before any healing can be achieved, we have to release the need to meet what we perceive to be external expectations of who we ought to be. The more we try to control anything outside of ourselves—like people's opinions and thoughts about us—the less happiness we allow to flow into our lives, as we become inauthentic to who we truly are in our desire to meet these external expectations. The Truth is that we have absolutely no control over what others think, perceive, and do. Trying to manipulate those into becoming what *we* want them to be becomes an exhausting and never-ending war that simply cannot be won. We are truthfully waging a war against ourselves by choosing to be inauthentic and in Ego. The Ego is the only one that worries about outside opinion. The Soul knows our inherent worth and is completely unbothered by the outside world. The Soul understands never to take anything personally, as nothing external to us is ever really about us.

Therefore, let's turn our total focus inward. Let's discover what our emotions have to say about our own inner workings and the wars that are already being waged there. We already know how to distance ourselves from our perceived reality mentally to become aware of our current thoughts and identify our subconscious patterns of thinking by becoming the silent observer within. From the previous chapter's work, we are already analyzing what goes on in our minds in daily life—in as many instances as we can become aware of—and eventually seeking out hints that reveal our inner wounding. Now, we will seek to attain balance within our hearts and emotions as we continue our process with the mind and our thoughts. Doing this will allow us to dive deeper to uncover our hidden truths.

The best way to identify our hidden truths is to observe our impulsive reactions and learn from what they communicate about our inner workings. As stated previously, there is always a driving force in everything we say, do, think, and feel. These four components of ourselves are tools for us to understand what is happening in our external 3D reality, and to further understand what is happening within us. Discovering our inner truths and wounding will allow us to heal, grow, and live authentically as our true Self, our Soul Self. Living truthfully and authentically to the essence of our being means that we are aligning both with our Soul and with our Soul's purpose. By denying who we are and what we are called to do in this life, we are being detrimental to our Self and all the Souls we are meant to help out along the way.

Alignment facilitates our living in 5D bliss, and doing what we love and what calls out to us automatically raises our vibration. Everything becomes easier when we are not fighting against the currents of our personal desires for the life we truthfully want to live. The true battle is in accepting that we are capable and deserving of achieving everything that we can dream of. We simply have to align with the current of our intuition, allowing it to guide us along the steps that will take us where we need to be. We need to align with our own energy, allow our inner guidance to surface, and take the necessary actions and steps we feel inside we must take in the energy of faith and surrender. We need to trust without tangible, physical proof that things happen perfectly for our highest good when we follow our inner voice. Sounds easy, right? In theory, yes, very much so. In practice? We will get there as we progress through the chapters. Trust in divine timing (alignment) and take things one step at a time.

We can understand this concept as though the Universe is this huge lazy river, and we are meant to drift in it happily, stopping whenever we want something on the shore, where everything is readily available to us at all times. When we resist, we try to swim against this current and ignore that everything we could ever need is within reach if we just stop and look at our surroundings. What calls to us can and will be found within the easy, fun current of the Universe. We are the ones who choose to splatter about and make things difficult for us to see clearly. Life is meant to be easy and fun, although not devoid of challenges, which means it is safe to surrender to the current. When something is simply not working in our lives, we are meant to let it go. If it is truly for us, it will come back to us in divine timing, which is being in vibrational alignment. What is important to understand here is that what is truly meant for us will never miss us.

The reason that we find ourselves fighting against the current of the Universe is that we are in Ego, and the Ego believes that it has to be in control and does not trust that the Universe knows what is best and will provide. The Ego does not understand that the current is pure, unconditional love and that it will *always* bring you exactly what is needed, exactly when it is needed. Any belief otherwise is the Ego manifesting itself. In light of this, I would encourage you to start a list of moments in your Journal where you have felt like a victim of your circumstances and choose to see what those instances were meant to teach you or bring to you in hindsight.

The first thing we want to take a closer look at in this chapter is our impulses, along with what triggers their action or associated thought processes. What actions do you perform impulsively? What creates the impulse within you? What do you catch yourself doing impulsively repeatedly? Digging deeper, what core wound is the driving force (or forces) behind your impulses?

If you have not done so, I encourage you to read the core wounds and wounding entry in the QRG. Understanding what they are and where they can come from helps us see how they affect us and why seemingly random things affect us so deeply. These are, in fact, the driving force behind every thought, emotion, action, and reaction we have. We are always guided by what we have learned, regardless of whether the knowledge is in our conscious or unconscious minds.

Whenever we act unconsciously about something, when we do something out of habit, it is because we believe internally that whatever we are doing or saying is 100% justified and true to us. We never revisit beliefs that we hold to be 100% true internally, so regardless of whether they actually are true or not (if they are even relevant to our current existence), we act on them by impulse. We do not stop ourselves and gauge the pertinence of our thoughts, emotions, actions, or reactions because we do not see the need to do so, since we believe it to be 100% right and warranted already.

When we are triggered, pressure is placed upon our inner wounds, which causes a strong knee-jerk reaction. This always happens as an attempt for us to identify our wounds so that we can heal them. These situations are drawn to our reality by our own vibrational energy. Your Soul wants to heal, yet your Ego stays stuck in the illusion of what is happening literally as a physical manifestation instead of taking in the lesson and healing that is trying to be brought forth internally on a vibrational level. A trigger is always a call to our attention for what needs healing. Triggers are always about the Self, never about external things, people, and situations.

We can look at it this way: our internal unhealed wounds are open, and they freely bleed about. The deeper the wound, the heavier the bleeding, and the quicker, stronger the reaction to a trigger, which we have described as applied pressure to the wound. If we do not take care of our wounds, patch them up, and heal them along the way, we will simply end up bleeding on the people around us constantly, often without being aware of it. Obviously, this does not result in a positive response from those we are bleeding on and is rendered worse if they are simultaneously bleeding all over us with their own unhealed wounds.

Becoming aware of our wounds opens up the possibility of healing them, but the choice to do so is still ours to make and to take action upon. Most people will stop themselves at: "Yes, I have this wound. It's part of who I am, so YOU have to deal with it." Which is not only extremely unhealthy but is part of the victim mentality attitude we are here to shift out of. The whole idea of "I have been broken by the world, and now I have to live with it, and so do you" is a lack of self-accountability. We may not be in control of the circumstances that happen in our lives or of others' behaviours toward us, but we *are* responsible for how we choose to respond to these things. If we allow ourselves to give away our personal power and then claim to be a victim, we are only hurting our Self and limiting our possibilities in Life.

To understand this, it has to be crystal clear in our minds that we are a Soul on a mission of self-love, self-discovery, healing, personal empowerment, and return to divinity or Oneness. In turn, this allows us to understand that we have created Soul Contracts that serve a higher purpose of healing and learning, but it is

69

ultimately up to us as human beings with free will *to choose* to learn, heal, and grow from these events, or stay stuck in a cycle of Ego victim-mentality which is bound to vibrationally pull in similar events over and over again in our life until we do choose to learn and break the cycle.

We are taught to see struggle, loss, and other "negative" events as bad things when, truthfully, they are opportunities to learn and grow. We resent them, fear them, evade them, and choose to dissociate from them because of that conditioning instead of facing them and accepting them for what they truly are: an opportunity to support us and propel us forward in our personal journey. It is once again synonymous with the Ego trying to control the show and throwing a hissy fit because it cannot control everything all the time. If we had never encountered adversity and pain, we would never be able to appreciate the beautiful things in life, simply because contrast illustrates value. We could never become proud of our achievements because they would appear to be meaningless without having first experienced failure.

This also relates to personal wounding. We can choose to ignore the wounds and spend our lives in the victim mentality of "Why do these things always happen to me?" "What did I do to deserve this?" "This isn't fair," etc. Or we can choose to face them, learn from them, accept them for what they are, and dig deeper into understanding ourselves and the reasons things have been showing up in our lives the way they have been. We can start to understand our subconscious mind by analyzing the why of our actions/reactions (the driving force within), finding out the root cause of those beliefs being pulled into our 3D reality, and reshaping them to become a belief that actually serves us beneficially.

To put things into perspective, our wounds are created by traumatic events in our past (in this life or previous ones), which have led us to believe "something negative" about life, which is being replayed repeatedly in our current reality so we can retrace that belief to its reason of being (the wound) and can understand that we were wrong in believing what we believed from that situation because we could not see the bigger picture then. As we were not meant to *because* we had to experience that end of the spectrum to understand, as a Soul, that it is not something we want in our next life experiences. The event itself becomes insignificant, yet *learning from it* is the goal and was the very reason for the event to need to take place.

If it had never happened, we could not now use it as a means to further our understanding of life and Soul evolution. This is the motive behind the saying that "everything happens for a reason." Our Ego sees in too small a fashion to be able to really understand the whole picture, while the Soul knows the Truth of it. The Ego focuses on the unpleasantness of what had to happen, while the Soul understands the higher purpose behind it, which is to create a strong contrast for true appreciation and gratitude to occur. If we never experience the ugly, we cannot truly appreciate the beauty. If we never experience the pain and the solitude, we cannot truly appreciate the joy and abundance of life. We have to experience what we do not want to uncover the truth about what we do want.

This being said, we have to get to a point where we can take accountability for all the blood we have (unconsciously) spilled all around us in our lives and how it can and has affected others. The purpose here is not to blame anyone or anything, but simply to accept what is for *what it is*, then make the necessary amends and move forward from there—a metaphorical clean-up of our spilled blood. To stick with the analogy, this clean-up can only come successfully from a place of healing since there is little point in cleaning up spilled blood just to keep spilling blood where we have just cleaned. Our own wound has to be patched up and bandaged first for healing to occur, both internally and externally. You would be surprised at how many people you have bled all over who can still be affected by that today. That is why it is so important to get over our Ego and see all the hurt we have caused others in our life, especially when we are not aware of it (or choose to remain ignorant of it even though we already know better).

The tricky part about self-healing is that, as explained earlier, we are not always aware of the fact that we are bleeding all over the place all of the time. We are not aware of our internal beliefs and how we impose them on others. We are not aware that our unconscious is dictating our perception of life, that our vibrational frequency attracts everything we experience, and that our chosen (consciously or unconsciously) mindset is what causes those experiences to affect us the way they do. The Truth is that life is always an outside reflection of our inner world. Knowing and accepting this means that if we can reset and reshape our inner world to our liking, we can then have the life we actually want to be living in the external world. Creating Heaven on Earth comes from within. It is an inside job, the results of which are brought forth externally from our internal vibrational Truth.

That is why the focus of healing has to be on our internal world. Beliefs are kept in the mind, while inner wounds are held within the heart, which is the pain center of the inner body. Connecting with our emotions means connecting with our heart chakra, which is our emotional center. Wounds can take various shapes and forms in our outer reality and stem from various experiences. Every single human being in existence has their own sets of wounds and will evolve at their own pace, depending on their free will choices, yes, but also if their current Soul contract with themselves requires them to heal specific wounds or not. Therefore, we can never compare ourselves to others to establish "how far we are" on our own healing journey. That is an Ego need for self-validation. Also, just because we are working on a certain wound that may have been caused by another person in our life, does not mean that they are also working on that wound on their end. We heal ourselves for our own sake. Forgiveness is a huge tool we will dive into in a later chapter, which expands on this concept.

The fact that you are here reading these words reflects that you are ready and willing not only to face yourself, but to grow and evolve from your doubts, fears, self-destructive behaviours and patterns, limiting beliefs, and, most importantly, to right your personal wrongs. Wrongs that you have done to others AND to yourself over your current lifetime. This is in no way meant to blame or shame you. It is an exercise in self-accountability. There can be no healing if we do not hold ourselves accountable and call out our own bullshit. In this book, we will be focusing entirely on the SELF. We may observe outside circumstances and encounters to understand our inner workings, but ultimately, these observations should always come back to understanding the Self.

Self-healing takes time, effort, consistency, resilience, self-accountability, self-kindness and care, forgiveness, and the willingness to be open and honest with yourself. It takes humility and perseverance. It requires you to be okay with being wrong and accepting the Truth of things for what they are. It requires us to dive deep into the dark corners of our true selves and shed light on things we would rather disregard and forget, things that shame us, things that make us uncomfortable. I know you are capable, and I

75

know you will succeed. More than anything else, healing is done one step at a time. It is something that simply cannot be rushed.

Keep in mind that healing is an everyday journey: it is a marathon, not a sprint. Things you will have thought healed and done with will come back full force and throw you on your ass. That is okay. Some days, you will feel amazing and powerful and as though you are perfectly healed; other days will have you crying in your bed for hours while you might not even know why. Those are okay, too. Healing is a roller-coaster of highs and lows until your energy eventually stabilizes into a peaceful plateau. Always honour what comes up for you. It comes up for a reason. Listen to your inner wisdom. Take what is given and look for the "why." Seek to understand, always and in all ways.

Going back to personal wounds, how do we assess ourselves in regard to what these wounds even are? We objectively look at what messages our thoughts, emotions, actions, and reactions are trying to bring to light and what they objectively reflect about what we hold to be true. To make this practice easier, I want you to start going through life as though everything is a mirror, reflecting to you something you need to see about yourself. Keep in mind that this does not have to make logical sense at first. This will help us gather the puzzle pieces so we can get to the full, complete image. Start noticing what makes you feel a strong emotion, then seek to understand why. Emotions are a great tool for figuring out our triggers, which help identify the deeper layer of wounding.

Furthermore, start noticing what you appreciate in others; these might be signs of what you need to implement more in your own life. The most wonderful thing about life is that it is so easy to make it better for others simply by doing things that make us happy. As cliché as it may sound, there is no greater gift than giving back. See how you feel about this concept and what it reveals about you. It could be that you feel closed off to giving because you yourself have never received it in a meaningful way, which could indicate a deeper wound in how safe you feel in the world. We will look into the individual chakras and the types of wounding that come from their over- and under-activeness in a later chapter, but for now, the exercises are about becoming aware of our inner Self.

What I will ask you to pay special attention to are all the moments when someone's behavior, actions, or words annoy you. Or a specific trait about them that just gets under your skin. Looking objectively at yourself, you will notice these traits are either something you do, an energy you hold, or exactly how you behave under the same specific circumstances. When we are triggered by someone else, it is almost always because we see a part of ourselves in them that we do not like about ourselves; one we tend not to notice is actively within our energy. Cue in the immediate rejection reaction to the very thought that we could be the same way as someone or something that annoys us, and hopefully, this will help you realize that this is a great place to start digging into yourself. Again, this requires great humility and a willingness to see yourself objectively with an open mind of "Could this be true about me?"

We are all flawed human beings, and there is no shame in acknowledging that. On the contrary, it demonstrates the will to become better. If what annoys us in others is not something we end up doing, and we can fully, 100% confirm this through thorough introspection, then what we should do is seek to understand why we were triggered in the first place. The purpose of triggers such as these is to spark self-awareness. We would simply not be triggered if there was nothing sensitive being poked at within us, like a wound, insecurity, or belief. This is why it is so critical not to be judgmental of what we uncover. Instead, we must be in the energy of self-compassion and self-love. We cannot change the past, so we must not hold it over our heads while we are healing. By all means, make amends to those you should make amends to, but also allow yourself your mistakes. Allow yourself to heal and become a better person as a direct result.

Whenever we judge another person—or experience a negative outburst towards them (internal or external)—it is always fundamentally about us. It is always a product of our own insecurities or discomfort. It is never really about the other person or circumstance. This is what I mean when I say the world is a mirror of self-discovery. In the same lens as our rejecting of things outright that we do not want to believe could be true about ourselves, when we are triggered by other people, we are actually triggered by things we do not like within ourselves. These things are usually aspects we are afraid to admit to and which we do not want to consider to be true. The Ego often uses self-deceit when faced with an uncomfortable truth about the Self it would rather ignore. It is part of the blame and shame game.

A person with an unhealthy Ego will believe they are flawless and will admit to very little of their wrongdoings, if any. They believe they are blameless in everything; they take no responsibility whatsoever in any aspect of their lives. They "know" everything, have all the answers, make no mistakes, and have nothing to work on in themselves. They always view themselves as just such a blessing to have around. What would the world do without them? Nothing is EVER their fault; they are always the victim. I believe narcissism and self-righteousness are symptoms of a rampant Ego. In this society, it is no wonder that narcissism is running rampant because it refuses to acknowledge its mistakes and to make choices that ensure the world becomes a better place. Our societies hold little to no accountability. Therefore, why should its citizens? Blaming individuals without understanding what shaped them is nonsense. As we know, there is always a root cause for everything being the way it currently is.

Until we hold ourselves responsible and accountable for our own shit, we are stuck in an unhealthy Ego. We may not live the entirety of our lives the way described above, but when we become defensive and feel threatened, we tend to fall into these patterns. It is important to learn to recognize these patterns in our daily lives. Start recording all the little (and big) moments when you can identify an unhealthy Ego in a section of your Journal, even if you can only spot it in hindsight when revisiting the memory of what happened. Remember that healing requires humility and 100% self-honesty, especially when what we uncover is unpleasant to consider. The first step for this to happen is to understand that we are all human. We all make mistakes, we all carry baggage from multiple lifetimes, and we have to acknowledge that we are not perfect. We have to open up and see where we have been less than stellar and accept that we have been in the wrong at times in our lives and have not held ourselves accountable for it.

Another key component of what you should write down in your Journal is everything that you take offense to, along with what you take personally; any (and every) kind of trigger you experience. There is no bigger indication that Ego is present than when we are triggered. Figure out the *why* of the trigger or what you took personally. What/how did it make you feel? What were you trying to hide from or protect yourself from? What "accusation" was perceived? You have to start understanding yourself at a deeper level for healing to start occurring. You will know you have healed fully when the same circumstance/thought/person leaves you indifferent instead of sparking a reaction.

I want you to start considering and opening up to the idea of being wrong. About yourself. About others. About the world. About your beliefs. About the stories you have told yourself over time. About the roles others have played in your life. About the roles you have given yourself over time. About everything. Opening up to possibly being wrong and broadening your perspective are both very powerful tools. They have the potential to shift your world upside down. They are also essential to healing. We cannot fully heal if we do not use and eventually master these tools. We will remain stuck in an unhealthy Ego instead. Believing otherwise is your Ego getting in the way of healing.

"What if I am wrong about _____?" "What would the outside perspective of this be?" "How did the other person feel about what happened?" "Where did I jump to conclusions or allow my emotions to get the better of me?" These are all questions to push further into your introspection and look for the bigger picture. We have to forget the Self to see the Truth. The very act of asking those questions is a step towards healing because it takes away the pressure of having to be right. It takes away the illusion of being a victim. It forces us to acknowledge that other people have a life just as rich, vivid, and intense as our own. We are not the main characters in other people's stories.

Any resistance you feel towards all that was expressed above comes directly from your Ego getting in the way, which means it is another excellent opportunity to identify it and start countering it. Ask yourself this question when you experience the most resistance: "What if…?" Where in your life can you affirm that you are so right you could never potentially be wrong? Keep in mind that there are billions of people in this world, all of them living a life as intricate as your own. Ask yourself just how many of us are experiencing the exact same situations, in essence, yet claim the experience to be unique to us and, therefore, completely impossible to relate to for anyone else. You guessed it, this is a huge Ego tendency. The whole "you could never relate because our experiences are not exactly the same to the last detail" trope is just that. An Ego trope.

Another question to ask yourself, which is integral to personal growth and healing, is: "How is this person/situation/interaction serving me and my highest good?" Remember that we are a part of the Infinite Consciousness that is the Universe. Everything that happens in our lives is always ultimately happening for our highest good, even when it seems the least likely. Everything happens for a reason, and this reason will often only be understood when we can access the bigger picture. Until then, the Ego will likely rail against the unfairness or focus only on the pain. Pain is (unfortunately) often what humans need to be able to grow. It is again the idea of creating contrast in life to have access to greater happiness.

We are incarnated today to heal and grow. Deep healing would be impossible if we could not access our wounds. Positive and negative, good and bad, are part of the duality programming of humans, not of Soul Truth. The above question will help you to keep this in mind as you observe quietly, without judgment, for answers and your personal truths. Keep writing down everything you observe about yourself in your Journal: the good, the bad, and the ugly. It will all make sense for you in the end as we go through the healing process together.

I want you to start looking at the possible causes of your triggers without setting anything in stone. Allow yourself to be surprised by your discoveries as you keep at it. Things do not need to make sense, but there is no harm in engaging in thought analysis. For example, you notice when people share good news that you react with envy instead of being happy for them. What does this reveal about you? What possible core wound does this come from? Write every possible answer without prioritizing any of them, making sure you write down those you want to reject outright as possible explanations. In this example, the driving force could be a lack mentality or self-worth issues, as in "Why don't good things happen to me?" It could also be a wound of abandonment showing as jealousy, where your needs are never met outside of yourself. Additionally, it could be a wound involving feeling powerless, where no matter what you do, you never seem to get what you believe you deserve. It could be a combination of all of the above. The possibilities might be numerous, and it is good to get them out on paper to eventually be able to trace things down to the Truth. This way, you will be able to start seeing trends pop up that will facilitate your investigative work.

Since we came here as Souls to heal and grow, we have agreed before incarnation to multiple contracts that will force us to acknowledge the need to heal. The way this works is not about one situation happening, and boom, all your problems will go away. On the contrary, it will start off slowly, with situations, encounters, and events becoming more and more frequent in your life until you notice the repeating pattern or cycle. We go through cycles of lessons that loop over and over again with more intensity until we simply cannot ignore them anymore. It has been my experience that the more we choose to ignore the lesson and stay stuck in Ego, the harder the hits come until we are forced to let go of control, accept the lesson, start healing, and move on. Letting go of control was probably my biggest lesson so far in life, and it took me years before I was able to embody allowing fully. So do not be too hard on yourself. You will never get it right on the first try. Take that kind of pressure off your shoulders and allow for growth to take place. We cannot harvest a crop the day after the seed was planted.

Like I said, healing comes in cycles. Lessons come in cycles. A single event that triggers you could have multiple wounds attached to it. You may heal from it once, but discover there are still multiple aspects to what happened that affect you differently. This is why it is important to keep track of them and dig into the multiple possibilities of *why* this affects you. You will be building a web of cross-references to figure out what kind of wounds you live with. All of this knowledge will eventually help you recognize a trigger before it overtakes you and your reactions, so you will be able to either stop yourself or make something better out of what is happening. This kind of awareness happens over time. You will change from being aggressively reactive to choosing how you consciously want to react. At first, becoming aware of a trigger can lead to simply distancing/removing yourself internally from what is happening so you do not blow up externally. This is an excellent first step.

Becoming aware of how we will respond or react gives us the time we need to change the course we were unconsciously on into a course that will feel better. We are not our triggers. Our triggers have something to teach us. Our end goal here is to be in a place of pure, unconditional love towards everyone on this planet, especially ourselves. That is the final destination. The journey starts with being at peace with who we are at any given moment, so we can evolve into a better version of ourselves. We get to that by observing and consciously choosing how we want to live. We will start shifting these thoughts/emotions, actions/reactions into loving ones. If you cannot hold space to be loving during a trigger, then at the very least, choose to remove yourself, regroup, evaluate, calm down, and choose to approach things differently. Just this last part is already a huge step forward in the realm of self-healing.

As stated at the beginning of this chapter, our emotions are tools for us to understand our wounding with the purpose of healing. However, there is a big tendency in today's world where people allow themselves to become overwhelmed by their emotions to the point where they will "lose their shit" on just about anyone. This looks exactly like a cornered, wounded animal trying desperately to protect itself. That is exactly what is going on within these people. Not only is it unacceptable behaviour in someone, but it is also a very telling sign of a very wounded person. There is a saying that goes: "Hurt people hurt people." It is also a very clear sign that we are not supposed to take anything others do personally because it is simply never about us.

Reactive people like that tend not to know who they are outside of their association with feeling "outrage," "anger," "self-righteousness," or whatever emotion they associate their whole personality with. Instead of treating their emotion like the clues it is, to look within for healing, they use them as a way to escape the fact that they hate their reality or themselves, refusing to acknowledge that their salvation lies within their own hands. They lack total accountability and responsibility. This is why it is so important to learn that emotions are messengers. We are not our emotions; therefore, we cannot keep allowing them to overwhelm us. The purpose of our emotions is to draw our attention to what is going on within so that we can process the emotion before releasing it.

At this point, please review the QRG entry for "Raising your Vibration & Being Centered."

Being centered and balanced means we do not live in excess of *anything*. Raising our internal vibration allows for our Center of Being to be surrounded externally and upheld internally by the more positive and good things in life. Our natural state of being then becomes lighter, easier, and happier. Raising our vibration and healing our Self guarantees an easier state of living, as it removes the "negative," the unwanted. This is why it is important not to hold onto our emotions. They are meant to be fleeting. They come and go because they are temporary. They are messengers. Clinging onto the good feelings or chasing the highs means we are afraid of letting them go because we fear we will never experience something quite as good as this again. By fearing this, we also prevent even better things from coming into our lives. The Universe wants us to live our best life. It is just waiting for us to get on board with this and actively work on doing the inner work.

Fear of lack and loss are two of the biggest reasons why we hold onto things that are honestly detrimental to our well-being. These come from the belief that the best life has to offer is behind us. It portrays the future as being bleak and uncertain, and that we are better off holding onto what we currently have instead of potentially getting something worse. There are also other fears and wounds at play here, but on the broader spectrum, it comes down to believing we are not worthy of receiving better. People are afraid of being left with less than what they currently have. They forget or ignore that letting go of what they have allows for something better to take its place, for this is the Truth of the Universe when we choose to heal, grow, and evolve.

This is why so many people are stuck in jobs they hate that are unfulfilling. It is also why people stay in toxic, abusive relationships and friendships. There is the common belief that having or holding onto something is better than having nothing at all. Let me ask you: Is it better to hold onto something that hurts you or be free from it? This type of thinking is based on fear. Fear always holds us back. We often stay where we are uncomfortable because it might feel safer than not knowing what comes next. We tend to assume that the unknown is worse than the known.

Our fears can help us figure out what kind of wounds we have. For example, the belief held from the wound of abandonment is often that we live in an unsafe, dangerous Universe that is out to get us. This is, of course, the opposite of the fundamental Truth that the Universe is unconditionally loving and accepting and wants the best for us. This illusion of separation is what causes the fear. Free will allows us to choose where we want to invest our energy and beliefs. When we know that we are one with the Universe, then everything becomes possible, and we understand we are always safe and taken care of. We will address all of this in-depth in the next chapter on fears.

For now, let's get back to overwhelming emotions. When we understand that we are not our emotions, and those emotions do not define who we are—that, rather, they help identify triggers—it makes the dissociation process easier. This means it becomes much easier to be the silent observer and objectively witness what is playing out in both our external and internal realities. We will come to recognize when we do not need to feed into experiencing a heavy emotion. At this point, all I ask is that you start noticing your emotions, which ones become overwhelming, and always, always, always open the door to ask *why*. It will take a lot of practice before you can detach fully to observe. Start with noticing what is going on in the moment, what the trigger was (or were), and how it progressed over the course of the situation. What thought or additional emotion came up to fuel the fire or, on the contrary, appease the situation? At first, bringing conscious awareness will mostly be done in retrospect instead of in the moment itself, until we start catching ourselves earlier and earlier and get a hold of our out-of-control emotions.

You might start catching yourself when you are already overwhelmed; do not worry about this. It is normal at first, and you will gradually learn to identify and build this muscle over time and with practice. Awareness is the first step to reclaiming personal power. Remember to always be kind and patient with yourself: you are learning. Progress happens with consistency and effort. Whenever you catch yourself wishing you were further along in your journey, recognize that feeling as being in your Ego. Impatience is Ego. Living in the past and fretting about the future both keep you from grounding in the present moment. We learn from the past and then let it go. The future does not even exist and never will, so do not worry about it too much. Focus on the present moment with what you want to see happen in the eventual future. There is literally no other moment in time than now. Where you are right now is perfect as is. Give yourself a chance and somewhere to start.

The most important thing to do when we become aware of our emotions is to breathe. Do not fight against what is coming up. Every emotion always comes up for a reason. Honour that emotion, sit with it, listen to what it has to say, then allow it to flow out of your body and into the ground below. Witness, judgment-free, the message it brings forward. It is time to stop vilifying and fearing our emotions. What we are learning here is to detach from the emotion internally to observe its message. Why are we feeling what we are feeling, when and where we feel it? Who is around us when this emotion comes up? Allow the emotion to come alive within you, but not to control you. Never deny your emotions, but do not succumb to them. It is very important to validate the existence of our emotions and then release them from our being so that we may achieve internal peace.

What does this mean in practice? Feel your emotions to understand them. Understand where they are coming from and why. Let's take a breakup as an example. In our first relationships, most of us enjoy the bliss of believing they will never end. We see the other person as an important part of our lives. If we get into a relationship without really knowing ourselves and who we really are, we tend to lose ourselves in the relationship and the other person. We tend to put our relationship first and attach our intrinsic value to this relationship. We put a lot of time and effort into making things work. In most cases, we stop being our first priority.

However, when a break-up occurs, it feels like our whole reality comes crashing down around us. My experience of the break-up of my first relationship was completely shattering. My whole world had been flipped upside down, and I felt broken. Unlovable. Worthless. All of these intense emotions were constantly flooding my system. For the life of me, I could not understand why the person I loved more than anything in the world (myself included) would just decide to leave. For seemingly no reason at all. He could not even give me a reason. He did not even know himself or could not admit it to himself; in either case, the reasoning belonged to him. Our relationship was honestly great. We always had fun, and we clicked on multiple levels. We never had big arguments, and there was frankly nothing negative about it. I could not comprehend the break-up because I could see no flaw in the relationship, which then felt as though I was the problem. I kept chasing after him for a long time in an attempt to validate my worth through his acceptance and approval of me.

This being said, who I was energetically could never have sustained that relationship. I was starved for love, and that, along with all of my energetic baggage, wounding, and subconscious beliefs, probably made me view that relationship in a biased way. Regardless, I was crushed when he broke things off. There are many reasons why relationships do not work or end seemingly abruptly; most (if not all) happen because of the Soul Contracts we have signed before incarnating. The relationship had served its purpose, and now it was time to move on or repeat the cycle of lessons. This cycle can be a repeat of situations with the same individual or a different one. In my case, one of the major lessons I had to learn from this was that I was worth so much more than how I was allowing others to treat me, including this ex-boyfriend. This is something I can see now, in hindsight, as I was pretty young then and had in no way started my healing journey, nor did I have much knowledge of interpersonal relationships, as I was always an outcast growing up.

Looking back on that experience, I can see how my lack of self-worth, self-love, self-appreciation, self-respect, and seeking outside validation and approval led to this relationship not going any further and has sabotaged other relationships in my life. I was putting this man on a pedestal and believed I was inherently worthless. Why would anyone want to be in a relationship with someone they consider inferior? I was considering myself inferior; therefore, my energy held that belief. I came to see that my energy probably became the reason why he left. My subconscious beliefs, my baggage, and my wounds all repelled him energetically. Yet this break-up was already pre-ordained as a way to trigger me into healing, which did happen eventually. At that point, I felt my emotions deeply and was often overwhelmed by them, but I had never looked into the why of things until later. I was in

Ego and accepted my victim role by taking that break-up extremely personally.

As my story illustrates, there are lessons to be learned from old emotions from the times before our awakening to consciousness. This is a form of practicing witnessing our emotions by looking back with an objective, inquisitive eye. One that holds more understanding and more experience to uncover the underlying possibilities and truths held within those emotions and events. This brings me to address victim mentality, which feeds entirely on overwhelming emotions to survive. Victim mentality is not objective; on the contrary, it is a very emotional state of mind, and it is always self-imposed. It is also entirely an Ego state of being.

Society has normalized victim mentality to the point where it becomes the default way of being for most humans. However, when we remove the Ego from any given circumstance, we can realize that what is happening is never about us as an individual. Anytime we use phrases like: "I've invested too much in this person to let them go," "There's nobody else in the world for me, it *has* to be them," "Why is this happening to me," "I don't want this to be happening," "The world is so unfair," "Everyone else always gets what they want, why can't I," etc., we're obviously in unhealthy Ego, even though as we are experiencing these moments they are quite intense. It takes a conscious effort to take that step back and see exactly this attitude for what it is: victim mentality.

No situation that happens in our lives is ever truly about us as individuals. Everything and everyone we encounter serves a purpose: our higher learning and healing. No matter what the circumstance is, when it is outside of our personal control, there is absolutely no use fighting what is happening in the same way that we cannot change another person. We also cannot single-handedly stop a fire from consuming a burning house. The idea here is to identify what *is* and what *is not* within our means to control. I am talking about events and moments where there is simply nothing you can do to change their course. I am not saying to be a doormat to people who would jump at the opportunity to abuse you. Please use your common sense and discretion. It is important to recognize what is within our personal power to change and what is not so that we may focus only on what we can work with instead of wasting time, energy, and effort on what we cannot control.

A good example of this from my personal life is when I was working as a waiter in a specific restaurant. My boss had decided to take even more from waiters' tips as tip-outs to the bartenders, kitchen staff, and runners, to the point where we were giving away a third of the tips we were making. Imagine having your boss take away a third of your paycheck to give to other employees because "they work harder and deserve it more," instead of actually paying them better wages. This was when we were coming out of another Covid closure, right after the holidays, with a whole month of us not having been working, so a lot of us were pressed for money. We all tried to have a conversation with the bosses, but were ignored and told to leave if we were not happy. I personally tried to keep talking to the boss to get things to change because of how unfair and draconic it was to waiters, but to no avail.

In this situation, I was often angry and carried a lot of resentment within me as I worked, eventually not caring at all for my workplace and caring only for the clients I served. I was expecting my boss to show some sense and compassion, and honestly, just appreciation for the people who actually run the business for them, and I was left very disappointed. This is a perfect example of me letting my emotions get the better of me. At that point in my life, I had gone through too much and had to heal from very bad situations; therefore, I had very little tolerance for bullshit and especially for being abused so openly. So I quit. I did what *was* within my control instead of waiting around for someone to save the situation. I took back my personal power, said no to being abused, and left so I could allow something better to come into my life instead.

I used to have a good relationship with that boss and thought he was one of the good ones, so I believed he would do the right thing. This turned out to be a lesson in standing up for myself and not fighting battles you cannot win, as in my wanting to change someone who was not willing to change. His mind was set on his decision. I hoped I could change his mind, and I held onto that hope when all the evidence pointed in the direction that there would be no change. I was refusing the reality I was living in and refusing that it was my time to do something else. I tried going to work at another restaurant, and I immediately felt it would be the same kind of disrespect and abuse, just painted a different colour. So, I became jobless.

When this happened, I decided that I was going to take some time off and just see what would come up for me. Everything happens for a reason, and it became evident quickly that it was a blessing that I was jobless with no other prospects. I spent a lot of time trying to relax and heal, which proved impossible as I was immediately ridden with guilt at the idea of doing "nothing" all day. I had grown up being taught that if you were not spending all your time working, then you were worthless. If you are not making money, you are not of any value and are a waste of space. It did not matter that I was on my last nerve, and my nervous system ended up imploding and throwing me out of whack for almost a whole year: I still felt terrible for being (at that point) simply unable to work.

It turned out that I had a lot of repressed emotions from my current lifetime of various intense traumas I went through. It all came to a head and exploded, finally, because I was making time to spend with myself. A lot of issues I thought had been resolved were showing back up. I actually had just stuffed them very deep inside, where I would not be able to feel them. With time off work and allowing myself to try to understand what was going on within me, everything I had shoved so far down and away from my awareness came bursting back up so that I could finally feel everything that had happened and how it still affected me unconsciously. I had to sit with myself and my emotions and allow them to show me where I was holding heavy energy against myself.

Do not get me wrong. It took me months to get to the point where I could truly access these repressed emotions. My body was carrying such stress that I physically could not relax. I felt guilty enjoying reading a book, so I would not read. I would spend hours and hours scrolling away on my phone, trying to escape my reality because I did not know how to cope with being alive. Doing something I enjoyed, like reading or playing video games, made me feel intense guilt, but scrolling for days on end on my phone numbed me completely, so that is what I did, even though I hated it and told myself repeatedly to get off my phone. I was stuck in being incapable of simply being present in my own body.

I ended up being able to confide in my then-boyfriend about what I felt was going on, and the more I talked, the more came out. This was so liberating for me, who never felt safe talking to anyone about what was truly going on within myself. I broke down crying in front of him multiple times on multiple occasions because so much was coming up, ready to finally be released. And I am talking ugly crying: snot falling out of my nose, barely breathing, uncontrollable, deep, deep, deep crying. I felt so amazingly light afterward. I had been holding onto childhood trauma and beliefs that were so detrimental to my well-being because that had been what I had been taught love was. I never knew better until I got into a relationship with my then-boyfriend, who taught me what true, unconditional love really was for a time.

For the first time, I was experiencing safety and a solid foundation of support, which led to my entire being crumbling into the broken mess it was holding itself back from being by sheer force of will. Unfortunately, my will broke when my body felt I did not need to hold myself together any longer because I had felt unsafe and unsupported in the world. It felt to me like, for the first time in my life, I could rest. I did not have to be strong. I did not have to keep going on and on and on without pause. I could finally breathe, and that first breath destroyed the faulty, disheveled, hanging-by-a-thread foundation that had been my reality until then. I was forced to process absolutely everything that had been done to me in my life because I simply could not keep going the way I had. My body wanted to be healed of all the abuse it had gone through, and it was not taking no for an answer.

All of this is to say that the emotions we refuse to feel and process stay stuck within us. We will carry that guilt, anger, disgust, whatever emotion until it has a chance to express itself. The longer those emotions are stuck within, the stronger they will want to come out. This is normal, especially when we have been conditioned as children not to feel our emotions, usually because the adults in our lives did not know how to cope with their own, much less with those of their children.

Starting off on this journey really is the hardest part, but look! You are already all the way here. It may not seem that far to you, but look at how much further you are now than you were when you started reading this book. That *is* progress. A little is way more than none at all. All we have to do is keep putting one foot in front of the other.

Remember that our Ego does not want to give up control or change. It will fight you on your healing journey until you feel deep inside your bones just how safe and loved you are in the world. As a parting note, remember to check in with your mindset here and then, as the Ego will make healing seem like it is hard work, a chore, or something otherwise unpleasant. Instead, choose to see this process as a gift you are giving yourself. Honestly, healing is nothing short of a great gift. What you invest in yourself and your well-being is never lost: it is the best investment you can make that keeps on giving. See this as the amazing positive that it is, and let the negativity flow down and out of you.

We are responsible for how we choose to see the world and our experience in it. Grow aware of how you are viewing your journey of healing and make sure it is a warm, positive experience for you, despite the effort and episodes of discomfort. Try applying this perspective or mindset change to other aspects of your life and see how the Universe responds.

Chapter 3
Your Fears and Wounding

———————— • ————————

As we start this chapter, we have already started uncovering some of our fears. Always keep in mind that your thoughts and your emotions are tools for you to help unravel your inner mysteries. How we think affects how we act, and how we feel affects how we react. All these, understood together, bring the greatest clarity to our inner world. The Truth is that we constantly limit ourselves. I believe there is a point in life—when we are told to become an "adult,"—where we lose touch with trusting ourselves. I also believe this is rooted in our upbringing, in how our parents talked to us and made us feel. Children are sponges, especially at the energetic level; they absorb so much more than just the words spoken around them. This is why, unless we actively work on ourselves, we will grow up to become another version of our parents, as they are all we have ever really known of what being an "adult" looks like. Looking objectively at both of our parents, we need to ask if this is really something we want for ourselves.

Society tries its hardest to destroy individuality, so when we are asked to become adults, we tend to lose our True Selves to fit that mold of what society dictates we should be, do, and look like. Here is a heavy question to consider as we get the ball rolling: What is the point of living your life if you are not your true, authentic Self? What is the point of being you if you are holding yourself hostage deep within? Why would you be here if not for your uniqueness? What is it about you that truly makes you you? True beauty in this world is found in contrast. The magic of this life is found in following our inner compass, the Truth of who we are. There is literally no one else like you, and that is to your advantage. No one else can do what you can do, the way you do it.

So, what keeps us from accessing our true, limitless potential? Subconscious beliefs about our capabilities, lessons we have learned in childhood, societal conditioning, and most importantly, our fears. Anything can be a reason why we hold ourselves back, but *fear* is what keeps us from moving forward. Fear is what has us stuck in place. There are many different types of fears, but they all play the same role. In my experience, unless you actively look for them to detach from them, our fears dictate most, if not all, of our actions and inactions.

Society, as we know it today, thrives on fear-based conditioning, such as pressure-packed ads of now or never, limited-time-only products, missing out on life if you do not conform to certain standards, rejection for being different, the rat-race mentality, only the strong survive, everybody for themselves, tear down the competition to get on top, destroy others to make yourself look better, crabs in a bucket mentality, etc. The list goes on and on. The idea behind all these is to use our fears against us for personal gain. Fears of missing out, of being left behind, of lack, of loss, basically of survival, as there is a rampant belief that we have to hustle and always be on the look-out for the next big opportunity and always work, work, work, grind, grind, grind. We live in a fast-paced world of now, now, now. This means that we never get to stop, breathe, and just appreciate being alive.

There is so much pressure placed upon individuals to accomplish things, which creates so much fear of being perceived as less deserving when we do not meet these hypothetical standards. This is ingrained within us from a very young age, and it becomes a very limiting cage we trap ourselves in by buying into that narrative. However, we are starting to see a growing discontent with living that way, which is beautiful to witness and be a part of. We are well on the way to reshaping reality as we currently know it to be for it to become more Soulful. Right now, society is absolutely miserable because it refuses the innate connection to all that is. There has been a domination of distorted masculine energy in the leading forces of the world, which creates the whole rigid, greedy, and unforgiving structure we know today. Things are going to snap soon as the world tries to regain its natural state of balance. There will likely be a pendulum effect, where we drop drastically away from dominant masculine energy into dominant feminine energy and so forth until an eventual balance is found. More on all of these themes in a further chapter.

To start, we will familiarize ourselves with Maslow's hierarchy of needs as a tool to understand why fear exists in our lives. Abraham Maslow theorized that human needs are five-fold: physiological, safety, love and belonging, esteem, and self-actualization. As you can see in the image below, the bottom needs are the strongest ones when they demand our attention; the lower the need in the pyramid, the higher the importance of its being met. As long as those needs are not met, we cannot thrive in self-actualization as we are meant to. The moment one of the lower needs is lacking, we may revert to a survival state of being, which closely resembles the behaviour of wild animals fighting for their lives.

These can be further divided into deficiency needs categories (the bottom four)—where we cannot perform at our best if they are unmet and which grow more insistent until met—and a singular growth need category, which we can only begin to meet once all other needs have been met to a satisfactory degree (meaning they do not need to be fully met, just enough to feel satisfactory and no longer urgent). For example, thirst is a physiological need that gets more pressing the thirstier we get and disappears when we have drunk our fill. The thirstier we get, the more insistent the need becomes to the point where we can focus on nothing else until it is satisfied.

Self-actualization needs, on the contrary, become more insistent the more we fulfill them, to the point where if we do not fulfill them, we will start feeling worse in our natural neutral state of being. The reason for this is that being able to work on self-actualization means we get to work on becoming more our True Self. Once we start claiming our authenticity, it becomes harder to ignore or revert to being less authentic, as that state of being will simply feel too wrong for us to remain in. Authenticity is where we can share our unique gifts with the world. It is where our Soul's purpose lies. The more we tap into that delicious energy, the better we feel and the better we understand why we are here. Self-actualization is a state of personal bliss. Once we get a taste of it, nothing else compares or makes sense to be in. Nothing else is worth wasting our time on.

Having esteem needs fully met is the prerequisite for opening ourselves up to self-actualization. These needs act as the wings we need to propel us to the next level. There is no mistake in using a pyramid to further the understanding of this concept. The bottom two needs are the foundation we need to create for basic human functioning. They are also known as the basic needs. The following two are classified as psychological needs, while the top part is known as self-fulfillment needs. All of these needs are important to living a good life; however, the lower ones will become overwhelming and will move aside the higher ones until they are met. However, our Souls crave being in the highest need category to evolve and expand as individuals.

Notice how safety is the second-lowest need. Our most fundamental need is to keep our body functional; only then is it possible to focus on feeling safe, which is the next foundational level of Self. The energy of fear keeps us in a state of feeling unsafe. Being in the energy of self-actualization—where we are free to achieve our highest potential, follow our calling, and be 100% authentic—is impossible as long as we remain stuck in the energy of fear. We cannot achieve our intended greatness until we believe we are safe to do so. Then, we have to believe that we *can* accomplish our true potential by fulfilling both our love and belonging, as well as our esteem needs.

One would think that a society that classifies itself as "advanced," "civilized," or even "first-world" would be meeting at least the basic needs of all of its citizens, that they may all be able to focus on their growth/being needs instead, which may further advance said society through the wonder of discovery and caring for all living beings. Unfortunately, because society is deeply imbalanced, it cannot provide the stability needed to achieve this. It is designed specifically to keep its citizens chasing their three lower needs while actively hurting their esteem needs so they cannot rise to their self-actualization needs. If this makes you sad to read, it should. However, we can change the world as we know it by working on ourselves and sharing this knowledge and growth with others. We have to put aside the crabs-in-the-bucket mentality and help each other instead. This is done most easily when we truly understand how there is more than enough for everyone to have a piece of the pie, and that even by doing this, there will be plenty left over.

Money holds a similar energy frequency to love. Your relationship with money is the exact same relationship you have with love. Look deeply into what this means for you personally, and Journal about your thoughts, feelings, and observations as you dig into your relationships with partners and money. I used to have a very bad relationship with money, as I saw it as the root of all evil. I threw money out the window because I refused to acknowledge its importance. Then, I wondered why I had zero success in my love life and even friendships. Money, like love, makes our lives so much simpler and more manageable, better than the bartering system ever could. Instead of wasting our time scavenging for the necessary materials for a trade, we have money. This relationship is one I encourage you to look at honestly and objectively to actively work on it and develop what you truly wish that relationship to look and feel like. We will address this in-depth in a later chapter, but it is interesting to investigate the levels of fear or lack we associate with our current money story.

The reason I address this now is because we live in a society of lack mentality, where we believe resources such as money are limited and that we will never have enough. We are meant to believe that we have to take what we can get and move others out of our way to do so; otherwise, we will have nothing. We are conditioned to believe everything is always a competition, and there is only ever one prize. Success is measured by what you have on a material level, which pushes us to constantly compare with others to see how "high" we rank compared to them. This is obviously unhealthy Ego behaviour and mentality. More than that, it is entirely false. The Universe and what it provides are infinite. It is not a pie where nothing is left for anyone else when the last piece is gone. Abundance is infinite. It always depends on what we make of what we have, along with our levels of appreciation for what **is** in our lives.

In the context of always needing to be better than our neighbours, we are taught that what we enjoy should come second to what must be our duty: making money. We are taught that life is unfair and that we are not inherently worthy of getting what we want and need out of life. We are taught to be grateful for the crumbs given to us, tossed on the ground like food for an animal. We are all measured, assessed, and evaluated on an extremely specific, limited scale, disregarding everything that makes an individual unique as waste. We are taught to shut up, sit down, and never think for ourselves, never question the content of what is force-fed to us. Original thoughts are dangerous and useless and only serve as a tool to get you cast aside, shunned, and rejected.

We are taught to stop being curious and to follow the program, no questions asked, so we can be shaped and molded into silent workers to serve our invisible overlords. We are taught that being authentic to ourselves is inherently wrong, especially if it does not fit the picture of the 2.5 kids, white picket fence, and nuclear family. Anything that stands out has to be pushed back down. We are taught that appearances have way more value than substance. We are taught to be the best or not to bother trying at all. We are taught that mistakes and failures are shameful and make us garbage individuals, not worthy of any attention or praise. We are taught to bend over backward for our betters, accept abuse with gratitude, erase ourselves completely to not bother anyone, and forget who we are to satisfy the "people who really matter." We are taught to never rock the boat.

I do not know about you, but for me, writing these words and acknowledging how we have been brought up and are expected to live did not sit well with me. It fired me up at how ridiculous and useless all that drivel is: how toxic it is and how it needs to change. Thankfully, we are starting to see this change already. It is coming, one person at a time. The above does not resonate with me, with my sense of Self, nor with how life *should be* on this Earth. So, let us change that by healing these internal wounds and releasing those fears and false beliefs. We can, in turn, help others do the same. We must break our own chains to help break those of the people around us. Remember to write in your Journal all the emotions and triggers that may have arisen from reading these previous paragraphs. Read them again to really feel into what has been coming up internally for you. And look into *why* those emotions are present.

Our society has been fashioned for the control of the masses by the select few. An interesting fact to look at is how the overly rich are clearly not in a self-actualization state of being. Money is love. Love is the third need. If these ultra-rich people feel like they can never have enough money, it means they cannot meet the third need of Maslow's hierarchy. When we look at someone, and I mean *really* look at someone, we can always see in their non-verbal ways of being which needs are not met within them. I encourage you to practice truly looking at people. This, in turn, will lead to you being able to look at yourself more objectively. We do not look to judge. We look *to see what is already there* and understand.

Let us now take a closer look at control. Why do human beings ever seek control? If we look at nature, it is in perfect harmony with itself to the point of creating massive ecosystems where even a slight change in one of its elements can wreak havoc within. Yet, over time, it will always find a way to rebalance itself perfectly. Humans seek to control everything because they have no faith in the perfection of the Universe. Humans seek to control everything because they do not believe they can be safe and cared for. Humans are constantly fighting against the natural flow of the world because they believe they know better and can do better themselves. Human arrogance is a terrible blight we have to live with for now. Hoarding excessive amounts of wealth is a mental illness and is indicative of a deeper, bigger hurt or wound.

When we truly believe that all our needs will be met and taken care of by the benevolence of the Universe we live in, we will never worry about money again. We know our inner guidance will show us what to follow to get all our needs met. We will not be hoarding money in case we run out. We will happily share with others around us without expecting anything in return because we know we do not need more. We know that we will always be all right. The point here is not to blame these hoarders or the society they created, but to open our eyes to the truths all around us. Choosing to blame is always choosing to be victim-mentality and throwing away our personal power. Always.

Most of us are currently struggling with our psychological needs, which is why there is a massive increase in mental health issues, including depression, anxiety, and much more. We live in a society that refuses our humanity. It is up to us to reclaim it. As stated earlier, we are now on the descending side of the dominant masculine pendulum. There are waves and waves of Souls coming in with the mission of facilitating this shift. We are some of these Souls, identifiable by choosing to heal ourselves and help others along their own healing paths, consciously or not.

The healing work we are doing now will not only affect us and future generations; it will also help older generations heal and evolve. These are parts of the contracts we all have with each other. Our personal healing becomes healing in our ancestral lines. As personal healing affects us on a cellular level, we (as Souls) choose our parents for specific reasons; the family within which we are born is never by mistake *because* we choose our incarnations and the path our lives will take. Our healing will help them heal and heal the generational wounds we have all been carrying throughout the familial lineage. The lessons we learn, the subconscious beliefs we unlearn, and the healing we do clear all of these things for our children and their children, and so on. This is why this work is so important. By healing ourselves, we are healing humanity as a whole.

The important thing to understand about Soul contracts is that the very essence of the Universe is Unconditional Love. We are the Universe experiencing itself. Therefore, we are also, in essence, Unconditional Love. All the Soul contracts have been made through the lens of unconditional love. This means that all of our life experiences, regardless of how painful and unwanted they were, were done in essence in unconditional love to help us heal and grow. This does not mean we are given free rein to hurt others. It does not mean that rapes and violence are justified, not at all. It simply means that on the grander scale of things, they were agreed upon as necessary for our personal growth by both our Soul Selves and the perpetrator's Soul. It does not excuse it, it explains. It allows understanding, and understanding leads to healing. This can be hard for the Ego to accept, but it is a Soul Truth.

This particular lesson is essential to remember when we have difficulty reconciling what has happened to us in our 3D lives. It is okay and normal for this to be difficult to assimilate, as it is a very big shift in perspective, but it is necessary to be aware of it if we want to understand the greater meaning of Life. You will learn to become grateful for adversity because there is no growing as an individual otherwise in our current reality. One day, this will no longer be the case as humanity will be mostly healed, but until then, transcending pain will be another tool for us to use to further our healing.

At this point, some of you will be wondering why we have gone through all of this information when this chapter of learning is about fears. The answer is simple. We cannot get over fears we ignore that are even affecting us. Societal conditioning has anchored numerous fears within us, so it was important to outline most of that conditioning. It will be up to you to dig up what I missed in your case. Healing occurs with acknowledgment, acceptance, understanding, and release, which we will dive deeper into in the next chapter. For now, we will keep working on understanding where our fears come from. That was the purpose of exploring both our societal conditioning and our intrinsic needs, along with personally exploring how these are directly relevant to us.

In addition to our upbringing, we will also hold fears in our energetic bodies from previous lifetimes. If you have any kind of inexplicable phobia, I am willing to bet you have a past life in which you died by means of your current phobia. There is absolutely a trauma associated with irrational phobias, which is why we react so strongly to them without knowing why. Our energetic body remembers past life traumas, even when we do not. This is true in this current life as well. We see so many stories of women who were abused, often by relatives, when they were very young, only for them to have repressed those memories until they dig into their subconscious with another person's help to reveal the Truth.

As stated previously, not having our needs met triggers a very imposing internal motivation to get them met. This creates a panic inside of us where we are completely in reaction mode to get that need met, sometimes at all costs. We are in unhinged, visceral survival mode when even our Ego is pushed aside and stops running the show in favor of raw instincts of self-preservation. Survival mode can be overwhelming and primal. There is very little conscious thinking going on unless it is to meet the current demand. Survival mode can also occur when we do not feel safe (basic need #2), which means we fear being in danger and, therefore, are constantly on the lookout for anything that could potentially harm us.

Get your Journal ready and start thinking about times in your life when you have felt overwhelmed by needing to get a basic, fundamental need met. Think about when you were *desperate* to have something, experience something, or achieve something, like being with someone, receiving someone's attention, being part of a group, going to a party, gaining someone's favour, a brand-new pair of shoes, a book, etc. Regardless of what it was specifically, you wanted something, and nothing would get in your way of obtaining it. Sometimes, you went against your own better judgment and what others cautioned you against. Or, it did not matter if you hurt others while in the process of obtaining what you desired. You just *needed* it. Look into these events and seek to understand exactly what was going on within yourself and *why* this need was so strong to the point of disregarding both Self and others to satisfy it.

These moments will help you pinpoint what kind of fears are attached to these needs. Ask yourself what it was that you were actually chasing in those moments. What hole did it temporarily fill? Remember that the outside circumstances are always just a reflection of what is going on within. Write all these things in your Journal, along with any possible whys. This time, use Maslow's hierarchy of needs to see how much deeper you can uncover your own secrets. Go back and use this tool with the previous discoveries in your Journal as well.

As I have mentioned before, we are in the energy of fear when we do not feel safe, loved, or supported by the Universe. These are all illusions created by the false beliefs we hold to be true subconsciously. As we slowly become aware of more and more of our wounds and false beliefs, we will see how they both play on our fears and are fueled by them in turn. We are energetic beings, meaning that whatever we put our energetic focus on will be attracted back to us. For example, if you genuinely believe yourself to be unlucky (even if only unconsciously), then bad luck will follow you around because that is where your attention/belief lies. The Universe always conspires to prove us right by giving us what we are asking to attract energetically.

In the same vein, whatever we fear will never be too far from us because our fears are powerfully contained within our personal vibration. Once, I was in a car with a guy who was deathly terrified of praying mantises.

We were exiting a secure, fenced-in building and had to swipe a key card. I had very rarely seen praying mantises in my life, never in a city, yet there was one right on the box where you had to swipe your key card. My friend never saw it, but it stuck out to me as very odd because there was no vegetation nearby. In my mind, there was no reason for a praying mantis to be there. It was only when I pointed it out that my friend panicked and revealed his phobia to me. I sincerely believe that if he had not been in the car, there would have been no praying mantis on that metal box.

Our vibration is a magnet for what is already subconsciously present in our energy and for where we place our focus. Our subconscious beliefs are the ones that hold the most space in our energetic vibration because we hold them to be 100% true. This means they are beliefs we simply never revisit and are, therefore, hidden from our conscious mind. Our conscious beliefs may still hold doubt, which is why they are part of our awareness. Even if we consciously believe at 99% that we will receive something, if we hold the unconscious belief that we cannot have this thing, we will not receive it because our vibration says no at 100%. This is why it is so important for us to uncover these subconscious, false beliefs and clear them so that we can have the life and bliss we truly want and deserve. Uncovering our deepest fears helps to shine a light on what we subconsciously hold to be true, both about ourselves and the world we live in.

We will never consciously revisit any belief we hold to be 100% true because we classify it in our minds as untouchable, as a fact of life itself. These particular beliefs can be found in both the conscious and unconscious minds. The work we have been doing up to this point is meant to depict a trail leading to these beliefs. Becoming aware of beliefs we have made in our current lifetime will help uncover unconscious beliefs that are bleeding through from previous lifetimes, which is why we are doing the work in the first place. We aim to make the unconscious conscious to heal and be free from it. We can do this by seeing the proof of its existence being reflected in our lives, a.k.a. our internal reality being reflected without.

There will be a segment later on about how to receive proper assistance in healing the unconscious. For now, we will just explore the topic briefly. What we will be looking to heal within the unconscious mind are all the core wounds we have experienced in previous lifetimes. A core wound is the initial wound that creates the false belief we unconsciously still hold to be 100%

true about life. As long as the core wound is not found, identified, and healed, it will continue to affect us as it is directly stuck within our energetic field, or personal vibration.

First, we have to understand that the human body is composed of 4 different aspects, or bodies, which are physical, mental, emotional, and vibrational/energetic. We have started identifying our mental and emotional bodies in the previous lessons, and here, we will explore the vibrational body further. Since we are energetic beings, our energy is our signature. This is why we get different feelings from simply looking at different people. Our energy always picks up on someone else's energy. When we get a good or a bad feeling from someone, it is always because we sense the Truth of their essence, even if our eyes do not see what we feel. Energy is impartial; it cannot lie, deceive, or pretend to be something else. Every single one of our physical senses can be fooled, but what we pick up energetically will always be truthful because it simply is what it is and cannot be what it is not.

Just because we may pick up a bad vibe from someone does not make them automatically a bad person. This kind of energy first tells us that we have a history with this Soul. Our energies have mingled in a previous lifetime, and we probably parted ways with "bad karma." Karma is about unresolved, energetic attachments. It is not the commonly misunderstood idea that the Universe strikes down bad people for perpetrating bad actions. Karma is not "do good and you will receive good," and "do bad, and you will receive bad." Karma is the energetic link between people and situations. Suppose there are unresolved wounds between people or between a person and a significant occurrence. In that case, that wound stays in our vibrational energy, and we are karmically linked with it until healing can occur. Our own wounds can be seen as our karma, and it has nothing to do with whether we deserve them or not.

When we talk about wounds created in past lives, we are really talking about what our human perspective learned as an absolute truth through the tiny lens of our then-life experience. What does this mean? For example, I had a healing session where we visited some past lives to see what kinds of wounding I was subconsciously holding onto. In one of those lives, I was a little girl who ran away from her village while it was being massacred, pillaged, and burned by raiders on horseback. I had felt that we were in the Mongolian Genghis Khan invasion times, and I was living in this coastal village, around 7 years of age. When the attack happened, my parents had told me to run away and hide in a nearby seashore cave, where I was to wait for them. They promised me they would come and get me and that I was to stay hidden until they did, no matter what.

As you may have already guessed, my parents never came for me. All that little girl knew was that she was alone, terrified, cold, and waiting for someone to come save her. She prayed and prayed and cried and could not understand why this was happening to her, why she had been abandoned this way, not only by her parents, who had *promised* they would come to find her, but also by her god, who was not answering any of her prayers. This was the lifetime where I subconsciously learned that the Universe was not a safe place, where the ones you love, whom you think you can rely on, would ultimately let you down, forget about you, and never keep their promises. This created the false belief that I would always be alone and could not trust anyone to do right by me.

Seeing this lifetime and understanding what this little girl had gone through and the beliefs she created from her experience explained to me exactly why I felt so revolted by the idea of a loving God watching over us, why I could not open up to people, and why I felt like everyone I loved never had my back and always abandoned me when I needed them. I had a deep core wound—not only about trusting others but also about abandonment and betrayal from my loved ones and the Universe, the god that was supposed to watch over me and care for me.

Healing the wounds created in that lifetime has drastically changed my relationships with my family and friends and my relationship with the Universe. The tricky thing with experiencing our past lives and seeing the lessons we learned from traumatic incidents is that, as human beings, we often do not understand the *why* of things or only ever understand them from our flawed, biased, tiny little human brains. Why did that little girl have to go through such trauma? As Souls, we seek to experience everything life has to offer—to create a total understanding of the human spectrum of experiences—and learn what we want more of in future lifetimes and what we do not want to re-experience.

We, as human beings, cannot understand the vastness of the bigger picture at play here. It is too big, intricate, and ultimately complex for our brains to comprehend. Simply because we are not meant to. As Souls in human bodies, we are tasked with learning our specific list of things and then moving on. We are but a small gear in the whole system, tasked with doing our job, just like every single other Soul. Our contract is not limited to only one lifetime, although specific lifetimes have specific items added or removed from their particular list. Some have to create wounds for later healing, to experience living with and without said wound. We cannot fully appreciate the without if we have not fully experienced the with.

Everything in our lives indicates what we have signed up to experience in this lifetime. Wounds always serve a purpose; we become ready to heal those wounds when that purpose expires. Wounds are not to be seen as negative: they are a tool in our Soul's evolution. As unpleasant as a situation in our lives might have been, if we have experienced it in this lifetime, it is because we are capable of dealing with it. Our Soul signed up for this lesson. Our fears are also tools to indicate the possible wounds we have to deal with. By uncovering our fears, we can follow the thread of our otherwise unconscious wounding to the same degree as our triggers. Otherwise, we will never be led to revisit the false beliefs we hold to be 100% true subconsciously because we perceive no reason to.

A core wound is where the wound first appeared in our vibrational energy. From that lifetime on, we carry that wound, which repeats itself as a pattern in multiple lifetimes, so we can follow the trail back to the initial wound and heal it. Healing a core wound clears all the subsequent related wounding because by removing the initial energy, it pulls out all of the same energies that were created from that core wound, just like pulling a plant by the roots brings out all of the plant, not just the surface root. This is why we have been working at figuring out our triggers, fears, unconscious actions, and reactions: because they lead us to understand what our core wounds could be. By doing this initial digging into ourselves, when we do book a healing session with a facilitator, we have access to much more healing than if we had done no work on ourselves at all.

Another great tool to help us understand our wounding and what affects us is to look into our chakras. We will cover these in a separate chapter later on. Before we get there, we will have to practice hearing our intuition and truthfully listening to ourselves first. As learned earlier, exposing our needs is the first step to looking inward. The needs chart is a basis for a more logical approach (masculine energy), whereas the chakras will be more intuitive (feminine energy). These energies, too, will be explained in greater depth later on. We will be developing the introspection layer by layer throughout the chapters.

Everything we have explored in this chapter will give you a lot of introspective work to start doing. Healing is a lengthy process, so remember to be patient with yourself and always be honest with what you uncover. There is no shame in exploring our depths. There is no shame in revisiting moments that are hard to look at. We are practicing objectively looking at ourselves and our inner workings. We are working on removing our own judgments towards ourselves. We are practicing self-honesty and acceptance. We are removing attachments we have created in our beliefs. The self-exploration we are doing has to be done with the utmost respect for who we are by honouring our journeys so far.

One last thing to consider as we start digging into ourselves: self-acceptance is essential. What you will find may not always please your Ego, but remember that what your Ego wants is irrelevant. Learn to identify and shush that voice, which is trying to hide your inner depths and truths from coming to light and being seen. Our fears serve to distance us from something unpleasant we do not want to revisit. They are linked with traumas we have experienced in the past and current lifetimes. Whatever we refuse to acknowledge is something likely important for our healing, so we must identify and push through that initial resistance. Fear will be your greatest indicator that you have to dig deeper into a given subject. Remember that whatever you outright refuse to consider could be relevant or true and will also be important to dig into.

Start noticing when you refuse something you actually want, and look at *why* you are refusing yourself this thing. What are the true underlying reasons for the refusal? Look at when you refuse to accept gifts, invitations, and compliments, when you let an exciting opportunity pass by because you do not believe yourself worthy of accepting it. These are all indicators of deeper fears and wounds at work. It is your job to uncover what really dictates your behaviours and actions, not to accept the excuses your Ego provides as cover for the underlying truth.

Also, take a look at where you doubt yourself and undermine your own natural talents and abilities. Why are you shutting down your gifts or disbelieving in yourself? Look into where people have complimented you on your skills, and you downplayed it or flat-out refused or redirected the compliment. Where are you sabotaging yourself in your own self-appreciation? Start taking risks. Start accepting compliments. Start doing things you enjoy for their simple enjoyment without holding onto guilt. Do what you love, regardless of the possible results. Stop thinking you are not good enough or valuable enough to do what fires you up. Leave your fears behind and choose to be brave. To be brave means to go forward despite fear, not to never feel any fear; it means not letting your fear win. Embrace yourself for exactly who you are in this present moment. This is your starting point. There can be no other. Go from here and know you can only get better.

Chapter 4
Your Prison

———————— • ————————

The first three chapters have been about getting acquainted with our inner Self: our thoughts, emotions, actions, reactions, needs, fears, and whatever imbalances we may have started uncovering within. Now, we are going to start identifying the box or container that holds all of these things: the prison we keep ourselves caged in. We have started scratching the surface, and now we will dive in deeper and start unlocking some doors of personal truths.

We already know that our lives so far have been dictated and run by our untamed Ego. What we may still be unaware of is that we have been living in a self-imposed box of limitations. We started exploring this concept by the end of the last chapter. Our box is our comfort zone, yet it is also a prison based on our self-perceived limitations. The Truth is that we are infinite, energetic beings who have lived multiple lifetimes, mastering multiple different things. Our potential is limitless, yet we limit it ourselves with our beliefs of what is possible. We create the beliefs of what we can and cannot achieve, and we hold onto them for dear life because we have been taught that if we are not perfect at doing something on the first try, then we are hopeless in that domain and should never try again.

The phrase "you can do anything you set your mind to" is one of the most powerful, truthful statements we can live by. Our mindset is what will dictate the outcomes of what we do. Every single one of us has hopes, dreams, and goals we want to achieve. Yet, most of us abandon those goals and dreams because we believe they are unattainable. We believe that we could never get what we want because of "insert excuse." Our society conditions us to extinguish the fire of our passions by repeatedly telling us that our dreams are not meant to be achieved by everyone, that only a select few get to achieve and do what they dream of achieving and doing when the truth is that you absolutely can achieve every single one of your dreams, goals, and ambitions. It is all just a matter of mindset and belief. And also choosing to do the inner work to be energetically aligned with our intentions.

These limitations come from fear-based sentiments and conditioning when, truthfully, we are meant to achieve our goals. Why would you feel passion or be fired up about anything that is not meant to be yours? What is meant to be your driving force if not *what makes you feel alive*? Why else would you be so motivated internally and driven to accomplish something otherwise? We sabotage ourselves, consciously or not, because of our ingrained fears and false beliefs, which are based on untruths. When we uncover the truth, these false foundations crumble, and we become free and driven to pursue our passions anew.

We tend to live life constantly disbelieving our true potential, saying "no" to what we truly want, and holding ourselves back out of fear or the false belief that we do not have the time or we are past our "prime." These are the walls of the prison that keep us small and "safe"; the floor is held by the foundations of our core wounds and false beliefs, while the ceiling can only ever go as high as our faith and trust in the Universe allows for it to go. All of these create our "comfort zone." No matter how many times we shut ourselves away from what we truly want, we will *always* find our way back to these dreams, goals, ambitions, whatever you want to call them. They are always there because they are a part of who we truly are. They are a part of our Soul essence, part of the very reason we exist in the first place.

So, how do we shift all of this? How do we free ourselves from our prisons instead of staying in the status quo of living a life that leaves us feeling miserable? By doing inner work and understanding that we are safe to trust ourselves and safe to follow our individual, unique paths. Everything becomes easier when we trust and believe that we are always *safe*. The world is a safe place. The Universe is a loving, benevolent force that wants to see us succeed. The Universe loves you and takes care of you. If any of these statements revolt or trigger you, write them down in your Journal. As you may have guessed, it greatly indicates the wounds you carry. Try to pinpoint why and where the trigger comes from. What is the driving force behind every thought and feeling you are experiencing?

Also, take a look at every instance in your life where you have felt unsafe or abandoned. What can you uncover in those instances that reveal a truth or belief you hold? How can you shift your perspective from that of a victim to one where you acknowledge you were never unsafe to begin with? What has happened to get you out of those circumstances? How can you look at it differently from an outside perspective? When you learn how to connect with your Higher Self, try to look at things from a Soul perspective. How was this situation meant to help you heal and grow? Remember that everything in life happens to show you something about yourself. Every interaction is a Soul contract to help you heal and grow, as unpleasant and destructive as some of those experiences might appear to be in our physical reality. This being said, just because an event has a higher purpose for you to find out about does not mean to minimize the potentially devastating effects that same event can wreak upon us. We still have to honour all parts of the event, especially its effect on us, either physical, emotional, or otherwise.

I have come to realize that some of the most traumatic experiences of my life have happened when I was the least in touch with my Truth. When I was completely dissociated from the Truth of who I am and doing things that were not aligned with what I truly wanted for myself, I would always find myself in painful situations and not understand why I had to go through some genuinely horrific things. I had to realize that I did not want to keep living these things. I had to make certain changes in my life. I had to trust that things would improve if I followed the Truth of who I am and what I genuinely wanted for myself. Whenever you ignore yourself, something unwanted always tends to happen. Use that for the lesson it truly is: that you can want and get better for yourself than what you are currently settling for. This happens the most when we follow the path we believe we are supposed to follow instead of the one we genuinely want to pursue.

By lowballing yourself, you are creating a reality you will want to escape because you inherently know you deserve better. And you are *the only person* who can give that to yourself. There are no princes in shining armor waiting to swoop in and save us. This means that whenever you give your power to someone else, you will never be happy. By disrespecting yourself, you will never be fulfilled. You will never get somewhere better by staying in situations that make you feel like dying inside. You have to want to give yourself better. You have to believe you deserve better. You have to want a change and follow through with it. If you keep waiting for change to happen independently of the effort you put into it, it will simply not happen. Ever. You have to create it for yourself. You have to choose differently. You have to do different things. You have to get yourself out of the hole you have dug yourself in. Remember that blaming others is a complete Ego state of being. The Ego is afraid of change because it cannot control things. Do not let your Ego keep you where you do not want to be simply because the known feels safe compared to the unknown.

At first, the fact that you are the sole person responsible for where you are currently in your life may be hard to come to terms with, but the simple act of coming to terms with it will help you regain some of your personal power. You always have access to your personal power; you simply choose to let others make decisions for you, and you go with it. Because it seems easier, it seems less painful, and less dangerous than to stand up and claim what you want. But it keeps you miserable and unsatisfied. People-pleasing is a sign of having little to no self-love or self-respect. It means you value everyone else above yourself, which is ridiculous. We are all equal. We are all the same. Human beings, one and all. We must learn to value ourselves fully, independently, and accurately before anyone can reflect that worth back onto us.

All of this is especially hard to accept when we have gone through some heavily traumatic life experiences. In my own trauma experience, I have been through multiple scenarios of abandonment by people I love who were supposed to support me, such as my parents letting me down and discouraging me from believing in myself and going for what I wanted in life, my first ex walking away from our relationship without ever giving me a reason when on paper it seemed a perfect relationship, my beloved cat running away and never coming back, my closest friends backstabbing and abandoning me, etc. What I have come to realize with much hindsight and work on myself is that these were all a reflection of *me abandoning myself.* I was projecting the blame of my internal vibration externally onto other people and situations, unconsciously. These are all instances of the Universe showing me my inner reality in an attempt for me to see my internal wounding in order to heal it.

Nothing is ever random or coincidental. Coincidences simply do not exist in this world, which is so mathematically precise and calculated. We attract all of our experiences vibrationally, which is exactly why relying on blame is useless. We may not be responsible for a situation happening in our reality, but if we are experiencing even a part of it, it is for a reason. We have called it into our 3D reality experience vibrationally, and our job is to figure out and understand why.

These above personal situations of mine have created wounds in my younger years that allowed me to see a pattern once I started awakening to the Truth of our energetic world, which facilitated my past life healing of wounds such as believing I was not interesting nor worthwhile as a person, thinking that I was worthless, believing that those I loved the most did not care about me at all, believing that no one would ever want to spend time with me willingly, believing I was easily replaceable. My self-worth has been a huge wound for me to heal. Truthfully, it is a wound I am still working on that is heavily triggered by my writing this book. My fear of being seen also comes up, but the fact that I am identifying, acknowledging, and accepting these fears for what they are—choosing to understand the message they are trying to give me— allows me to release the crippling hold they could have had on me otherwise. There can be no personal progress when we choose to stay in the dark and ignore our shadows. We have to embrace them in order to liberate ourselves from them.

You will know that you have hit the nail on the head with your self-assessment of your beliefs when just thinking about it will make you want to cry or feel overly emotional. If what you believe is a core wound you hold does not trigger any kind of response within you, then it might mean that you need to keep digging, as you clearly have not found the true source yet. Follow the pain trail to its source. The imagery of a physical wound works perfectly for this concept, as you may feel pain when touching around it, but you will have a physical jerk reaction to touching the worst part of that wound: its core. We need to find this to heal all branches of pain caused by the core wound.

When referring to my own experiences, I was completely unequipped to understand what was really going on at those times. I was completely stuck in Ego, ignorance, and victim mentality. Looking back now, with the tools I am sharing throughout this book, I could see and understand that something greater was at work. My energy attracted these scenarios so that I could uncover my core wounds and heal them. I can now understand what happened from a Soul-level perspective instead of on humanity's default wounded Ego level. Now, when something happens in my life, I can internally distance myself from the unfolding event to see it differently—from a Soul perspective—and thus understand why such things are attracted to my reality in the first place, and how to best deal with them.

This does not mean that I never experience extreme emotions. It simply means that I do not let those emotions overwhelm me anymore. I have gotten to a point where I rarely take anything personally anymore. When I do, I search for *the reason why I did* and also for *what wants to be seen about my internal reality* and wants to be processed within myself as a result. This book aims to get you to a place where you can understand and process life from a Soul perspective, regardless of current circumstances. This does not mean you become something other than human. It simply means you are consciously creating the reality you want to live in instead of just going through life's motions powerlessly. Every day becomes an exciting reality you can shape to your will instead of the dull standard that is the "going-through-the-motions-mindlessly" norm of living we experience otherwise.

Along with what I have shared with you previously and more, I began uncovering the events of my life from a Soul perspective because I wanted to understand why these things had happened to me so that I could save myself from experiencing that kind of heartbreak and pain over and over again. I grew up profoundly hating myself. I had zero self-confidence, I was extremely defensive and incapable of communicating and opening up, yet I was also desperate for love and acceptance. I also had severe depression, crippling anxiety, and was a complete doormat and people-pleaser, allowing others to treat and use me in any which way, just as long as I could feel that – for a tiny moment at least – I had some kind of value to someone somewhere, at some point in time. All in all, very destructive mindsets, behaviours, and decisions on my part. I was incapable of loving myself and treating myself with any kind of respect, which I later came to understand was because I held the subconscious belief that I was not worthy of receiving either love or respect.

Looking back at my own life was not only eye-opening in what I held to be true, but it was also a very hard, painful exercise I had to go through to accept myself exactly as I was, exactly where I was in my life at any and all given moments, despite all my perceived shortcomings and flaws (of which I believed I possessed no redeeming qualities whatsoever). I had to accept all of these unkind beliefs I held for what they were telling me, and I had to forgive myself for allowing others to use and hurt me so that I could feel *something*. Because it felt to me that feeling something (even pain) was better than feeling nothing at all.

I had to learn to lower my defenses for my own good if I wanted to be able to allow softness in. I had to learn to accept what had happened in my life without placing blame on anyone, including myself. I had to accept that I chose this reality for my life, even if it was not entirely conscious. The hardest part to acknowledge was the understanding that I was allowing all of these bad things to happen and to continue happening by choosing to let them happen, knowingly making decisions that were obviously detrimental to me, and doing so simply because I could not fathom the very idea that I did not deserve to be abused, in any way, by anyone, ever.

It was a long road to recovery, years of consciously choosing better for myself (more often than not forcing myself into better decisions despite not feeling worthy of deserving better), of falling back into terrible, destructive patterns, of (very) slowly learning to love and respect myself, of learning to say "no" and to stick with it for my own sake. It took a lot of time and conscious effort on my part when I felt I had absolutely no energy to waste on these things. I had to constantly fight the feeling that I was not worthy of being saved, much less of being loved. It took me years to come into a healthy, loving space within myself. Some things were easier than others, but everything I was uncovering in my past and experiencing in my present moment was helping me establish exactly what my prison walls were. All of my self-limiting beliefs were holding me back from achieving any kind of potential I *knew* I had inside me. I had to learn to accept myself exactly as I was in my present moment over and over again, and each time, acknowledge that I do have value and that I was worth investing in, regardless of how broken I felt and was.

There are still days today, more than ten years into my personal healing journey, when I want to give up on all of my ambitions because a small part of me still believes myself unworthy of being seen, of receiving the accolades and the merit I know myself to be worthy of. Healing is an ongoing process; we can always become better people, better versions of ourselves, through authenticity, humility, and self-respect. The moment you believe you are done healing and that there is nothing more for you to dig into, always realize that this is your Ego talking. If you had nothing further to learn or embody in this lifetime, you would not be here physically anymore (since the goal of incarnation is to grow and evolve), so be patient with yourself and always stay open to seeing more than your own perspective. Be wary of anyone who tells you they are fully healed and have zero self-work to do, as they are strongly stuck in Ego. There may come a time in the future when the people who have been actively working on their personal healing come to a place where there is no more healing work to be done, but that day is not here yet, and these people are not there yet.

Going back to identifying the composition of my prison walls, I had to dig into every time I had told myself "no" for something I really wanted, every time I found excuses to limit myself and stay small, every single time I sabotaged myself in meeting my goals and going for my dreams. I had to look into every single time I let someone else get what I also wanted, where I let everyone pass in front of me, where I made others come first, and list every single way I was keeping myself in my "safe space" and never made too much noise. Our job in this chapter is to uncover every single time we betrayed ourselves, where we were not allowed to be authentically our Self. Our "safe zones" keep us from personal progress. They keep us small and hidden; they are more aspects of our self-imposed prison walls, which keep us from our true potential.

Staying in our "comfort zone" may feel warm and comfy, but it is still a prison. It completely limits us from being who we truly are and reaching our true potential. What is comfortable is often just a matter of perception. We can never be happy in a space that is too small to contain all of the Truth of who we really are. Our comfort zones keep us stuck and living in fear by limiting the range of our perceived capabilities, meaning that the truth of our capabilities is not adequately represented by where our comfort zone ends.

The most important step in our healing journey is to get to know our true, authentic selves, not the image we project for the benefit of those around us (even ourselves). Most of us grew up being told to stay small and unnoticeable to not "rock the boat." Most of us never even got the chance to discover and experience life as our true, authentic selves, even in small ways. This is also a journey of self-discovery that goes hand-in-hand with healing.

My kind of self-sabotage looked like:

"I won't apply for this job, I don't meet *all* the qualifications," when I was short maybe 1 or 2 optional traits.

"I'm not pretty nor thin enough to be taken seriously in the acting industry," so I never bothered to apply for agencies when acting has been my childhood dream and passion.

"I'm not good enough to ever be noticed," so I will not even bother trying, even though that choice is killing me inside.

"Who am I to think I could ever succeed and be recognized by others?"

"My body type is terrible; nothing ever fits me well."

"I look terrible all the time, why bother trying to look pretty? Everyone can see it's a scam."

"Why bother opening up to anyone? They'll all just leave me anyway."

"I can't do this, there's obviously someone better than me to do it."

"What if they're secretly thinking I'm a joke?"

"Who am I to believe I can do this?"

"What if I fail and make an utter fool of myself? No one will ever take me seriously…"

"It's better not to try to do anything if it won't be perfect the first time. I am obviously just incapable."

"People don't even try to understand me; they certainly don't care about me."

In my life, I was constantly being taken advantage of because I could not stand up for myself, which is the interesting part because I would always go out of my way to stand up for others. At my then job, I was doing the work of a manager, yet was still at minimum wage for months and months until I finally grew the nerve to ask for a raise, which was initially shut down hard. I eventually got it because my employer recognized my merit. When I left, he needed to hire three employees to cover what I was doing alone, but if I had said nothing, I would have stayed at minimum wage. I had to learn to stand up for myself, realize my worth, and choose to honour and respect it. I had to overcome all of my survival instincts to downplay my role and to keep accepting the scraps I was given as though they were my just reward. I had to choose that I deserved better for my Self and act accordingly. I had to recognize my own worth instead of waiting and hoping someone else would.

What I discovered was that all of these scenarios, limiting beliefs, and inner monologues were all based on fear. Our prison walls are all made up of our fears, both conscious and unconscious, which are always indicative of deeper wounding. The main driving force behind staying in our safe zones is always fear. Fear of being seen, fear of being hurt, fear of being disappointed, fear of failure, fear of not being good enough, fear of outside forces that are out of our control, etc. We have been exploring our personal fears in the last chapter—and getting to know ourselves better in the chapters before that—by impartially observing what is going on in our lives (whether thoughts, emotions, actions, or reactions), accepting everything unconditionally for exactly what it is, and digging into what it reveals about our inner reality.

The entirety of what we have been doing so far stems from a technique I have developed for myself that I am now sharing with you, which I call the AAUR technique. AAUR stands for Acknowledgement, Acceptance, Understanding, and Release. So far, the chapters have focused on acknowledging our inner workings and accepting what we are finding when we are digging into ourselves. Unless we acknowledge what we discover, we cannot accept what has happened and what is. It is impossible to truly understand something about ourselves if we have not accepted it as a truth first. Accepting what we uncover opens the door to understanding the *why* of things being present both internally and externally. Once we understand the why, we can start the process of letting go and releasing, being free from the hold of whatever wounding we have uncovered.

Fundamentally, the AAUR technique is about casting an honest, impartial, judgment-free look upon ourselves, including how we act, react, think, feel, and treat ourselves and others. This technique asks us to become a detached observer of how we go through day-to-day life so that we may understand the underlying currents that drive us. We can make our unconscious conscious by looking at all the clues and hints we are always dropping for ourselves and receiving as an answer to our vibrational energy. By becoming aware of every automated gesture and thought, we uncover the road to our inner blocks and false beliefs. This technique is the very essence of the entirety of the work we have been doing in Part I of this book. It can serve you for the rest of your life if done properly.

We know the Ego always seeks to justify itself—its behaviour, its actions, and its defense mechanisms—by placing blame outside of itself and refusing responsibility, accountability, and ownership of all that it does. If you do something hurtful to another (regardless of intention), your Ego will always claim that the other person/circumstance/event made you do it and that you truly had no choice in how you responded. Acknowledgment is how we start to outmaneuver the Ego. The Ego refuses to acknowledge the Truth of what happened—specifically, the role you played in the situation—because both you and your Ego are terrified of being seen as the "bad guy." The Ego wants to be the hero, the saviour, etc. A person in Ego tends to be narcissistic in that way. No fault can be laid bare at their feet because they are too "good" and "perfect" to have possibly done something wrong. Our Egos put us on an unreachable pedestal, completely disconnected from reality, to protect us from it. The first step in liberating ourselves from our Ego is to open up to the possibility of being wrong, of failing, of being hurtful, of reacting too strongly, of acting badly, of being a flawed human (which we all are).

When we stop fighting or ignoring what is plainly in front of us, we become open to seeing the truth of a situation. We have to actively recognize and see beyond the protective filter that our Ego surrounds us with. In defense of the Ego (which is but a tool for our human experience, nothing more), most of you reading these words will have come from a household where, as a child, you were not allowed to do anything wrong. You probably lived with an abusive or emotionally unavailable parent(s)/parental figure(s)/caretakers, where you learned to fear punishment. By default, you learned that you could not admit to your shortcomings, your faults, your curiosity, etc., because it would always land you with a punishment you believed to be disproportionate to the "bad" you had done. This is your Ego learning how to best protect itself within the circumstances of your upbringing. Our job as adults is to reparent ourselves into understanding that it is okay to make mistakes and to be who we currently are, as long as we keep working on our personal evolution of becoming better people in general.

By understanding that the Ego operates as a defense mechanism, it becomes increasingly fascinating to watch other people around us. When we start to understand ourselves from our prior history, which explains how we have become the "today" us, it becomes much easier to understand others and where they are coming from. It becomes easier to be patient and empathetic towards them as well. This absolutely means that we should cultivate patience and empathy for ourselves, also. The Truth our Ego always tries to keep from us is that we are the ones who need to heal. An external event or circumstance will always give us a clue as to what needs to be healed or worked on internally. (Quick note that you absolutely should come to the point of embodying empathy, but this *never* means allowing disrespect, abuse, or enabling the person you are feeling empathy for. More on boundaries in a later chapter.)

This does not mean that we will instantly understand and heal what is affecting us with the snap of our fingers. We might need multiple different clues before getting to the bottom of the message. Healing is a puzzle where we are constantly finding new pieces and trying to make them fit into the bigger picture we already know exists. Sometimes, we might have all the pieces and still cannot understand how they fit until we experience something that allows all the pieces to naturally fall into place to start making sense together. Healing is a lifelong journey, where we can always keep self-improving.

Going back to removing the Ego filter through acknowledgment, it becomes fundamental that we incorporate here the practice of being an impartial observer, which we have already been working on in the chapters thus far. What we seek to do is to own our responsibility for what happened. This does not mean taking all the blame: the moment we think in terms of "blame," we are still viewing things in terms of Ego. As impartial observers, we analyze our behaviour: our thoughts, actions, emotions, reactions, and whatever else draws our attention (and, more importantly, what is trying to escape our attention). Our subconscious will guide us to what we need to see, so listen to your intuition and to what calls to you. We will explore inner guidance in depth in a later chapter.

As a Soul experiencing life on Earth, our goal is to experience great contrast (throughout multiple lifetimes) so we can sort through what we do and do not want to experience in an optimal life, which is why we now have multiple wounds to heal. We have already lived countless lives, rich with their own experiences and contrasts, and we are now coming to a distilment of what we wish to remove from what we will want to experience both for the rest of this life and future lifetimes. We can view this self-healing work as the point of transformation, as the caterpillar builds its cocoon so that it may become a butterfly. This process takes time and dedicated effort, but the results make all the struggle worthwhile. As the caterpillar, we also have to melt down and rebuild the essence of who we are to reveal our inner beauty and potential. Even the ugliest caterpillar can make itself into a most beautiful butterfly, but we have to do the work of transformation first.

This is where acceptance comes in. Once we have acknowledged the existence of a wound or identified its underlying factors, we have to accept it both for what it is and how we have been behaving as a direct result of this wound. This means taking back our power and owning our responsibility for the actions, reactions, outbursts, and so on that we may have done due to being wounded. The fact that we understand we were reacting and acting out of wounding does not give us a free pass to disregard accountability. By taking responsibility for the pain we may have caused others, we are opening a door directly into our capacity for self-healing. This is often where shame steps in and stops us in our process of healing.

Most people I know who have wronged others are ashamed of themselves (often unconsciously), making it very hard to acknowledge and accept what they have done. People are often ashamed of their behaviour, and instead of acknowledging this, they will go above and beyond to justify themselves by placing blame elsewhere. This is the vicious cycle we want to observe and understand. To let shame win means to let our Ego stay in control. Acceptance demands true humility and forgiveness towards the Self, in spite of the intense feelings of shame and/or guilt that may be present.

Acceptance demands personal vulnerability, which is a gateway of absolute importance for self-healing. This is why I have been asking you to practice silent, judgment-free observation: there is no other way you can access your inner healing than by accepting your shortcomings. The Ego believes itself to be beyond reproach and error. Acceptance allows us to be kind, gentle, forgiving, and nurturing towards ourselves and others, without which inner healing cannot happen.

Next comes understanding. When we seek to understand the why behind our actions and reactions, we are truly uncovering the wound at the source of our unwanted behaviours, so that we may put a definite stop to its effects. This step supports the previous work of acknowledgment and acceptance and acts as the stepping stone to being able to release that baggage. As long as we hold onto the energy of the wound by not actively seeking it out and healing, its effect will always keep showing up in our lives. When we understand our motivations and their roots, we can actively work on changing them. Our purpose in this lifetime is to heal. Healing on an individual level brings about healing at a collective level.

Following are a few examples of ways we hold onto the energy of the wounds (more often than not through identifying with victimhood and giving it importance): associating with and giving importance to the story we have fabricated around an event to justify why things happened the way they did; being addicted to the drama of what happened and milking reactions in others; actively seeking out empathy and sympathy from others for "what happened to you"; constantly reliving and revisiting what happened with no effort to make peace with it; wearing your pain as a badge of honour and as a way to feel superior to others; holding onto the energy of victimhood and badgering those who "couldn't possibly understand"; making your whole persona revolve around the event; believing your wound allows you to dictate what others can feel, or belittling another's experience by comparing with your own; etc.

The Truth is that when we have done our healing work, letting go becomes not only possible but wanted and needed as closure. As long as we associate who we are directly with our wounding, we cannot heal, release, and grow from it. You will know you have done the work when recalling the event no longer triggers an emotional response. This does not mean you feel nothing; it just means that you are not overwhelmed by its memory, that it does not touch anything sensitive within, and that you can truthfully affirm being at peace with the matter as a whole. You are now content within yourself despite what has occurred. That event does not define who you are anymore; it becomes a part of your life experience instead, without your entire world revolving around attachment to it. This kind of release will make you feel lighter both within and without. Healing wounds is like shedding energetic weight and can be felt physically. Low-vibrational energies feel heavy in the body where they are stuck.

Which brings us to the question: *how do we release?* Understanding requires us to dig deep within ourselves to understand the *why* of things. Understanding brings clarity and reveals answers we may not have known were within us the whole time. There is always an explanation for why things are the way they are, and we, as humans, are no exception to that. At this point, I will ask you to expand your mind and open up to the reality that we are entirely energetic beings living a physical life. Our Souls are energy, and time is not linear.

As best as I understand it, all of our lifetimes are piled up onto one another, with the single thread of our Soul linking every single one of them, as a straight line spearing through and connecting them all together. This means that what happened in a past life, which traumatized our Soul in a specific way, can be—and is—carried into our Soul's energy in this lifetime through that thread. Our current memories are specific to this lifetime, but our Soul knows all of them from all our lives at all times at the same time. Everything is happening simultaneously for the Soul while individually for the lives.

This not only explains irrational fears and phobias (deaths and/or traumas occurring in another lifetime that mark the Soul) but also explains why certain people feel instantly familiar to us – our Soul recognizes their Soul's energy. There is a whole invisible web connecting every single person on Earth, and nothing is ever random. Coincidences are not random occurrences; they happen for a reason – to catch your attention. The Ego view is too small to understand this, but the Soul *knows of and sees the bigger picture*.

Your outside world is a rich vision of your inside circumstances, always. When it comes to wounds, the source, or core wound, is almost never in this lifetime *because* this is a lifetime with a mission of healing. What we experience in the here and now is often a bleed-through from a past life that seeks to be healed. There are two layers to healing here: the physical repercussions in this lifetime and the source of the wound in a past lifetime. We heal the physical to ensure a better life ahead of us, and we heal the energetic level of the past life wound to ensure the energy is cleared and will not keep showing up as lessons in this life for us to heal from and address the underlying wounding.

This is where I categorize healing work into three separate categories: Current Accountability healing (CA), which is performed on a physical level; Energetic Release healing (ER), which combines physical and energetic healing; and Soul-depth healing (SD), which is a purely energetic practice. The first two can be done on our own. The third requires outside help as it digs deep into the subconscious and Soul knowledge we hold, but simply cannot access by ourselves. We cannot yet dive into our subconscious consciously, hence we need a healer to assist us. If we cannot see what we need to see in an unbiased manner (to understand where our wounds come from), then we cannot release the guilt or other emotions that keep us stuck within a specific pattern. The release is about self-forgiveness, seeing the higher purpose of an event, and understanding that what happened was not our fault; therefore, this energy is not ours to carry around. It is about letting go of guilt (imagined or real) felt towards the situation.

It is very important for me to stress at this point that no healer will ever "magic away" all your wounding for you. It is simply impossible. There is no benefit to "blindfolded" healing, where the healer does everything for you and tells you that "*you are all better now.*" Sure, you might *feel* better for a little while, but as long as you do not facilitate and are present for your healing, the wounds always come back *because there is no understanding happening*. Simply put, ignoring a problem does not make it go away. Only when you identify the problem, understand where it comes from, seek out the source, and then consciously choose to heal, learn, let go, and move on will you see real, lasting results.

An easy way to understand healing is to picture a massively dirty car, and I mean crusty, mud-caked, dirty car. A healer would be the water hose. Different healers have different kinds of water pressure, but simply using a hose (even a pressure washer) will never completely clean your car. You have to be willing to soap and scrub if you want actual results that last. Just using a pressure washer on your car might make it feel like dirt is coming off, but the true gritty parts that are important to get off will stay on and cling until they are scrubbed off with soap. But you have to find the dirty spots first to know they exist and need cleaning. This is why I always suggest doing some work on yourself before consulting a healer; this way, you already know where to apply the scrubbing pressure. Sometimes, in a healing session, when you come prepared to heal one thing, the work you have already done within allows for a few other different aspects of healing to be ready to be "cleaned" at the same time.

Let's start by exploring the first type of healing work: current accountability (CA). We have already been working on this level of healing through the regression journaling and self-analysis exercises implemented since the first chapters, culminating in the AAUR technique. Release can be done on a personal level through CA healing when the pain/unresolved trauma is experienced first-hand in this lifetime, aka childhood and early developmental years, through early adult years, up to where you are today. CA healing is always about this lifetime.

Have you ever experienced recurring memories that keep coming back in an incessant loop? You think you are done thinking about whatever the situation was, yet it always sneaks right back into your thoughts. These memories show us our stuck emotions that want to be healed. Have you ever been so hurt by someone that you do everything in your power to never cross paths with them again? This is a Soul connection asking for you to find forgiveness within. Forgiveness is such an important and powerful tool in our healing journeys, and we will dive in-depth into this subject in a chapter entirely dedicated to forgiveness. Needless to say, avoiding someone or blocking them always means you are holding onto that energy because you are choosing not to face it. True release is found in letting go, and when you truly let go, you become completely and healthily unbothered by that person, regardless of what happened between you. Blocking and avoiding mean you *are* bothered. Therefore, you cling to that energy, meaning you are still clinging to that connection and person.

The AAUR technique is truly about regaining our personal power. What does that mean? Our personal power is how we move around in the world, our level of confidence, happiness, contentment, joy, etc. All the good feelings in life come from being in our personal power and recognizing our own sovereignty. What does this have to do with CA healing? As long as we do not believe ourselves worthy of love and respect—namely, our own—we will never receive them from outside sources, regardless of how much healing we do.

Before anyone else can give you love, you have to give love to yourself; same with respect and every other positive interaction. If you want to be taken care of by someone, then you have to take care of yourself completely on your own first.

This means, out of pure self-love and self-respect, we have to look at all of the times in this life when we have been and acted as "the bad guy." We owe it to ourselves to hold ourselves accountable where we have been less than stellar, both towards our person and towards other people. We have all been assholes to other people at least once in our lives, regardless of whether it was intentional or not. We have all been assholes to ourselves countless times. There is no denying our humanity in the process of healing. This is why I have been hammering in for chapters now to look at yourself objectively and judgment-free, so you can start forgiving yourself. We are all human; we all do hurtful things. It is up to us to choose to become better, and that starts with self-honesty. The goal of healing ourselves is to evolve beyond our current limitations. We want to become better to receive better and simply feel better in general.

Keep looking objectively at yourself and using the AAUR technique to finally be able to release. Review the steps daily, if you have to, so the natural flow of the technique sinks in and becomes second nature. Release is a conscious choice we have to make to let go of all the negative attachments we hold onto with given situations in our lives. We always need forgiveness to release. Forgiveness is the key to letting go.

Let's focus now on the second type of healing: Energetic Release healing (ER). When it comes to ER healing, we are using both tangible physical aspects of healing, combined with a powerful boost of energetic healing. What does this look like? Reiki, acupuncture, massage therapy, hypnotherapy, etc. This type of energetic healing has a physical anchor point or modality. Even if you do not believe in energy work, energy still works on you. It is not so much a question of belief but one of open-mindedness and allowance. What we resist persists.

Throughout your healing journey with this book, one of the goals is to get you back in touch with your own body and intuition. As you start doing healing work, you may not yet be in tune with your energy or vibration, and that is okay. As you become more comfortable within yourself and make your body your home—and really start listening to what your inner workings are telling you—you will begin to feel your energies simply because you are attuning to them by coming back into your body. This will also help you understand what kind of blockages are held within you, both on a physical and energetic level.

Energetic Release healing sessions will only ever go as far as you have. What do I mean by this? These are *release* modalities. Using the AAUR technique, we understand that there needs to be acknowledgment, acceptance, and understanding before there can be release. In some cases, understanding and release are intertwined, but there has to be acknowledgment and acceptance happening before release can take place. Why? Because how can you possibly release something you are not even aware you are holding on to? We release what feels like unwanted excess. Therefore, we cannot release what we have not yet identified as excess, just as we cannot free ourselves from something we believe is vital to who we are.

Other than seeing professionals offering the modalities listed above and others, energetic release becomes something you can do on your own with personal rituals. I recommend starting with the help of professionals first, as you start getting a sense of your own energy. Still, when you are attuned to yourself, you can start doing symbolic rituals to help release stuck energies within. The key needed here is to be able to work with our energy to help it flow out through our body.

I personally love using the elements as assisting cleansing tools. Water is the element of the emotional realm, earth is the element of the physical realm, air is the element of the mental realm, and fire represents the energetic realm. Most of us have an element that speaks to us more than the others, although all can be used at your discretion. Since the goal in working with the elements is energetic release, what really matters is the ritual and the intentions, not the element itself. You can intuitively come up with your own ritual as long as the steps remain consistent with what you have learned so far.

Whatever element you choose to work with, the focus is always to set intentions of release. Let's use the example of working with fire. You could have had a bad breakup and cannot get rid of the person's energy, or they blocked you, and you cannot receive in-person closure (which is only necessary for the Ego). You could write down everything that is bothering you in a letter addressed to them, where you lay down everything you could possibly wish to communicate, which would give you closure. Remember that closure only ever comes from within, never without. You can ask the Universe, Mother Earth, or whatever it is you believe in to help you release all of these things, then burn the letter while thanking the fire for its wonderful cleansing properties, while feeling grateful for the love and support they both offer you.

All the elements have amazing cleansing properties. Soaking in any body of water while intentionally asking for it to remove all unnecessary energies attached to you, to wash away all that no longer serves you, is a powerful cleansing ritual that can also be done in a shower or bath. The trick is to really let yourself connect to the element first. Working with air can be as simple as standing outside in a wind gale or working with your breath, while the earth element requires direct skin contact. The element becomes a tangible anchor point for energetic release. To be clear, ER healing is about releasing what has already been uncovered. You cannot wish away a lesson or wound, as they must be learned and/or healed for them to be able to leave our bodies and for us to progress on a Soul level.

Working with the elements becomes a very personal process. I could give you any number of examples and rituals, but the best results will always come from how you intuitively feel you should proceed. You may have a default element to fall back on, but in some situations, you may be drawn to use another. It entirely depends on you as a person and a Soul and on the element required for optimal healing and release. There will be a later chapter on intuition—listening to and trusting the inner self.

Most holistic healers in today's world focus on this kind of work. They can be a good starting point for your healing journey and help you navigate what needs to be addressed. Keep in mind that you will never get as good results with someone who "does the work for you" as you would with someone who acts as your guide and assists you in your healing. After all, it is YOUR healing journey, your work to do. A helping hand can be welcome, but we cannot grow dependent on it. Otherwise, we miss the entire point of healing, which is to face ourselves and cut away our own bullshit. You will probably encounter the healers you are meant to work with naturally, as they all have Soul contracts to work with you. Pay attention to your intuition to feel for what will work best for you. Remember that there are no mistakes when things do not turn out how we think we want them to. There is only information to gather and lessons to learn.

Whenever we engage in a healing session, planning for time off afterward is always important. Some sessions will leave you drained because some blockages are just that strongly ingrained that it takes a lot of energy out of you to let go of them, or that they were so heavy that existing without this extra weight is destabilizing. You and your body have to adapt to its new capabilities. Carrying energetic baggage takes a lot of energy from us. Therefore, getting all of that empty energetic space back through release can leave us feeling exhausted. Give yourself time to see how things change in your life afterward, and welcome those changes as they come. Do not worry about the changes manifesting themselves, and keep working on yourself in the meantime. Detachment is how we allow things to come into our physical reality.

Some changes will be instantaneous, and others will take a little longer before showing up in your everyday life, but whenever they do, make a note of it in your Journal. By keeping track of your unlearned beliefs and healed wounds, you will be able to see when a pattern starts repeating or if the wound has deeper layers. Layers in wounding are normal, as the deeper you dig, the more you can unravel different aspects of the same wound. As you do more healing, revisiting what was before can help shift your perspective, or your new perspective will allow deeper insight into what was before.

Moving on to the next and final healing modality, we will look into what Soul-depth (SD) healing entails. This type of healing cannot be done alone, simply because accessing our Soul knowledge is done in the subconscious. We cannot consciously enter the subconscious yet. However, we can understand our intuition as being whispers of guidance from our Soul, which comes from the subconscious. When we talk about healing on a Soul level, this implies working with past lives as they are simply another aspect of our human experience as a Soul because time itself is not linear as we understand it to be.

SD healing entails diving into your Akashic Records (your Soul's history library) to uncover core wounds, karmic cycles, and false beliefs you hold to be true so you can free yourself from all of them. Most struggles you experience in this current life come from these past wounds, and they attract situations that should grab your attention to focus on healing that particular aspect. Obviously, these instances are never feel-good moments because why would you want to heal something that feels good?

In my experience, the more you ignore your healing and inner guidance, the harder you perceive life to become. The Universe will keep looping you into the wounded cycles until you decide you want to grow and learn, but each cycle will become more and more unbearable until you have no choice but to choose to free yourself by healing. After all, the reason you have incarnated now is because your Soul *wants* to heal. Therefore, the Universe will keep nudging you in the right direction even (and especially) when your Ego does not want to follow suit until you feel you have no choice in the matter anymore. This is how we should understand free will: you are free to choose not to learn and heal, but it will come at a steeper price later on, regardless. This is why we have to learn to be brave in facing ourselves, because the cost of not doing so often comes at a very high price. Doing the healing work leads to personal freedom and fulfillment simply because we are removing all that is keeping us from attaining our highest good vibrational truth.

Truthfully, sometimes, we do need a good metaphorical slap in the face because we would never become aware of something being awry otherwise. What we have to understand here is that these situations come to light in our lives out of pure, universal, unconditional love. The Universe loves us and wants us to be whole, hale, and happy. We cannot be our best, brightest, fulfilled, and loving selves when we carry around trauma energies. However, most trauma we have accumulated in past lives stems from false beliefs created in situations we misunderstood as our Egoic Self. Diving into the Akashic records allows us to understand the Soul-truth of a given situation, so we can release the false belief and associated core wound created then and there by seeing how wrong the person we were then was in the lesson they chose to learn.

This dissolves the belief, as it simply is not the Truth of the situation from a Soul perspective and, therefore, cannot remain in our energy. Releasing that in this review of a lifetime allows for that energy to drop from our current lifetime and vibration since all of our past lifetimes, future lifetimes, and current lifetimes are connected by our Souls. And since time does not exist outside of the Earth sphere, we are simultaneously experiencing all of these lives at the exact same time. There is no real beginning or real end. Just as we start life as a baby, and we grow and mature into adulthood and eventually into death, we may start the process all over again in the next incarnation. Our

Soul had a preliminary first life as a baby and grew throughout all of its incarnations until their last one, where all intended lessons have been learned, and growth has been topped out to the point where there is nothing left to learn, no more way for our Soul to grow. This is called ascension, which means we are fully merged into Oneness as a Soul being. It means we are attuned to all that is and live from a Soul perspective at all times, as there has been the full realization and acceptance that there is nothing else.

An example of this in sessions I have done myself would be the process of healing my relationship with God, along with my abandonment wound. I saw that lifetime as a young girl living in a coastal village in Asia somewhere, where her parents had instructed her to flee and hide in a cave by the shore as the village was being invaded by Huns in the middle of the night. I could see flames, and I knew death was around, so I ran. My then-parents had told me they would find me in this cave and to stay put, no matter what I heard, that they would come for me when it was safe. Obviously, they never did, as they had been murdered while protecting my escape.

But that little girl died in that cave, waiting for her parents and praying, praying so hard for her parents to come and get her so that she would not be alone and terrified anymore. She prayed so hard and shattered when she understood no one was coming, and she cursed God for having abandoned her like this. She drowned with the tide, as she was too terrified to leave the perceived safety of the cave, and she had been told to stay put no matter what. She had believed that everyone she loved had abandoned her, including God, translating the experience into the belief that she was not worthy of feeling safe, warm, and loved. She chose to believe that the world was unsafe and out to hurt her. She chose to translate her experience into the belief that those she loved dearly would always abandon her when she needed them the most.

These beliefs that the little girl died while creating and holding onto have shown prominently in my own life here and now, where I was always on my own growing up. Neither of my parents was emotionally available, and they never gave me what I felt I needed. This was the abandonment wound showing up, along with more instances here and there in my life. I greatly resented God with all my heart, even though I grew up in a Catholic community. I was completely closed off to people, as whenever I tried to open up, I would be rejected and shut down hard by others. I was, in essence, alone in the world. I had to rely only on myself, as everyone else in my life always let me down or made me feel like a burden when I asked for something, so it reinforced those false beliefs in me, the very beliefs that attracted these situations to me vibrationally in the first place. I had to become aware that I was carrying these energies through living them and seeing them as my truth.

I can see now that I grew up with those circumstances because my Soul wanted to be rid of these false beliefs. Viewing that lifetime and how I came to learn these lessons—while also realizing from a Soul perspective that God never abandoned me, and neither did my parents (they just could not come to save me because they were dead)—meant I could let go of the thought that I was a burden, not wanted, not enough, and not loved. On the contrary, I was extremely loved and supported, but I had given in to fear. I learned afterward from that session and being able to see the Soul's perspective of what had happened, that what was intended for that little girl (had she exited the cave instead of giving in to her fear), was to be found by other survivors busy restoring their village, and that a family member who had survived was looking for her and would have taken good care of her.

This little girl had chosen fear instead of her intuition, which was softly whispering to her that she should go back to the village. She exercised her free will and made the easier choice of giving in to her fears, which were much louder within her, instead of confronting them and moving beyond them to trust that her inner voice would guide her to safety. There is no need to place blame on this little girl. Her choice still helped me grow and evolve today, and so I am thankful for her and her experience. As stated previously, we live in a world of contrast. The worst of our experiences allow us to rubber-band-stretch-explode toward experiencing the absolute best in contrast. I had to experience choosing fear to be able to see that it is never there for my best interest. Fear always keeps us small, isolated, and alone. We always have to choose to overcome fear, as fear is always an illusion.

After that session, my whole relationship with the world and with God shifted. A lot of us will have bad relationships with religion because of past life trauma. It is important not to mistake religion for spirituality. God, Allah, Source, and the Universe are all the same thing. Any and all deities are just this idea of a higher power that governs all. The word God has been abused and humanified too much nowadays to hold any real value compared to what the Universe really is, so it can be easier to connect with this ideology by using words like Universe and Spirit, or Source. If God is a triggering word for you, as it was for me, know that it means you have a wound attached to the Divine. We have to understand that the Universe is a safe, loving place that wants to give us everything we need by reconnecting with our true selves, by understanding that we are One with and within the Universe, but that it will not enable people who refuse to work on themselves. Rewards come from overcoming our traumas, not by ignoring them.

By embodying the Truth of who we are as Souls, we can live a blissful, easy, satisfying life of undiluted happiness and joy. It may seem impossible at first, but just take the time to imagine a world where everyone is connected and knows of this connection. There would be no hardships. There would only be love and support in every corner of the world: we would live in peace and harmony as a species, as we were always meant to. This may sound like an unattainable ideal, but you would be wrong to assume so. I have pondered on how to actually get the world to change for the better like this, and the answer came to me swiftly and strongly, as though it was the simplest thing to grasp: we change the world one person at a time, by choosing that we want better for ourselves. Doing this inner healing work individually leads to our changing the entire world from within.

PART II

CONNECTING WITH THE SOUL

Now that we have a basic understanding of who we are and how we function in this world (and keep digging into it), and we have accepted that there is more going on than our base human senses can pick up, it is time to start the process of connecting with our Soul. Shifting realities, or perceptions, from the 3rd dimensional to the 5th dimensional way of living translates to moving from living in our Ego perception of life to living from our Soul understanding of life by transcending the lesson, or illusion, of the 4th dimension: time.

Just like any other talent, intuition is a skill that can be developed, and some people have an easier time accessing it. Just like a naturally talented musician connects with music easily, some people are more naturally intuitive than others. However, just like any other skill, everyone can practice and master intuition, given that they put in the time and practice. It all depends on the willingness and effort of an individual. Yes, some people will need to put in more conscious work than others, and that is okay. Every one of us has our own unique path of healing to do, and some of us have particular wounds to heal with Divine energy before our connection with intuition becomes crystal clear. Some Souls have worked at it for lifetimes to be able to have an easier connection with their own intuition in this lifetime. Some Souls are very young and simply do not have the same amount of practice from other lifetimes to guide them.

Regardless, what is important to remember as we start our journey into Part II of this book is that we have to learn to trust ourselves and trust the Universe. Nothing ever happens without reason, just as nothing is ever coincidental. Whatever happens in our current reality is there for our highest good, especially when we do not understand how or why. Therefore, when we are confronted with difficult-to-digest situations, it becomes easier to know that the situation is not really about us personally but rather that it is meant to help us learn something important. This understanding may be difficult while in the situation, but time and other circumstances will help bring about understanding later. This has been true for every circumstance I would deem horrible that has happened to me, or that I have witnessed for others. Hard situations, while never easy, always offer guidance in some way.

In this Part, we will examine the self-imposed ceiling of our prison (which we have been outlining the contours of in the previous chapters) while also learning about intuition and other clairs or "psychic gifts." Afterward, we will examine the Chakra system and how it functions, then wrap up with the power of forgiveness and how to best utilize it for our personal growth and Soul evolution.

Throughout the rest of this book, continue working on the Self as we have previously learned how to. Healing is a lifelong process. As we focus on self-healing, this becomes the energy we put into the world. Do not be surprised if, in the coming weeks or months (however and whenever it shows up for you), many triggering events will facilitate your healing process. Also, look for the underlying clues of why these situations happen, what is triggered within you, or what wants to be seen and addressed, and Journal about your thoughts and discoveries. Keep re-reading the previous chapters as needed until the information becomes second nature.

At this point, keep an awareness out for whatever repeats or draws your attention, things you cannot help but notice, which stay in your awareness over time. These may indicate possible healing modalities for you to try or a new path you should follow in your life. Be discerning and trust that you are safe to follow these clues. Trust and have faith that the Universe is now placing these things in your path intentionally so that you can pick up on them more readily. Investigate and see what wants to be seen without judgment, as judgment clouds intuition! Always use what resonates with you and upgrade your own understanding and self-healing techniques as you go. Use these opportunities to identify when your own fear gets in the way. There is no wrong way to heal, unless we are simply choosing not to.

Feel safe knowing that everything is always perfect and in service to the highest good of all (including your own). I am very proud of you for having come this far, and I hope you will be proud of yourself and your personal progress as you keep witnessing it happening.

Let's keep digging!

Chapter 5
The Glass Ceiling

———————— • ————————

In the previous part of the book, we have started exploring the confines of our self-imposed prison by understanding that we are the creators of our own limiting beliefs. We are expanding upon the limits of our prison—including its foundation—by starting to seek out and heal core wounds. We push back these walls by exploring beyond our comfort zone, through understanding that they are only held up by our fears. Now, we begin exploring what makes up the ceiling of our cozy little prison: that which keeps us from our natural connection with our Soul and the Universe.

Let's take a closer look at the elements that compose this glass ceiling. Why have we severed our connection to Source, and why have we decided to shut out Divine energy from our lives? This barrier we have erected ourselves (regardless of whether it originated in this life or a previous one) comes from a belief of betrayal and/or abandonment. We have come to believe that it is not safe to connect and trust in the Universe, and that we will always be let down or disappointed because we are not getting what we want and/or asked for.

There is an incredibly important distinction to make here: what our Ego wants is rarely aligned with what our Soul wants for ourselves. By mistaking an Ego want/need for a Soul want/need, we may have fooled ourselves into believing that the Universe has let us down. The Truth is that as long as the Ego is driving the car, we will never get to our intended destination because only the Soul knows the way.

The wounded Ego is amazing at throwing tantrums over nothing. It demands the true path to follow while simultaneously completely refusing to listen to indications because it believes it knows everything and does not need anyone's help. This is the energy we want to identify and disentangle from our True Self. Believing we can control life from an Ego perspective is ludicrous because our Ego is not aligned with our highest good. It is still in survival mode, protecting us from any and all perceived threats, regardless of whether these are indeed real.

We may also be nurturing beliefs that it is not safe to connect with, nor trust, the Universe, that we need to fight to have our very basic needs met, and that we cannot rely on anybody other than ourselves (and even there we usually do not trust ourselves fully because we are disconnected from the True Self). Imagine living in this state of extreme tension, as though your cord is constantly taut and nearing its breaking point. Some— if not most—of us are probably living like this right now. I know that I was, *and* that I was not even close to being aware of it at the time.

My own cord did end up snapping, and everything within me unraveled. I have been subjected to incredible amounts of abuse, to the point where my brain was completely burned out and not functioning properly. I was severely depressed and suicidal because it felt like life itself just wanted me gone, and I simply did not have it in me anymore to fight against this. The only reason I am still alive today is because I knew for a fact no one would take care of my cat if I chose to follow through with my suicide plan. I valued my cats' well-being above my own life because I felt like I had no reason to keep on living just to endure endless abuse.

However, when I did reach this absolute rock-bottom point in my life, I was forced to drop everything I was doing and just rest. I could not function. I was on medical leave and still could not rid myself of the stress that had taken over my body, essentially paralyzing me in more ways than one. What saved me was to turn toward my spiritual side, which had started showing up more strongly in my life prior to arriving at this point. I had that spiritual foundation to rely on in my lowest, darkest times, and it was the only foundation that survived my unraveling. I had nothing else to fall back on, but it was there when I needed it most. Not only did it stay with me, but it also ended up being the only thing that stayed in my life that actually made sense. People could not help me. They simply were not capable of understanding or reaching me. But Spirit was always there, guiding me, reassuring me, and helping me keep the hope alive that life was worth living.

This is something each and every one of you will come to understand, although hopefully not when you have let your wounded Ego drive you into the ground as mine had. I was so attached to my outside circumstances that I could not let myself see the truth of reality. The 3D illusions were all I put my faith in. I was very much the "I need to see it to believe it" type of person, thinking science had all the answers and nothing else was real. But energy does not work that way, and so I had to learn. Energy does not care for any personal belief; it simply is what it is and works how it works. It does not change on a whim; it is constant in its presence and flow.

A typically strongly held belief I encounter when talking about energy is that if a higher power truly did exist, then there would not be so much evil in the world; it would be a much better place to live in. I am also rebuked often with the "fact" that we have no physical proof of a higher power existing in the first place. Both of these statements are wrong and framed entirely from an Ego perspective. The simplest to start with is the one claiming there is no proof of a higher power: all you have to do to see it is to look around. I ask you now, assuming you have done the work from the previous module up to this point, if there has truly ever been a coincidence in your life? Or have you started to realize just how interconnected everything truly is? One door shutting in our face leads to another, better one opening.

When we start doing healing work, and we get to a point where we have done enough that we start seeing the truth of our everyday reality being nothing more than a massive illusion (and that energy is the only driving force in the Universe), we get to see the patterns of the Universe working through and around us in this 3D reality. We realize that nothing is ever random and that it is, in fact, the Universe communicating with us by dropping hints and clues. Whenever we see synchronicities, as in repeating numbers or animals or any other sign we ask for and identify, that *is* the Universe communicating with us. The answer to the meaning of this communication can *always* be found within, but we have to learn to listen and trust what comes up.

As for the reason why there is so much "evil" in the world, we first have to remove ourselves from taking it personally. The fact that there are people who hurt others deliberately is not about you, even when it affects you personally. It is part of their own Soul process. Just as you have lived lives where you were an abusive, sadistic person who hurt others deliberately, you also have lived lives where you could be compared to a saint. Every single Soul has to experience both sides of duality to its fullest before being able to return to Oneness. This is never an excuse to deliberately hurt others, but it does explain the assholes in our lives and worldwide.

Planet Earth is a school of creation magic and is about harmonizing order and chaos as One. This is why we have Soul contracts that link us to others. Whenever we have a Soul contract with someone where one of us (or both) deliberately hurt one another, that contract is always done in the most profoundly unconditionally loving way *from a Soul perspective*, with the goal of evolution and learning as an outcome. The web of Life is too complex for the human mind to comprehend, but the Soul *knows* the Truth of these things on a scale that the human mind ignores and cannot comprehend *because* having that knowledge would take away the learning opportunity. Free will is the capacity to choose between growth and stagnation.

This does not mean we should lie down and take whatever abuse comes our way for the sake of evolution, absolutely not. Part of life is to experience contrast. This means to experience both what we want and what we do not want so that we may get to live the best life has to offer. We are all part of the Universe, experiencing itself and the possibilities of life as a human being, as a vessel that can carry all of the colours of the rainbow. This is why we go through both negative and positive experiences, so we can learn what we truly want and desire, and then learn to focus on what we actually want to attract more of through our energetic output. Whatever we focus on is what we attract more of. Right now, in 2025, we seem to be experiencing a collective shift of standing up for ourselves and demanding a better quality of life for all. There are many examples of this coming up in our everyday reality, but they are happening through experiencing the contrast of what lack of proper care for all is shaping up to look like and how undesirable it is on a global scale.

How we resist connecting with the Universe stems from our wounded perception of the world we live in. This is why shifting our perspective from Ego to Soul, as we have started doing in the previous chapters, is crucial to healing and growing. It is time to stop taking everything we see with our eyes at face value while believing there is nothing more going on than what the surface shows us. Shifting perceptions is one of the greatest tools we can use to start shifting into the life we have always wanted for ourselves.

Having an open mind about all you have been reading so far and what you will read in this book is another crucial tool, as it goes hand-in-hand with shifting perspectives. We cannot grow and evolve if our minds are closed. We will keep staying stuck exactly where we are, which is not where we want to be, nor should be, which means our current reality will keep growing more and more uncomfortable until we choose to open ourselves up to possibilities.

The example from my own life of hitting rock bottom is exactly this lesson that if we refuse to go, be, and do what/where we are meant to go, be, and do willingly, the Universe will step in and ensure we start aligning with our purpose regardless of how our Egos choose to experience it. The beautiful thing with this is that when we start going the wrong way again (usually out of fear and lack of trust/faith in the universe or our Self or true calling), the exact same warning signs will start popping up again. It will be our choice to heed them or fall back into the exact same pattern and problem. When we are meant to learn a lesson, we will repeat a cycle until it is learned over and over again. When we *think we have* learned the lesson, it is not the end of the tests: we are always further tested to ensure the learning is true to the point of second nature instead of being a self-delusion of understanding.

How can I affirm this so confidently? From my personal experience, yet again. My previous burnout adventure in pursuing a career in a field I cared not for, but would bring in massive amounts of money. I was good at it, but was brought down continuously by the other players' wounding and projections, and the establishment that masquerades as abuse and teaching incompetence as resilience and "only-the-best-succeed" attitude to the point of my rock-bottom experience. After trying (and failing) at pursuing my spiritual practice because of my own wounds, trauma, and mostly lack of faith in myself, I decided to go to university and try a different career path.

I wanted to further my knowledge and understanding of how the "educated" world understood things; therefore, I chose to major in psychology, but I already knew that the potential jobs were of no interest to me. I felt immense pressure at that time to just get with the program and do what everyone else was doing, because what else could I possibly do? Who did I think I was, not doing what everybody else was doing? How dare I think I could get away with being different and making different choices for my life? Hadn't all of my failures proved I could never achieve anything on my own? Better to just follow the crowd, keep my head down, and be just another number amongst numbers.

Again, I chose not to follow my guidance in favour of my Ego and the expectations others placed upon me. And so, while still reeling from my burnout/depression/suicidal state of being, I went back to school.

In December, right before the final exams of the first term were to take place, I experienced a mysterious illness that made me spend the night at the hospital, where no doctor had any way of knowing or explaining what had happened to me. Even though it seemed like it could have been an epileptic seizure, none of my symptoms (other than the physical ones) matched up, and nothing was found following all the tests and blood work they did afterward. I had no after-effects and have not had another episode to this day, although the experience left me in a state of complete mental and physical exhaustion. My brain could not retain any information if I tried studying. Therefore, I was incapable of doing any of my exams, meaning they would all be deferred to the following semester's reading week.

Anyone who has been to university can understand how much more challenging (and in my state of being, impossible) this would have been, as it would have involved studying new classes while keeping up with the old ones, having the previous term exams crammed between new term mid-term exams, and no rest period as that would have been the purpose of a reading week.

All of this while still physically and mentally recuperating from my episode, having extremely low levels of energy, and living with the fear that this mysterious, debilitating illness might strike out of nowhere again and leave me worse for wear once more. I was under so much pressure while not regaining any energy and feeling more exhausted by the day, until I chose to drop out of my classes because I knew I could not keep pushing myself that way; otherwise, I would burn out again. Making that decision for my own well-being filled me with shame.

The Universe made sure I understood I had to let it all go by creating a semester where the workload would be ridiculously costly to my well-being (meaning midterms before my previous semester's final exams, all crammed within five days, with more midterms afterward and then more final exams within a month after that. This meant I would have had to do the equivalent of two full semesters of work and studying within a single term, with no break whatsoever in between. Madness. Especially since my personal energy levels were still very low and slow to come back from my rock-bottom episode.

What came up for me then was that very distinct memory of that rock-bottom burnout from my previous career choice, and I knew that if I tried to follow through with that insane semester, odds were I would end up right back there, in the exact same mental place again, and there was no way in hell I would allow myself to go through that again. Once was enough. I realized then that I loved myself enough to say no to things that were destructive to me. And so, I quit university out of self-love. It took longer than that period of my life for me to truly start following my purpose because I kept trying other ways of being just like everyone else out of Ego and fear, which all kept failing me over and over again, simply because I was not following my inner guidance and instead doing what my mind thought I ought to do. This was to show me how the Universe is always guiding us toward our true purpose when we step aside and decide to listen. Ultimately, it is always our choice to trust it and follow its guidance, but the Universe will always keep redirecting us until we choose to flow with life instead of fighting against it.

I realized with hindsight that I was once again following a path that would not serve my Soul purpose, though I did not want to see it. I wanted to be normal, to have a normal life, but we simply cannot fight against our Soul and the plan we made for ourselves in this lifetime. This path made me focus on external things instead of my own internal journey. I chose it to appease the expectations others placed upon me, not because I was genuinely interested or invested in that pursuit. I was once again following a path that was not mine because it was a tangible/physical way for me to get to where I thought I wanted to be. But the truth was that I was putting aside what I really wanted to do for what I thought I ought to be doing. I cannot stress enough the importance of the distinction here.

The Universe is always the energy of unconditional love. Always. As explained in the previous chapter, any and all labels associated with a higher power (God, Allah, Source, etc.) always refer to the same essence: the Universe. The religions themselves are all irrelevant, especially when they impose beliefs and teachings that are violent towards "unbelievers" or otherwise promote fear, separation, and hate instead of unconditional love of all for all. Regardless of whether it is physical or verbal violence, or even arrogance and self-righteousness, religions are always a means of control of the masses since they ask for blind obedience and mindless repetition of whatever tenets they hold. There is a huge difference between religion and spirituality, and it is of absolute importance not to mix the two up with each other.

Religions nowadays are mind-numbing. They are tools to keep people from trusting themselves or listening to themselves, and much less thinking by and for themselves. Religions seek to impose their beliefs as unquestionable truths, and if you question or do not adhere to the faith, then you are evil and a heretic. This is especially ironic as most claim to be religions of love and acceptance. Religions today are based on threats and fear-based manipulation (ex., going to Hell if you do not obey what is dictated). Fanaticism is always a lack of connection with Self and, therefore, with the divine essence within. Religion imposes; it never allows. Religion is purely Ego-based.

Spirituality, on the other hand, *is* this inner connection, this understanding that we are all one and the same. Spirituality is seeking out the Truth of things and embodying these truths as we come to understand them. It is also understood that we all have our different journeys and that it is wholly and inherently perfect *to be different*. It is perfect to be our True Selves. It is perfect to be exactly where we are currently on our own path: there are no real mistakes, only loving guidance, even when we do not understand it yet.

Spirituality allows; it never imposes. Spirituality is Soul connection.

This being said, religion as a concept in and of itself does not have to be vilified, but we have to see the truth of it as the tools of control of the masses that they are. There might be some very good and pleasant religious communities that allow personal choice and freedom without ever shunning or judging anyone within and outside of the community. I am not personally aware of any, but they might exist somewhere out there. The point here is to look and see if a community brings joy, peace, equality, and lightness to everyone, regardless of whether they adhere to the movement or not. Are the members treated equally? Are they given choices, or is everything imposed? Do the women play the role of a servant, or are they free to be unapologetically themselves? The need to exclude and control is entirely wounded Ego energy. Acceptance is a Soulful state of being.

Seeing things in the light of duality while believing one side to be inferior/superior always indicates that we are in wounded Ego territory. Whenever someone (or we) insists on white OR black, good OR bad, dark OR light, without ever allowing for both to be present nor acknowledging the grey areas in between, they are stuck in 3D perception. Anything or anyone that imposes differences as absolutes that cannot be reconciled as a whole or as varying aspects of the same thing is stuck in separate, dualistic thinking and, therefore, stuck in Ego.

At this point, we will drop the belief that anything can be boxed in as good or bad. *Things simply are.* For some reason, people need to shove them under a labeled box as though these labels or boxes have any real significance. And they attach themselves to these boxes, or significances, often in ridiculous ways. We are so much more than one box or label. These boxes and labels come with extensive lists of what allows you to be part of them. You do not need any of these things to figure out who you are. All you need is to be authentic and genuine with your Self. This absolutely can be scary, but why choose to be so afraid and averse to meeting and accepting your own Truth?

The truth is, it does not matter what you choose to identify as, regardless of what we are talking about. It never matters how you identify as long as you are being your true, authentic Self. Mostly, I have found that the people who attach themselves to labels do so because they have no other way to understand themselves, and therefore seek external answers, validations, and acceptance. Someone secure in themselves is someone who knows and understands the Truth of who they are and *does not need to prove or validate any of it with the external world.* Secure people *do not care* for labels on themselves or on others. We understand that we are all fundamentally the same, regardless of whatever outside differences we may show. These details are completely irrelevant to the Truth of things and have no impact on how good a person we are and choose to be.

Consciously choosing to put yourself in a box or adhere to a label and everything these things entail always reinforces the walls of your own prison *because you are choosing to limit yourself to what this box is externally perceived and allowed to be.* Always. Putting importance on outside appearances, perceptions, and other factors like that is a purely Egoic way of being. The Soul does not care about trivialities like gender, sexuality, or skin colour *because it knows that you are so much more than all of these things combined.*

You, as a Soul, are so much more than reducing yourself to your sexuality, or gender, or skin colour, or any other detail of the human vessel. Because, bottom line, who cares? And more importantly, *why would anyone care (other than yourself) about your personal settings, and why in the world would it matter?* The important thing to be aware of here is that those who do care seldom matter, and those who matter will not be bothered. Be your SELF. Love your SELF for who you are, and never mind the rest of the world. They will figure their own shit out on their own time, or they will not, and either way is not your problem. Put all of your energy into figuring out the truth about who *you* are, what *you* like, and what drives *you*. The envelope is not important; the content is. We have to learn to detach from details like these that carry no real consequence, only socially constructed ones, which ultimately are of no consequence.

Imagine for a moment that I attached my entire identity (and therefore value) to having blue eyes and that I was to judge others who do not have blue eyes as lesser simply because they are not like me. It is utterly ridiculous and nonsensical. We all have to celebrate our differences in order to appreciate them, but that does not mean having unhealthy attachments to these differences. You are so much more than what "sets you apart" because, in the end, we are all one and the same. We simply express different facets, or layers, of this same thing. Humanity is a rainbow, and different people are different colours of this rainbow, but it takes all of the colours to make one.

If these last few paragraphs have triggered you in any way, make a note of it in your Journal. Seek to understand *why*. What wounds are associated here with these topics? Why is your worth attached so strongly to what you perceive as your identity? Why do you seek unnecessary external validation, and how can you give it to yourself instead? Give yourself permission to embody the Truth of who you are.

Let's put it this way: whenever we seek to attach ourselves to physical reality anchor points such as appearance, gender identity, and so on, we are rooting ourselves in the 3D dimension of separation consciousness. Being attached to outside circumstances and definitions and whatnot takes away from our personal power because now, instead of being able to just be ourselves openly, we are forced to live up to the expectations and standards that these labels and boxes enforce instead of just letting these burdens fall away from us to truly embodying the Truth of who we are. By attaching our identity to external Ego factors and boosters, we are keeping ourselves from embodying our genuine Soul Truth. The Ego takes everything personally, but the Soul knows better than to take anything personally.

This in and of itself can be a tremendous point of contention for you, and that is okay. It is a part of your process, and it is perfect. Just learn to detach from needing to have these kinds of shields up. As stated, they are part of the walls we hide behind. Just realize that anything imposing differences as separating humans into distinct, "irreconcilably different" categories is an Ego thing. The need to be and feel special and distinct is purely wounded Ego energy. It enforces separation or 3D living. I have come to realize that getting the fuck over ourselves is the greatest gift we can ever give ourselves.

When we get over ourselves, we free ourselves from all the useless crap we hold onto and think is of utmost importance but are actually ways we are rejecting our Soul truth. Soul (or 5D) perception recognizes the Oneness of things and how everything just *is*, without needing to be more or distinct, separated, categorized, or classified in some way (which is just a way of feeling in control). Everything is just part of a bigger whole. It is like arguing that the index finger is the most important finger when, in reality, it is just a finger. All fingers are important in their own way. Just because they serve different purposes and have different names does not mean one of them is worth more or less than the others. They are just different, meaning they can bring different things to the table, so to speak. But in the end, they are all the same thing: fingers. Now replace the word finger with human and re-read this paragraph. That is the understanding we need to move with for our healing.

Once we do get this understanding, we realize that however we personally perceive things to be is always irrelevant to the actual Truth of things. By focusing on details, we are missing the bigger picture. The need to categorize and assign meaning to things disappears, as acceptance that things simply are what they are—without needing to be more, or to be justified in their existence—is the only thing that makes sense. This understanding renders useless the need to "fit the mold" because we understand that every individual thing is just a tiny part of a greater whole and should be what it is in Truth instead of trying to be something else. We may play the role of a toe, while another is meant to be a lung. We should not aim to be the same when our role is to be different.

We can then understand just how inconsequential we are, which therefore leads to the understanding of how consequential we can be when we follow our Soul path. We can be the connection in the spider web of life that just does not want to pull its weight, or we can be the part that allows the whole to function. When we understand that we are just a tiny piece of a massive puzzle, we become fulfilled with finding our proper place. All pieces are different, yet they are all valuable because we cannot finish the puzzle if there is even one piece missing. That is why it is important to know who we really are, but it is also important to realize that we are just another piece of the puzzle in the grand picture of Life.

It takes true humility and grace to understand this. The Ego hates this fact because the Ego has delusions of grandeur; it needs to prove itself and to be worshipped. If what we do does not matter, then what matters is what we choose to do. The Ego has difficulty accepting that what we do does not matter because accepting this would shatter its illusions. Whenever we think in separation terms, we are thinking in Ego. Always try to zoom out and see the bigger picture, the higher perspective, when you feel triggered. When triggers happen, note them in your Journal, even when unsure why you are writing them down. It is likely a clue to figuring out your wounding or a way to check your own progress.

It is important to understand that when we force conformity to an ideal, we force limitations. Whenever our state of being is not genuine, we disempower ourselves. We are creating the idea that things *have* to be a certain way and that if they diverge ever so slightly, then they are out. Rigidity in any way of thinking represents closed-mindedness, and we already know that we cannot evolve and grow from these states of needing to control our reality. We always try to control our environment when we do not feel safe. Control is always a fear-based state. Allowance and flow are indicative of a state of growth. We have to recognize that by forcing labels on a person or multiple people (or especially on ourselves), we are effectively cutting their wings. By forcing someone or ourselves into a box, we take away the possibility of being so much more than our limited perceptions and perspectives.

Take a moment to think back to every single instance where you have been labeled something that you felt did not represent who you were. Yet somehow, because someone had labeled you as such, it became known, and more people started putting you in that box, too. How did it feel when someone decided on your own limitations for you? Who put you there, and *why*? How else have these people tried to clip your wings? How did that environment feel for you afterward? These are all things to write in your Journal. Remember that your 3D reality brings you what you expect of it while also pulling in situations to trigger your healing. What do these words, labels, or boxes trigger within you? Especially when they are forced on you, and you do not associate with being these things to begin with?

In turn, we have all participated in these terrible labeling acts. Whenever we insult people and call them certain names. Whenever we gossip. Whenever we say, "Oh, so and so is so clumsy," and other such labeling. Sure, you may believe you have evidence to further your claim, but have you considered that you may just be seeing what you want to see to prove yourself right? Is the "clumsy" label even remotely part of that person's Soul truth? You may consider someone to be clumsy who has no personal attachment to the thought and who does not consider themselves to be, but it is your view of them, and you are imposing that view on them. Speaking in vibrational terms, perhaps your belief that that person being clumsy is what brings about events that "prove" their clumsiness, but which only ever happen when you are around. You send them vibrational intentions, which the Universe responds to.

Do these events actually prove you right over that person? Or is it just the Universe reflecting your beliefs back at you?

This brings up another question: why do people judge others? More often than not, they judge based solely on external appearances. Judging another is always a form of control. By labeling and judging others in advance, individuals feel more secure in themselves and how they compare to their environment. By deciding who people are in advance, they cannot be surprised by a different facet unless they go looking for it. Their interactions will always be filtered through the initial person's lens of judgment. I say this is a control tactic because instead of letting another person show who they really are on their own terms, a person will judge and label, and then never touch that box again unless exceptional circumstances force them to reconsider. Very few people decide to reconsider their initial judgments simply because they cannot admit to themselves that they may have been wrong.

It is important, then, to wonder why people do this: shut themselves out from others without ever giving them a chance. The obvious answer is fear, but also because they do not connect with the Universe:

they do not feel and understand the Truth of things, and they do not realize how safe and loved they are. Therefore, they protect themselves by shutting the outside world out and keeping a safe distance from what they feel they cannot control and/or comprehend. People always fear what they do not understand.

The illusion of safety we can get from controlling our environment is incredibly brittle. The moment something happens that we cannot control, we break down or double down on trying to manipulate things into the way we want them to be (usually to no avail). This illustrates perfectly how unsafe we feel and how unconnected we are. When we *are* connected, there is complete trust and faith that the Universe will always provide for us, regardless of what our outside environments appear to be.

The difference here is that the Ego controls and manipulates to get what it wants, while the Universe provides what you need as a Soul. The Ego believes its wants and "needs" to be above everything and everyone else. The Soul understands that there is more than enough for everyone to go around. The Ego is the captain of the Survival ship, while the Soul captains the Thriving ship. When we are in the energy of the wounded Ego, we do everything out of perceived necessity and urgency. When we are in Soul-truth energy, we do things because we feel called to do them in the time and place necessary.

I want you to start remembering how you feel when you do things. The way feelings work in your body is like a compass to your true path in life. When doing something feels heavy, draining, and unsatisfying, it means you are not doing something aligned with who you are and your Soul purpose. Why choose to remain in this energy? What are you actually yearning to do but are stopping yourself from doing? You can try out a simple exercise of considering doing two different things. Feel between the choices. Whatever feels easiest and lightest in your body and mind is what you should focus on doing at present. What feels heavy, unalluring, and draining is not what you should be doing.

For example, when I was debating quitting University, I asked myself if I preferred to continue part-time and see how I felt or if I should just quit outright. My mind loved the idea of staying part-time because this quitting decision was meant as a "leap-of-faith" type of decision for me to make, and staying part-time allowed me to cheat on that decision to keep myself feeling safe in the illusion that I might belong on the well-beaten path. Obviously, when I made the decision to go part-time, I felt a tiny bit of relief, yet after the cooldown of that emotion, I was still bothered. So, I sat down with myself, in honesty, and felt into my decision to remain part-time. The answer was crystal clear: I was simply not meant to stay. To leave completely left me feeling high and free, while remaining part-time felt low, bogged down, and chained. My mind did not want to agree, but the Truth was there.

It is essential to remember that we are the co-creators of our reality. We can always choose to follow the paths that feel heavier because they feel safer. But will we truly be happy on that path? What is the point of living a life that ends up being unfulfilling because we did not listen to our True selves or were not brave enough to stand up against our fears? We have to remember that F.E.A.R. stands for False Evidence Appearing Real. Fears are illusions of the mind. We cannot embody faith and trust when we allow fear to dictate our lives. We cannot surrender to the Universe and our perfect life if we hold on to fear. We cannot surrender if we cannot embody faith and trust. Yet the key to unlocking and experiencing our own Heaven on Earth *is* surrender.

With all of this information, we can conclude that our glass ceiling is made up of our inability to trust and have faith, regardless of whether we are speaking about trusting and having faith in people, in ourselves, in God, or in the Universe, etc. When I started on my own healing journey—through a friend who ended up teaching me Reiki and unlocked the start of my awakening process with a session she did on me—I was completely closed off from the world. At first, talking about chakras and energy was very foreign to me, and my highly analytical/practical/scientific mind disbelieved it all, yet I could not help but be drawn in by these topics. I was also in a very miserable state of being, and I figured I had nothing to lose by giving her healing session a try.

To say my mind was blown wide open afterward is an understatement, as in that first of many sessions, I came to a place where I could feel, see, sense, touch, and taste my own divinity; that parcel of the Universe encapsulated within each and every one of us. There was no possible way for me to deny it afterward. It was like tasting a sample of Eden that became a driving force in my own healing journey because I wanted to have access to that limitless power within me at all times, to that sense of perfect contentment and happiness, of warm, nurturing, unconditionally loving, and accepting energy existing in every cell of my body. It felt like a miracle to me because I was living in such a huge contrast to that energy. I became addicted to healing and uncovering my Truth to experience that miraculous feeling in my everyday life and to become able to naturally feel it as strongly every day as I felt it then.

This opened my eyes to the fact that I was living life feeling absolutely unsafe and utterly alone, being completely shut off and isolated in this alien world full of chaos, suffering, and hurt. That session happened at the end of 2016, and I can only look back at my incredible journey since and what seems like the moment where my life truly started. When I realized that there was more to life than what I had been taught and that there is more to living than just going through the motions and completing the "success checklist" of life, it was then that I started rekindling the tiny flame of hope within me. Hope that I was not limited to where I was then, that there was actually more to life than I could physically see, and that it could be my reality.

It took *a lot* of facing myself and accepting difficult truths about who I was being. It required me to wrestle my life out of my Ego's hands, recognize my own stifling victim mentality attitude, take back my personal power, shift awareness and consciousness, and heal so many aspects over and over as more layers of hurt were uncovered as I went. Nearly a decade later, after many dramatic shifts in my existence resulting from my inner work, I know I still have work to do, but we are not doing the work to reach an end goal. We are doing the work to give ourselves a better Life so that we may fully enjoy our present moment as it is. Going back to the story of the little girl in the cave, by rejecting and hating God, I was truthfully rejecting and hating myself since we are all One, connected, and hold a piece of the divine essence within us, a.k.a. our Soul.

The concept of Oneness explains why what we reject outright is always something to do with our own wounding. Whatever we judge and dislike in others are things we judge and dislike about ourselves, often in a mirrored, inverse way. The world is a mirror to our wounds. The world contains all the information we could ever need and want, but we have to look to see. Everyone knows how to physically *look*, but few know what it takes to actually *see*. As Soul beings, we come to see ourselves in everyone and in everything, realizing that there is no true separation. We know that to judge and criticize another is, truthfully, just judging and criticizing a disowned part of ourselves. It is never truly about the other.

This chapter is about starting the foundation of our relationship with faith and trust. When we deconstruct surrendering to the Universe, as we did previously, we see that the requirements are faith and trust. The question becomes: do we require faith in order to trust, or trust in order to have faith? I personally find these two states of being to be complexly intertwined, as in you cannot have one without the other. You cannot have true faith without trusting in the potential outcome, and you cannot trust if you have no faith in a person, situation, or Self. It feels to me as though faith is the energetic component of trust, which is a focused form of faith. As though trust is the vessel for faith: the practical action to the spiritual state of being.

So, if these two are interconnected and are on the same level (or stepping stones), how do we reach them? What comes first, and where or how should we start this process? What is the first stepping stone here to attain trust and faith? What allows us access to them? In my experience, I believe the answer to be hope and detachment. We have to start with hope. Hope becomes the light in the dark, the flame that illuminates what is possible even when it seems improbable. Hope is an energy in which we can release the logical, analytical mind. In fact, too much brain, calculation, and probability hinder hope, which is why I attach detachment to hope in the same manner I find faith and trust to be attached. We have to learn that our minds do have their place, but that we heal from the heart space. Detachment removes the blockages our own minds put up against our healing, both consciously and unconsciously.

Beginning our foundational work on the premise of hope and detachment and building upon them will allow for faith and trust to have a solid, level grounding to land on. The stronger the foundation, the more we can rely on trust and faith to the point of accessing the next level of surrender. Each level has to be strong enough independently to support the next one before we can move on.

So, how do we cultivate hope? Quite simply. It is a choice we have to make over and over to shut off our brains and be open to what is possible. Leave probability behind in favour of possibility. Hope is about the perspective we embody and the lens through which we live our lives. In the previous Part, we learned to be aware of our perspectives so that we may shift them into ones that serve our highest good. Hope thrives in a positive environment; therefore, we have to identify where we are being negative, either deliberately or unconsciously. This is why we have been working on being a distant, silent observer within, so we can see where we are being negative in an objective fashion.

We have to be willing to allow people, life, the Universe—everything—to surprise us pleasantly. If we start thinking that they could also surprise us unpleasantly, just remember that the Universe always conspires to prove us right. Where and how we choose to place our focus is up to us. This is not about wishful thinking and optimism but about how to reframe how we choose to attach expectations and emotions to people and events. If we cannot control a turn of events, how we choose to approach it will dictate how much it will or will not drain us energetically. Pessimism drains us. Optimism puts a pep in our step. Why would we want to choose to feel heavy when we could choose to feel light and positive? This is the difference between hope and resignation. Obviously, our wounding plays a role in this perspective, and that is why healing techniques were shared previously, so that you may actively work on decluttering your energetic space.

We always attract what we focus on; that is how energy works. We get to choose what we want to focus on and how we want to approach a problem or a person. It is always up to us to control our attitude. This being said, even though we may consciously choose to think and feel a certain way, what is in our vibration is what will show up in our lives. By not cleaning out our energetic field, we may still attract stuck beliefs of being unlucky or having bad experiences despite our healthier mindset. Start looking at how to heal the unconscious so it does not keep dictating your experience.

Furthermore, I hope that by now, you have started a process of conscious self-love and appreciation, as this will only help and facilitate your progress moving forward in this book. It is okay if it is an on-and-off thing as long as you keep bringing yourself back to it. You should already have a section in your Journal where you have been documenting your judgments about other people and situations, along with any self-judgment. We are going to revisit and add to this section.

So far, we have been using this tool as a means to physically track and understand our wounding to facilitate healing. Now, we will add another layer of evaluating our own levels of optimism and how we perceive the world around us. Meaning how safe and secure you feel at different times of day in different places. How optimistic you are when you think of future projects. How do you feel in regard to certain activities or people? Document when you feel positive and when you feel negative every time you identify these feelings within you. The goal is to start seeing patterns. What brings you joy, what does not, and how can you shift things into a more positive light?

This does not mean betraying yourself by having to feel positive about everything all the time. Not at all. There is such a thing as toxic positivity, where one never allows what they perceive as "negative" to exist in their lives, but ignoring our problems does not make them go away. Positivity is understanding that even a negative circumstance can shift or bring about something positive. True positivity is about removing the fear associated with experiencing negativity. Positive and negative can exist in the same space. They simply are. It does not have to be one *or* the other. Negative is not to be vilified in light of positive. They are simply two sides of the same coin. Negativity helps us understand what we want more of. Or less of.

This exercise requires a daily commitment so you can keep track of your current state of being. Identify what you allow, refuse, ignore, or run away from. Notice how the energy in your body changes when faced with something perceived as positive and when faced with something perceived as negative. Doing this while being honest and objective for a few days or weeks will grant you an eye-opening gauge of what your mindset looks like at present, what you allow to pull you down, and where you allow things to pull you up. It may be shocking to see to what extent you betray yourself in everyday circumstances and encounters just to keep the peace or otherwise not rock the boat.

As a secondary task, I challenge you to go back and find situations, events, and people with which you have associated incredibly negative thoughts and feelings, and I dare you to choose to see how—from a SOUL point of view—they may have, in fact, been a blessing in disguise. This is an exercise in broadening the openness of the mind. You may not be ready to face this yet, depending on your trauma, and may never wish to do so for certain people or events, and that is perfectly okay. But keep it in mind as something to do later on in your healing process if you get to a point where you can be open to the idea. It is important to listen to yourself but also to understand what really motivates you to keep certain doors shut, and if they are genuinely worthwhile to ignore in your own healing process.

I also challenge you to choose the emotion you truly wish to embody daily. Give yourself reasons and excuses to choose to be happy and to spread joy. Do it consciously for no other reason than it would lift your day up, as feeling optimistic and positive about life, in general, would lift both you and your energy up. As an example, when you are in line and waiting for your coffee, and it seems to be taking longer than it should, choose to find reasons why this could be perceived as a good thing instead of a bad thing. Since good and bad are always subjective and part of dualistic thinking (instead of the Oneness thinking we should seek to embody), seeking what makes you feel good and actively choosing to feel good regardless of external circumstances will bring about more "good" moments.

I want you to start noticing when you are unnecessarily negative in your life. Does a small inconvenience send you off the deep end of negative thoughts and heavy feelings like impatience, anger, name-calling, annoyance, complaining, whining, and whatnot? How harsh are you with strangers, regardless of whether they are making mistakes or not? How harsh are you with yourself when *you* make mistakes? What about how you treat your loved ones while in a bad mood? Become aware of these things and consciously choose to shift them. Choose to be kinder and compassionate with others, as with yourself.

When faced with negative situations and your Ego despairs that there is nothing to be done about the given person or situation, take a step back and re-evaluate if this is actually true. Do not be afraid of how creatively you can counter your own Ego. Any reason to shift your mentality is good enough, regardless of how silly or small you may think it is. My favourite tool to use here is to find the humour in whatever is happening. Let me tell you that there is always something funny to find and run along with. Instead of focusing on drama, choose to lighten the mood for your own sake if for no one else's.

Using the prior example of waiting extra perceived time to get your coffee, it could become a great reason to check out the hot person who just joined the line, or you could perceive it as a lesson in patience and unconditional love, or you could realize that you take every minute of your life too seriously and you need to loosen up that part of yourself, or you could notice a beautiful painting you had never taken the time to notice before. Any reason to shift seeing the situation from a negative light to a positive light is a great reason. Roll with it. It is always up to you how you choose to deal with a situation, and if you really want to load it up in your unnecessary baggage cart or leave it behind with a smile.

Another great way to help focus on bringing about more positivity and reasons to just be happy is to focus on the present moment. This moment here and now, as you are reading these words, is all that we really have. The past can never be again. It is unchangeable, while the future will always be out of reach, and since the future is only ever about potential, it is not reality and, therefore, cannot be seen as reality. This means that what really matters is always just the here and now. We should absolutely keep doing certain things while having a broader future in mind, but our focus should always be on the present moment. Living for the future is no life at all, just as being stuck in the past keeps us from enjoying the present. We have nothing but our present moment and what we choose to do with it.

This being said, wasting time and energy both on clinging onto the past by regretting and lingering in memories, as well as constantly worrying and stressing over the limitless possibilities of an unknown future, are both fundamentally detrimental. It is of absolute importance for us to make peace with *all* aspects of our past. Feel free to dedicate a huge part of your Journal to doing this. Any recurring memory that brings about unresolved emotions needs to be processed consciously by sitting with it and allowing it to share what keeps it coming back to us on a loop.

The past serves as a teacher, whereas the future is constantly shaped by the present. What happens in the future depends entirely on our actions in the present. Living consciously in the present moment allows us to regain our personal power and peace of mind because we realize we are the only ones in control of how we choose to exist. When we realize there is no point in stressing over the future since it will never exist, we can let go of all the unnecessary self-imposed anxiety. It is only from being completely in the present moment that we can start feeling the natural flow of life and feel which direction is beckoning us forward. This is how we can begin connecting directly with Source, and the highest version of ourselves, meaning the "us" that is already living and embodying our dream life. Our Higher Self is our guide to rejoining them as One.

When we start embodying this principle by choosing to always be in the present moment and allowing it to guide us (instead of our attempts at controlling Life through our Ego), we have reached faith. It takes a leap of faith to let go of the reins. When I stated earlier that faith and trust are interconnected, it also means that we can use one to access the other through hope and detachment. To live in the now requires us to have faith. Faith in ourselves and our personal power, yes, surely. But more importantly, faith that the Universe will never let us down when we are actively following our Soul path. This means our true Soul path, and not what our Ego thinks is the path they want (then tries to force things to happen how it wants things to be).

This entails using the energy of hope to dip our toes in the pool of faith to learn what it feels like. When we are hopeful, we are allowing the Universe to present itself to us with the best possible outcome. Remember that this outcome does not involve pleasing our Ego. This is why I have been having you practice differentiating your true Self from your wounded Ego while also learning to see things as a blessing in disguise when you cannot understand why something is happening from a human perspective. This whole work practices the energy of hope, leading to faith. The more we practice this, the more we see just how wonderfully and perfectly the Universe operates. The more we accumulate this proof, the easier it is to relax into the energy of faith and trust and eventually into complete surrender.

We deepen our faith and allow it to reconnect us with trust by practicing mindfulness. The more aware we become of our environment and what we allow into it, the more we can witness the little miracles that happen daily, and the more we can see how wonderful life and this world truly are. Try trading your eyes for those of a child and see just how magical life truly is, each and every single day, when we remove the weight we place upon our shoulders as adults. Mindfulness and positivity go hand in hand in this process as we seek to acknowledge life's deeper meaning and perspective of Oneness.

This is when we become able to truly appreciate the intricacies of the Universe at work as we start noticing more and more of it both in and around us by practicing what was taught in the first module. Faith requires us to shift our perspective of life into the vision and belief that we are unconditionally loved and supported in our journeys while understanding that *everything* always happens for our highest good and the highest good of all. Especially when we cannot yet see or understand how it unfolds. This is the key to deepening our relationship with faith and trust. We have to be at peace with the fact that we cannot know everything and, therefore, can never truly control anything, which is why we choose faith instead.

The next time you are confronted with a situation that just seems terrible in every way and where there could not possibly be a point to it, much less a positive outcome or reason, I want you to hold back on judgment and consciously choose to wait and see. To allow things to unfold as they wish. Tap into the energy of hope to be open to the possibility of this situation bringing in some unforeseen blessing. Whenever we are confronted with a reality we do not like, and there is nothing we can possibly do about the circumstances, we need to learn to let go and consciously choose to believe that whatever is happening is, in fact, happening for the highest good of all involved and that something better will come and replace it for us if it creates a void in our lives. There needs to be endings before new beginnings can appear. Endings are not to be feared and held onto; they are here to teach us to accept what is and detach from material needs.

The Universe adores us and wants to give us the best possible things. It is our own level of wounding that dictates what we allow to trickle in. When the Universe shuts a door in our faces, it *always* lets us know that a much, much better door is opening somewhere else. The Universe will never throw at us more than we can handle. We can use this knowledge whenever we feel overwhelmed or distraught because it *always* means that we can get through whatever hardship we are currently experiencing in our present moment. Some potential examples of this could be as simple as missing a bus or someone ghosting you, while it could also be bigger, like being fired or being cheated on.

The simple truth is that the Universe always knows better than we do what is perfect for us. This is true because the Universe holds the entire picture in its metaphorical hands, while we only have access to a tiny, minuscule fraction of a glimpse of the entire work. The thing is that the Universe is so committed to our growth, healing, and happiness that it will not let us get away with truly sabotaging ourselves in the process. Whenever we choose not to let go of things that do not serve us or are actually damaging to us, the Universe will keep forcing our hand until we are simply no longer capable of holding on. This is free will in action. We can sabotage ourselves all we want, but the Universe will keep making the choice of self-sabotage either harder to make—or appear totally ridiculous and immature—until we are simply forced to face ourselves and let go.

When we are in wounded Ego energy and allow it to steer the ship by trying to control everything—from our environment to our appearance (and being otherwise shallow and the opposite of who we authentically are)—and we still believe the lies we tell ourselves about how we have to "fit in" and follow a certain path because "that's how it's always been" or "everyone else is doing this"—or whatever other bullshit—it can be very hard to let go of these things, as they feel secure. They feel safe. We have built our entire prison around these things, after all. What is familiar is not necessarily satisfying. Whatever does not feel satisfying, what does not fill us with peaceful contentment, simply is not meant for us in the long term. This does not mean everything will be easy, but we will not mind difficulties if we know the end result is what calls to us on a Soul level.

When we refuse to let go of what is not good for us, we become stuck in a repeating cycle that keeps winding around tighter and tighter until something breaks, and we are simply incapable of holding on any longer. Usually, the Ego likes throwing a little tantrum at this point: "But why can't I just have what I want?"—to which the Universe replies, "Because there is something much better for you trying to enter your reality." And the Ego continues ranting, "But this is already perfect, and I want it," to which the Universe just laughs—because the Ego really knows nothing.

This simply means that when we identify resistance of this sort in our lives, it always, always, always means that we are not being truthful with ourselves. When we are aligned with our Soul Truth, everything flows easily and effortlessly. Therefore, when we struggle and fight against the current, we are just keeping ourselves from our greatest good. More often than not, it is fear of change or of the unknown that keeps us going in cyclical loops or even beliefs conjured by what society decrees as "normal" and "the way forward." The truth is that we are the only people who can truly identify our Soul path or guidance on how to move forward by listening to our bodies' responses and sensing what feels best and in alignment with our highest good. What feels exciting is our flow, and following it is our test of faith.

Since we established that faith and trust were interconnected, whenever we build up our faith, we are also building up trust. We have to choose to have hope and to have faith, and the results will naturally build up trust. Keep in mind that when we detach ourselves from desiring a specific outcome and instead allow the Universe to provide what is best for our highest good, we are consciously choosing to let go of being controlling, and *that* is how we allow the Universe to show us just how much we can trust it. The key is to let go of needing to be in control, as we cannot manipulate the Universe to provide for our Egoic desires. The Universe listens to our Souls' needs.

Usually, when we want something, we have a very specific image in mind. The more specific this image is, the more controlled it is; therefore, the less the Universe is likely to provide it, or it will provide something similar, but we will never be satisfied with it because it was not what was best for us to have *in our Egoic mind*. We have to learn to broaden our desire or simplify it entirely. For example, say you want to start dating new people, and you meet someone whom you think is perfect for you, but they do not seem as invested as you are. If you start asking the Universe to end up with this specific person, you are entirely controlling in your manifestation of a loving relationship instead of asking for the best possible person for you.

Let's be honest here. When we are looking for love, we are looking for the best possible relationship and connection with someone who complements our strengths with their own. We are all looking for the love of our lives, even when we do not feel we deserve it for whatever reason/wounding. The best way to get into a great relationship is to ask for the best possible match-up and release the desire for specifics to the Universe. By asking for a specific person (who is likely not intended for us), we are making it impossible for our perfect match to be brought into our lives. We have to learn to trust that the Universe knows best. Not only does it know *you* best, but it also knows every single other person in the world best. How could it not provide us with the best possible outcome? Why would we believe that our Ego opinion is worth more than the infinite knowledge of the Universe? We also have to be careful not to mistake attraction for love.

Trust asks that we relinquish the need to be right and that we open up to the possibility that we can receive something or someone much better than we even know or can possibly be aware of. Trust requires us to differentiate between what we think we want and what we actually want. For this example, we may think we want that specific person, but what we actually want is a great, satisfying, fulfilling relationship. We have to learn here to get our minds out of the way of our heart's true desire. Remember in the first chapters when we introduced the mind and the heart as tools? Our heart is our manifestation tool because we connect with the Universe through our heart space. The mind always gets in the way of authentic connection.

Trust also implies patience. When we ask the Universe for something, it may take some time for it to arrive from our human perspective. We cannot be fussing about not physically seeing our manifestation yet, as that simply delays the process further. We have to learn to trust in Divine Timing, meaning that everything always happens at the perfect time: in the Universe's time. The thing is, though, that the Universe does not deal in time. It deals with vibration, which means that we receive what we ask for when we are in vibrational alignment with it. We have to be receptive to and aligned with the energy of what we want, meaning that if we hold onto contradicting beliefs (especially subconscious ones), we will not be able to receive our manifestations, which is why the work we have been doing in this book until now is so essential.

We access the stage of surrender when we attain solid foundations of hope, faith, and trust. When we surrender, we release the desired outcome to the Universe, knowing that as we flow with our Soul, we will be brought to the perfect place we need to be at that present moment to meet the perfect people we need to meet. If you still believe in coincidences at this point, ask yourself how a Universe that has been proven to be so perfectly mathematically accurate could possibly be wrong and make "coincidental mistakes."

To wrap up this chapter, practice (and journal about) identifying when and where you are controlling your environment and instead actively choose to leave things up in the air from time to time. We do not always need to act on things as they happen. Observing, taking a step back, and allowing things to play out on their own are great steps in learning to let go of control so that we may flow with life instead of fighting against it. Find what your own personal Flow feels like within yourself and practice surrendering to it. Practice holding within yourself the energy of hope, faith, and trust. Journal about all the manifestations that you consciously choose to leave up to the Universe and their results when they happen. Most importantly, learn to detach from expected outcomes by being patient and open instead.

Mastering all the content in this chapter will bring us to a point where we release the need to have our expectations met, meaning that we release the need for set outcomes we have decided are the only possible solution. We tend to find ourselves disappointed when we give our personal power to others by having expectations of them. We tend to create stress when we have high expectations of ourselves. Expectations are a measure of control, and they always feel heavy and irritating.

Let's not mistake expectations with the need to ask for help or have our needs met. Better yet, do not associate your needs and happiness with external expectations. We should be able to give ourselves everything we need. We cannot remain in the energy of needing others to satisfy us and also believe we own, and are, in our personal power. We should never require permission to be ourselves. By placing our needs on someone else's shoulders, we are essentially betraying ourselves as we are literally giving away our personal power to another. Any time we force or coerce someone into doing something they do not really want to do simply because we want them to, we are in wounded Ego energy, not in Flow.

By having no external expectations, we remove the possibility of feeling disappointed, frustrated, angry, and other low vibrational energies. We must learn to rely on ourselves first. Feel your Flow, let it guide you, and you will meet people who choose to help make your life easier instead of harder, purely out of goodwill. Whenever we try to force things to happen the way we want them to, it will *always* backfire on us in one way or another. Learn to allow and let go. Become self-sufficient and self-reliant.

Give to yourself first what you wish to receive from others. The more we bring our power back into our own hands, the easier it is to flow with the Universe, as we are not waiting for someone to feel good or to meet our needs. When we take care of ourselves, we invite the Universe to take care of us as well, since we embody this vibration. It is also a great way to keep the Ego in check since placing expectations on others is another form of control. Your job here is to start realizing when, to whom, how much, and for what "reasons" (read excuses) you justify placing expectations on others to yourself.

With time and practice, you will start realizing how much better you feel when you drop unhealthy external expectations. To be clear, expecting to be treated with kindness and respect is a healthy expectation. Expecting to receive certain things from others that they are not entirely willing to give to us is unhealthy. Shift meeting your needs into your own hands and watch as you open the door to becoming genuinely independent and thriving of your own volition.

Chapter 6
Inner Guidance

<hr />

Following our inner guidance and inner knowing—our Flow—in the present moment, when we are aligned with Source energy, will always guarantee us a bright and supported future. By following the guidance of the Universe, we literally never have to worry again because we understand that everything is already taken care of. *You* are already taken care of, and it becomes only a matter of following the steps given to us intuitively. When we fully, consciously live in an energy of alignment, we understand how fundamentally true this is. And the best part is that every single one of us can access this by decluttering the trauma in our mind, our body, our emotions, and our overall vibration. These are also referred to as the mental body, the physical body, the emotional body, and the energetic body, which are all different layers of our physical being.

Now that we have started learning to connect with the Universe and are practicing being in our own energy of Flow, it is time to become acquainted with our own "psychic" gifts. I use the term psychic here loosely, as these abilities are innate to all human beings; it is simply a matter of practicing them. There is also an unfortunate stigma associated with any such gifts. Take the time to Journal about what feelings come up when hearing of psychic gifts and elaborate/investigate why such feelings exist within. The Truth about these abilities is that they are just another talent anyone can cultivate. Some people are born with an easier connection to them, just like some kids are born with natural, phenomenal singing voices or athletic abilities.

We are talking here about connecting energetically with Source, learning to trust and feel the vibrational Truth of things in our bodies. We have to open ourselves up energetically to receive messages and insights, and to feel the difference between what feels truthful and what does not, while also making sure we are not being "receptive" while in Ego. While we can receive such messages while in Ego, the trouble becomes that the Ego hijacks the narrative and forces meanings onto the messages and actions to take, consequently, which may not be in line with the actual messages received. Whenever we find ourselves trying to prove we are right about something, we are in Ego. We have to become okay with the idea that we can be (and often are when in Ego) wrong, but we especially have to let go of the idea of fixed outcomes. Anything rigid is not flowing.

Since we live in a world that does not yet understand or widely accept these gifts and mostly shuns them or is fearful of them, we learn as children to tune them out. We do this because we are taught that ghosts do not exist and other such nonsense, while also being taught that our parents know best about everything and should never be questioned. This is an early first step in forcing us to stop listening to our inner guidance. Whenever parents force their personal beliefs on children, their innate connection to the Universe is either severed or severely dampened. It is important to let children grow and learn at their own pace and to nurture what feels important to *them*, not what seems important to the parent (unless we are talking about basic needs and necessities). Children need to figure themselves out at their own pace, not be imposed a personality by parental preferences.

This is part of the reason why people are always so amazed by children when they dabble with these gifts and show how naturally in tune they are with spirits and energy. Children are naturally in a Flow state; they have not yet been "rigidified" by society. We have to learn to be like these children: open and receptive, while also not shutting down what goes against our personal beliefs. Beliefs and opinions never trump facts and physical experience. Further, we are often pushed to believe that listening to our innate gifts is the work of the devil and other such nonsense. We are taught to be fearful and distrustful of them with talk of possessions, dark forces, evil intent, etc. The truth is that people simply fear what they do not understand and, therefore, try to force control over what they cannot control in order to feel safe.

When we truly understand Oneness and that the Universe is an energy of pure unconditional love connecting everyone and everything, we can understand that the only things really holding us back from our full potential as living beings are our fears and conditioning. We have allowed fear to be the driving force in our lives, unintentionally or not. Some people were either fearful or envious of others who had clear connections with the Divine energy, and so enforced control and fear to shut them out. The fact that people who are comfortable being in their feminine energy have the best connection to Source comes from the fact that feminine energy is softer, permissive, attractive, and flowing.

This means that the (mostly) women who were persecuted (witch hunts, for example) were persecuted because of their trust and faith in their innate connection. They felt which herbs had healing properties and trusted them. They could perform energy healing. They were connected to nature, in tune with higher guidance, which freaked out the people who were not connected, as they could not explain this inner knowing and seeming "magic." While the energy of Flow may not be visible, it can be perceived when one attentively looks at nature.

In the same way, we cannot physically see the wind itself, but we can feel it and see its effect on other things. Prior to the development of technologies, there was not much else to look at other than nature, as there were no TVs and internet, but even then, not everyone could be bothered to actually *see*. Some were more dependent on nature and, therefore, more in tune with its flow, such as farmers and fishermen. They had to understand weather patterns to know how to handle their jobs, what was safe, what was risky, and what was a hell no.

Nowadays, the world has been forged by distorted masculine energy; just look at how rigid and unyielding it is. It is all straight lines and black or white because that is how masculine energy is. It is linear and logical and "achieving goals" oriented. It is not permissive energy; it is "take charge" energy. Keep in mind here that we have thrown into the garbage the idea of good and bad. Both feminine and masculine energies can be distorted and harmful. We will learn more about these energies in a later chapter, along with how to heal and fully embody both of them, as all beings carry both energies within.

The people who are not in tune with their own connections to the Divine and energy are usually fearful and envious of those who are. Whenever people are envious of others, they always try to bring them down in order to feel better about themselves. Non-acceptance comes from envy or a misplaced sense of superiority (which always hides wounds of self-worth), as they see people who are in tune with their gifts as having something more than them, something they believe they can never get for themselves. Therefore, they seek to silence, discredit, and control the perception of others upon those they deem as a threat to their own self-worth or image. They feel inferior and threatened, so they try to bring those who are in tune down to their own limited level, just like crabs in a bucket.

These kinds of triggers are to be expected from people who have done no inner work on themselves and believe they have nothing to work on at all. My advice is to just ignore them because whatever we give our attention to, more of it flows into our reality. Besides, when our own energetic vibration rises from the healing work we do, we become incompatible with people stuck in lower vibrations, and it is completely normal to feel ourselves let go of the people who are not upgrading their own energies. Some people will be very triggered by this, and that is okay. Remember that any relationship that tries to hold us down and make us feel small is a relationship we have to surrender for our own well-being. Never hold on to someone who does not want to see you heal and grow, regardless of who they are to you. If people choose to upgrade themselves by doing their inner work, they may come back into our lives as better versions of themselves. Or it could be that we are meant to attract better people who have a higher vibration similar to our own instead.

We must always put our own well-being first in our lives. Some attachments are just not meant to last, and that is okay. It is also okay to feel grief at "leaving others behind," but we should never keep ourselves small and stuck because we want to "wait for someone to catch up." If they are truly meant to be in our lives, the distance and separation from our energy might trigger them to evolve for their own sake. But if they do not, getting them there is not our job. We can only ever really lead by example. Anything else is a lie. Do the healing for yourself and watch as it forces others out of their comfort zones purely energetically. Drop those who try to hurt, judge, and control you, and keep those who keep on loving and supporting you, even if they do not understand. We do not always need to be understood; we only need to be accepted as we are, so we must stay away from those who refuse to accept us. We cannot change them, and we should not allow them to keep hurting us by sticking around, especially out of "love" for another. It is never Love to choose to hurt another, deliberately or not.

When it comes to hearing our inner guidance, we have to be quiet enough within to be able to listen and hear. We have learned so far how to distance and detach from our conscious reality enough to become an impartial observer of our external reality. We will take this same exercise and apply it to our internal reality to see what is happening within. Some of you may have already intuitively picked up on how to do this from the previous exercise, regardless of whether you are even aware that you have been doing it. From here on out, we will be doing this exercise intentionally.

Our body is, in and of itself, another tool for our human experience. The fact is that our Souls have chosen this body piece by piece and fashioned it inch by inch perfectly in how it would serve us best in our current lifetime. This is true for every single person in the world. Our body communicates with us constantly as it is always telling us what it needs, with feelings such as hunger, tiredness, and thirst, but also with how external things make us feel. It signals to us what is meant for us and what is not, what we should avoid, and what we should go for. Our job as a Soul is to learn to listen to our body, as it acts as the physical compass to our spiritually desired experience. We cannot hear it well if we make other kinds of noise (especially if our mind is very loud), as the body's communication can be very subtle. It does not communicate with logic but with physical symptoms. This is often referred to as a "gut feeling."

Going back to the principle that our psychic gifts are just another innate ability of the human body, it is important that we cultivate a healthy relationship with our physical vessels. We have to drop down into and exist within our bodies fully and embrace ourselves exactly as we are in our present moment reality. There will be a whole chapter dedicated to self-care later on to practice this further. For now, we have to learn to identify and rid ourselves of every single judgment we hold against our bodies. Of course, this is something that will become an entire section in your Journal.

Catalogue every thought you have about your body when it enters your consciousness, regardless of how negative or positive you perceive them to be. And *do not be ashamed* of the instances where you are being terrible to your body; highlight them instead. Keeping our heads in the sand in the face of truths such as these may feel good in the short term, but I promise that addressing them head-on will make you feel wildly, vastly better in the long term. We have to learn to respect and love our bodies to be able to work well with them. Where there is a disconnect, there will be physical symptoms.

Some people will want to either stop reading from here on out or skip this chapter entirely because of trauma and/or false beliefs that there is no "magical connection" to be had with the Universe. Some may believe that we cannot possibly all have psychic gifts. The truth is that they are wrong. Our innate psychic gifts are just like any other talent, and we can all choose to cultivate and work on any talent, regardless of where we start out on its "competence" meter. All of us can cultivate a solid singing voice with dedication, time, and practice, for example, even if we are considered to be tone-deaf. It is always only a matter of believing in our own capabilities and giving no power to detrimental feelings such as doubt, shame, or guilt. We are the only ones who can permit ourselves to give our all in order to achieve whatever "success" we want from it. We define our own success however we choose, as it should never be dependent on external sources.

In this world, we are constantly shut down and regarded as worthless in any artistic capacity if we are not a natural at something and are not simply perfect from the start. I am now asking you to let go of that pretentious bullshit. Being imperfect is being human. Human beings can learn anything if given the proper time and training. Making mistakes is what allows us to grow and learn. Never discourage yourself from doing something that lights you up inside just because of your perceived level of "being good at it." Do what feels good and fun to you, regardless of what others think. We are here on Earth to create and have a fun experience, bottom line. We are here to learn how to shape our perceived reality into one that brings us absolute joy and abundance. Are there some hurdles to achieving that? Of course, absolutely. But these hurdles are what allow us to determine what we actually want more of while also understanding what we want less of. Failure is seen in such a negative light when it is often simply an opportunity to learn and redirect ourselves. This does not mean to give up, but perhaps simply to choose our audience better.

Whenever we use excuses of not being good enough at a given discipline or that we cannot do something because (insert bullshit reason), we are betraying ourselves. We choose fear instead of believing in ourselves and our capabilities. Drop the idea of being perfect, drop the idea that making mistakes reflects badly on you, and drop the idea that you are not allowed to be patient with yourself as you learn to do something. Drop the idea that you are a lost cause. Rome was not built in one day, and neither will you heal and achieve your highest potential in one day. Invest in yourself, be loving, be patient, and be brave in the face of your own evolution and progress. Remember how we learned that we are keeping ourselves trapped in our prison? These are just more layers to the walls we are imposing on ourselves.

Any and every single time we give in to excuses as to why we cannot do something, we are creating our own limitations. We are staying in our comfort zones. We are staying small and "safe." But this "safety" is an illusion because we will never be satisfied with our lives by constantly betraying our desires and interests. It is time to stop saying "no" to ourselves and start saying "yes" instead. No more enabling "I can't." Choose to enable "I can" instead. Do you want to try something new? Try it. *Then,* decide if you like it or not, never based on how "good" you were at doing it. Be truthful about the reasons why, regardless of the answer. There is absolutely no point in lying to ourselves because we do not feel good enough or worthy. Just because we are not great at something is never a reason to stop doing what we genuinely enjoy doing. We never need to be perfect at anything; let go of putting that kind of pressure on your shoulders.

The human brain and body are incredible things. Our will is one of our strongest assets, and it, too, can be developed positively. We have the potential and the tools to do whatever the hell it is we want to do with our lives. And what we genuinely, from the bottom of our gut and heart, want to do is likely what we are meant to do. This means that the Universe *wants us to succeed in what brings us joy, happiness, and contentment.* The trick here is to identify what makes our hearts sing, what lights the fire inside, and what triggers personal Flow. What excites us authentically, like a little kid, is part of our Life compass. And we can get all this information simply by looking within. We contain the keys and clues to what we should be doing—what we want to be doing—with our lives. There is an infinitely huge difference between what we *feel* we should do and what we *think* we should be doing. One is our Truth, the other our conditioning.

We can master anything we put our minds to, regardless of how much talent we start out with. It is all just a question of effort and dedication. Give yourself the chance to grow in whatever department brings you joy and happiness, regardless of how terrible you believe yourself to be. Who cares? If you do not enjoy what you are doing, why are you bothering to do it in the first place? Note these reasons/excuses in your Journal to contemplate how they feel. When you enjoy what you are doing, it means that what you are doing is perfect in and of itself, regardless of how you feel/think about it. The odds are that you are just being unnecessarily harsh with yourself.

Remember, we were saying that our bodies are our compasses? This means that what feels good to us is what we should put our energy into. What feels bad or what we have no feelings for is something we may have been forced to believe we should be doing. Listen to your body. Let go of the fear that you will "make a fool of yourself" because even if you think you are, those who will judge you for it are people you should stay away from. Be weird. Be creative. Be *yourself*, and let those who do not like that never be in your presence again. You will be better off for it.

This is not the time for us to use our brains. It is time for us to follow our hearts, *especially* when our brain tries to bargain that we cannot or should not. Our brain will always impose limitations in these matters because of fear and being too scared to be open and to trust that we are safe. Our mind is scared of letting go of control. It does not feel safe to surrender because surrendering means consciously relinquishing the outcome. It does not feel safe for humans to let things unfold naturally. If you notice having these limiting thoughts and beliefs surrounding things you love to do, write them down in your Journal and deconstruct *why* they are present. Have your parents always discouraged you from following your interests to pursue something more "practical" instead? Have you ever been given the speech, "But how will you make money"? "What's your plan"? "What do you mean you don't have a plan? And a backup plan for your plan? And another plan after that, just in case?"

Here's the thing about plans: they are rigid and unyielding. They do not flow when a problem is encountered, and odds are, we are forced to make new plans to adapt to what has happened. Having a plan means needing to be in control. Having a plan means that we do not trust the Universe to provide the answers and the way forward in due time. Whenever we need to have answers, we are in Ego. When we are listening to our inner guidance, we do not need a plan because we are connected with our Soul. The "plan" becomes to follow how things feel and trust the signs and guidance we receive on a daily basis. The plan is to *not* have a plan and instead just flow and follow what comes up intuitively.

Intuition is a major tool in how to live our best possible life. It is also intricately subtle and whispers from deep within, meaning that when there is noise or dissonance within, it becomes very hard to hear and heed its advice. Intuition is quiet. It does not scream and does not force our attention to it. When our mind is loud and our Ego unchecked, it becomes nearly impossible to hear our intuition, which is exactly why we had to go through the previous chapters first to get to a place where we can quiet down the noise within and learn to listen. We have to empty the chaos within in order to be able to listen. *Empty* to listen. Learning and applying this to correctly identify our intuition instead of following the "quieted down" version of the mind and Ego thoughts is very important.

Permit yourself to trust in your true Self, in what you hear, feel, or see that cannot be explained conventionally. Learning to trust ourselves and giving ourselves permission to trust in what we feel but cannot necessarily explain is key to moving forward here. Keep practicing and trusting in yourself and the universe, as it is such an important process to go through. We hold ourselves back from experiencing many things because we are not giving ourselves permission to just do them, usually out of fear of what others will think or how they will perceive us.

The thing about caring what others will think is that whenever we give in to that fear of judgment, we are always, always, always betraying ourselves by giving our personal power away. We have to learn to stop betraying ourselves. Women, especially, have been conditioned to self-betray constantly, in many outward ways, but also in highly insidious and hidden, subtle ways, most of which we may still not be aware of. This is why we should have a section in our Journal where we recognize and detail the ways we are betraying ourselves. When do you say no when you really want to say yes? Or say yes when you really want to say no? When are you letting opportunities pass you by when you really want to do and experience them yourself? When are you letting others get what you want to get instead of you? When are you saying, "Oh, it's okay, I didn't really want this," when you did, in fact, really want it? When do you actually get to live your life for yourself instead of for others? How often do you self-sacrifice for others?

These are all instances of self-betrayal, which we will address in depth in the self-care chapter. For now, start exploring what comes up for you on your own, and practice giving yourself permission to do and feel what you actually want to do and feel. Honor your body and emotions, and always analyze if you are doing things out of fear or not. When it comes to you and the things you want to do, who better than yourself to determine what those are and allow them to happen? Give yourself permission, believe in yourself, and get started.

Going back to intuition, the best way to summarize it is to view it as the needle in the compass that is our body. Intuition is the piece of our Soul within our body that knows the path to our best, most fulfilling life. To our intended destiny, if you wish to see it that way. It is the feeling of the best possible direction to take or a decision to make. As stated previously, it is a very subtle feeling that the Ego disregards with ease. This is why we have been practicing zooming in on what we reject in our minds immediately. The Ego always does the immediate rejection of something it does not want to consider true. When our Soul rejects something, it is always shown to us in the form of a physical feeling and/or sensation of deep unease or sickness.

This does not mean that overwhelming emotions are to be followed as intuition, not at all. When talking about what feels good in our body, it is never an overwhelming feeling. Intuition is more like a little push or a little pull in any given direction, thought, or sensation. Intuition is *subtle*. Whatever reaction we may experience within, if it is not subtle, gentle, and soft, it is likely not our intuition. The Ego is reactive, the Soul is passive. The concept of free will represents our choice of following the Ego or the Soul. We can follow what we *think* is the best possible path for ourselves or trust that the Universe has already laid out the perfect path for us and that our job is simply to follow it leisurely, at our own pace, by following our intuitive nudges.

Intuition becomes impossible to perceive when we live our lives entirely from our mental space, just as it is impossible to perceive when we are overwhelmed by emotions. This is exactly why we have learned to detach from both of these states in favour of observing objectively and actively choosing to heal. Healing ourselves gives us stability and solid ground to stand on and allows us to contain and work on triggers as indicators for more necessary healing to occur. How easily some people become triggered and offended and choose to lash out externally directly indicates how much healing they need to do, but refuse to give themselves.

Healed and healthy people are not easily triggered, and when they are, they can contain themselves instead of exploding all over the place on everyone around them. What we have to understand here is that other people's reactions are never, ever about us, just as our own reactions are never actually about anyone outside of ourselves. To blame our internal emotional state and follow-up explosion on someone external to ourselves is to refuse personal accountability. Our wounds may not be our own fault or making, but this never justifies unleashing ourselves on anyone, ever. This is why choosing to heal is so important: it makes our own lives better, and by default, the lives of others around us as well, because they are no longer exposed to our own volatility.

With all of that being said, we can understand why it is so important to be in a place of personal stability and integrity to truly feel and identify our intuition. The strength of our connection with our intuition depends entirely on the balance between our head space and heart space, which depends on how little we allow our Selves to be dictated by either or both. There is a misconception that intuition comes from the heart. In fact, it comes from the center of our being, where our connection with the Universe is accessible through our Soul tether. You may have heard this connection being referred to as the "higher heart" or the "inner heart." From this point on in the book, we will refer to this space as the Soul's Essence Energetic center.

This Soul's Essence Energetic Center (SEEC) is not to be confused with our chakra points. It is our energetic connection to Source and can be found directly underneath the heart chakra, before the solar plexus chakra (more on chakras in a later chapter). This is our energetic center of being, and it is our direct connection to Source. It is the drop of divine energy we all carry within us. Whenever we hear someone instruct us to drop into the heart space, they are actually asking us to drop into this energetic center, which is *not* the heart chakra. We can understand it as the central cog of our energetic being, which spins the Yin-Yang (feminine and masculine) energies within.

The SEEC within us is our direct link to the Universe; it is our energetic umbilical cord. It is the piece of the Universe, aka your Soul's seat, which interlinks every single living being together in the interwoven, intricate web that is the Universe. It is the spark of life, the spark of *who we really are* deep down inside. This is the *you* that your human vessel carries, where your vibration originates from, where your Contracts are stored, and the blueprint for your divine life is kept, where your individuality comes from as connected to the greater whole. It is our divine anchor point. It is where our intuition whispers to us from, as it reads the blueprint and whispers the next step, always.

The location of the SEEC between the heart and solar plexus chakras, while also being the energetic center of both our masculine and feminine energies, is the reason why we have referred to intuition as a "gut" feeling. When we feel pulled by our Soul and spirit guides, this anchor point is where the feeling is coming from, but it is physically transmitted through our masculine energies in the solar plexus chakra and our feminine energies in the sacral chakra. Our wounding determines what we can and cannot "hear" within ourselves. We know it does not come from the heart because it physically feels lower than that. When our Soul warns us to turn around and leave or not to trust someone we can feel is shady and potentially dangerous, it tugs at us from deep within. The gut feeling and our own instincts are more primal, physical intuitions that come directly from our Source connection. It is where our intrinsic, unexplainable *knowing* comes from, directly from the Universe, which holds all knowledge.

The SEEC remains a smaller, subtler kind of connection to the Universe than connecting through our crown chakra. When we connect to the Universe from our crown chakra, it is because we have done the necessary work to uncover this crystal clear and easy connection coming through the top of our heads and into our being. It represents our *conscious* choice to connect and heal, to follow divine guidance. It represents our ability and willingness to recognize the link we have to the Universe and the fact that we are actively seeking a deeper connection because we have learned to trust and rely on the Universe willingly.

The SEEC allows for the "sleepers" and non-awakened folk to still have a connection with the Universe, albeit unknowingly. Everyone has the potential to start their own healing journeys and have access to higher guidance whenever they choose to. We always have a connection to our own Soul and divine sovereignty, but free will dictates that we must choose this by and for ourselves if we wish to evolve further consciously. This proves, however, that we are **never** disconnected from Source. Most of us have started this life *feeling* completely disconnected from the Universe because of past life beliefs, trauma, wounds, etc.

This was the case for me, especially since I started out with such a huge wound concerning the divine, as illustrated in the past life of the coastal village's little girl. I was angry and outright denying the existence of

God or a higher power because I had misunderstood a past life experience and created trauma around it. Yet even though that was in my vibration as my unconscious belief, I have always felt safe and secure in following my intuition and instincts, my gut feeling. I was verbally rejecting the Universe, or God, while also heavily relying on its guidance, unbeknownst to myself. This goes to show that we are never cut off from the benevolence of the Universe, even when we think we are or want to be.

Comparing how I was (unknowingly) guided then with how I consciously choose to receive guidance now, the only real comparison for me to make is the ease with which I now receive guidance. My gut feeling has never led me astray, even when I was not sure I was understanding it consciously correctly. Even though I might have had doubts, I always ended up trusting my gut feeling because it came from within. It always felt like a tiny little nudge or pull. I was never really certain of feeling it, wondering if I was just imagining it. Comparing that tiny, subtle feeling with my crystal-clear intuition and direct Source channel today — of which the pull and flow are simply undeniable for me now — the overall sensation or feeling of guidance is the same one, with the volume dial turned all the way up. The only difference is that my access to it is not limited to a hole the size of a pinprick anymore (the SEEC), but a wide open, clear communication channel (the Crown chakra).

The funny thing now is that since my guidance is undeniably strong and clear, I cannot reject it. Not that I ever really could because of my divine Soul blueprint, I could, however, delay my evolution through my free will choices. Now, whenever I try to ignore my guidance or delay following through with it, it will always come back stronger and fiercer until I *make the choice* to follow through. In the same way that sometimes the Universe will force us to let go of a cycle by making it impossible to keep choosing it anymore, the Universe will always guide us in the right direction for our highest good, even when we think we want something different. Remember that whenever we think we know what we want and yet things do not align with what the Universe is guiding us to do, we are undoubtedly always in Ego.

Every single time I have followed the Universe's guidance despite what I thought I wanted being a different path, I have always, always, always come to a place that felt like the perfect fit, and most times, it felt better than anything I could have imagined for myself.

That is the magic of the Universe. And I would always feel afterward like kicking myself for thinking that I knew better what I wanted, much along the lines of "Why did I choose to wait so long when this is obviously awesome for me?" This is to help us realize that following our Ego's lead never serves our highest possible good. It never serves our higher purpose to stay stuck in wounded Ego energy.

If anything, all the excuses we throw out there as to why we should not follow our Soul path are excellent pointers for hidden wounds to investigate. This is part of why I say it is so important to get over ourselves. We never know better than the Universe, and it is absolute hubris to believe otherwise. As an example, I have always been regarded as being lazy and a procrastinator because I often was not able to motivate myself to do much unless a deadline was due the next day. Hello ADHD. When I began the journey of writing this book, I had difficulty sitting down and channeling. I had not yet uncovered and healed the false belief I held, which stated that whatever I did or tried to achieve would never be good enough and people would never see its value. Much like the self-worth wound I held that made people see no value in my physical self because I do not fit societal norms of how a woman "has value". Talk about impostor syndrome.

However, this was just me projecting my inner wounds onto my work, meaning that I held the belief that *I* was not good enough and that people would never see *my* value because I could not even see my own. Both of these wounds have been heavily reflected back to me in my life. The blessing for me in this was that in every big chapter of my life, at least one person had always seen me and my inherent value. This person always ended up being older and wiser than I, and definitely had been through interesting/difficult life experiences AND chose to work on themselves. They were people I looked up to, whom I thought were so far above and beyond myself, and I viewed them as figures of authority in their respective fields.

This symbolized, of course, that even though the masses of "normal" people would look at me and see nothing of value, nothing important, there was always someone "above their level" vibrationally who saw me and my worth and communicated it to me. This means that even though the people surrounding me could not understand me and see the truth of who I was, including myself, these people I viewed as a "higher power," if you will, always had my back. They uplifted me, encouraged me, picked me up and dusted me off, always saw my worth and value, and communicated that to me, even though I rarely accepted their praise due to my wounding. They believed in me when I could not.

This goes to show that, despite how I perceived myself—and how others perceived me—there was always more going on behind the scenes, which the people who mattered picked up on. We have a nasty tendency to not be kind to ourselves and think the least of our capabilities. This shows us that even when we do not believe we are capable of great things, someone else can, will, and does. Just like the Universe loves and sees us for who we truly are, and knows what our Souls can accomplish and achieve.

Looking back on your own past experiences and cycles of repetition (which should be listed in your Journal as you uncover them), notice your life patterns and who was rooting for you. Try to recall when you followed your intuition, even when you were not particularly aware that this was what you were doing. Take note of all the times when you *did not* follow your intuitive insights and where these have led you. Also, start doing this with your everyday reality, tuning into your intuition, and following what it says. It does not matter if you mistake your Ego for intuition at first. With more practice, you will start feeling the difference between the two energies, the more you work with them. We have to remove the idea that making mistakes is a sin.

There will be moments when you think you are following your intuition when you are not. There will be times when you are not even aware that *you are* following your intuition, yet it will feel good, so you follow through with the idea anyway. The goal here is to start tuning into the energy of your intuition, to differentiate it from your Ego's voice. We can learn to identify it by how good we feel when we follow the guidance it provides and noting how we feel when we do not follow it. We also must identify when fear is trying to cloud our intuition or speak over it. The more you practice identifying and following your intuitive hits, the easier it becomes to connect with that energy, and to realize when the Ego slips in to interfere.

When you start tuning into your intuition, you will be receiving messages in different ways. This is where we introduce the clairs: clairvoyance, clairsentience, claircognizance, clairaudience, clairgustance, and clairalience, or seeing, feeling, knowing, hearing, tasting, and smelling things that are not in your immediate physical area. We have access to all of these forms of insight, although we are more naturally inclined to receive specific clairs. However, just because we have a stronger sense of one clair does not mean we should disregard information we receive from other clairs. All of them are ways for us to receive or perceive messages and information.

At this point, you may or may not have done enough healing to have a clear connection with Source, and wherever you are in your own journey is perfect and okay. What to do here is to relax, surrender, have an open mind, and allow for whatever messages want to come in. If nothing comes, then nothing comes. This is not a process that can be forced, and you should not feel discouraged if it does not happen quickly. Having this knowledge in the meantime means that you will not feel so lost or confused when they do start kicking in.

At first, it may be hard to hear, trust, and believe in what we receive. I recommend you keep tabs in your Journal on what you receive or think you might have received, regardless of how you feel about its validity. This will allow you to come back and see if you can find some kind of confirmation in them later on, if they warned you of something, or whatever messages show up for you. Their meaning will reach you when it is meant to. Get rid of the idea that you need to understand the messages immediately upon reception. More often than not, understanding comes later, so we do not want to get lost in the spiral of self-doubt by searching for meaning that does not necessarily exist yet in our physical reality. We can see Source messages like puzzle pieces; sometimes, we need to find more pieces before the image can be made clear.

Let's start exploring the clairs and how they can show up for us, starting with clairvoyance. This one really is as simple as it sounds: we see things in our mind's eye, or the third eye chakra. There are different levels of clarity with which someone can see, most often depending on what other clairs they have strong connections with. Additionally, we may begin to see more clearly as we clear out imbalances or wounds blocking the third eye chakra and the crown chakra. Some will see bright, clear images or flowing storylines, others will have a black-and-white imprint they can refer to, or simple flashes and quick glimpses, and there are other varying options in between. When we see it, it will look like watching a movie or a picture in our mind. Random flashes of images can appear, stemming from a thought or from seeing something in the physical world.

Clairaudience is also pretty straightforward, as it implies hearing things internally. We may hear random song lyrics pop up in our thoughts, distinct words being whispered in our ears, although no one could have spoken them around us. We can hear a ringing or a high-pitched whine that asks us to pay special attention to what we may have just said, heard, or thought. Wherever the source of what you hear comes from, external or internal, trust that there is a special significance to whatever draws your attention. I have noticed that when I receive clairaudient messages, the "voice" that speaks them to me is quite different from my "thought voice" or even my "Ego voice"; therefore, I know it does not come from me, but it whispers with a feeling of deep benevolence.

When it comes to clairgustance, we may experience random flavors in our mouth even though we are not drinking or eating anything. Certain phantom tastes may bring us back to specific circumstances, so there may be something that happened then that we need to pay attention to now. It may also refer to a specific person who leaves either a "bad taste in the mouth" or a good one. Trust what comes up and be curious enough to dig into it. Specifically, for this clair, it may also be an indication of something we should eat or drink that our body is asking for. Whenever we are urged to drink or eat a specific food or beverage, I would advise you to respect and honor that. Be careful, however, when it comes to junk food and drinks that lower our vibration, as this may just be our wounded Ego showing up with cravings to satisfy a wound.

Clairalience is closely related to clairgustance due to the close nature of our mouths and noses. The principle for clear smelling is very similar to that of clear tasting: whatever smells pop up in our nose when there is no potential source around us physically can be indicative of something we need to have more of around us. Smells can bring up memories of people and places, even events and circumstances ingrained in our memories, just as they can communicate an emotion associated with the smell. Whatever shows up for you, be curious and investigate in your Journal.

Next, we have clairsentience or clear feeling. This one shows up particularly strongly in empaths, as it allows the person to feel another's pain, discomfort, and any other emotion or sensation as their own. Clairsentience implies a physical reaction or sensation. This may also be phantom sensations about events that have happened to you or others. Clairsentience can become unbearably uncomfortable for us in the body if we are tapping into very traumatic experiences. We have to remember that those experiences are not our own, or not happening right then and there, and that our physical discomfort is temporary. It may feel intense, but it is never harmful.

Phantom limbs are a great example of clairsentience, and when someone keeps feeling their phantom limbs, it is mostly because they have not really allowed themselves to process that physical wound emotionally, with every aspect that entails for them individually. This refers back to the AAUR technique; knowing we have lost a limb consciously does not mean we have done the healing work of acceptance, understanding, and release on an energetic level. Phantom pains occur when there is a disconnect between the physical and energetic bodies, where one knows the leg is gone, but the other does not, therefore sending signals of "something is wrong here."

Lastly, let's explore claircognizance together. This one is trickier to trust and identify because it is simply pure knowing. This is direct communication from Source through our SEEC, dropping accurate, factual knowledge in our lap. Whatever we feel coming from claircognizance will feel absolutely right, will never come from the mind, and we will never be able to explain how or why we know something. We just do. It has always felt to me like I had a sudden epiphany, and the information always came as an unshakable, distinct, powerful feeling of awe, freedom, and Truth. It feels like a proven fact, a non-negotiable truth being illuminated inside, as though it was there all along, and a veil was simply lifted that we may have access to an answer, none of which has anything to do with logic. I once revealed to my best friend that her sister was having a miscarriage, while she did not even know her sister was pregnant, and she contacted me a few weeks later, saying it had been true. I had no way of knowing, yet there it was from within.

All clairs are attuned to giving information through the vibration/energy of Truth. Once we develop our clairs and intuition, we get to see how we can never be lied to again. We will feel the difference between someone who is being truthful and someone who is not because those energies are vastly different in how light and heavy they feel vibrationally and energetically.

Obviously, all of the clairs are susceptible to the Ego trying to run the show and drop misinformation. Claircognizance is the one clair that the Ego can get away with meddling with the most. People stuck in Ego love thinking they know everything and will claim to have direct knowledge from Source, but whatever they claim to be true will always feel wrong when communicated to us because of the difference in frequency between Ego and Truth. This feeling of wrongness is also our intuition. People who display arrogant certainty and refuse to listen to other people's thoughts and opinions, and who are unwilling to have a simple conversation on a given topic, are stuck in Ego. Closed-mindedness and a belief in being superior are purely Egoic states of being.

When our Ego tries to hijack our claircognizance, we can always check within ourselves where this "knowledge" is coming from. Our minds and thoughts are the realm of the Ego. Our SEEC is our Soul's seat. If we feel under any kind of pressure or fear, that is when the Ego steps in, as its job is to protect us. When we step away from the energy of fear and take off the pressure we put on ourselves, it becomes easier to dissociate from our Egos. The Ego is a defense mechanism crafted for our survival. When we feel the need to prove ourselves, we are in Ego. Fully accessing and tapping into the clairs can trigger in someone the Egoic need to feel special or better than, or smarter than, etc., which are all indications of self-worth wounds. The Soul never needs to compare itself with anyone else, ever, and so whatever is said reactively during times of stress and fear, or to feel superior to another, never comes from the Soul.

Keep an open mind about all of the clairs, and you will quickly see which ones are strongest within you. You may experience all of them in your lifetime, as you may only ever feel one or two. It really does not matter or mean anything other than these are the tools you have to work with that will serve you best in this lifetime, as chosen by your Soul before your incarnation. We are all different and have different gifts, experiences, and life paths. Therefore, we will need different things. The Soul is never in competition, as it does not need to "win." The need to win is purely an Ego thing, again based on the idea that people are better or less than ourselves. The Soul does not care for superficial "rankings."

Connecting with Source is a skill to develop, so give yourself time to connect and practice feeling into your SEEC to attune to its frequency. However, this is not a process that can be forced; it absolutely has to be allowed. The Ego forces, while the Soul allows. The best advice I can give for this practice is to sit in complete silence, preferably surrounded by nature if you can, so that you can start recognizing divine energy within while being supported and surrounded by it from without. As you develop that connection with your SEEC, you will need less complete silence and stability to connect with it as it becomes easier to feel or sense its presence within, but this will not happen overnight. If you think it does, you are in Ego.

This leads beautifully to understanding the craft of meditation, which is the process we utilize to connect with our SEEC. At first, you may need calming music in the background to occupy that space of background noise while you let yourself connect and slip inside the Self deeply. Meditation is about coming into communion with the Self. The best way to do that is to seek out the SEEC, as it holds our true essence. It is our direct link to the divine, Source, the Universe, and it is our key to truly feel into and understand Oneness.

In today's world, there are so many modalities highlighted as being meditative, and so many platforms that can teach us how to do it. As we are all different, we will all have different ways to learn how to meditate effectively. So I advise you to follow your intuition if you wish to learn with a modality outside of this book, which is perfectly alright. You should be able to feel what works and is right for you, as you will always feel pulled back to it when you choose to disregard it. We can also feel what is not meant for us by being attentive to how we respond physically. We cannot miss what is meant for us. We will also feel when it is time to step towards something else, generally when we do not feel it resonating anymore. It is useful to consider that anything we practice with complete mindfulness (embodying the present moment and being completely within our physicality) can also help us attain a meditative state.

Here is where I am going to ask you to start a daily meditation practice, the length of which is entirely up to you. You can spend half an hour to an hour or more to reach a truly meditative state of awareness and full-body consciousness, or even a few minutes a day of tuning into yourself fully if you feel tight on time or energy. Multiple little check-ins throughout the day are great, too. One specific teacher I have been following for a while recommends doing it when you are going to the washroom since we all have to go multiple times in a day, and there is not much to do in the meantime. What is important is consistency. Do what you can within a day, but make sure to always do it at least once, even if it is as you wake up or before falling asleep.

As touched upon briefly with mindfulness, practicing anything that allows us to center ourselves within and become mindful of the body and Soul connection, or that has a single point of intense focus, is an excellent exercise for practicing the connection with our SEEC. The goal is to push away all forms of distractions for a single point of focus that allows us to be completely in the present moment, anchored within the whole of our body, from fingertips to toes. Self-expression in its pure, unfiltered form is a connection to the Truth of who we are, to our Soul. Losing ourselves mindfully in the process of creation is the key to living our best lives, regardless of how that looks.

What is meant by this is that the goal should never be the focus. The journey is. In essence, a journey is how we choose to get to the end goal, ideally by enjoying every moment given to us. When we dance freely or play music, paint, build a deck, or whatever creative craft feels good to us, when we are being powerfully creative, we allow a window to our Soul to open and our personal Truths to simply exist in the moment. But when we do lose ourselves in a hobby we enjoy, we do not focus on being done with it. We do not expect the end to hold all meaning; rather, we aim to find meaning in getting to the end result. We would not read only the last page of a book and claim to have read the book.

When we understand that meaning is found in what we do and how we do it, we start connecting with our Soul Truth. We understand that the end depends entirely on our process to get there, making the process itself the true container of the value derived from achieving the end goal. If there is no process, there is no end. We are constantly in different processes at the same time, and when we finish a process, we start on another while appreciating the ride we had with the previous one and being satisfied with its completion. By constantly chasing end goals and never appreciating the road we are on, we tend to lose faith in ever achieving it, or get frustrated because we feel we are not there yet, or too slow, or whatever Egoic concept attached to "failing" comes up as a wound for us. However, it is normal that halfway through watching a movie, we are not at the end of it yet, so why let it frustrate us and make us wish it was just over already? This is part of the process of surrendering to the Universe: enjoying every single moment we experience for what it offers currently, without needing to be "further ahead."

A practice that has greatly helped me understand, develop, and trust my own intuition has been playing with tarot and oracle cards. I had always been drawn to them, fascinated by the concept of receiving direct guidance through such a cool medium as beautiful tarot and oracle cards. My family enjoyed playing cards and would do so often, so I grew up constantly having cards in my hands and learning new ways to think and figure out who held what in their hands. I was then unconsciously already developing my intuition through cards; therefore, switching to tarot cards (which have roots linked with regular playing cards in the first place) and oracle cards felt natural to me.

At first, I had to get to know the specific meanings behind each card, as I could pull them but did not always know what they meant or how to interpret them individually or as a group. Then, when I was comfortable enough with my logical learning of the cards, I would cross-reference what I thought the cards were saying to me with what was written in their booklets, which was honestly hit-and-miss. When I started wondering why that was, I realized that sometimes a specific item or image in the card speaking to me, not necessarily the logical meaning of the card itself. And so, I transitioned from relying on what the booklets and my logic told me to trust what I *felt* the cards were telling me, and *then* my readings began being accurate for the few people close to me with whom I allowed myself to open up and share this passion of mine with. I had to trust in my own clair senses and intuition, my own wings, instead of relying on the cut-and-dry method others used. I had to learn my own way of reading cards, which is specific to me and my gifts.

Obviously, when I feel drawn to read the description in the book, I trust my intuition and follow it. This is why I now have multitudes of decks to use, which all have different pictures for their respective tarot cards and sometimes wildly different book definitions, and I always respect which decks I am drawn to for specific people. Sometimes, it is a feeling; sometimes, I see the deck I am meant to be using or one of its specific cards in my mind's eye, and other times, they will look like they have this indescribable shine to them only I can see. Practicing with tarot and oracle cards has been an awesome way for me to practice my intuition and learn to trust it, along with identifying and trusting the knowledge that came from Source.

In the same line of thought, I also enjoyed watching readings on the internet, mostly pick-a-card readings, because I could feel the energy of the piles and sense if a message for me was held within. I also learned from readers what certain cards or aspects could represent in ways I did not know from just reading about tarot. When I was not certain of a choice, I would ask my guides if there was a reading for me, and they would "highlight" the one I should watch, which was always the one I thought I should, that had drawn my eye, but did not trust myself to choose because the feeling felt too faint. This is to say that it is okay to seek confirmation from your guides when you are not certain, but this cannot become a crutch for you to rely on. There were also readings I was not certain of that simply repulsed me energetically when I started watching them, telling me I had no messages within.

The most important part of learning to trust our intuition is to understand that we cannot force it. We have to feel and listen, not force and take the lead, as that is us falling back into Ego control mode. Being in a neutral state, devoid of desires, open to anything and everything being possible, and accepting whatever comes and feels right deep inside is the optimal state of being to be able to perceive intuition adequately. Being in a state of allowance is necessary to be able to feel that subtle poke.

The more we are in our minds, the less we can hear our intuition. This is why it is important to learn to let go of stress and expectations, to learn to be patient with ourselves and permissive of mistakes, and to also learn to be quiet and comfortable within our own bodies. "Mistakes," as we perceive them, are actually a fantastic tool for learning. We can use them to follow the patterns of what works for us and what does not. Sometimes, we may feel our intuition and doubt it; other times, we will think we heard our intuition, but every time the mind is involved, it is not intuition. We must learn to let go of the fear of being wrong, as there is no such thing as being wrong being a bad thing if we are willing to grow and learn from it. Mistakes serve a purpose in our growth and evolution and, therefore, should not be inherently villainized.

Being right or wrong is always irrelevant; the process is what is important. Attaching importance to being right is an Ego pattern that will keep us from growing and evolving as a Soul. We counter this problem by being open to the possibility of being wrong and knowing that even if we are wrong, it is not a bad thing. Being wrong is not the end of the world, nor is it something to be afraid of, nor is it something that lowers our worth. On the contrary, admitting to being wrong is a wonderful skill very few people seem to possess. Being wrong or being right are both expectations we hold over ourselves, and thus, they limit our growth. The important thing to do is to re-center and ground ourselves to be able to let go of expectations altogether.

The less we allow stress, fear, and anxiety in our lives and bodies, the easier it will be for us to relax into the present moment, and then the knowledge of intuition will be easier to detect and access. Allowing ourselves to be overtaken by fear, anxiety, stress, and other heavy, draining emotions means that we are resisting something in our current circumstances. It is important to make peace with where we are in our lives so we can use that as a solid stepping stone to move upwards into the life we actually want to be living. We have to learn to follow our path of least resistance to access our personal bliss. This refers again to using our bodies as a compass to guide us toward this path of least resistance. What feels good in ourselves is meant for us. This state of being will become easier to follow with dedicated practice and trust/faith that the Universe will not let us fall.

Sometimes, we may start feeling crazy by following this process, as although it feels intuitive, our minds can easily freak out because we are stepping out of the comfortable limits it has imposed on us regarding what is possible. We have to learn to be okay with feeling out of control because that is exactly what we want to do: let go of control. We are shifting the focus from trying to control the uncontrollable (our external reality) in favour of controlling what we can control (our internal state of being). This being said, practicing letting go of external control can be very challenging and exhausting because it will feel like you are fighting yourself along the way, and in some ways, you are. We are fighting our conditioned fear that we are not the masters of our own lives, that we are not the sole sovereign power over our path forward, when the truth is that we are. We have to unlearn the limitations we have grown to believe dictate our lives.

When you have started to feel crazy and overwhelmed, it is always good to take a break, take a step back, look at the whole picture, and reflect on it for a while before tackling these problems again. This may allow us to access a much-needed shift in perspective or to learn something we cannot see until we take a step back and reassess what has been going on. Oftentimes, when we are so focused on struggling against something that is just not working the way we wanted, or intended for it to work, and we struggle against allowing it to unfold how it wants to unfold, we are simply shooting ourselves in the foot. This is purely refusing to let go of control. We need to practice humility here and accept that it may not be within our hands to shape.

Intuition will always feel easy and simple. It will feel *right*, as it is part of the natural flow of the Universe. Learn to let yourself be carried by the current of life instead of struggling unnecessarily upstream. Whenever things start feeling heavy, draining, and complicated, it is *always* an indication that we are not following our personal Truth and are instead trying to force or control an outcome. Let go. Stop creating your own resistance to your own personal path. Surrender, acceptance, and flow are essential at this part of the journey. Therefore, if they do not feel strong enough for you to rely upon, keep practicing and growing them consciously.

Feel free to explore your intuition and experiment with how to best connect with it. For me, it was tarot and oracle cards. For you, it might be another interest. Follow what calls to you, what draws out your natural curiosity, what you may have been denying yourself the right to try out for whatever bullshit reason (trust me, they *always* turn out to be bullshit reasons and excuses). Listening to what calls to you is already practicing intuition. Now, you have to choose to trust it. It may feel terrifying, and you may have to try a few times before you actually allow yourself to really try, but keep going back to trying, however many times you need before it clicks. Even if you put it aside, you will find that you keep coming back to it, thinking about it, and considering it. Trust that and choose to follow through. Give yourself permission to take that leap and surrender to the fall.

Practicing all we have learned so far in all the previous chapters will help ground and center our Self, and this stable state of being will eventually be accessible to us even in times of intense conflict. The end goal is to always be in a loving state of detachment and flow where we understand that every single person in the world is on their own journey, and we are all individually responsible for our personal healing and growth. This is why our own inner guidance is the most powerful tool at our disposal in terms of figuring out what is meant for us. More than that, it is the only way we can truly get to know ourselves and, in turn, learn to love and respect ourselves for who we truly are.

By seeking to understand ourselves and our unconscious ways of being, we can become more empathetic and understanding of others and their own unconscious ways of being, which allows for detachment from their outbursts *because* we understand it is never actually about us in the first place. We are all of us living out our wounding in hopes of healing; some of us are simply choosing to do something about it. When we become aware, we can direct our own healing, but we can never do it for someone else. We cannot heal others; we only guide them in their healing with unconditional love and compassion, often through the example of our own evolution and healing. It always starts by giving to ourselves first.

Chapter 7
Understanding the Chakras

·

There are multiple sources that speak of chakras already in the world that go deeply into the details of them. The point of this chapter is to give a satisfactory overview for comprehension and application of knowledge into our healing journeys, meaning that all the important information can be found here, but if you wish to further your knowledge of chakras for yourself, there are more detailed and in-depth information books and teachers waiting for you.

This chapter offers a comprehensive guide to what chakras are, where they are located energetically in our bodies, their function in our human experience, what overactive, underactive, and balanced chakras feel and look like, and tools to help heal and balance them ourselves. Even if you have prior knowledge or experience working with chakras, it is highly recommended not to skip this part and to read it in full at least once, as reading through offers more than just knowledge on the chakras. It is part of the process that reading this book accompanies you in. Since being open-minded is a big part of healing, you may find information within these next pages that you were not anticipating, or something clicks differently, or something completely catches your attention and becomes a sign for the next thing needing to be worked on.

The first thing to understand is that we are not separate from our chakras. On the contrary, they are very much part of who we are. They are an energy source within our body that overlaps our physical bodies and translates our inner workings into our outer reality. What does this mean? Every chakra is a center for specific aspects of our human existence, and we can identify if chakras are overactive, underactive, or balanced exclusively by someone's behaviour and reactionary output. Everything internal is visible externally for those who know how to look.

Each chakra is different yet equally important, as they all serve separate functions. They reflect on our inner workings and wounds and are an excellent key to observing what is going on in our own subconscious mind. They help us see where we are not in alignment in life. It is important to note that there are many more chakras than the main 7, but for the purpose of this chapter, we will view only the main ones. Again, if you feel called to research them further, please do so and keep following your intuition in every aspect this book brings up for you.

Since working with chakras is purely an energetic practice, we have to make sure we can connect with and feel ourselves energetically while also being able to hear and heed our intuition before any real change can be brought within these energy centers. As you continue to practice recognizing and developing your intuition and other spiritual "psychic" gifts and aspects of life, the easier it will become to connect with your chakras. The first step for some might simply be tapping into the energy centers and feeling when they are connecting with them or not, and listening to what they feel is coming up. Be curious, and Journal about your findings, intuitive hits, and any other type of information received or perceived, including speculations.

Being aware of what chakras are and what they individually represent, while also understanding how their distorted energy shows up in our lives, will help us identify and understand our own wounds more easily. Let's make it clear here that we are not affected by our chakras; rather, they reflect our inner state of being. A healed and balanced human has healed and balanced chakras. We can use tools, however, to help us heal and shift the energy of the chakras so that they force an external shift in a situation in our awareness to help it heal and be balanced in turn.

Furthermore, it is important to understand that colours carry a vibration. Take a moment to observe your space and belongings. Are there colours that are more common to you that you actively seek out or are drawn to? On the flip side, are there colours that repel you and make you feel uncomfortable just looking at them? The answers to these questions will also help identify potential wounding and chakra imbalances. We will not go further into colour therapy in this book, but if the medium calls to you, trust that.

When it comes to crystals and stones, the idea is the same: they carry vibrations. These marvelous jewels of the earth hold frequencies in a similar way that colours do, which is magnified by the colour they show up as. Naturally, then, colours and crystals will help balance the chakras they are associated with *because* everything is just a question of energy, meaning frequency and/or vibration. The more sensitive to energy we become, the more we can feel into the Truth of these things, as Truth carries its own frequency. Trust when you feel called to either a colour or a crystal, and dig into the information it provides to your inner workings. Be curious about yourself and your world, as curiosity is a great tool for our intuition to communicate with us.

As we get along with these chapters, it would be perfectly normal to have doubts and resistance show up toward the information imparted. This could be as simple as the Ego feeling uncomfortable and acting out, or a specific wounding that made you refuse your connection with the Universe resurfacing, but the recommendation here is to just work on having an open mind while reading, even if you do not believe anything you read. It might simply be that you are not yet ready to go deep and need to clear out some more surface wounding before being able to access the deeper layers. This is totally fine and part of the journey. The thing about beliefs is that, ultimately, they are completely irrelevant in the face of Truth. As stated before, Truth holds a specific frequency to it and can always be identified this way with practice.

Practicing tapping into energy will help you find out the Truth of things for yourself, but remember that it is always easy for our Ego to start taking over when we embark on a spiritual journey or healing of any kind. This is true for both beginners and seasoned players because sometimes healing has to meet external circumstances (when they are meant to happen in divine timing) before the healing process can start. If the Ego did not take over from time to time, then we would not be able to identify the next step of healing work required within us. It is part of the process, but we have to remain attentive to identifying our Ego so it does not run away with us for too long.

Since Earth is a world of contrast, we cannot identify what we do not want more of in our lives if we do not experience the lack of it first. Obviously, this refers to all Soul timelines—or lifetimes—at once, meaning these experiences of intense contrast have happened through multiple lifetimes, not just this one. It would be impossible to expect someone to go through everything life has to offer within one life. This is why, at this point in the timeline, we are now ready to clear out what is unwanted so we can look forward to experiencing living in bliss in this lifetime and the ones that may come after. By creating the contrast of experiencing what we do not want, we create a strong desire for what we do want more of, and desire is just another vibration through which we manifest our physical reality.

To summarize, many people who have started a healing journey will get stuck in Ego for an indeterminate amount of time because they believe they have done all their healing when the truth is that they have done *some* healing and then decided they were better than everyone else. Obviously, this is Ego taking over, but it is always such a sweet song to get lost in when thinking that we are more spiritually advanced than anyone else and, therefore, can rest on our laurels. What to remember here is that being judgemental and working with the idea that there are people who are "superior" or "inferior" to us is complete bullshit and shows clearly a person stuck in Ego with a rather large wound around self-worth.

Which brings us back to chakras. Let's first explore the question: What exactly are chakras? They are energy centers that act as a direct connection to our own life force energy, also called Prana, Ki, or Chi. They are the key translators of our human experience and keep a record of our wounding throughout our lifetimes. They are consciousness centers where we can access different levels of embodiment, meaning embodying the Universe or Source in a human state:

embodying our own divinity. This can only happen when all chakras are healed and balanced, because otherwise our bodies are not high-vibrational enough for us to fully accept receiving our Soul within. This is the actual reason why we choose to work on healing ourselves so that we may truthfully incarnate fully as our Soul instead of just embodying a sliver of it by default.

The first chakra, commonly known as the Root or Base chakra—Muladhara in Sanskrit—is red in colour and located at the base of the spine. This energy center is our direct connection with Mother Earth and the physical world, with associated keywords of survival, manifestation, and grounding. The Root chakra further indicates one's individuality in direct relation to the greater whole and the amount of energy at our disposal in facing everyday life. It dictates our sense of safety and belonging in the world.

This chakra invites us to look at how safe we feel in general in everyday life and how connected with the rest of humanity we feel we are. An easier method to identify this is to look at the opposite, or how detached and alienated we feel towards humanity as a whole. These become direct answers to how safe we feel within and how connected we really are with our own bodies.

How we view humanity as a whole is how we view ourselves. How safe we feel in the world is how safe we feel within our bodies. How is this true? It is the very principle of "as above, so below; as within, so without; as the Universe, so the Soul," or the principle that our outside reality is a direct reflection of our inside truth.

When the Root chakra is overactive, it shows up within someone as an unhealthy obsession with all things material and perceived "success" attached to how many material things they own. Materialistic people, who are focused on appearances and "status", decide if others are worthwhile based on what they own or how rich they are or seem to be. This and focusing strictly on physical appearance indicate an overactive root chakra. The same goes for people who fear and resist change of any kind and are very controlling and dominating, because these are ways for them to feel safe. They feel threatened by everything outside of their control. This can also show up as people who never share with others yet take all they are offered (and often more than just what they are offered), who are overly selfish and self-involved or obsessed with themselves, who are narcissistic, greedy, and prone to outbursts of anger in general, but especially when their shallowness is pointed out.

The overactive Root chakra summarizes people who do not feel safe in the world and whose sense of identity or individuality is heavily distorted. They believe themselves untouchable, yet are terrified of losing their possessions because they have made their materialistic world their personality. They translate one's material possessions and wealth as someone's value as a person. Therefore, they constantly compare themselves to others to see how they "rank" in life. They constantly need to feel "superior" to others and treat those they deem as "inferior" terribly, with contempt and a great lack of basic respect and decency.

They also tend to be overly sexual but rarely satisfied because they never actually experience a connection during sex, just physical sensations, as true intimacy would require vulnerability on their part, which does not feel safe to them. They see vulnerability as a weakness because they are terrified of people seeing through them to the truth within, just as they are terrified of their own truth and seek to distance themselves from who they really are in favour of who they appear to be. Generally, they are incapable of seeing themselves in a bad light, regardless of how true it is through their behavior and actions. Wounds of self-betrayal tend to be found in this chakra.

Dealing with an underactive Root chakra, however, will look like people who have little to no sense of self. We find here the people-pleasers, the doormats, who always betray their own wants and needs in favour of providing them to others. This is where we will encounter people who copy others or forge a personality based on what they think others want to see and would approve of, since they are not grounded in the Truth of being who they are. They likely have no idea who they really are, and they do not see their own power and value, likely assuming they have neither to contribute. We are also talking here about people who are depressed about life and the state of the world we live in, and cannot reconcile there being any good left in the world. The underactive root chakra is akin to being unable to connect with our physical reality and life itself.

General despair and giving up on life are also indicative of underactive Root chakras, as this energy center is the direct link we have with the world and the amount of vitality we are allowing in from Mother Earth herself. We need this energy to be balanced so that we can feel the love and support coming in from the Earth. Otherwise, an underactive Root chakra translates as a disconnect from the 3D reality, from the world, and from the Self. There is this sense of abandonment attached to it, of feeling alone and isolated, of feeling unsafe. This can also show up as anxiety, insecurity, financial struggles, low drive in life, low sexuality, potential drastic weight fluctuations, or illnesses appearing frequently, and a strong sense of general instability in everyday life. This also means living with very high amounts of stress and the illusion that we can only ever rely on ourselves, that others are inherently dangerous to us, and that the world is out to get us. It is fear of existing.

Both underactive and overactive Root chakras house people who are easily triggered by what they perceive as attacks to their sense of self, or to be more precise, the image they have created about who they think they should be, who they pretend to be, and who they know they are not. Anything that asks them to be authentic will be treated as though it is a threat to their very existence.

When a person's Root chakra is healed and balanced, they carry an undeniable, authentic sense of self, of being safe, of belonging, and they can feel the unconditional love and support from their energetic connection with the planet. They are very stable and grounded and have no difficulty receiving an abundance of all kinds with little to no effort. These people will be in a state of peacefulness, healthy detachment, and acceptance of the states of the world and others, and they will never feel the need to prove themselves to others. They feel and connect deeply with Mother Earth and her children and inherently know they will be kept safe and provided for at all times. They trust in the Universe and the flow of process. They know who they authentically are and consciously embody themselves fully and confidently while also being able to manifest what they need easily.

There are many tools available to assist in healing and balancing the Root chakra. Since we already understand that this is a vibrational world and that everything carries a vibration, it should come as no surprise that we can use existing vibrations to help activate our own. Crystals that help with the Root chakra specifically include garnet, smoky quartz, black tourmaline, hematite, and black onyx. Wearing the colour red, eating red and/or root foods, listening to musical tones of "C," and any and all grounding exercises are other ways to work with the Root chakra.

Working directly with the element of earth is also beneficial since this is the chakra of connection with the energy of Mother Earth and is also our "waste disposal" chakra. This simply means that all energy transformed and transmuted within us through healing that kept our energy low vibrational will exit through the Root chakra, through the soles of the feet, and into the earth. Being in nature, spending time in silence focused solely on feeling that connection with the Earth's core, feeling the breath of the world and its soft song, and tuning into the energy of life it provides are great ways to help ground, which is a strong tool to heal the Root chakra.

It is important to make clear here that all of the healing, transforming, and clearing of past wounds essentially means breaking loose and rejecting all the energetic waste that keeps us low vibrational, weighed down, and holding us back as individuals. All of our blockages and limiting beliefs are energetic weights, keeping us stuck at our current vibrational level. All blocked and unbalanced chakras have physical effects on our bodies. The energetic weight we hold on to can reflect as physical weight we can never seem to shake off, no matter how hard we try. This excess weight can be understood as a physical layer of protection we subconsciously choose to hold onto in order to feel safer in the world.

The key to healing the root chakra is to ground and connect with our own body fully, as in reconnecting with disowned parts, loving ourselves unconditionally exactly as we appear to be, and other body mindfulness exercises. Physical exercise is very important as it helps us ground our Selves in our bodies. Therefore, anything that practices deliberate body mindfulness is important for healing, such as yoga, tai chi, and dancing. We have to reconnect with and own our body as the temple it is for our Soul. It is crucial to understand that our Soul chose our body exactly as it is and chose every transformation it would go through.

Of utmost importance is the understanding that our Soul has made no mistakes in crafting the perfect vessel for itself. This may be triggering for some to read, so Journal honestly about the various triggers that can arise at this point and revisit them when calm. There will be an entire chapter dedicated to the physical body and the role it plays, along with explanations of feminine and masculine energies within and how they function. For now, the purpose is full acceptance of — and unconditional love for — Self.

Next comes the Sacral chakra, or Svadhisthana in Sanskrit, which is orange and located just below the navel, centered where the womb is located on the female body. This chakra encompasses emotions, relationships, sensuality, sexuality, and creativity. It is the center of feminine energy, of desires in all forms, and is the home of self-expression. This is where we uncover the authentic self, as we are *beings of creation,* and the Sacral chakra is the *center of creation* within our human bodies. We, as humans, are here as creators. We are all artists of our own kind. The very blueprints of how and what we are meant to contribute to society as Souls are stored here. Svadhisthana means "the dwelling place of the Self"; I would simply add the *creative* self, as all chakras are centers of Self, just different aspects of it. The Sacral chakra offers us the magic of creation through emotion and desire.

Being known as the processing center, the Sacral chakra is also referred to as the assimilation center. This means that this chakra is the physical center of balance in our human bodies in regard to the physical world. Being the seat of processing emotions means that all the emotional turmoil we fail to express vocally gets pushed down and stuck here. Unexpressed emotions accumulate here over time through a lack of conscious emotional processing. We have to allow ourselves to feel and live out our emotions without letting ourselves be controlled by them so that we can understand the

311

message they are trying to convey to us. We can only receive these messages by feeling our emotions in the Heart chakra before they can be processed and released through the Sacral into the Root, then down into the Earth. Unexpressed emotions cannot leave until they have conveyed their message because the very purpose of experiencing emotions is to inform us of something.

When we reject our emotions and otherwise refuse to deal with them (meaning keeping them from being "dissolved" into processable components by the Heart chakra once the message is received and accepted), we are simply shoving them down into the Sacral chakra, where they cannot be processed because they have not fulfilled their purpose. This is why we can accumulate very old emotions dating from the beginning of this lifetime and from previous lifetimes. Emotions are energy, and that energy is stuck to our Soul essence. This explains phobias in people who have "no valid reason" in this lifetime to carry such phobias. They are untreated emotions (fear) that have followed us through this lifetime.

When dealing with an overactive Sacral chakra, we will see people who are emotionally explosive or reactive, who are easily overwhelmed by their emotions, and who experience extreme cravings and desires. Completely irrational bouts of intense emotional outbursts will be common, as well as insatiable addictions to all forms of pleasure, be it in the form of sex, food, alcohol, drugs, or other forms of escapism. They will also be addicted to drama, either their own or by creating situations themselves for no other purpose than self-entertainment or to feel powerful when otherwise feeling powerless. They will be people who show up as attention and validation-seeking individuals, who are manipulative, who gaslight, and who are very self-centered and self-serving. They will have little to no empathy for others, they will want to be the center of attention constantly, will always throw pity parties for themselves, play the victim in all circumstances (especially when they are the ones at fault), and will have no respect for others in general.

Other things to look out for include self-obsessed behaviours, or main-character syndrome, where no one else exists or is important unless they serve them in some capacity. Narcissistic tendencies and full-blown narcissism stem from an overactive Sacral chakra. They have a completely distorted sense of Self because they have so many unprocessed emotions fighting a battle to be seen and freed from within them, which means they cannot absorb any kind of criticism of their person that touches their self-delusions of grandeur. They are incapable of self-accountability because they prefer to believe they are perfect as they are instead of being honest with themselves, which is another reason why they experience complete emotional breakdowns over trivial things. They have a distorted positive view of themselves where they paint themselves as a martyr who simply cannot be understood by others and who can do no wrong. Others are always the problem, never them.

On the other hand, dealing with an underactive Sacral chakra will take on the form of people who have difficulty making connections with others, who do not trust nor allow themselves to be creative (their own harshest critic), are closed off to or are fearful of sexual relations, while also being unable to relax during and allow themselves to feel pleasure. There can also be an inability to trust in others and themselves and an inability to feel pure, undiluted passion, excitement, or even enthusiasm. They prefer to keep themselves small, hidden, and unnoticeable. An underactive Sacral chakra also shows up as a complete disconnect from genuine personal feelings and emotions, along with difficulty recognizing, identifying, and processing them adequately. They have a distorted negative view of themselves, which translates as a lack of faith, belief in self, and inability to do things for fun. They lack a proper sense of Self.

A healed and balanced Sacral chakra allows a person to be wide open to intimacy of all kinds without self-betrayal or needing to be dependent on another person to validate their worth. There is a secure, loving sense of Self and a deep respect for Self. This person does not betray themselves for another, and they fully embrace their creativity and creative gifts. They are comfortable around all others and are friendly and compassionate towards all, even strangers. They are attuned to their feelings and are sexually free to experience deep connection and pleasure *shared* with another. This balanced and healed chakra is great for effortless surrender and vibrational attraction of everything a person wants and needs when aligned with Source and their highest good. This chakra being healed and balanced allows for emotional self-mastery.

Emotions are associated with the energy of water. Therefore, water is the best element to work with when it comes to working with the Sacral chakra. Crystals associated with this chakra include carnelian, amber, tiger's eye, and opal, while moonstone and aquamarine boost the connection with the water element, as do shells and sea salt. When working with crystals, make sure to properly inform yourself on their individual properties and how to best work with them individually, but also ensure you select those that call to you intuitively for best results. The ones listed in this chapter serve as suggestions and may not be suited to your specific needs. What may work very well for another may not work as well for you because you may have different wounds needing to be addressed at certain times. Different crystals have different vibrations and, therefore, heal different things.

Other vibrational matches to working with the Sacral chakra are the musical tones of "D," eating orange foods, wearing orange, spending time in water, allowing creativity, using orange in your creative practices, or using sandalwood. Consciously processing stuck emotions is also part of healing the Sacral, which is what we have been working on for the entirety of the first four chapters (AAUR technique). This *is* the emotional processing center, after all. Stuck emotions in the Sacral will need to rise up to the Heart chakra to be felt and heard before returning to the Sacral to be processed and dissolved energetically.

At this point, it needs to be clear that there is no "order" in which to clear and balance chakras. Follow what is calling your attention the strongest and go from there. Your healing will happen how it needs to happen for you to fully clear layers of wounding before the deeper layers can be uncovered. A chakra can feel balanced without being healed entirely. When another layer is accessed, this can shift a balanced chakra into being either over- or underactive again, and we need to start healing all of them again until we access the final layers of wounding and can be free of the whole process. There are as many different healing journeys as there are people on them. Trust in the process and know that you will be guided to what you need along the way. Let go of the idea that the finish line is the goal; otherwise, you will make yourself miserable by chasing after it. Healing takes time and effort, and simply cannot be forced.

The third chakra, and the final of the lower chakras, is the Solar Plexus chakra, or Manipura in Sanskrit, which is yellow in colour and is located just above the navel, between the lower ribs. This chakra is the center of personal power, be it willpower, self-belief, self-confidence, self-esteem, or self-discipline. This chakra is also the seat of masculine energy, and it further governs the mental or intellectual aspects of life and is where the energy of the Ego resides. This means that people who are stuck in Ego likely have a distorted Solar Plexus, as the more we heal and balance it, the easier it is to circumvent the Ego in survival mode until it goes back to being the tool of personal power that it truly is in its healed state.

The Solar Plexus is considered the "Sun" chakra, the center of joy and warmth within our bodies, which houses our inner child. This is where the mental processing of our relationships happens. A distorted Solar Plexus energy can only ever offer a distorted view of our relationships, including the one we have with ourselves. It is why, when an external relationship does not work out how we want it to, it is taken so personally by our wounded inner child residing here, who throws random, massive temper tantrums when they do not get their way. How we choose to perceive ourselves and the people around us is directly influenced by the state of our Solar Plexus chakra, just as is the depth to which we can experience joy and deep laughter.

When this chakra is overactive, we tend to see patterns of strict rigidity and an overwhelming need to be right, to win, to be seen as "superior" or an "alpha" at all costs because we unconsciously directly attach our sense of worth to those outcomes—being wrong, losing, and being seen as "less than" are seen as a direct hit to their worth as an individual. There is a huge difference between healthy and unhealthy competition, which is dictated by the state of people's Solar Plexus chakras. Our deepest self-worth insecurities are rooted in this chakra, and an overactive one takes the shape of a big superiority complex. In contrast, an underactive one shows a big inferiority complex.

Other noticeable traits include being overly stubborn, controlling, aggressive, short-tempered, and judgmental, while also pretending to be a leader but never actually being one through leading by example, only dictating with words. These are the "do as I say, not as I do" types, believing themselves above their own rules and regulations of others. We can also find here intense coldness and lack of humour (unless it is their own, which often denigrates and degrades others to appear better than), along with bursts of pent-up rage and an inflated sense of self-importance. These are the big-babies-throwing-temper-tantrums types. They are all about bravado while lacking actual character, integrity, and substance.

On the other hand, an underactive Solar Plexus chakra presents as shyness, evasiveness, an inability to assert oneself, and a weakened or non-existent state of genuine personal identity, which leads to creating mask after mask and trying to fit in by blending in instead of celebrating their true Self. These people will be unreliable, riddled with self-doubt, unable to see their own worth, and are all too willing to throw others under the bus to preserve themselves, as they have no strength of will and never take responsibility for their own actions. They have little to no character or integrity, which is true of overactivity as well.

Underactive Solar Plexus energy means these people will constantly be seeking guidance from others as they do not trust or value their own judgment. They are easy to manipulate and are doormats in general, as they have no personal boundaries and would bend over backward to please and gain a sense of worth or value from external praise. There may also be addictions present and other types of obsessive behaviours in an attempt to appear better than they are or to escape their own insecurities. They use and do whatever they can to try to feel better about themselves, not caring for the potential damage to others that their actions and decisions may cause. They tend to only look out for their own self-interest and act as a trapped, wounded animal that lashes out at all perceived threats.

A healed and balanced Solar Plexus, however, is truly a wonderful thing, as it is quite literally likened to a person being a beautiful, warm ray of sunlight. They are strong in the Truth of who they are, confident and reliable. They are people who are accountable and are not afraid to take responsibility for their actions and words, regardless of how it would affect them personally. They keep their promises, and their word is their law. They will be warm, kind, compassionate, and full of life and laughter. They will be quite playful as they will be strongly connected to their inner child and will love and appreciate life for all it has to offer. They treat everyone with kindness and respect and are always willing to help. They are responsible and will not fear taking on challenges or standing up for those in need. They do not take anything personally; they are true to themselves and intimately know who they are. They are self-sufficient yet know when to ask for help and do so when needed. They are humble and can create a safe space for others to exist and communicate in.

Working with this chakra involves the element of air, as this is the mental processing center (meaning our perceptions are affected by the state of this chakra), but we can also work with fire energy due to its nature of warmth and stability, and connection to the inner child. This implies that techniques such as aromatherapy and deep conscious breathing are excellent tools to use in healing this energy center, just as allowing ourselves to indulge in and relax into moments of intense, deliberate joy and laughter. They do say that laughter is the best form of medicine, after all. Any kind of assertiveness training and group exercises that develop self-worth and self-esteem will be particularly useful for underactive Solar Plexus chakras. Anything that heals and nurtures the inner child is also recommended to work with.

This is the energy center that stores everyday mental stress. Therefore, all relaxation methods that allow you to connect deeply with your Self and inner child are great modalities for healing this chakra. Listening to tones of "E" in particular and engaging with the colour yellow by wearing or eating yellow items is also beneficial. Spending time in direct sunlight or communing with fire through candles or campfires will also help heal this chakra. Crystals that can be worked with include peridot, rhodonite, golden tektite, rainforest jasper, tiger iron, topaz, yellow tourmaline, or citrine.

The three chakras we have explored thus far are part of what is called the "lower" chakras and are directly linked to our understanding of the physical experience, the 3D world. They are the chakras we work through when we need to ground ourselves in our physical experience. The Root encompasses our energetic waste disposal and overall connection to the world, the Sacral holds our emotional processing and our relationship connections with others, and the Solar Plexus sticks to the mental processing and the relationship connection with personal identity. They are the chakras that facilitate grounding, connecting with, and communicating with the world at large and its people, with the Self, and with Mother Earth herself.

Just like a tree, the more stable our connection is with the 3D and the planet through grounding—growing our metaphorical roots within earthly reality—the stronger and more stable we become, allowing us to expand upwards and welcome the Universe and its energy of Truth, metaphorically growing our trunk and branches higher and higher. This foundation is essential, as without solid roots, a tree topples. Just as we have been living in a toppled state and are now seeking to rectify ourselves. We need to have a strong and solid foundation for us to be able to bring down the manifestations we want and need.

Manifestation is about creating something energetically and then allowing it to manifest physically, which cannot happen if we are not properly grounded and solid enough to receive it. It would be like trying to reel in a massive fish while trying to stay afloat in the water ourselves: we would only ever end up being dragged around as we have no solid footing to rely upon to give us the strength to pull back.

In between the lower and higher chakras, we find the 4th chakra—commonly known as the Heart chakra, Anahata in Sanskrit—which acts as the bridge connecting both the 3D (lower) and 5D (higher) dimensions. It is green in colour and located just under the collarbone, slightly above the breast. It acts as the connection point for physical manifestation. A blocked Heart chakra cannot manifest consciously. This chakra can be summarized in 3 main principles: unconditional love, compassion, and unity. It represents infinite Divine Love and the meshing of our connection with both the Universe and Mother Earth. It encompasses our relationship with Life itself within the acts of giving, receiving, and sharing.

The biggest indicator of the state of this chakra is the relationship we have with Love, both general and specific: how we treat and value ourselves and, as a direct reflection, how we treat and value others. The Heart chakra is the seat of Self-Love. One's personal generosity is a great indicator of the state of their Heart chakra, as someone who refuses to give freely is clearly underactive. In contrast, the ones who give abundantly but to their own detriment are clearly overactive.

When it comes to the act of receiving, those who have great difficulty—or outright refuse—to receive from others likely have overactive Heart chakras, since the root of this wound is the belief that others deserve to receive, not themselves. On the other hand, those who take, take, take everything and more have underactive Heart chakras and have a strong lack mentality that they have to take all they can when they can because they believe there is not enough for everyone. As for sharing, overactives will make sure everyone gets equal portions, though they likely will not keep enough for their own fair share, while underactives refuse to share what "belongs to them" yet expect others to share all they have with them. Both types reflect a wound of lack: overactivity through harmful self-neglect, and underactivity through selfish hoarding.

Before diving deeper into the unbalanced states of the Heart chakra, we will quickly address the smaller, associated chakra, called the Higher Heart chakra. The problem I have encountered while tapping into this energy is that it has been constantly mislabelled. What people have been calling the Higher Heart chakra is, in fact, the actual Heart chakra, and what they have been labeling as the Heart chakra – located at the center of the breast, the lower half of the sternum – is, in fact, the Soul's Essence Energetic Center (SEEC), as we have explored earlier.

The confusion is easy to understand since the Heart chakra is understood as the center of unconditional love, but what carries greater unconditional love energy than Source: the Universe itself? The SEEC, being our own personal sliver of the universe within, was misunderstood as a chakra center, when it is in fact our direct connection to our Soul and Source. The difference between them is that the Heart chakra is where we process feelings and emotions into loving energy when it is balanced, and that loving energy will become, with healing, unconditional love for all. The goal of healing and balancing all chakras is to make our human bodies compatible with the true energy of unconditional love, which *is the very essence of* the Universe, so that we can one day fully embody our Soul through our SEEC and share that beautiful energy with the world as a way of existing.

Once we become able to embody pure unconditional love for ourselves and every other living, breathing being in the world, be it animal, human, or the Earth itself, that is when our Soul can start the process of becoming embodied in our human vessel. As long as our vibration is not high enough, we cannot safely embody our Soul; the pain would be too great, as the pure energy of Universal unconditional love would force rapid healing to occur within all of our essences. The more healing we still need to do, the harsher that energy will rip through us in an attempt to heal us.

This is why healing is done in layers, so that it does not feel as overwhelming as it could be if the process were done all at once. That shock would be too great for the body to withstand. This is why our Souls will sometimes dip their feet into us to help boost the process, where we will feel this amazing, electrifying high that shows us what is possible and what is to come when we are diligent in doing the inner work. They show us how amazing and worthwhile things can be if we continue to trust in and surrender to the Universe by choosing the path of healing. These moments also produce dark nights of the Soul, where we have no other choice but to face our healing head-on or suffer our pain on repeated cycles until we choose to heal.

This is exactly why the Heart chakra will be the last chakra to be fully healed and balanced, as it requires all of the lower and higher chakras to be healed and balanced on their own first, so that the Heart chakra may have access to its true centered state. The higher and lower chakras will balance individually before balancing as lower and higher chakra groups and then balancing one off of the other to allow access to the Heart chakra's true balanced state. As long as that balance between higher and lower chakras is not attained, the Heart chakra will not be able to find its true center of healed energy.

People are only now starting to reawaken to the Truth of the Universe, thanks to the brave Souls that have come before our time to start the awakening process. It is up to us to acknowledge the Truth and pick up the torch to bring about change, to bring about true Heaven on Earth. This will be seen and felt strongly in the generations to come, as lighter beings will arrive in great numbers to pick up the torch once we, at the forefront, are out of energy to continue. We are now doing the heavy lifting so they can come in and sketch out the finer details. The promise this Earth holds is beautiful to witness, and we must believe in it and do our own part to be worthy of accessing its greatness.

All of that being said, let's refocus back to identifying overactive Heart chakras, or the overflow of love for others while neglecting to love the Self. They often present themselves as uncontrolled strong emotions of distorted needs, such as jealousy, being clingy and demanding, being co-dependent, offering love conditionally, over-sacrificing the Self in the hopes of being loved in return (which never works), and otherwise needing to please everyone considered of value to them. They can be selfless in a detrimental way, with the goal of "earning" the love they crave, have no boundaries, and are constantly betraying themselves and their own needs to fulfill those of others. They believe that the more they give of themselves, the worthier they are to receive, yet they also keep themselves from receiving because they inherently do not believe themselves worthy.

Because this chakra often operates as a safety valve, when it is overactive and a person reaches a breaking point (feeling overstretched and under extreme pressure to please and appease everyone else), the Heart chakra can "implode," causing a complete emotional breakdown to try and clear out all the pent-up energy. The Heart chakra is the seat of all feeling, which transmutes everything into the energy of unconditional love when it is healthy and balanced. We already know that emotions need to be processed to be released.

In an overactive Heart chakra, the space is too big, and many emotions become tangled up into a chaotic mess that is too intricate and complex for the Heart to assess properly. It becomes a jangled tangle of a little bit of many different emotions intertwining and trying to express themselves simultaneously, which is what creates the processing overload and, therefore, the implosion, but also is responsible for the initial feelings of being stretched too thin and consequently feeling under extreme pressure. This is how being too hard on ourselves manifests energetically, and self-love is the key to healing that.

On the flip side, dealing with an underactive Heart chakra will take the form of someone who is cut off from their true emotions in favour of self-preservation.

Being anti-social, feeling rejected, hating people, feeling lonely and/or isolated, being highly critical of others (and therefore Self, but this is never understood as such), lacking empathy, feeling unworthy, and always being negative and reacting negatively to everything are all signs of an underactive Heart chakra. Again, the theme revolves around not loving the Self, but expressed differently. Rejecting responsibility and blaming others for all their personal woes (which they tend to create themselves through their actions and words), being cruel to people and animals to feel a sense of superiority, are other signs, which all can be summarized by the lack of connection with Source created by closing the Heart chakra. They will feel dead inside because they refuse the energy of life: unconditional love.

A balanced and healthy Heart chakra takes the shape of someone who is generous, compassionate, loving, kind, happy, joyous, peaceful, understanding, empathetic, and, overall, just embodies the essence of the Universe. They are a pillar of true, authentic love and light, and will feel the connection between all living beings with the planet itself. They are completely genuine and down to earth and never discriminate, as they have the capacity to love and accept all beings exactly as they are and where they are in their personal journeys. They have a calm, soothing presence and an uncanny ability to just listen and be present. They are reliable and do not conform to any type of self-betrayal, including letting themselves be manipulated or played emotionally. They are masters of themselves and their own emotions. They know their worth, love and respect themselves fully. They feel no need to cater to others' perceptions or demands of them. They have a great sense of integrity and fairness and will not accept being undersold or misrepresented. They stand up for what they believe in, yet do not do so in an uncontrolled outburst. They do not judge others.

These people will not depend on others, yet know when to seek help. They give freely without expecting anything in return, yet can graciously accept gifts and appreciate them for what they are. They are individuals who do the right thing for the sake of it being the right thing to do, and most importantly, they are humble about it. They do not show off "how great they are"; they simply are comfortable with the knowledge. They have nothing to prove to anyone, and they do not seek external validation or accolades and prestige. They see everyone as equals, with the very concept of "superior-inferior" being utterly ridiculous to them. They exude purity and unconditional love and are polarizing in how they trigger other people's wounding simply by existing because of their high vibrational level of being. They have an open heart and do not fear pain.

The Heart chakra holds all the natural elements' vibrations within it, and practices of healthy giving, receiving, and sharing are great tools to help heal and balance this chakra since they directly correlate with the state of our relationships and how we perceive others and ourselves. Underactives have to learn to give freely without attachment or expectation of return, while also making sure they do not take more than they need or what is fair. Overactives have to stop overgiving to others and start giving to themselves more while also learning to accept gifts and compliments without resisting them and believing themselves unworthy of the attention. Sharing becomes a test of boundaries and self-respect for overactives since it becomes about being included in the process and receiving a fair share instead of being abused, taken advantage of, and left out as usual. Sharing is a test of selflessness, fairness, and personal integrity for the underactives who seek to heal.

Other tools to help heal and balance the Heart chakra include musical tones of "F," eating green foods, and spending time out connecting with nature. Witnessing and basking in the beautiful energy of sunrises and sunsets can be extremely potent for the Soul. Crystals associated with the Heart chakra include jade, green aventurine, vesuvianite, green tourmaline, peridot, rhodonite, and rose quartz. We already know that the best tool to heal and balance the Heart chakra is Self-love, but it does go hand in hand with forgiveness. Forgiveness opens every door that seems shut. Forgiveness of others and the Self is done by understanding our own humanity and, consequently, that of others. In the next chapter, we will explore this healing tool in depth, but it is important to note that no true healing can be done without forgiveness.

Moving on from the Heart chakra, we will now be entering the territory of the upper or higher chakras, which are connected with the higher realms of consciousness. We remember that the lower chakras interpret the physical realm and human reality, our vessel's experience of the world. The higher chakras, on the other hand, encompass the ability to deliver Truth (Throat chakra), to understand/perceive Truth (Third Eye chakra), and finally to receive Truth (Crown chakra) from the Universe. Just as the lower chakras connect us to Mother Earth—nurturing, soothing, and stabilizing—the higher chakras connect us with the Universe: authentic, inspirational, and purposeful.

The symbiosis encountered here is fascinating to witness. The lower chakras are associated with masculine energy, yet commune with the feminine energy of Mother Earth, whereas the higher chakras are associated with feminine energy, yet commune with the masculine energy of the Universe or Father Sky. This effectively means that we, as human beings, serve as the balancing center between the two. We will dive in-depth into masculine and feminine energies in a later chapter. For now, we simply need to understand that we are the connection, the bridge, between Earth and the Universe, of feminine and masculine energies working together as one. We human beings serve as the Heart chakra of Life, which is exactly why unconditional love is the answer to everything and why Oneness is the only answer.

It is as though we are living, breathing embodiments of the Universe's Heart chakra seeking to heal and balance itself out. We are all either embodying overactive or underactive aspects of Life's Heart chakra. We can see it in how poor people stand together and help each other with love, hearts of gold, and generous natures. At the same time, we also have unbelievably greedy, stingy, and selfish rich people who are incapable of sharing their hordes of wealth and who keep amassing more of what they do not need while abusing others in the process. These are overactive and underactive Heart chakra symptoms personified.

Returning to the higher chakras, let's introduce the first of them: the Throat chakra, or Vishuddha in Sanskrit. It is blue in colour, is located at the center of the throat, and represents communication, creative manifestation, and integrity. This chakra is directly linked to communicating Truth and connecting with our personal part in the cosmic plan. The Throat chakra is also known as the center of purification, where Source energy is transformed into physical manifestation. It is the mirror of the Solar Plexus. Therefore, how the Solar Plexus connects us to Mother Earth is reflected in how the Throat chakra connects us to the Universe.

This is exactly why we must be careful of what we speak, as the Throat chakra is our physical manifestation tool. When we are talking negatively about ourselves and others, our energy takes that as Truth we wish to see manifest, and we will apply whatever is said to our own vibration. Saying unkind things about others will be interpreted as vibrationally true of ourselves due to our innate nature of Oneness, and will get stuck in our energy and drop our vibration. When we judge and hate others, we are only ever hating and judging ourselves on a vibrational level.

These become an unconscious belief that can turn into a wound of Self-hatred if repeated too often. On the other hand, by speaking lovingly and kindly about ourselves and others, we can create a new belief that we are worthy and loved. Words are powerful, as they are manifestation tools. Speaking the truth is a cleansing process that helps to balance this chakra, as Truth carries its own vibration, which is why we can always energetically pick up on when someone is lying, when we are familiar with our intuition and the vibration of Truth.

When identifying overactive Throat chakras, keep a lookout for people who simply never shut up and are uncomfortable with silence. People who always need to talk or overshare, above everyone else, yet are incapable of even listening to others, have overactive throat chakras. People who are immediately defensive on every topic, regardless of whether they are actually attacked by others or not, people who are overly critical of others, and people who have strong opinions on subjects they know little to nothing about are more examples. There are also underlying patterns of fear associated with overactive Throat chakras, such as not being/feeling good enough and/or being unable or unwilling to take responsibility for one's own existence and how they impact others in their everyday lives, which is a direct tell of how spiritually immature a person is. Additionally, we can find in these people the inability to appreciate life's beauty and the failure to receive inspiration or ideas. Because the chakra is overwhelmed, it cannot perceive or speak Truth adequately.

In the case of an underactive Throat chakra, we will see this present itself in people as a fear of speaking up and being heard, of being seen, of being in the present moment, and generally being unable to show up for themselves in their own lives. This is true even for events they love and could otherwise be excited for. They will have difficulty communicating both their feelings and their needs. They will have a tendency to over-empathize with others in hopes that the feeling will be reciprocated, but we already know we cannot receive what we do not give to ourselves first. Therefore, that hope will never be answered, and the person will not understand why they cannot receive empathy or even sympathy from others. The answer is that they are vibrationally rejecting receiving this from others because they are refusing to give it to themselves. Acting meek, keeping ourselves small, isolated, unnoticeable, and unreliable, and being shy, quiet, and withdrawn are all further signs of underactive Throat chakras. We have to remember that humans are inherently social creatures, animals of community, and an underactive throat chakra means that we essentially become invisible to society.

As such, a balanced and healed Throat chakra shows up as a person who freely expresses their thoughts and feelings with respect and consideration for others around. They never speak ill of anyone, as they understand that every single individual is living through their own trauma and wounding. They understand where a wounded person can come from, but will not stray from their personal character because of others. They are fantastic listeners; they live creatively, honour themselves, respect themselves, always speak the truth, have great rhythm and timing, and are easily capable of receiving, understanding, and communicating spiritual insights. Their integrity is palpable. They do not refuse spirituality as they understand how fundamental to human nature it really is, and as such, will likely not be religious because they can see how distorted religions have become and how they now harm more than help. Honesty and kindness are ever-present in a healed and balanced Throat chakra, and these people will lead a life that is a true expression of themselves. They carry no self-doubt and do not indulge in lies of any kind.

Balancing and healing this chakra focuses on speech. As stated previously, speaking and honouring the truth is a great way to heal, but also by speaking kind and loving words to all that lives. Pay attention to the content of the words you speak every day. Are they meaningful? Are they true? Are they always kind and loving? Are they worthwhile? Are they representative of your personal truth? Further, are you genuinely happy in your life? Are you following your passions, or are you following what you were told was "life's checklist," "necessary," or "the right way to do things"? Or are you even capable of just shutting up and listening for an entire day? Actively listening to others and allowing their words to touch you? If any of these questions are answered with no, then you have a hint on where to start working on yourself. To choose authenticity is to choose to heal this chakra.

Genuine self-expression of all kinds is helpful in healing and balancing the Throat chakra. Obviously, anything pertaining to using the voice authentically is particularly helpful, such as speaking, singing, humming, or otherwise just making sounds with your voice as you feel inspired. What comes out does not have to make sense, as we already understand that different tones bring about healing. By speaking random words, we can use their specific energies, and by making random sounds, we can hit certain frequencies that we cannot just by speaking or singing. Some of you may experience certain songs never leaving your mind until you either read the lyrics or sing the parts that keep coming up over and over again. Healing this chakra could also include talking with a therapist or person of trust and unburdening ourselves from our experiences through words. Verbalizing thoughts, pain, mental processes, and emotional venting without a particular audience are all ways to practice strengthening and healing the Throat chakra.

Crystals that can be worked with for the Throat chakra include lapis lazuli, sodalite, blue aragonite, blue kyanite, blue lace agate, turquoise, clear quartz, and chrysocolla. Listening to tones of "G," eating liquid or watery foods like soup, sauces, juices, and water-filled fruits like watermelon and cucumber, and spending time in nature with clear blue skies overhead and direct sunlight will also help. The element of water is especially potent in healing the Throat chakra, making the oceans extremely powerful to work with, as is any natural, clear spring source and body of water. Expressing the Self through art and/or sound therapy is also a great tool.

Moving on to the Brow, or Third Eye, chakra—Ajna in Sanskrit—it is indigo in color and located at the center of the forehead. This chakra is considered to be the seat of wisdom while also being the Keeper of Soul Memories; it is thus the center of intuition, vision, and spiritual perception. This chakra governs our discernment and Universal understanding. It is where we envision and create the image we want for our lives. It is the seat of the mental body, meaning that it is through this chakra that we process or re-focus our goals, ideas, dreams, ambitions, and values. As a gateway to both the unconscious and higher realms of consciousness, tapping into this chakra allows us to identify and clarify our purpose or purposes in this lifetime. We have access to our bank of Soul knowledge through this chakra, such as the Akashic Records.

Many mental health issues stem from an unbalanced and unhealed Third Eye chakra, ranging from psychosis to anxiety. It is important to note that certain illnesses within the human body, mental or physical, can stem from multiple unhealed and unbalanced chakras and likely will not improve drastically just from healing and balancing one of them, just as they might stem from past life-wounding and cannot be healed until that lifetime is addressed and the source of the wound healed. It always varies depending on the individual Soul. We have to remember that what shows up in our physical reality might need some deeper healing than what working with just our chakras can achieve.

Having an overactive Third Eye chakra will present itself as high stress, obsessive behaviours, being ungrounded, and thus experiencing intense delusions and/or hallucinations, some even reaching the point of psychosis. There might be nightmares experienced, and difficulty focusing and concentrating on a given task. Losing ourselves in daydreams is an excellent example of this, as the Third Eye chakra represents True Sight. Excessive daydreaming and creating obsessive illusions, fantasies, or stories about ourselves or others in our minds are also examples of overactive Third Eye chakras. Basically, they are living out their fantasies as though they are real instead of seeing things for what they really are.

This energy center is where manifestation is envisioned or processed to become grounded in reality through the Throat chakra and present itself in physical reality through our Root chakra. However, we cannot manifest anything that interferes with another's free will, meaning we cannot force or coerce another person into anything they are unwilling to do or be to begin with. We cannot force a relationship to happen with someone who is uninterested. We cannot manifest a specific house to buy if the people living in it do not want to leave. Whenever we try to force a manifestation by trying to control the outcome, it invariably backfires tremendously.

This overactive chakra comes with a sense of floating through life, untethered, lost, confused, completely ungrounded, and unable to distinguish reality from self-made illusion. It will show up as an inability to differentiate between Truth and Universal connection, and delusions of self, or others, and of the Universe. These people will abuse the insights they receive in order to hold power over others. They will likely tend to be the "love and light only" crew, who ignore their faults and believe they are fully healed and have nothing more to work on in themselves, but their 3D reality will clearly show how untrue that is. They will be out of touch with the Truth of who they are, yet believe they fully embody it. There is a lack of personal integrity and honesty, and a refusal to self-evaluate. They are not following their true purpose, but the one they believe shows them in their best light. They believe their Sight makes them superior to others.

In contrast, the underactive Third Eye chakra crowd will appear as people with little to no sense of purpose, who will seem lost in life and just drifting from moment to moment without ever really being present. They will have no sense of direction and will likely feel stuck and frustrated, but unable to do anything about it. In addition to feeling lost and confused, they will also have little connection with themselves, and though they might believe they are happy in their lives, they will not feel fulfilled or driven. Because their Third Eye chakra is underactive, they cannot identify and work towards their purpose, so they seem to just aimlessly float through life without real care or wonder. They may jump from job to job as they become restless if they are too long in the same environment that contributes nothing to their sense of Self, which leaves them feeling unsatisfied and unable to help themselves as they cannot understand what is missing.

This energy center being underactive can also show up as poor vision and poor memory, a lack of imagination, poor common sense, and difficulty envisioning the future and understanding both inner and outer reality. These are people who will lose themselves in the horrors of current-day reality and be outraged but do nothing to change things. They will be dependent on feeling a sense of purpose through others instead of finding their own, and they will likely confuse inaccurate information with True knowledge. They will have little to no grasp of there being a bigger picture, nor of their own role in that picture. There is much focus on the negatives of life, which forces a dissociation from Source and creates for them a reality of extreme disconnect and loneliness, and they may willingly lose themselves in despair as they cannot see a way out or things ever improving.

When balanced and healed, the Third Eye chakra will show up in a person as someone who is highly intuitive, who has heightened insight and understanding of life and the world, who connects with Source easily and effortlessly, who knows and feels the Truth of things without effort, who learns quickly and easily, and who can experience altered states of being without losing themselves in them. They will also be very imaginative, yet can see through lies and illusions easily. They are in tune with messages from Spirit and are excellent, clear channels. They manifest easily and quickly (though that could also depend on the state of other chakras), and they trust and surrender to the Divine implicitly, as they understand the true universal connection that binds all of us together. As this chakra is the realm of knowledge and wisdom, those with a fully healed and balanced Third Eye chakra can step easily beyond the mind and Ego and their respective desires and longings that do not serve the higher call of aiding all as One.

To help heal and balance this chakra, meditation, stillness, quiet, and introspection are key. Just as for everything else in the world, too much of one thing is as detrimental as not having enough; balance is essential. This is also true of meditation as a healing tool. Deep, aware meditation can bring up a lot of strong emotions and memories, just as doing truthful and conscious introspection can. The idea here is not to do as much as possible and then be out for weeks energetically because you went deeper than you could handle. The idea is to start uncovering unpleasant truths and process them as they come up and start showing up more strongly as a consequence of wanting to heal; to hold energetic space for ourselves to be able to process what comes up in as peaceful a manner as possible, in a manageable way that does not exhaust us.

Healing is not a process that can or should be rushed. On the contrary, healing works in layers. As long as there is still an uncovered aspect in a given layer, we cannot move to the next, deeper layer. This means that themes we may believe we have already worked on and healed may surface again from a deeper layer of wounding, and this will be true until we reach the source of the initial wound. We have to scratch the surface before we can find a good, strong vein to follow to the very root of the issue.

Exposure to direct sunlight on the forehead while focusing on the Third Eye chakra is another way to help activate it, listening to tones of "A," and eating foods high in omega-3 fatty acids and antioxidants. As for crystals, working with amethyst, purple fluorite, iolite, azurite, Angelite, Herkimer diamonds, and diamonds is ideal. Be careful, however, of placing them directly on the Third Eye chakra as it is a very sensitive chakra and could turn overactive from exposure that is too strong or direct from a potent crystal, depending on your personal "balanced" starting point. This means that if your chakra is underactive, light, periodical touches from crystals in the center will be helpful, but not if your chakra is already overactive. Carrying the stones on your person as rings, necklaces, or bracelets is enough for them to work on your energy. Again, make sure you research the crystals you want to work with properly, as well as how to keep them in good health and clear the energies they absorb.

Finally, we have arrived at the last of the main chakras that will be covered in this chapter, namely the Crown chakra, or Sahasrara in Sanskrit. This one is violet in colour, is located at the top of the head, and represents the direct connection with the Divine realms. Just as the Root chakra links with the energy of Mother Earth and grounds us, the Crown chakra links us to the energy of the Universe and expands us. This can be visualized as a lotus flower lying flat atop the head, with the open petals representing the strength of the connection between the human vessel and the Universe. It is the energy center through which we receive knowledge and insights directly into our consciousness, where our finite being can commune with the infinity of Life. It is where we can recognize, connect with, and truly understand our own divinity, where we can access infinite wisdom and reach enlightenment (although this requires all chakras to be fully healed and balanced).

An overactive Crown chakra will take the shape of people who believe themselves spiritually beyond others, but it is done condescendingly. These people will be very arrogant spiritually, believing in holding all of the answers and that no one can truly understand them as they are on "another level." They will tend to be narcissistic as well, as they will nurture their sense of being "special" or "chosen" and will see themselves as in a category apart from the "common folk." This is where we find spiritual teachers and healers who are all talk and no magic, who just like to hear themselves, and who worship themselves and their supposed "brilliance" but do not actually offer anything of value.

These are the people who are inherently fake in their manner of living instead of being genuine and authentic, who are obsessed with how they appear and are perceived, but who are hollow and do not actually care to help others but will constantly tell them how to be while sabotaging them in their process to ensure they keep coming back. They will usually use fear and pressure tactics to get what they want while invoking curses, dark spirits or energies, evil entities, and other such fearmongering. The truth is that this is a Universe of Love. As long as you do not buy into these things, they will not affect you because it is only your vibration responding to your beliefs that could cause unwanted situations to happen. No one can affect another person's energy or free will without their consent. We can feel energetic external pressure when someone tries to meddle with our energy, and from there, we can block and clear away their energy instead of allowing it to affect us.

Other ways to spot overactive Crown chakras include observing the level of personal integrity—more specifically, a lack thereof—or if someone displays a God-complex of some sort. Their perception of Self is distorted to the point that they are fully embodying the lies they tell themselves they are and have no grasp of the Truth of who they genuinely are. They will confidently point their fingers at all the flaws they perceive in others, yet deny the existence of their own. They seldom follow their own advice, and all the rules they impose on others somehow never apply to them.

This state of being often happens when a person "unlocks" this chakra or becomes aware of the Truth of Universal Law for the first time. They tend to assume that because they are now receiving direct channeled information from Source, it means all their healing is done, and they are now fully healed and balanced, enlightened even, which causes them to stop working on themselves and close their eyes to their own faults and limitations. Since they stop working on themselves, they can never actually access deeper levels of healing, and they become stuck in their current energy until a shift is forced into their reality, which is seldom a pleasant experience. They will appear grand but feel hollow.

In the case of underactive Crown chakras, it will transpire as a complete shut-off from spirituality and Source. These are people who will feel no connection to the world or humanity; they believe there is nothing after death and that we live in a cold, hard, cruel world. Feelings of alienation towards humankind, of depression or general confusion and solitude, of feeling left out and apart, or outcast, will be present. There will be a strong rejection of any kind of invisible force that is not scientifically proven, such as a higher power, angels, guides, ghosts, fairies, and other beings that surround us on other planes of existence (energetic planes). They are the "need to see to believe" crowd, who either have difficulty or cannot feel energy by refusing to, by cutting themselves off from that innate ability we all possess to feel energy. We can all always feel energy, though it takes practice for the connection to be strong and fluid. These people likely live with a profound melancholy that they cannot even explain to themselves, which is created by their very rejection of the connection with Source energy.

A balanced and healed Crown chakra will take the shape of people who are connected with and fully embrace Oneness and Divine energy, often meaning they exude love, kindness, and gentleness. They know their mission or purpose and follow it in bliss. They are patient, kind, understanding, and have a strong healing presence. They carry Universal energy strongly, which others feel and are either strongly attracted to or highly triggered by. They are never afraid of death, and no subject is taboo for them. On the contrary, they naturally create a space where it is safe to have difficult conversations and where all parties are comfortable and able to open up. They feel calm and soothing to be around and can seem to carry an inner glow. They have an innate understanding that life is a direct reflection of one's own state of consciousness and that everything always happens perfectly and for a reason, while also never enabling destructive behaviours from others.

These people will harbour warm, loving, peaceful energy for all, and they know that life is a learning playground where we are meant to thrive as the masters of our own reality. They know and understand that the path, purpose, and challenges they have chosen as a Soul for their current incarnation are not a prison meant to control them but a puzzle to be solved that opens up the pathway step by step to the most perfect life they could possibly ask for, beyond their wildest dreams and aspirations. They also know that this puzzle will not solve itself and that hints are constantly around us to help us move forward. They have complete trust in themselves and the loving guidance of the Universe. They will be relaxed and stress-free, and they will feel no need to control anything. They will have total acceptance of themselves, embody their genuine energy of personal Truth, and have no problem living their chosen Soul path. They easily and effortlessly intimately connect with their guides and Source and choose to always embody a state of surrender to the natural Flow of Life.

Healing and balancing this chakra is all about a deep connection with Self and with Source simultaneously, while understanding the separation and innate communion between both. Being both fully open to receive and fully capable of giving back while retaining a sense of personal identity that is based on

Truth helps with balancing this chakra. Connections of all kinds are important: with energy, with Source, with Self, with the Earth, and with others, human or animal, even with objects. This process will be very personal and unique to each individual since it requires us to identify where we have disowned Oneness and use whatever technique necessary to reclaim that connection.

There may be a need to access physical locations around the world to retrieve disowned Soul parts of Self or reconnect with the specific energy we were carrying or channeling in previous lifetimes at these locations. There may also be places of power in the world that call to you that will either activate dormant aspects of Self or that will help you rediscover something thought lost on a Soul level. Pay attention to locations in the world that call to you and that you feel a connection with that cannot be explained through this lifetime alone, as these are subtle indicators that something is waiting for you there. These may be strong energies that will put you on your ass for a few days when first contact is achieved, or you may feel nothing at all and simply exist in those spaces where all you need to do is either contribute energetically or retrieve a Soul fragment. We never know what awaits us, but it is putting all of these puzzle pieces together that sparks Soul Lifeforce and cosmic understanding.

Healing the Crown chakra may also necessitate healing broken relationships in our life; keep in mind this never means allowing toxicity and self-betrayal, but rather making peace with all perceived disappointments, either in people or in situations that have taken place. Forgiveness is key for this process, and we will explore that theme in depth in the next chapter. Other tools include deep meditation, direct sunlight, stillness, being receptive, eating foods grown in and/or dried in the sun, listening to tones of "B," and spending time alone surrounded by peace and quiet. Crystals include celestite, selenite, clear quartz, and blue sapphire. It is also important to seek out experiences that call to you, push you outside of your comfort zone, are different, and allow for a shift of perspective to occur. We have to allow for every opportunity for change that comes knocking on our doors, as this allows the Soul to bring forth things that are constantly better suited to our personal evolution, even if they do not appear as such initially.

This chapter will now become a key resource in gauging your personal growth and in understanding aspects of yourself that were possibly unclear or unexplainable. This chapter was meant to allow a higher perspective, detached from preconceived notions. Remember all of the lessons learned in the previous chapters and use this one in conjunction with your progress. Use this chapter to help shed new light on all of the entries in your Journal so far and what they really represent within yourself. Use this knowledge to help shift your present moment and fine-tune your personal awareness. Remember that healing is a process. It can be hit and miss. This knowledge can help shed light on how we perceive life and our perceived shortcomings or successes. It is important not only to look at what could be a potential wounding but also where we appear to be on the path of healing.

I invite you at this point to continue or restart daily meditations, even if it is only for the duration of taping into each individual chakra and writing down what pops into your head, what you feel, what you know, or what is possible, or what comes up in each of them individually: anything and everything you perceive, especially when it seems to make no sense. As stated previously, healing is like a puzzle we are trying to put together to get to the full picture. Mistakes can and will happen: who cares?

Have a new section in your Journal where you write daily what comes up in each chakra, so you can start keeping track of the patterns they will show you. Do not doubt yourself in this exercise and write down everything, from song lyrics to random words or sentences, to a specific emotion, to an approximation of what you have difficulty perceiving or naming properly; bottom line, there is no wrong answer, only possible puzzle pieces to uncover. Write from feeling, not thought.

Chapter 8
The Power of Forgiveness

———————— • ————————

The first thing to understand when it comes to forgiveness is that current society understands the concept all wrong. Forgiveness is not something done to another for another's sake. It is not a favour you bestow upon the offending party. It is, in fact, a profoundly selfish thing to do. Surprised at my use of the word selfish to describe forgiveness? Good. It should be if you misunderstand the concept of forgiveness altogether. We also misunderstand selfishness as something bad and shameful, which it can be if it is over-indulged in to the detriment of others around us, but never when we choose to put ourselves first in our own lives, when others have been trying to dictate to us how we should live.

However, being too selfish is just as bad for the individual as not being selfish enough. When we are not selfish enough, we tend to fall into self-betrayal patterns. We might have learned as a child that everyone else's needs have to come before our own. This is a typical lesson learned by children raised by a narcissistic parent(s). When we grow older and realize just how terrible our parents were to us, many strong emotions arise seemingly out of nowhere at the injustice of how we were raised. There is a deep sense of betrayal stemming from the notion of how badly our primary love figures have failed us, often accompanied by shame for thinking badly of them.

We have to understand that our parents, too, have their own trauma, and the older generations have made seeking help taboo, where psychologists were demonized or thought of as shameful for a person to get to the point where they require the assistance of a professional. In my own journey, it has come to a point where I have had to educate my parents myself, with varying degrees of success depending directly on how open to listening they were, but mostly on what they chose to do with the information given to them. This is a reminder that we cannot help those who do not wish any help, regardless of how desperately they actually need it. Deeply wounded people often do not have the courage or will to look at themselves objectively, especially when it paints them in a bad light.

Which would make healing parental wounds complicated if not for the exercise of forgiveness. Otherwise, how could we heal a relationship with someone who is most definitely not repentant and much less willing to become aware of all the hurt they have caused? Or better yet, who rejects the fault and returns it on us instead? Who would have been a clueless child at the time? As long as we do not heal the relationships that have hurt us, we will be carrying that energy for the rest of our lives. Healing a relationship, however, does not mean we are willing to keep the other person in our lives; we only wish to release the energetic burden tying us together.

There are some hurts that go too deep to allow forgiveness to re-admit a person into our lives, especially when they are not willing to accept their true role in our life: that of an abuser. And this is okay! We never have to allow anyone into our lives, regardless of their relation to us. The good news is that we can heal a relationship energetically without ever being in contact with a person again. *That* is the power of forgiveness. The idea that forgiveness can only occur in a face-to-face encounter is blatantly wrong. Forgiveness is an inside job. It is not something the other party owes us. Therefore, wanting a formal apology from them is likely never going to happen, nor will it be satisfactory *if* ever received. We have to remove the idea that physical conditions have to be met for true forgiveness. Remember that we choose to heal for our own sake.

Narcissistic people do not recognize this trait within themselves because they suffer from major main-character-syndrome. Nobody but them matters, and the most far gone of them will simply not comprehend that other people have actual lives of their own, with feelings, emotions, desires, wants, and needs all their own. If we make them feel uncomfortable or challenge their preconceived notions of being a gift from God to the world, they will likely just get angry and blame us for XYZ. We cannot help people who do not want to acknowledge they have a problem, and it is always doomed to fail when we try. The Truth is that some of us, regardless of being aware of the true extent of the abuse we experienced and how broken it truly left us, have a big heart and just want to see them heal and be happy. But we have to give this love and healing to ourselves first before we can hope that our energy might engage them in evolving through no conscious actions of our own towards them.

I speak here of narcissists and abusive upbringings because most healers and empaths incarnating at this time to help the world in its energetic shift will have had difficult upbringings to learn important lessons of personal growth. Most of us will have had a difficult childhood with abusive parents or parental figures in some way, shape, or form, or have had traumatic experiences very early on. Because this is a world of contrast, a difficult childhood would have been the fastest path to triggering personal growth and getting us into the energy of self-healing so we can engage in the true mission of healing the world at large, as this is the true reason our Souls agreed to come to Earth at this time. Not everyone carries this mission, and it can be seen in the ease of living they embody. Not everyone can do the intense shadow work, healing, and purging that a lightworker does.

We have to learn to make peace with this fact, as our Souls have orchestrated this lifetime perfectly for our upcoming success. It is, however, perfectly natural to have strong feelings of resentment and anger surfacing in the face of this perceived injustice, and that is why we must heal these and all of our relationships, for our own well-being. Forgiveness is about bringing peace to our internal world, as within, so without.

Bringing peace within will shift the energy of the connection, and surprising results may happen from that internal shift into the external reality. However, healing for the sake of hopefully triggering another into healing should never be the reason to engage in self-healing.

Forgiveness is selfish in the sense that we are always only ever healing truly when we are doing it for our own sake. Forgiveness is selfish in the sense that it is a completely personal process that ultimately has nothing to do with an external person, even though that person *seems* to be the reason for our pain. The Truth is that other people are never responsible for our experiences; our own energy and free will always are. Our vibration attracts experiences to help us heal and grow, while our free will dictates the level of ease through which we wish to experience those. Of course, this is seldom pleasant to hear when we are stuck in harsh energies and environments. Still, it should motivate the understanding that there is always a way to free ourselves from a reality we do not actively enjoy and no longer wish to partake in.

As Souls, we have chosen the family and wounding we wanted to be born into. We then get triggered to activate the healing process of these specific wounds.

Our external relationships show us what wounding we are carrying. By relationships here, I am referring to anyone who has triggered you in any way, as small as a stranger's comment, to a full-blown couple relationship, or a parental figure. Generally, if we have wounds with a parental figure in this lifetime, it represents a wound with its cosmic equivalent. This means that if your relationship with your own mother is dreadful or non-existent, then it reflects in your relationship with Mother Earth. The same can be said of a father figure with your relationship to the Universe. This applies to the energies parental figures carry more than their actual gender.

This is why it is so important to understand that we are never forgiving someone for their sake and healing because it simply is not about them. Forgiveness is a personal healing process of detachment, of creating peace within and finding our way back to the Universal energy of pure unconditional love. Forgiveness is selfish in the sense that we are choosing to actively release the hold we have given someone over us by taking back our personal power, which we have disowned when we have chosen to allow ourselves to feel hurt and victimized by another. When we hold a grudge and are unforgiving towards another, we are only ever hurting ourselves because we are actively betraying our very nature of pure, unconditional love. Re-read these last two sentences as many times as needed for the Truth of these messages to really sink in and be understood, as they are of the utmost importance in understanding the very purpose of healing.

This may sound counterintuitive, but remember that any emotion we allow to overpower us shows us where we are betraying ourselves. We can observe the truth of this by noticing how what we already know does not apply to us and will not affect us in the slightest. Being called a coward when we know we are brave and show up as such will likely cause us to laugh at the insult because we know the Truth that we are not, in fact, a coward. We are never deeply affected by what we know does not apply to us. When we doubt our worth despite being aware of being worthy, to begin with, it means we have wounds around self-confidence, nothing more. Therefore, the question to start asking ourselves is: Why am I allowing myself to be affected by this? What is triggered within me? What wound is being poked into that requires my attention?

More than anything else, forgiveness is self-liberation in action. It is the act of loving ourselves so deeply that we choose to remove the unnecessary weight keeping us down, regardless of whether that weight is perceived consciously or not. For example, if we choose to ignore someone or block them on social media, we are actively choosing to disown the part of ourselves associated with this person. We deny a part of the truth of who we are, an entire aspect or wound of the Self. Ignoring or blocking someone is not the "power move" people think it is; it is simply more self-betrayal, and it shows that these people still hold power over us. Instead of addressing the issue and healing the underlying wound, it is the equivalent of burying one's head in the sand and pretending the sun does not exist because one cannot see it. It serves no purpose other than self-avoidance. There is a big difference between distancing ourselves from people who have hurt us and blocking them out of our awareness. One is enforcing boundaries; the other is running away from our own pain.

Holding onto grudges or keeping score with people is simply more of the same principle as above. Whatever we hold against other people is, in fact, something we hold against ourselves, either the exact same thing or its mirror opposite. Forgiveness comes in as a clearing, cleansing, energetic tool, and we will never allow this tool to operate within us if we hold onto the idea of wanting to be a victim. Being unforgiving *is* us holding onto wanting to be a victim. These may be highly triggering words for people who are actively holding onto a victim mentality but do not want to admit it to themselves. If these words trigger you, pop out your Journal and write about why. Investigate yourself truthfully about why you are holding on to unforgiveness, what it truthfully brings you, and how it truly is still affecting your life. As long as this resistance to healing is present, it affects your life, regardless of your awareness of its effects.

Victim mentality can be a difficult wound to heal because it requires massive amounts of humility to admit to ourselves that we are taking things personally for no good reason. Note here that every single reason that can be listed to justify holding on to unforgiveness is a bullshit reason. As harsh as this may sound, whenever we choose to take things personally, we are always stepping into massive drama queen energy every single time. Why? Because you will only ever feel victimized if you <u>choose</u> to feel victimized. Some circumstances are harder to overcome than others, *but they can be overcome* through our choices and the power of will.

Otherwise, we are admitting that we have no control over our own emotions, and this should become an obvious starting point on our healing journey. Being victimized is only ever a game we choose to partake in by creating a false narrative in our minds. It is not always easy to admit this to ourselves, but it has to be done for healing to have a chance to occur. This is a great time to recall that the greatest gift we can ever give ourselves is to get over ourselves in order to deal with our pain instead of letting it run rampant in our lives.

As long as we are holding onto a victim mentality, forgiveness is impossible. This chapter may need to be revisited more profoundly at a later date when deeper healing shifts have occurred. Still, it is good to be aware of its contents first, as the energy of my writing and these words will start to work through your psyche, probably unconsciously. It is crucial to understand that as Souls, we choose our life experiences in order to trigger healing on a Soul level, that everything ultimately always happens for our highest good, but that it always comes down to our free will to acknowledge this as such or not. Free will allows us to choose between freeing ourselves through healing or remaining a victim of "circumstance." To be clear, this *never* excuses hurtful behaviour others choose to engage in towards us, but it does explain it, and it is up to us to do what we want with that information. It is always about how *we* choose to move forward in our lives.

As someone who has been raped and otherwise abused my entire life, I fully understand how difficult accepting these words can be. But let me tell you of the liberation their truth brings about. Understanding on a core level that these events are never our fault and have been expressly designed to trigger our healing is equivalent to total liberation in the mind. We have done nothing wrong and are inherently deserving of unconditional love. It is important to understand that when that person's Soul made a contract with your own Soul for that event to happen, it was done with the utmost unconditional love to propel your healing journey forward.

The Ego will never be able to reconcile the Truth of this because it will only ever focus on the suffering incurred and its perceived injustice. Life does not happen *to* us; it happens *for* us. Again, this never makes the abuse acceptable, but it does explain their purpose for being in our lives in the first place. This shift in perspective on forgiveness and the energy of unconditional love does not happen overnight. There may be people and situations you simply cannot bring yourself to free yourself from at this time, and that is okay. It remains our choice to make. Healing is always optional and often depends on our level of courage. Not everyone is brave enough to face themselves and their Truths, which is okay.

It is important to understand and remember here that we are the only people who can free ourselves from the hold others have on us, that we willingly give to them, though not always consciously. Ultimately, complete Soul healing is the goal for all of us. We must choose between total healing and unforgiveness, as they cannot co-exist by their very nature. By holding on to unforgiveness and refusing to deal with the emotions that are brought up by our specific circumstances, we are only ever hurting ourselves and limiting our personal progress. We are giving in to Ego tantrums as we resort to blaming others. Blame serves no purpose and is always just an Ego trap to deflect personal responsibility and accountability. In Truth, who is "responsible" is always irrelevant because it never contributes to any aspect of healing.

Forgiveness is a process that comes in waves or layers, just like healing. The deeper the hurt, the more waves and layers can be anticipated before true peace and detachment are found. We must also fully clear out one layer at a time to access the deeper layers that follow. Obviously, the longer we have held onto pain, the longer the forgiveness process can take, especially when we are talking about years and years of holding onto unforgiveness to the point where it has become part of our identity. We identify with this wounding, which becomes part of our personality, with the danger of our exploding or imploding always present if triggered. The process of forgiveness requires patience and loads of self-love. We need to be kind to ourselves as we unravel this wound with the intent to heal from it. Ultimately, forgiveness becomes one of the greatest gifts we can possibly give to ourselves when we have the courage to release our pain.

Another aspect of forgiveness that can be highly triggering is the complete change it can bring about in our lives. When we have been accustomed to a certain invisible weight weighing on our shoulders, it becomes our normal. Removing that weight is highly unbalancing as the center of our world shifts completely. We can be forced to face challenging questions of identity, such as: How will releasing this pain change me as a person? How will it change or otherwise affect my life, my reality as I know it? How will it transform me, and what will that transformation communicate to others about who I am now? It is possible that we have grown so accustomed to carrying this extra load that facing the perspective of it being entirely eliminated from our reality can be scary. We may be reluctant to let go of what we have always known, even if it is for our highest good, simply because we have grown accustomed to its presence. Our prison walls always feel safe because they are known to us, familiar in their enclosing.

When we are kept (by our own choice or not) in an enclosed space for a long time, we grow used to the limitations of our world and the comfort we have to find there. Suddenly, being exposed to complete freedom can be a terrifying experience, highly disorienting, as we realize that there truly are no walls for the first time in our lives. Knowing that life and opportunities are limitless can be highly intimidating. Living for ourselves for the first time in our lives is an entire adventure all its own. We have to relearn how to live from a personal perspective, from our own genuine wants and needs. The same can be expected from letting go of the pain we have held onto tightly for any amount of time. We have to relearn how to live without lugging that exhausting, energetic weight around.

Since some cases of forgiveness will be harder to bring ourselves to release than others, we should always start with the smaller perceived slights and hurts to build up our practice and understanding of how forgiveness works. From now on, it is important to stop taking things personally and to start viewing situations from a higher perspective. Remember that our unhealed Ego is always in the way of our healing. Start a section in your Journal specifically to catalogue what you believe you will have forgiven (in yourself and from others), and what possible underlying wound is being healed by the process of forgiveness. As stated previously, this process happens in waves and layers; therefore, there will most likely be repeated sessions of forgiveness for one person or one perceived hurt.

Onto the subject at hand: how do we forgive? Obviously, mere words do not do the trick. Forgiveness is an emotional process. Therefore, it occurs in the heart chakra. As we have learned in the previous chapter, all emotions have to be processed there before being transmuted and liberated through the lower chakras. The process itself can be personalized to our preferences, but the important aspect of it is how genuine we are about it. It has to be done within yourself, *for* yourself, and meaningfully. A cold, untrue exercise of forgiveness might as well not have been done in the first place, whereas a heartfelt forgiveness will yield results. We cannot lie our way out of this process.

Working with the elements in cleansing rituals will only help liberate stuck energy, but will not bring about true forgiveness, as it is an internal process. Some people will say that all we need to do is soak in a tub and ask the water to take away all perceived hurts or to write down what we would say to the person who hurt us and then burn the letter, but these do not go deep enough to the core of the wound to heal anything. Temporary relief may be experienced, but true liberation will not be attained in these ways. We can refer to the AAUR technique here to understand why.

As with our previous self-awareness practice from the first part of the book, we have to revisit all of the situations we are holding in our vibration through unforgiveness, such as grudges and resentment. We have to consciously go through the event and respect everything that comes up as a result. We have to allow ourselves to process all that has happened in the situation, all the emotions that result from it, and actively choose to forgive and release. We have to identify exactly what it is we are forgiving in order to be liberated from it.

In the first revisiting of a situation, a specific theme or person may be the first layer of forgiveness needing to be worked on, whereas when we revisit the same situation another time, forgiveness may be asked of another theme or person present in the same setting. We have to revisit the circumstances or memories that keep coming up for us to process as many times as they are coming back, because when we have fully, completely forgiven all aspects, there will be no need for them to keep coming back to our awareness. When we are completely freed from the person or situation, we have achieved total forgiveness.

Some hurts will take less than a day to heal from. Others will appear in multiple layers over time. The best thing to do is to focus on what is present when it appears, not to push it away for another time, as we are simply delaying healing. This being said, always respect your own levels of capability, meaning that there is no shame in recognizing that healing and forgiveness may be asking more than we are currently capable of giving at the moment. The key is not to mistake incapability with simply not wanting to. These memories can be painful to sit with, and that is okay. Past circumstances cannot hurt you again. Process your pain, allow it to tell you what it needs to tell you, then let it go. We can use the AAUR technique in our forgiveness practice.

Whatever the case may be, always be proud of your progress in forgiveness—no matter how small a step you think you have achieved—as it is the greatest tool for healing we can learn to use. Progress is progress, and is always meant to be celebrated and is worthy of recognition. As with every ongoing technique and aspect of healing, we are learning to incorporate into our daily lives, consistency is key. That being said, take all the breaks you need to replenish yourself, as releasing big energies is exhausting physically, emotionally, and mentally. Do what you need to do to ensure you are ready and *willing* to undertake more self-work. If that means taking weeks off from reading this book, then do that. Respect yourself and respect your intuition. Just remember not to stay away from your healing out of fear or Ego.

As the focus of this book is self-healing, it is highly likely that the more you dive into these pages and learn how to deal with yourself and triggers, the more outside circumstances will start to trigger your healing for you. This is part of our Soul contracts together. I give you the tools you need to understand your reality and process things in a way to heal deeply. You will be presented with opportunities to apply your newly learned skills. This is normal and part of the process. Creating these habits will make dealing with the next set of lessons that much easier. Keep in mind that the Universe will *never* give you more than you can handle, and rest easy in that comforting knowledge, as difficult as the present moment may be to deal with. Triggers for healing happen when they need to happen. It is up to us to choose to heal or repeat the cycle.

This chapter imparts two major forgiveness tools. As we have come to understand so far in this book, healing starts from within. This means that forgiveness also starts from within. Just as healing ourselves heals our immediate surroundings, forgiving ourselves changes our outside reality as well. The first tool is, therefore, self-forgiveness, and I teach it with a mirror.

Sit with yourself in complete silence, with no distractions, and look at yourself in the eyes through your reflection. Do not break eye contact for any reason. See yourself fully, honestly, and open your heart to this experience. This will likely turn into a very emotional and otherwise triggering experience when done deliberately, wholeheartedly, and openly. If you get nothing from it, you are not open enough. You are not really looking. You are likely avoiding seeing the Truth. This is a very intimate exercise and will also indicate the level of comfort you have with yourself. This is also a great exercise for practicing self-love and acceptance.

While looking at yourself in the mirror, identify all the places where you have a problem with yourself and write them down in your Journal. This may come up as appearance issues, as strong emotions of disgust or sadness, as shame, etc. The idea is to write down every single thought and emotion that comes from simply looking at yourself. You can start by being further away from the mirror for a more global look and writing down what comes up from a distance, then moving closer to the mirror and stopping at a distance that brings up more things until you end up nearly touching the mirror with your nose and staring solely into your own eyes to see what is reflected to you from their depths. The eyes are a direct link to our Soul.

Once that is done, look at what you have written and identify all the places where you are hurtful and/or harsh towards yourself, where you reject some parts of yourself. Analyze and seek to understand what the underlying wounds are and actively focus on forgiving yourself from the bottom of your heart for being so cruel towards yourself and your perceived shortcomings. Further, identify how you are being your own worst bully and forgive yourself thoroughly for what you have been throwing against yourself constantly, often subconsciously. Consciously choose to eliminate these habits by choosing to be kinder to yourself from this moment forward and choosing to forgive your own harshness and heartlessness in favour of consciously choosing to love yourself instead.

Doing just this is going to clear much of your energy field. Self-forgiveness can take many forms and is ultimately essential for complete healing. Make sure to identify exactly what you need to forgive yourself for and speak those words of forgiveness out loud on repeat until you wholeheartedly mean what you are saying. A shallow forgiveness changes and heals nothing. Your heart space needs to be open, and your intentions need to be genuine for a real shift to occur.

The other technique for forgiveness we will be looking at is based on Ho'oponopono. If you are already familiar with Ho'oponopono and prefer using it, that is entirely up to you. For this technique to work, we need to have a complete understanding and acceptance of Oneness, that we are all one and the same, linked by the Universe in unconditional love.

This is why holding resentment or grudges towards others only ever hurts us. By begrudging and resenting another, we are only ever begrudging and resenting ourselves energetically. Everything we think and feel about another is thought and felt about ourselves vibrationally. There is no distinction between the two, as *there is no separation on a cosmic scale*, only ever in Ego consciousness.

Before we dive into the process itself, it is important to understand that this work is done entirely from within. We have to feel every moment strongly, mean every word spoken, and fully embrace the energy of Oneness. Starting will likely feel awkward and as though we are just talking to ourselves; it is easy to lose its meaning when we stay stuck in our heads and in self-judgment, which is why we need the mind to go away first. As for everything else in this book, practice will make everything easier and more comprehensible as you uncover your deep, innate connection with the Universe.

The first step to this technique is conscious deep breathing. We need to fully sink into our bodies and connect with the energy of the Universe. There is no better way to do this than with deep, conscious breathing. While sitting or lying down comfortably, engage in a process of breathing in through the nose to the very depths of your stomach. Make sure your back is straight, and nothing gets in the way of the air flowing down to the deepest parts of your being, and never constrict, tense up, or otherwise pull in your stomach to make it small; always let it expand as far out as it will go. Never restrict your stomach from expanding with your lungs, and expand as much as possible with each next breath.

Exhaling is to be done through the mouth in a powerful burst, making sure we empty our lungs entirely. Always remember: in through the nose, out through the mouth. We do this until we feel internally an energy of stillness and connection taking root within our being. After a few deep breaths, start incorporating pauses between inhaling and exhaling, then between exhaling and inhaling. This does not mean cutting off respiration and "holding" the breath. It simply means taking a moment and feeling when it feels right to either inhale or exhale. Deep breathing like this is also an excellent relaxing method. Keep in mind that we are going to be doing deep breathing throughout the whole exercise, as it will help us stay connected and grounded.

The next steps require us to enter conscious states of emotional being, which we will identify later on, while also seeking the connection in our own SEEC to that of another. We journey energetically into our SEEC, located just below the Heart chakra in the middle of the breasts, and actively seek out the energy of the party we wish to heal with through this infinite connection to All. Once we feel that connection being established energetically, we can start the forgiveness process. It is imperative to feel connected with the energy of the other person or party; otherwise, the work we do afterwards goes nowhere and will not reach its intended recipient, which obviously means that no results will come forward. If the energy of forgiveness does not seem to work, then it is always because it was not done properly.

In addition to being connected with the offending party, we also have to deeply connect with the energy of our own wounding, which is asking to be addressed. The order in which we choose to connect with both of these energies is irrelevant. Some people will find it easier to connect with the wounding and then with the offending party, while others will find it easier to connect with the offending party and then with the wounding. The important thing here is to connect to both. The process becomes easier when we recognize that these separate parties are already connected to each other and that we are just following that thread to consciously bridge both in our own energetic being.

After that connection is established and fully felt, we can start the true process of forgiveness. We will use the sentences best known from Ho'oponopono, which are: I'm sorry, please forgive me, I love you, and thank you. They always have to be repeated in this order. More than just speaking the words, we will dip into the energies they represent *before* speaking them out loud. If our words are not genuine and do not come from a place of personal power, then no healing can occur. The words become genuine when we feel the energy they want us to access and speak honestly from being in that energy.

Let's start with the first sentence: I'm sorry. As with any apology, there is no point in apologizing if the words are hollow and hold no Truth or sincerity. I will repeat here that assigning blame to another for a perceived wound is useless, as we ultimately are all one and the same. This apology has to come from the energy of genuine repentance. If you are blocking here because you believe it to be ridiculous to ask the person who has hurt you for forgiveness, you need to deepen your understanding of Oneness. We have to see the Soul truth that this hurt was a contract made between both Souls in favour of our personal growth and development *on a Soul level*. The Ego hates this fact because it likes feeling victimized and powerless under external circumstances.

You, as a Soul before incarnating, have asked this other Soul to do this to you by Soul contract, and the only reason they have accepted is because their Soul knew this was essential for the experiences your Soul requires you to have in this lifetime for its evolution. They have only agreed to do so out of pure unconditional love. This means that to frame the event in Truth, we have to see the Soul perspective and understand that we are asking *their Soul* for forgiveness, for asking them to do this to us in the first place, as we are all beings of unconditional love. It hurt them on a Soul level to have to hurt you on the physical plane, even when this physical person shows no remorse.

This process cannot happen when we are stuck in Ego. Until we learn to identify and let go of our Ego, forgiveness will not happen. It is imperative to understand that we are all connected as One in the energy of unconditional love and that life never happens to us but for us. Believing otherwise is holding onto a victim mentality. This is why I strongly believe that getting over ourselves is the greatest gift we can ever grant ourselves, as we become free to experience life on a whole other level. We must understand that forgiveness is a process done by the Soul for the Soul.

Once we are fully in the energy of repentance, we can also say the "please forgive me" sentence. In my experience, when I have done this very process, these first two sentences may prompt us to specifically enunciate *why* we are seeking forgiveness. This means that either while saying "I'm sorry" or "Please forgive me," I have heard intuitively to speak in full sentences of *what* I am sorry for and also *what* I wish to be forgiven of. Whenever these come to mind while you are doing this process, always speak them. Spend all the necessary time you need on this energy, verbalizing all that you wish to come out. Remember that you always have to mean what you say.

The next sentence is "I love you." This is evidently where we are in the process of reconnecting with this person on the Universal level of unconditional love. It goes without saying that the energy needed to be embodied here is unconditional love. The last sentence is "thank you," which is again self-explanatory. "Thank you" requires us to be in the energy of gratefulness, and we are thanking the Soul for having had the courage and love to give us what we needed, even if it was unpleasant in the physical realm for all Souls involved. Again, if you feel longer sentences coming up for either of these ones, always respect them and add them as they come. Some connections require more words than others, and that is alright. What is true for one connection may not be true for another.

The entire process is going to take as long as is needed, meaning that we may be repeating all of these sentences 15 times each with their accompanying longer sentences, as we may also only need to repeat them 4-5 times to get to the end result. It will always depend on the depth of the connection and the importance of healing it. Be certain that your Heart has been fully freed of this energy before ending the forgiveness session. Otherwise, you may need to do it over and over again for the same encounter. If this happens, do not worry. Sometimes, we need to go through more experiences in life before we can fully uncover all that needs forgiveness within one connection. The goal is to end the session feeling liberated from the weight of that pain.

As forgiveness is a potent healing tool when done right, never stop using this technique whenever you feel the need to, and especially when you feel you do not want to. This is a mutual healing process, whether you like it or not. You cannot heal yourself if you do not accept that you are linked to others and, therefore, will heal them by default. This being said, just because we choose healing for ourselves on a physical level through Soul healing, it does not mean that the offending party will show any kind of physical changes and become a better person from receiving your forgiveness. They may or may not; it depends on the soul contract between you.

As Souls, forgiveness is of the utmost beauty and represents Oneness in its purest form. As humans, we have to learn to understand and accept this as the Truth it is. We have to come into an energy where we are able to take absolutely nothing personally, to be able to say that we are fully healed and balanced while also having complete acceptance of life and our experiences as they happen. We have to be comfortable with controlling nothing yet influencing everything. Just because we can influence things through our free will does not mean we can try to control outcomes, as being controlling simply shows us our wounding around feeling safe in the world.

As a last note for this process of forgiveness, it is always easier when we work with the energies of the Earth and the Universe by connecting with them prior to starting the process. I personally choose to visualize a ray of white, purifying light coming up from the core of Mother Earth into the soles of my feet and going through my chakras one at a time until it bursts through my Crown chakra and up into the Universe, tethering me to both. Then I visualize a beautiful blue ray of light coming down from the Universe into my Crown chakra, down through the chakra system, and out through the soles of my feet to join the core of Mother Earth, once again anchoring me to both. I ask that these energies work through me as a cleansing, purifying force that disintegrates all that no longer serves me, removes all negativity from my vibration, and helps me release all that was once stuck. Once those connections are done and the intentions of healing, clearing, and releasing are spoken aloud, I start the process of forgiveness.

PART III

BEING ONE WITH THE EARTH

Welcome to the third part of this book, the halfway point of the treasured learning and healing journey we are doing together. So far, we have uncovered fears and wounds to be worked on and healed. We have opened ourselves up to the possibility of being wrong, to learn from our "mistakes," and to grow into who we really are. We have started to love and value who we are in the present moment so that we may become who we are in Truth—at a Soul level—in order to embody this Truth in everyday life.

We also trust our Soul and our intuition to guide us towards the life of true, unfiltered bliss we are meant to be living: our Soul path. We are also learning how to properly identify our Ego, accept our current perceived flaws and limitations, and transform them so we can become hale and whole within. We are becoming better people by embodying our genuine energy. We are discovering our connection with the Universe and the Truth of Oneness. We are walking the path of balance and Ascension by casting an honest, impartial, and unconditionally loving gaze upon the truth of our current life experiences and circumstances.

By holding ourselves accountable and understanding that we constantly shape our reality by the frequency of our vibration, we are beginning to understand what our personal power is and how strong we can be when stepping out of a victim mentality. We are starting to see beyond the illusions of life and know that living is about so much more than what we have been conditioned to believe. We are awakening to the Truth of Life.

Now that we consciously understand there is a whole Universe behind us—supporting, loving, and rooting for us—it is time to recognize that the planet known as Earth is its own entity and loves and supports us in exactly the same way. We are children of earth and sky, who are made of water and who embody the flame of passion or creativity. It can only ever be through living our passions that we can truly feel alive. Just like a tree, we need to grow our roots deeply to be able to expand upwards and reach our full expanded potential. Mother Earth is our most solid foundation. Recognizing this and communing with her is where we start the process of our exponential growth.

Once we start on our spiritual journey, it can be very easy to lose ourselves in energy work and get a kick out of our newfound abilities and personal power. Take time to enjoy these new developments and how they reflect in your life. Find gratitude for your growth, then come back to working on yourself. It is always important to celebrate our achievements and our role in achieving them. However, when it comes to manifestation, if we are not solidly grounded in reality, the potential energy that is manifestation cannot come through to us on a physical level, despite our level of growth.

Energy is static, ever-present. The Law of Conservation of Mass states that nothing is lost, nothing is created, and everything is transformed. This is what energy work is all about. That is precisely what manifestation is. Energy cannot come forth in altered shape unless it has a channel. Energy takes the shape of the channel. Lightning is a great example of this. Electricity currents activated by a light switch are a prime example of how manifestation works. If you do not flip the switch to active, the energy cannot come in. If we are not grounded, we are not turning on the switch of allowing manifestations in.

It is up to you to consciously turn this switch on in your current life 3D reality to allow the manifestations you dearly want to appear. You direct this current yourself by allowing. If you block it by trying to control the outcome, then the energy has nowhere to go, and your manifestations cannot reach you in physical reality. Manifestation comes with a balance of energetic and physical actions and intentions, which start with grounding. The beautiful thing to keep in mind is that Mother Earth provides us with everything we could possibly need to succeed. It becomes simply a matter of attuning to this Truth and letting it do its work. Let's start uncovering how!

Chapter 9
Growing Your Roots

---•---

Everything we have learned so far has been about self-actualisation, detachment, spiritual understanding, and personal development. It has focused strongly on upper-body energy, such as establishing a preliminary connection with the Universe while also using our brains to step back and analyze ourselves truthfully, which is perfect. Now that we have started recognizing and working with our potential, we will need a solid foundation to rely on, rest upon, and build from. The work you have been doing on your own throughout reading this book and Journaling is also part of the strength of this foundation. You are the only one who can build it. It is up to you to invest in yourself and hold yourself accountable in your own life.

At this point in the healing process, we want to manifest the life and reality that best serve us. We will start feeling called to align with our Soul purpose.

Healing our wounds and fears contributes to removing all the potential obstacles in our way. Therefore, it is exceedingly important that we keep working on ourselves throughout our lifetime as the cycles of life continue to trigger what needs to be removed from our energy field: our vibration. Keep revisiting all that comes up in your awareness and work with your Journal accordingly, adding and expanding on the deeper levels of the wounds and fears you may have already identified. Each layer you clear out in any given wound or fear will unveil fresh eyes and understanding to be used on the others, which is exactly why you may want to revisit this book and what you have Journaled about over and over.

Remember that the Ego believes it knows all of the answers all the time, while the Soul is open to being wrong and discovering new perspectives and information. To shift into Soul living, or 5D existing, we must be living in a physical reality that reflects the Soul entirely and which has the highest vibrational state of being: that of pure unconditional love for all. The Soul cannot be embodied in any other vibrational state of being, as they are simply not a right fit to the energy of the Universe itself. This is exactly how we can come to manifest our Heaven on Earth: by living in a

Soul-sustaining vibration. You can refer to the Quick Reference Guide found at the beginning of the book to refresh your understanding of all things energetic, as we are about to dive deep into these subjects.

Since the focus of this journey is internal, it can only be gauged by comparing who we were previously to who we are now. That being said, what is truly being evaluated is the level of happiness and contentment gained. Progress can only really be measured by how much happier, freer, and lighter we feel in our lives now than we were before. The most essential ingredient in building our solid foundation of life is the happiness or joy of living.

As always, using our Journal, let's investigate some important questions to ask ourselves. Just how happy are you feeling in your current life situation? Are you simply going through the motions of life, feeling unfulfilled, depressed, or stuck because what else could you possibly be doing? Does your current employment motivate and spark joy in you? Does it excite you, or are you just chasing after money? Is your current relationship satisfying, loving, supportive, and uplifting? If not, then why are you with this person if all they seem to bring to the table is anguish, struggles, fights, and doubts? Or are you bringing these things in and not recognizing this about yourself?

One of our greatest human flaws is staying in familiar situations because we are comfortable with what we already know. This is done regardless of us knowing that we ought not to, especially when what we know and are familiar with, and therefore comfortable with, is toxic and hurtful. Even when we know better, we still seek out these environments because we fear change and that we could fall into something worse. By giving in to this fear, we also stop ourselves from accessing something infinitely better. We allow our fears to come first and our well-being second because we subconsciously believe that having something is better than having nothing at all, but the reverse is actually the truth. It is always better to have nothing than to have something that only ever limits and hurts us.

The vibrational Truth is that when we create a void in our reality by removing an element from our lives, the Universe always actively seeks to fill up that empty space with what best serves us at the present moment. What does this mean? It means that as long as we are holding on to things that do not serve us or actively hurt us, we are effectively blocking all the good things we want from coming in, simply because the space they need is already occupied. By holding on to the old out of fear of the unknown, we are keeping ourselves from experiencing our highest good. We need to make sure that we have access to healthy, fertile soil if we intend to grow our roots out to create a very solid and strong foundation. If we want better things to come in, we have to get rid of the old and rotten.

The best way to start creating the right environment for personal growth is to recognize what is holding us back and what is actively discouraging us from living our truth, from living authentically. As an example, whenever I had the courage to start writing as a possible source of income—or to explore other ways of earning that did not involve a "normal," physical 9–5 job—and I had made some progress, was on a roll, and felt proud of what I was doing, I would want to share that pride with my father and possibly receive encouragement. Every single time, without fail, I was let down. Instead of encouraging me and being proud of me for following my own path, he would tell me to stop what I was doing, that it was useless and pointless and a waste of time, that I ought to get my head on straight and be realistic about life and how it is supposed to be lived. Whenever I would say that some people make a great living out of these things, he would always tell me they were the exception and that I could never make it that way.

He would always shatter my confidence, and sometimes I felt that he enjoyed watching as he crushed me because of the surge of power he felt it gave him over me. I've seen that light in his eyes more than once, every single time he mocked or ridiculed my dreams and ambitions. But he was my father, and I loved him. I thought he wanted the best for me, so even though I was breaking my own heart in the process, I listened and obeyed. I let him break my spirit over and over because I did not know there was an alternative. I never thought to stand up against him because I had never learned this was an option. So, when I dropped out of University and started writing this book, you best believe it was never even a thought of mine to share that with him. Because I knew he would just discourage, judge, and criticize me all over again; same old, same old. He had proven to me that he did not deserve my trust. He had shown me this my entire life, but I had finally started choosing myself and putting myself first in my own life.

I was stuck in the belief that parents are supposed to inherently love their children and want the best for them, that they would encourage, uplift, and help them achieve their goals and objectives. I had to realize that this was never the case for my father: he preferred believing he was right about my never being able to succeed in what I wanted to do by constantly clipping my wings and slamming doors in my face. He preferred actively trying to prove he was right in discouraging me instead of ever helping me. My lack of success was the proof he needed. Therefore, he always ensured that it would be my reality. My father always needs to feel superior, that he is always right, and that he never does anything wrong. That I would dare to follow my ambitions instead of what he wanted for me was just an insult to his pride. That I was not following the path everyone else was going down and was choosing to be true to myself was just a mockery of his image. I became the "failure" in his eyes, and he has always treated me as less than.

I do not always believe my father is a bad person, but I do know he has tremendous wounding that he refuses to acknowledge and work on. This wounding bleeds through in all of his relationships, yet he chooses to remain blind to it. That is his choice to make for himself, but it does mean that I am no longer willing to compromise myself to satisfy his Ego. Appearance is all that matters to him. He loves his money more than he has ever loved any person in his life. He has always shown me that I would never be his life's priority, only a nuisance. I am now at a point in my life where I have recognized all of this and accepted it for what it was: that it is simply not about me but about his wounding. We cannot help people who refuse to acknowledge that they need help. Those who prefer pretending everything is fine simply cannot face their Truth, which is their choice. All we can do is let them go and choose ourselves instead.

Cutting off loved ones is never easy. But we have to be strong enough *to respect ourselves enough* to stop letting people who claim to love us abuse us. We have to put ourselves first in our lives, always, because we cannot help others if we are not taking care of ourselves first. We cannot help others if we do not intimately know ourselves first, which is why we have been doing the type of work contained in Part 1. We have to recognize that we need to let go of everything and everyone that is holding us back, that we are holding ourselves back. Ultimately, it is always a choice we make to give our power away to others, even unconsciously, but it also means that it is always a choice we can make to take our power back.

All we have to do when we choose to make these changes is to step out of the way for the Universe to provide us with what we need. By choosing to let go of what keeps us small and hidden, by releasing what we *think* we want, what we *think* we need, or what is best for us, we then allow room for the Universe to bring in what we *actually* need. The mind is a wonderful tool, but it often gets in our Soul's way by manipulating us with our fears. Even when we think we know what we want, we have to understand that we do not know what we do not know. Therefore, our brains cannot know what is best for us when it does not have access to all of the information. The Universe does not have that problem, as it *is* all information.

We may be holding onto something we believe is great for us, but is in fact only mediocre, when we could have access to something infinitely better suited to us. We are limited by our experiences and notions of what is and what should be by our own minds. This could refer to a job, a relationship, a friendship, or even a way of life. To think that we know better than the Universe what we need is a ridiculous Ego notion, nothing more. Think of it as comparing Universal infinite knowledge to one person's current life experience, and this person says they are infinitely wiser than the Universe and its infinite knowledge because of their one lifetime of experience; it is absolute hubris and quite laughable.

What is more, many people fear being alone and surrounded by silence because they unconsciously seek to escape their internal world. They fear themselves and what they can uncover within, which is deeply saddening and shows just how wounded and miserable they really are and how alone they really feel. They seek constant distractions from various sources, such as being around other people even when they do not enjoy their company, always having background noise to occupy their minds, escaping into another reality through video games, reading, or other forms of entertainment, extreme consumption of alcohol or drugs to escape, etc. Doing these things because we genuinely enjoy them while remaining in control of ourselves is not the same as using them as a means of escape because we are uncomfortable being by ourselves, with ourselves.

This leads us to the first exercise of this chapter: sitting alone with Self with zero distractions and just listening to (and Journaling about) everything that wants to come up. Entertaining every thought, exploring the depths of our minds, being comfortable within, with everything we are hiding from ourselves in there. Quiet personal contemplation, with absolutely nothing to distract us. This is not meditation, where we clear the mind and simply exist in the present. This is actively getting to know our own minds and hearts and secret desires and thoughts. This is a self-intimacy exercise that uncovers the Truth of who we are and what exists within us that wants to be acknowledged. It is time for you to face yourself from within, to spend time with your thoughts, emotions, and personal desires, to figure out what makes you who you are, what makes you special, and what you are truly here to accomplish. By becoming intimately aware of our inner workings, we start to uncover our Soul purpose.

To do this, all we need is peace and quiet. It can be done by lying down on your bed or couch, sitting in a chair, or whatever is most comfortable and least distracting. There cannot be any distractions, meaning the TV and radio are off, your phone is on silent in a different room, and you are alone or sufficiently isolated that nothing and no one can bother you. Make sure you will not become hungry or thirsty, that you do not need to go to the restroom, and that nothing will pull you out of this moment. Then, just be present with yourself and your inner truth. Connect with the

Universe and listen. Zone out within yourself and look at what has been waiting for your attention.

This may feel overwhelming at first, and that is okay, as you likely do not have a lot of experience doing this. What has accumulated in the dark over time will always be waiting for you to find it and will be eager to come out when given attention. This may also feel scary and daunting as we uncover things we did not even know about ourselves. However, emptying our inner vault this way by acknowledging what we have pushed down and ignored of our own desires will become one of the most satisfying, liberating exercises we will gift ourselves. How long we have been denying our own Truths simply adds to this vault of personal secrets, as our desires never leave us; they have simply been silenced.

Ask yourself: Why are you here on Earth today? What are you here to accomplish? What sets your Soul on fire and has always called to you since you were young? What are your deepest desires? What have you shoved deep down and out of sight because you have believed it was a ridiculous dream or ambition to have? This is where you will want to start a new section in your Journal, with the main focus being self-discovery. Use the AAUR technique from Part 1, and do not allow yourself to retreat. Being uncomfortable is normal and part of the process: do not fear it. The more you allow yourself to get comfortable with your own internal discomfort, the faster your progress will be. Face yourself truthfully with love and compassion. Do not resist or fight what comes up. Accept everything as it is for what it truly is and represents.

Allow yourself to be a silent witness to your inner world. See what you love and like, what does not belong, and what drains you. What is truthfully yours? What were you conditioned to believe? What does it teach you about where you have betrayed your true self? What can you learn about your true desires and ambitions? More importantly, when most of the information has been processed, where do you truthfully want to go with your life? What do you want to be? What is missing? What calls to you that you have chosen to ignore? It is of primordial importance not to limit ourselves to thoughts of "Well, that is never going to happen, so why bother?" Ask yourself, what do you actually know about what is possible? Then, realize that you know nothing in comparison to the Universe and its endless possibilities.

This, again, calls us to get over ourselves and our assumptions. To realize how little we know individually. Find your personal truths and give them the chance they deserve, and give *yourself* the chance you deserve, both of which are inherently deserving by the very fact that they exist. You are worthy of all that you desire as long as it does not impact another's free will. You just have to get out of the way of achieving or receiving these desires. At this point, the best possible thing to do is to find out what your personal truths are and start actively honouring them. My advice is to revisit everything you think is a certainty in your life and figure out if it really is or not.

As humans, we love to believe things that make us feel good, but are not necessarily the truth. Bluntly, this means that we prefer to live a lie rather than to face the truth, which ultimately serves no one and only serves to delay personal progress. It means being stuck in a pile of shit and choosing to stay there because we have decided we were comfortable there instead of admitting to ourselves that we are actually stuck in it. It is not always fun to discover that our current reality is a flaming pile of shit, but we have to admit it to ourselves if we ever want to be able to move on. Just because our current reality is a flaming pile of shit *does not mean that we are*. It just means we have been stuck in the same place for too long and are more than ready for something new and a little less odorant as a lifestyle.

This could mean leaving a relationship we have settled for, moving from a current living space because we are not happy there, setting manageable goals for a new future we will actually enjoy, taking risks, making changes, losing friends, making new ones, trying new things to push our limits and see our true capabilities. Saying yes to ourselves when we have only ever said no before. Whatever comes up as a desire that we have should be acknowledged and honored as such. We owe it to ourselves to give ourselves a real chance, not a pretend one where we expect failure. Whatever you truly expect is always what you will receive because what we put out vibrationally comes back to us. The Universe responds to the beliefs carried in our energy. If we want something but deep down believe we could never have/attain/achieve it, then we never will. We have to shift our mindset of what is possible and what can be achieved. We have to uncover our subconscious beliefs that dictate our vibration and, therefore, what we attract into our lives.

Make a section in your Journal where you list all of the desires you uncover within yourself, regardless of how likely you believe they are achievable. Do not bother with how realistic they may be, meaning that if one of those deep-rooted desires comes up for you as "I wish to ride upon a star," then write that down exactly as the words are presented to you. Comprehension and the likelihood of it actually happening are not important or relevant at this point. Honouring what comes up regardless of perceived impossibility. The goal is to dare to be honest with our dreams. Also, continue/start a section in your Journal on your deep-rooted beliefs, the ones you know of at least. By going back through your Journal and looking through the first sections, you may be able to start uncovering the patterns in your subconscious beliefs when you analyze the driving force behind your fears and limitations. Perhaps repetition from various episodes of Journaling may become apparent at this time.

I recommend doing this stillness and inner listening exercise at least three times a week to start with, if you cannot do it daily. When this process becomes easier and more like a habit, you will be able to tap into your inner world more easily, as the mass of initial clutter will have been sorted through and will have started to diminish from your previous visits. Keep updating your journal when you uncover more truthful desires and when you think you have uncovered a subconscious or conscious belief. Compare if your conscious beliefs actually reflect in your outer world to see if they are the actual beliefs driving your vibration. Do the same exercise with what you believe you have identified as unconscious beliefs. Your outside reality will always show you the truth of things by reflecting it back to you or not. Simply be careful not to be in Ego and look for validation instead of Truth. Use your intuition as a guide.

The next exercise offered in this chapter starts with making a list of every possible thing that makes you genuinely happy. I mean by this that the very thought of doing or being around a certain person or place makes you giddy with joy within. Do not write down what average happiness is. I do mean true, unfiltered, unbridled joy of living. This could be doing an activity like a sport or a craft, being in the presence of a specific animal, or even in a specific location with a certain person, being around a certain colour, a flower, eating a specific meal, or anything else! Then, your task is to incorporate being around, doing, or experiencing one of these things every single day. Add a touch of unfiltered joy every day from now on. Do what feels fun and inspired! Do not turn this into a chore in your mind. Instead, let yourself perceive what would make you happiest to do that day. It comes down to permitting yourself to love life and, by extension, to love yourself. If every day feels like too much effort or too daunting at first, at the very least, try to incorporate this once a week. The goal is to give yourself a moment of bliss as a highlight in your daily monotony.

Now that we have decluttered the mind and given it some love, we are going to do the same in our home environment. Holding onto things that no longer serve us means that they become useless clutter. Clutter is just another word for junk. When we hold on to junk instead of disposing of it properly, not only are we encumbering our living space, but we also happen to clutter up our energy. Having an excess of something is just as bad as not having enough—the more cluttered your living space, the more cluttered your energy. Energy is meant to be free-flowing, just as our living space is meant to be clean and stress-free. Items can also hold vibrations, and our relationship with them can affect us unconsciously.

Remember that your outside world reflects your inside world. If you live in a messy and dirty home, imagine what that says about your energy. You may be carrying years of old junk and trash in your energy because you refuse to remove certain items from your home. Ask yourself what it is you are actually holding onto. This does not have to limit itself to the specific item, but the energy, the memory, or even the feeling it brings up for us. Sometimes, we just need to shake up our energy for all of the old to fall away on its own. By removing all the excess in our lives, it becomes easier to breathe and move around. We get to experience vibrational lightness and freedom. This exercise may be hard to do at first, as it may require emotional processing and release, but it will feel like a breath of fresh air and make our environment feel brand new.

Go through everything that you own at your own pace, and release what is no longer needed or wanted. Make sure to set up a schedule or otherwise hold yourself accountable during the decluttering process and take it one step at a time. Instead of viewing the process as a mountain to climb, give yourself a few boxes or wardrobes or rooms as objectives for the day. Make sure that one task a day is manageable, but keep going until you are done. Throw out everything that is broken and give away everything you do not use anymore that is just gathering dust. Do not hold onto things that are worn out and desperately need to be changed. This shows that you have a subconscious belief about not deserving new, shiny, fully functional items, or in other words, that you do not believe yourself worth investing in on a personal level.

Any item that you do not use regularly or seasonally needs to be cleared out. The more space you have, the better you will feel. Ask yourself why you accept living in a cramped-feeling space to begin with. Do you not believe you deserve breathing room? If not, then why? What does that say about your beliefs? How do you consciously choose to treat yourself? The same can be said for holding onto sentimental items. What are you actually holding on to? Is it healthy? Does it make you feel good, or is it grief that you have not processed, that is kept stuck in your energy? Is it really beneficial for your highest good to keep around? Or is it keeping you stuck in the old energy, stopping anything new from coming in? Is it really, genuinely important to hold on to? Why do you refuse to let it go? Keep your Journal handy, as writing things out as they come up can help achieve a much-needed perspective.

Regardless of how much we use it, anything that brings us joy should stay, but we have to be honest with ourselves on the whys. Holding onto things for the sole sake of holding onto them is pointless. I, for one, love books. I cannot have enough books. Looking at my filled-up libraries makes my heart sing. But if I do not enjoy a particular book or series, I do not keep it. I give it away because the energy of those books does not reflect my own. That is what we are looking for in deciding what to keep, what to give, or throw away.

The same principle applies to clothes. If you have not worn a certain item in a complete year, get rid of it. Throw away anything that looks old, torn, or has holes. Give what is in good condition, and get rid of everything that no longer fits you. Do not hold on to these old energies, even if it is a goal to lose weight. Accept yourself as you are now. If things change in the future, then you will get the chance to get brand-new clothes that reflect your current energy. For example, I was holding on to old pairs of jeans in case I ever got "fat" again. All it did was remind me how unhappy I was when I had excess weight. These jeans held the energy of how I felt about myself in those days, and that was not energy worth holding onto because I was not kind to myself back then. I was better off ridding myself of the "what if" than holding onto it "just in case."

Another question to ask ourselves about clothes: Do we enjoy wearing what we have? Would we prefer to change our style to be more representative of who we are now? As we grow and evolve, our preferences will also grow and evolve. Have you been gifted clothes you loathe and would never wear, but feel like giving them away would insult the person who gave the gift? Give them away anyway. Clothes are a completely personal choice. Do not feel forced to wear clothes you do not want to wear, especially if it is to "save someone's feelings." If someone buys you clothes, they have to make sure they know you very well and know for a fact that you will love the piece in question and that it will fit you perfectly. We do not have to endure misery to ensure another's happiness. Adults can deal with disappointment alone without needing another to placate or validate them.

Keep the clothes that suit you, that you love, that you feel comfortable in, and that carry positive energy for you. Keep what truly represents you, not what you want to be like or what you fear you will become again. Honor yourself through your clothing choices and by having a clean, tidy, and uncluttered home. How you treat your home is a reflection of how you treat yourself. Do not let yourself be an afterthought for your own health and living space.

Clean living also means clean eating. A great way to practice self-love is to become aware of what we put into our bodies to have a healthy and nutritious diet, one that suits us and our lifestyle. This does not mean going on a rigid, make-you-want-to-end-yourself, ridiculous, and self-shaming diet while obsessing about weight, nor succumbing to societal pressures of what is deemed "acceptable" or "desirable" on a physical level. It means to start being accountable for how we choose to treat our bodies. Sugar intake is the first thing to start becoming more aware of, as it is terrible for the body but also insidious in the sense that huge amounts are found in *all* products (in North America, at least). Food portions are also incredibly disproportionate here, and most people live with a stretched-out stomach (internally) because most people have been taught they have to finish their plates even when they are not hungry anymore, which is, in fact, an act of self-betrayal.

Clean eating means eating healthy foods, absolutely, but also becoming aware of the quantities of food ingested. Start the habit of eating only when you start feeling hungry and stopping just before getting that "full" feeling, as this feeling occurs only when your brain receives the message that your stomach is full, when, in truth, the stomach is full before the brain gets the message. Identifying that delay and how it feels when your stomach is truly full, versus when the brain gets the message that it is, will be key in resetting our eating habits. This does not mean never eating "junk" food, but becoming aware of how regularly we are doing it and if it is healthy to do so.

Another important thing to consider is just how quickly we eat. Are we wolfing down an entire meal in seconds? This is one of the biggest reasons for over-eating: we eat so quickly that our stomach cannot keep up with registering the amounts ingested. Therefore, there is a greater delay before the brain tells us to stop because we are full. If you regularly feel sick after a meal because you have eaten too much, this may be an important factor to consider. Try to slow down your eating habits by taking smaller bites, taking more time to chew, taking pauses between bites, and allowing your stomach time to take in what you are giving to it. Learn to savour and appreciate each bite and to be thankful for your meals.

My advice here is to transition slowly from your current diet to where you want to be in healthy eating habits. Start by incorporating more fruits and veggies slowly, while also cutting sugary and other less healthy drinks, snacks, and desserts. If you are capable of giving up pop and energy drinks completely, do that, as they are easily some of the worst substances health-wise and have absolutely no beneficial aspect to counter just how harmful they are. Keep in mind that what you choose to ingest has effects not only on your physical health but also on your energy levels and how you feel about yourself overall.

As our bodies begin to feel better from the direct results of eating better, we find that we become sick less often, we gain more energy in a day, our hair and nails grow out healthier and thicker, we are naturally more relaxed and positive, and this obviously culminates into a boost of self-confidence. We do this to feel better within, which translates into feeling better about our own physical appearance. We can start this process and look exactly the same as we did before, and yet still feel happier and better within, which leads to more exterior self-acceptance as well! This may be triggering to some people to read, and if so, Journal about it. Realize what kind of wounding is the driving force behind the emotion and why you would choose to let that dictate your life.

The goal here is to fall in unconditional love with Self. We honor our body by taking good care of it. If you are not taking good care of yourself and are unhappy with your looks, instead of wallowing in that energy of self-pity, identify why you are holding onto wanting to feel miserable with yourself. Where do you believe you are not worthy of your own love? And why? When we truthfully love ourselves, we want to take good, loving care of our bodies. This means choosing to love ourselves exactly as we are and identifying the places where we can take better care of our bodies. Again, this has nothing to do with weight and appearance. This is about feeling good about our Selves from within in order for that energy to be reflected back to us.

Every single human being is unique. Every single human body is unique. Our Souls fashioned our bodies for this current existence perfectly. Perfectly, in each and every case. Remember that we are currently incarnated to heal past life trauma. Whatever triggers you about your own physical vessel needs to be addressed in depth. It goes without saying that the "standard of beauty" of societal norms is pure garbage and should always be taken as such. The important part is to feel good about ourselves, inside and out. In Truth, someone's level of attractiveness is derived more from their level of self-love and confidence than their exterior looks. Although looks may give some form of confidence, one's personal internal worth makes one beautiful.

This being said, it goes without saying that physical activity is a must, in the sense that we should honor our bodies' capabilities and learn to appreciate them. You may be terrible at team sports, but you can dance like nobody's business. You may be one of those people who genuinely enjoy running. Yoga may be your thing. What is meant here by physical activity is to use your body in a way that forces you to become aware of it and appreciate it, where it feels comfortable to be embodied within this vessel. If all you can manage is to go for walks, then walk. If you enjoy shooting hoops but have no basketball talent, shoot hoops anyway. Physical activity and exercise are two separate subjects. Exercise is important as well. The goal is to be the master of our own body instead of feeling limited by it; however, this shows up for us individually.

If you are reading these words and you have a physical disability that keeps you from doing most/all physical activities, then ask yourself what you *can* do to connect with your body. Accept your Self and your disability for what it is, and do not let it victimize you. Never allow outside perception to victimize you, either. If you need further inspiration, take a look at all of the Paralympic athletes, or even Stephen Hawking. Our mindsets and personal judgements are the only things in the way of our self-happiness and acceptance. This is true of able-bodied people as well. Choose to connect with your body despite its perceived limitations and honor it for what it can do, never mind what it cannot. And remember that you are already perfect, exactly the way you are. Our vessel is our Soul's chosen temple in this lifetime; what we choose to do with it, how we choose to honour it or not, is always up to us. Self-improvement will only ever make us feel better about ourselves, regardless of whether we are talking about physical or mental self-improvement.

The next exercise in this chapter will be to keep track of your natural eating habits for a whole week, then keep going for a full month. Write down everything you choose to eat and drink, as well as the quantities, to the best of your ability. The idea is to start seeing unhealthy patterns and tweaking where you can to ensure you are moving in the direction you want. It will also help to see just how much sugar is ingested and how few fruits and veggies are consumed. The idea is to find balance. See how much water you drink and how much you eat out in a week, and hold yourself accountable with healthy objectives. Remember that progress is progress, regardless of how "much" or "little" we perceive it to be.

At the same time, keep track of how much exercise and physical activity you get in that same week and month, and note your energy levels throughout the days. One week may not be long enough to see the full pattern, but with time, you will become aware of some truths that may not be that obvious in how you treat your physical vessel. Keep track of your life choices like this beyond a month. This way, patterns will become more obvious, as will your progress. You will start noticing naturally that on the days when you eat better and move your body more, you automatically feel better physically. Taking care of our bodies is a huge act of self-respect, and if you are actively neglecting yourself, look into the whys.

An interesting concept to remember around these subjects is that unowned or unrecognised guilt seeks punishment. When we choose to punish ourselves by overeating and overindulging in sweets, it is because somewhere deep down, we do not value ourselves and feel guilty about something, often unconsciously. In my process, when I realized that I was choosing to satisfy my mouth cravings above the well-being I felt in my body by constantly over-eating and consuming massive amounts of sugar, it clicked for me how it was, in fact, an act of self-loathing. I was purposefully eating way too much food because I was deeply unhappy with myself, and eating became an emotional crutch, a way for me to cope with existing. Growing up in an environment that offered no emotional connection and support meant that I had made good-tasting food my source of comfort.

Remember here that exercise, physical activity, and healthy eating are three very important aspects of our physical experience. All three are mood boosters and a medium for self-love and self-respect. If you are experiencing resistance towards one or all three of these things, ask yourself why you are actively choosing to betray your body this way. What is the underlying wound that motivates the need to stay unhealthy and unwell within? Why do you fight against taking good care of yourself? Why do you resist treating your Self and your body with respect? Why do you choose to self-sabotage and withhold affection for your body?

On the other hand, are you overworking yourself physically? Are you eating so little that it makes you the other kind of unhealthy? Are you trying to uphold the barbaric "standard of beauty" in today's society and betraying your well-being in that pursuit? Again, this whole process is about self-honesty and balance, and you will only ever go as far as you allow yourself to.

This does not mean giving up; it just means making small adjustments that are not seen as major, "threatening" changes that can be perceived as too much to handle all at once. Before long, baby steps will have gotten you further than drastic changes ever will, simply because small adjustments are sustainable in the long run. This is not a process to rush; we are not in a race. It is a process of self-care and acceptance. Start slow and upgrade your self-love and consequent lifestyle progressively as the previous change is fully incorporated and deemed effortlessly sustainable.

The main idea for change to occur somewhat naturally in our health is to take things slow, regardless of whether we are talking about changing eating habits or exercising. For exercise, maybe start with a little promise to yourself to do something three times a week, or even a small walk every day. The idea is to find a pace that is a little challenging, but achievable without feeling overwhelmed, that will end up being something you look forward to. Same with changing diets. Small steps taken progressively assure success. If, for some reason, you have been doing great, then hit a wall and fall back into bad habits, do not be hard on yourself. Maybe you have been doing too much changing with not enough sustainability. Find ways to encourage yourself throughout, and do not push yourself too hard that you become resentful of the process. We have to implement these changes with long-term goals, never instant gratification.

Celebrate where you have gotten in your goals, and when the need for going back to the bad habits leaves you (and it will, let it ride out instead of wanting to punish yourself for indulging in them), do not rush back to where you left off. If you have taken a break, never expect that you will be able to start off where you left off. Accept where you are presently, at all times, and always go from there. Give yourself the chance to start again. Make sure you are comforting yet firm with yourself. This is a process of re-parenting ourselves, so make sure that you are kind to yourself. Support and focus on your current progress instead of lamenting not being "further ahead." There is no further ahead. There is only ever the now. Wanting to be further along is just another form of non-acceptance and self-judgment and is ultimately detrimental to progress.

Since doing things one step at a time gets you where you want to be, your goal then is to enjoy the process. It may not always be easy, but it is important to recognize that it is worthwhile. Give yourself reasons to be happy in the here and now. Choose to appreciate new experiences instead of dreading them. This mindset does not limit itself to exercise and healthy eating; it is invaluable advice for everything in life. Find fun in exercising, discovering, eating healthy foods, cleaning and decluttering, and taking care of yourself. Stop viewing life as a list of chores and shift your mindset to viewing life as opportunities for joy. How we choose to approach a challenge determines how willing we are to accomplish it.

Change your perspective on how you approach all facets of life. Why choose to be miserable for what you do not have when you can choose to be grateful for what you do have? Reconsider how you feel about things and look into why they make you feel what they do. Choose to change your own narrative about your life. Growing our roots is all about reconnecting with the Truth of who we are and honouring that truth consciously within and consequently without through our bodies. Our foundation grows stronger and healthier when there is no more inner conflict, and we choose to be authentic.

We are here to learn and grow as Souls, but this cannot be done without understanding and fully connecting with our vessel. To be able to embody our Soul essence, our body needs to be able to contain that pure energy first. Again, this has little to do with physical appearance and everything to do with how comfortable we feel within our own skin. Furthermore, we were gifted this beautiful, wonderful planet as a playground to learn and grow. Having fun while being responsible is a balanced way to approach things. Having perfect harmony between those two is the key to making our existence pleasant and worthwhile. All work and no play is just as bad an energy to be in as all play and no work. Being all work is no life at all, while being all play makes life meaningless.

Finding balance in all aspects of life is essential to following our Soul purpose. Being constantly busy, or on "the grind," is what we pretend is the best way forward, when all it can lead to is burnout when we are not following our Soul purpose. Being constantly busy is the equivalent of cluttering our time. Having time to do nothing and relax is of utmost importance. Mammals are not designed to be constantly on the go, and humans are mammals too. There is a reason why our society is so dysfunctional and keeps showing symptoms of potential collapse. It is because the way it works goes against humanity's very nature.

Additionally, the busier we are, the more opportunities we miss. This may sound counterintuitive, but think about it. If the Universe is trying to give us something and we are too busy and tired to notice the signs and follow through with them, when are we supposed to be able to make the necessary space to allow it all in? As a general rule, the people who need to have every minute of their time planned out, reserved, and busy are not well within themselves. They use being constantly busy as an Ego boost for a sense of worth, as they are so popular or so in-demand that they do not have the luxury of free time. The Truth is, however, that they are betraying their very real need for rest, peace, and quiet. They also embody the notion of a lack mindset in terms of never having enough time, when they choose to leave no room open for themselves.

The thing about being constantly in busy mode is that we do not realize just how exhausted we are until our body crashes, and we are then forced to rest. We do not realize how stressed and unhappy we are because we literally do not have the time to sit and feel our emotions; we push them away because, again, we have no time to deal with them. What is ignored always builds up until it eventually explodes. On the other hand, only ever having free time may be exhilarating at first, while we catch up on rest. Still, it becomes boring over time as we constantly search for new ways of entertaining ourselves, become restless, and feel unfulfilled by mindless activities. This is why, ultimately, we always need a good balance of both purpose and relaxation.

This does not mean that doing one thing automatically means the other one is not present. We can accomplish our purpose while having moments of fun, and also have fun while achieving our purpose. It comes down to a matter of perspective. If we are in a work environment that brings us no joy, then it may be time to look for other opportunities. On the other hand, turning fun into work can be more harmful than good if the work conditions are not conducive to joy. Turning joy into obligation is the best way to kill the mood. Part of the importance of this chapter is to bring more joy into our lives deliberately and to do so in all aspects of our lives. Thinking work and fun must be separate; they are irreconcilable opposites and can never share space, which equals being stuck in duality thinking or duality consciousness.

Early Eastern and native Western philosophies are some of the most advanced states of understanding of the world and how we fit in it that are known to us to this day. The best way to explain the concept above is with the Yin-Yang symbol, which is the ultimate expression of Oneness in today's symbology. These philosophies embrace the symbiosis of life and flow instead of seeking to control everything and force things into shape. The varied ancient Eastern and Western cultures were seemingly quite different. Yet, most had similar, if not identical, spiritual founding principles of communion with the Self and nature, explaining that individuals are a small part of a greater whole. Further than the individual, life itself is always repeated in smaller and smaller identical patterns. Or we can understand it the other way, where the same pattern can repeat itself multiple times on increasingly bigger scales.

If we look at traditional Eastern medicine, such as acupuncture, the logic underlying the theories is that a single problem, or symptom, can never be understood at face value; that there are underlying currents and patterns that reveal the true source of the problem. This means that the problem cannot be truly understood if we do not understand how it interacts with its surroundings and its relation to the bigger picture. The same applies to us when it comes to traumatic experiences and wounds. Therefore, we cannot fully understand how to heal ourselves if we do not understand the logic, the "whys" of things that happen or have happened, and root out the source of the pain. This speaks of not only our actions and reactions, emotions and thoughts, but also of the circumstances that brought us to these events, the repeating patterns, and the unconscious vibrations we project that attract lessons and opportunities for healing.

It is by looking back and tracing the patterns to their source that we uncover the truth of their reason for being. Yet even those are shaped by more elements of their own surroundings. It is a law of nature that everything constantly affects everything else. Just like an ecosystem needs the symbiosis of all its parts to thrive, so do we. And just like how we can research and document exactly just how intricately and complexly all the different parts of an ecosystem work separately to reach the intended results of survival together as one whole, so can we uncover the complexity of our own symbiosis with Life and the Universe to understand our own function in this lifetime. This helps to understand how all who participate in our lives, every single interaction, regardless of how big or small, are all part of the symbiosis of our smaller network of being in the larger network of the world.

Understanding our place in the Universe, how we fit into our own ecosystem, and how we affect those around us—and how they affect us in return—is an important part of understanding ourselves. Keep in mind here that as rich, varied, and intense as our own lives are, so is the life of every single person in the world. In any given ecosystem, the smallest imbalances in one small part of it can upset the entire system and cause its destruction. All the parts need to function properly individually for the whole to function healthily as one.

Taking the metaphor further, our own body is its own ecosystem in and of itself. Yet it is part of a larger ecosystem (family) that is part of a larger system (neighbourhood), that is part of a larger system (city), that is part of a larger system (region), which is part of a larger system (province or state), which is part of a larger system (country), which is part of a larger system (continent), which is part of a larger system (Earth), which is part of a larger system (galaxy), and so on into infinity. This was done in the focus of zooming out. When zooming in, we can see our heart as a separate ecosystem, our lungs as another, our liver as yet another, and so on, with every single organ and system within the body, all the way down to our very cells, to the atoms composing those cells. This is the same principle of the Yin-Yang symbol, the idea that there is always a smaller thing present in a bigger thing to make it whole and to illustrate how everything is interconnected.

There is a common misconception regarding the Yin-Yang symbol that claims the symbol is about the fighting of good over evil, which is extremely duality-based thinking, also known as Ego perception. On a Soul level, good and evil are not a thing. There is only ever experience. The Ego wants to believe that human nature is war, fighting, or competition with the need to be superior to others. These are profoundly Egoic notions. Humanity's pure essence is Unconditional Love. We never feel bad when we give love. We only ever feel bad when love is perceived to be taken away, rejected, or insincere. Needing to compete, assert dominance, and being crowned victor comes from deep self-worth wounds. When we know we are worthy to begin with, then we are not chasing external validation through competition.

There is nothing inherently wrong with competition when it is truly about testing skills. Healthy competition can have great intensity without being toxic. The toxicity of competition comes in the form of needing to win at all costs because the "worth" of a person, or even a nation, depends on a win. This is why people feel the need to cheat; the importance of external validation is greater than their sense of self-integrity. They have no integrity because they inherently do not believe themselves worthy and, therefore, believe that having a win is what will give them proof that they are worthy. Because they do not feel good about themselves, they need to feel "superior" to others to fill that void.

The Truth of life is that when things do not work out as we expected them to or how we want them to, it is a message for us to uncover our true motivations for needing this thing to work in the first place. Is our Ego the one truthfully in charge of our desires? Probably. When we are in Soul living, we fully understand and embrace that when one door seemingly closes for us, it means the one we are truly meant to go through is open elsewhere. Receiving "bad" news, such as a job termination or the end of a relationship, is never, in fact, bad for us. Only the Ego perceives it this way. The Soul accepts these things for the opportunities and new beginnings they really are. It is healthy to let ourselves grieve what we thought we wanted, what we thought was meant for us, but then we must choose to move on in our quest for the bigger and better things waiting for us through this redirection. We must help our Ego understand that an ending is just a new beginning in disguise. Do we choose to focus on the "negative" or the "positive"?

There are no flaws in the grand scheme of things, only in our Ego perceptions of things. There are no mistakes, only redirection toward our highest good, and it is up to us to choose between struggling against the change, accepting it, and moving on. Everything is always perfect exactly as it happens, especially when we do not understand how or why. It is always only ever the Ego that refuses the Truth and struggles against it because it believes itself above it all by believing it should be in control of all things. The Ego believes itself far ahead and beyond the knowledge and wisdom of the Universe. It is hilarious when you consider that the Ego is simply one human being's perception of what is.

The principle of the Yin-Yang symbol asks us to detach from the belief that we are consequential, that we as individuals matter. We do not. We are fundamentally irrelevant and inconsequential to the grand scheme of things. We are but a fleck of dust in a fraction of a millisecond in time. Ultimately, we are absolutely *nothing*.

I am placing a lot of emphasis on the above paragraph, not only to shatter the reader's Ego but also because it is of the utmost importance for us to understand how little importance we hold individually. We hold none at all. It is when we truly and deeply understand this that we can put our Egos aside entirely. We need to get over ourselves completely before we can do any good in this lifetime. Only then can we understand the true importance that we hold. But we need to experience that Ego death first to truly understand the depth of this principle.

By understanding exactly how we are absolutely *nothing of consequence,* we can understand that we are *everything of consequence.* Thinking this second part without understanding the first one is exactly what is wrong with this world and its people to begin with. By understanding just how small, irrelevant, and inconsequential we are, every barrier we have ever chosen to believe existed to limit and contain us, to keep us small, has no reason to exist anymore. By being nothing, we can be anything and everything. Since we do not matter, all that matters is what we do, which means that we can accomplish anything we want to.

We can understand that there are no limits to our creative potential, only the ones we impose on ourselves.

By shattering the illusion of self-importance, we stop giving importance to things that hold none. For example, our physical appearance, what others think of us, what is "expected" of us, what we expect of ourselves, the pressure we place ourselves under to "perform," what we believe success looks like, any and all social "conformity" norms, all of these things are truthfully all bullshit ideas of no importance whatsoever. They are self-created, limiting barriers. None of these things matter in the slightest on a Soul level. What *does* matter is how well and how happy we are within. Are we listening to and following the Truth of who we are? That is the only gauge of importance in this lifetime. Nothing else matters. Because if nothing we do matters, then what matters is what we choose to do.

When we come to the realization that this society of ours is fabricated on lies, bullshit, and appearances, we blatantly see how trivial and useless these ideals really are. Our society is based on illusions, not Truth. It is all a fabricated web of lies to distract and control the masses, to stop people from achieving self-actualisation. Our society is fear-based. It is of self-preservation in an "everyone for themselves/crabs-in-a-bucket" kind of way, which is the furthest from our human essence as we can possibly get. The Truth is that the pack survives while the lone wolf dies, but we have been painted the false picture that the lone wolf is the powerful one. It is by helping each other and loving each other unconditionally that we can all truly grow and thrive. Humans are meant to thrive as a community, not as individuals. Otherwise, what is the point of having differences?

We have the power to shape our reality. We have to acknowledge that we are our Souls, not our Egos, and that, therefore, the plan our Souls have fashioned for us to follow is quite literally the best possible life we could ever dream of achieving. All that is required of us is to identify that path, trust it, and choose to follow it. Fear is always the energy that gets in the way, as are our Egos and the indoctrinated notions of what our lives "should" be. Living in our Soul energy means living with limitless freedom and opportunities. THIS is what life truly is about. It is an adventure of fun and self-discovery, healing old wounds along the way so we can be free to attain the bliss of living our Heaven on Earth. But we will never be able to attain that if we choose not to work on ourselves; if we choose not to heal and follow our Soul path. The challenges we face are always for our growth and benefit. Everything always happens for our highest good, and it is always up to us to fight against it or embrace what is meant to be learned in order to evolve.

Grounding ourselves is all about understanding this perspective and living its truth. Slowly embodying the higher perspective and choosing to connect and honour the energies of the planet and the Universe above while accepting our physical reality for the adventure of growth and healing that it is, is how we start the true grounding process. It is the path to growing the strongest possible foundation. Do not worry if this seems alien and strange at first; that is normal. This chapter intends to start accepting this as Truth, but we all get there in our own time through our own experiences. This is normal and part of transitioning from Ego perspective to Soul acceptance.

Grounding also involves freeing ourselves from our fears and self-imposed restrictions. By accepting and connecting with the current truth of our 3D reality, we now grant our Soul a way to reach through and connect with us. Grounding is the first half of the bridge between both energies, the bridge of which we are the center of— the connector. We are preparing our physical reality to receive everything our Soul wants us to have, all of the abundance and unconditional love we are inherently worthy of. Remember that joy is the biggest magnet that attracts the manifestations we want and deserve while living in the energy of gratitude and happiness.

We have been put onto this Earth to experience all the beauty life has to offer, and sometimes, that means experiencing its complete contrast for us to truly and deeply be grateful for and happy with what we have. Beyond that, raising our vibration levels automatically raises that of our surroundings. Choosing to be happy and to grow and evolve on a personal level is all we have to do, and it is done by following our inner guidance and trusting that the Universe always has our backs.

Chapter 10
Balancing our Inner Feminine and Masculine Energies

———— • ————

This chapter encompasses much of what we have already been working on and funnels it into a deeper understanding of who and what we are. First and foremost, with the principle of Oneness we have explored, it becomes interesting to investigate the elements that make human beings distinct individuals. We are more than just our human bodies; otherwise, we would all act, feel, and behave in the exact same way. It is our separate personalities that make us who we are individually. But, other than our Soul essence, what makes us so distinct while being similar? The answer is the energies we all carry of feminine and masculine essences, and where we fall into that spectrum.

To start, every single human being (to say nothing of animals) carries both feminine and masculine essences. This can be understood with the principle of the Yin-Yang symbol, as complementary equal opposites. Some of the best relationships we will ever have in our lives (romantic and otherwise) will be with people who match with us energetically in a complementary fashion. Being in too much of the same energy will just end up with butting heads constantly, while being too different will simply not connect long-term and become incompatible after the sparks fizzle out. Keep in mind that when I refer to these masculine and feminine energies, I never speak of gender.

It must be understood that we all start off embodying more of one energy. People who claim to be androgynous do not escape this rule. Claiming to embody certain energies does not equate to truthfully embodying them. A perfectly androgynous being would be someone who has attained enlightenment, who is perfectly balanced within and without, with no wounds present to affect self-understanding, and as of yet, the Earth is not carrying anyone with that energy. Those claiming to do so verbally show a completely different reality through their actions and behaviours. This shows a wound around self-worth as their actions tend to show them chasing after being recognized as "special," "different," and "apart," basically wanting to be worshiped for their "uniqueness."

This idea of being androgenous is due to their refusing to acknowledge the energies within, disowning parts of themselves, or being unknowingly disconnected from either feminine, masculine, or both energies as a direct result of present or past life wounding and trauma. A lot of trauma centers around disowning one or both internal energies as a way to feel safer in chaotic environments. Once completely healed, their claim may be true, but as long as wounding is present, they themselves cannot know. If they cannot connect to either or both energies within, they are simply in self-denial, as every living being contains both energies within. Feeling triggered? Journal. This is a quick note to remind you that when we feel triggered by anything, we still have wounding to work on. Therefore, our self-perception is still warped.

Which energy is strongest within us has nothing to do with gender or sexuality. Feminine energy and masculine energy are fundamental human elements. We have to remember that energy is purely energy. It holds no biases, no preferences, no ideologies. Energy is simply energy. It is there regardless of whether we want it to be or not. And both feminine and masculine energies are part of what makes a human being human.

A fully healed and balanced human being has healed and balanced feminine and masculine energies that coexist perfectly within the most beautiful symbiotic dance of equilibrium.

Some of us will outright reject the energy we are uncomfortable with, which is part of our wounding. We reject it because either we do not feel safe being or existing in that energy, or we have previously disowned our connection to it due to trauma. Using myself as an example (biologically born woman and heterosexual), I had completely disowned my own feminine energy, growing up as a complete tomboy who hated the colour pink and everything considered to be feminine. I viewed femininity, and consequently women, as weak, useless, and only there to be of service to men because of how I was brought up. I never wanted to be seen as weak and useless, and I always felt the need to prove myself against my gender. I understood that being born a woman made me automatically "less than" in the eyes of men, even if they viewed me that way solely through unconscious conditioning. I was unfortunately brought up in a Catholic setting, where the misogyny is very strong and ingrained; insidious in nature.

The perfect example is that little boys are given many opportunities to try and fail and are taught that it is okay to make mistakes and that they should use them as learning and growth opportunities. In contrast, little girls must be perfect every time they try something. Otherwise, their spot would be given away to a boy because they had "proven" that they could not be trusted with it if they made a single mistake. It is incredibly frustrating for the little girls when they see the boys being encouraged to learn from their mistakes and to try things over and over again, that hopefully, they will end up performing better the next time when the girls are themselves ushered to the side and told to be grateful that they were given a single opportunity to begin with.

I, therefore, completely rejected and hated "girl activities" like shopping, dressing up, and doing nails in favor of doing "manly activities" such as playing sports, getting dirty, being physically active and fit, playing video games, and otherwise just doing what felt right to me. The above paragraph's reality fired me up to the point where I constantly had to show I could do everything the little boys could, but better. I always needed to show I could best boys over and over again at anything society said was for boys only. I needed to prove that I was not a "weak, helpless little girl," a "damsel in distress that always needs saving," and that

I was more than "just a woman." In hindsight, it is infinitely sad to think that an entire gender is treated this way and that this treatment is what is socially acceptable because it goes unseen and unacknowledged. Just imagine the pressure that little girl put on her shoulders because she was continuously told through both actions and words that she was inherently less than others, that she felt she had to prove her worth over and over again, or risk being discarded like the others.

I grew up knowing I would constantly have to prove my worth to men before they even considered giving me a begrudging chance. And this struggle is completely invisible to boys and men. Their experience tells them, "No, of course, girls are given a chance! I watched them on the field for a second. She just was not good enough!" The Truth is that girls are never given a chance to learn and grow into becoming good to begin with, unlike boys. To this day, I still see so many examples of girls having to fight to be included, to fight for what they want, while being belittled and mocked for it. Women still have to "prove their worth" if they want to belong in certain spaces before men will choose to acknowledge them. There is this disgusting idea still prevalent today that women always have to prove themselves above and beyond men to receive the bare minimum in return.

Of course, my experience is due to the patriarchal stereotypes of my upbringing in part, but it also stems from past life wounding that I discovered later on in life, which I have since understood and healed. I had a deep-seated wound that made me believe that women were lesser than men by nature, which is made prevalent in the Bible with the story of Adam and Eve, where Eve is blamed for everything while Adam made the exact same decision by his own free will to eat of the apple, instead of having a backbone and discussing it first or even just saying no. The point is that Eve is villainized for being manipulated by the snake and making a mistake, while Adam is excused for making the same mistake. This ideology was reflected back to me in my upbringing, giving me the burning desire to prove this belief wrong over and over again because my Soul knew the Truth of the equality between feminine and masculine natures. They are simply different: equal, yet complementary.

This is the basis behind the saying, "If you judge a fish by its ability to climb trees, then it will believe itself to be stupid its entire life." Society is built in favour of men's abilities, and women are judged by masculine standards. The Truth of this is reflected in everything, but especially in modern medicine, where all previous studies and research were done solely by white males on white males, and the results were used as the basis for the entire human spectrum.

I have just recently received the preliminary diagnosis of being both autistic and ADHD, known as AuDHD, which flew completely under the radar in my youth because I was an "overachiever" in school, but especially because I was a girl. How these things show up as behaviour in boys and girls is completely different in most cases. Yet, the standard of diagnosis is entirely based on how it shows up externally in boys because their "symptoms" are generally more obvious. In my experience, the worst part about mental conditions is how doctors and specialists have no clue how they *feel and act within a person*. They base their diagnosis entirely on what someone can *see* from an *external* perspective about how it can be bothersome *to others* and, therefore, how to make it containable for others' sake, which is absolutely ridiculous. They look for external symptoms instead of internal patterns and then try to make them manageable for the poor humans who have to "deal with" these people.

Things are starting to get better at this point, but it is still far from where they should be. This does not mean that all of modern medicine is garbage. On the contrary, we have numerous wondrous advancements that help many people in many ways. However, the problem with modern medicine is that it has a purely masculine approach: find the problem, remove the problem, end of story. This is, again, looking for the external symptoms instead of finding and addressing the root cause. It is an entirely visual approach, which is fundamentally incomplete, as removing a symptom does not treat the underlying condition. This works up to a certain point for physical ailments, but is useless with what is invisible to the eye. Because modern medicine is purely a masculine practice and approach, it does not seek to understand, only to fix what is apparent.

All of this is to say that feminine and masculine energies are more than just energies affecting us within. They are also part of how we act and react, think, and feel. They also show up in external settings as ways of viewing the world. As some may have guessed at this point, feminine and masculine energies are more tools to help us navigate our human experience. And just like everything else we have learned so far, the goal is to achieve a balanced life by balancing these tools within, so that it may translate without.

When it comes to struggling with our personal identities, we are really struggling to accept the truth of who we are and accept ourselves exactly as we perceive ourselves to be. We can start out in life and have absolutely no idea who we are. We have to find ourselves and figure out who we really are within before we can stop caring about the details of what makes us, us, and just choose to live our Truth. To simply exist as we are. Ultimately, life is about self-acceptance and making the choice to evolve into the best possible version of Self, but this can never happen if we refuse the truth of where we are currently standing. Whenever we seek external validation and acceptance, we essentially betray ourselves by saying we do not trust our judgment or that our opinion is worthless.

A lot of people struggle with self-acceptance because our societies forbid it. Society is based on appearances, not substance, and therefore cannot endorse a genuine person who does not buy into the fakeness of needing external factors to be whole. Factors such as "makeup is essential for women, and they cannot walk out the door without it," and "men have no real worth if they are not sporting a six-pack."

Ultimately, this creates the pressure that we must always be agreeable to the public eye. It creates the illusion that we need to follow these rules to be seen as worthy by society, when the Truth is that we are inherently worthy regardless of our appearance. The important lesson here is that we find true peace, ease, and wholeness from within, as we will never find them from without.

Often, when we struggle with self-acceptance, we try to figure out where we fit in. This usually causes people to create personas they know fit into certain circles to see if that circle is right for them. However, this creates a cycle of depending on others to validate our existence and give us a rush of feeling good about belonging. Belonging for the sake of feeling like we belong when we are not living our Truth rapidly becomes a toxic way of living because we then enter a constant cycle of needing to prove that we belong when we do not. We become addicted to chasing acceptance from the group instead of focusing on uncovering our inner truth and choosing our own self-acceptance. Anything inauthentic will always crumble, no matter how much we try to sustain it.

The relief we get from feeling like we belong in a group we do not belong in will only ever be temporary, as it has no solid foundation to rely upon and is just more self-betrayal. It also creates the belief that we cannot trust and rely on ourselves, and it also never feels good when others constantly need acceptance from us. It becomes draining for people when they constantly need to reassure a person that they are accepted, and it creates the need for distance and peace because that person's energy just demands too much. It becomes toxic in the sense that that person drains us of our energy to feel stable in their own self. They become dependent on our energy, which forces us to produce more for ourselves. Still, because that drain is constantly present, it becomes unsustainable as we never get to fill ourselves up. We become stuck in a constant production mode to sustain another.

Neediness created from being incapable of taking care of ourselves and meeting our own needs is extremely repulsive energy for others because of how desperate it feels. Of course, some people can (and do) take advantage of this by selling us superficial quick fixes, which ultimately never work because they never involve self-work. People in this energy are desperate for change but refuse to give it to themselves. They are waiting for the knight in shining armour that does not exist, and will take anything and everything they can from any source available to them.

The important thing to understand here is that though we can find acceptance from others to be gratifying, we cannot become dependent on receiving acceptance from outside sources. This will lead to us not being able to give acceptance of ourselves to ourselves, but it will also, over time, lessen the hit we get from receiving acceptance from others to the point where we find ourselves needing more and more to achieve that same feeling, just like a drug addict. It is important to understand that emotions can be addictive. People who create drama just to be in the presence of that adrenaline rush are prime examples of this. The same applies to people addicted to outrage and self-righteousness; they are addicted to the feeling of empowerment by their overwhelming emotions instead of recognizing they are just completely out of control of themselves. When we are healed, the energy of drama is repulsive to us because of how profoundly disingenuous it is. Drama equals bullshit. When we are healed, we do not tolerate bullshit in any form from anyone, especially not from ourselves.

Another thing to remember when we rely on outside sources to feel whole and complete within is that what is given can always be taken away. The Truth is that relying on outside sources for anything in our lives equates to giving away our personal power. This does not apply to contracts and services we pay for; this refers to having crutches in our personal development instead of choosing to heal. If, instead of dealing with a problem on our own, we run and find help at the first sign of a potential difficulty instead of seeing if we can figure things out, it removes the possibility of personal growth, learning, and self-sufficiency. This is why we have to be capable of *giving ourselves what we need before* we can choose to let someone help us out with it. This does not mean we should never rely on others for help, but it should not be our answer to everything.

For example, how can we ask someone to love us in a relationship when we do not currently love ourselves? Or even, how can we be independent and self-sufficient if we never try things out on our own? Being independent and allowing others to help us out when needed is an entirely different vibe than being unable to do things because we are dependent on other people's help to achieve anything. One is empowered, and the other is completely disempowered. We need to learn to stand on our own two feet (metaphorically) and give it our best shot to realize if it truly is beyond us, and we then need some help. This does not mean we should start messing with a car engine to prove ourselves if we have no mechanical training whatsoever, but it could mean getting as far into a problem as we can go without creating more problems for ourselves. We need to identify what is truly out of our depth and what is not, what we can learn along the way, and what we cannot.

The only real way to truly discover who we are is through experimenting. How can we possibly know the truth of what makes us "us" if we cannot identify likes and dislikes? And how can we truly know what we like and do not like if we never try anything new? This means that if you were imposed beliefs as a child, imposed things you were told you had to like, and some you were never allowed to experiment with, how can you know anything about yourself if someone has made all of those decisions for you? How could we possibly know our own strength if we are lifted up by others all the time instead of seeing just how far we can manage on our own?

We need to give ourselves the acceptance we want to receive from others. We have to be able to stand up for ourselves to achieve anything of value in our lives. Otherwise, it is only ever other people achieving these things for us, meaning we never achieve anything alone. Healing always depends on the Self, not on anyone else. Give yourself the permission *to be who you truly are*, and to figure out that part for and by yourself. Do not allow yourself to depend on others to validate your identity. No one else in the world can be you. Only you have that superpower. Just be yourself, and the right people will find and love you for it. And those who do not, or cannot, are meant to leave your life by this point. Keeping yourself small and out of the Truth of who you are to be able to keep these people around is just more self-betrayal.

By becoming self-reliant and self-sufficient, we never have to fear that the source of our personal power might disappear overnight. The key to self-healing is understanding that we are our own power source. How much we allow that flow within is always up to us. This does not mean always refusing outside help; it means that we do not depend on outside help to exist. It means that if all of our external help sources disappear overnight, we will be fine regardless. This is the energy we need to find ourselves in to be able to create our own Heaven on Earth, it is the prime energy conducive to manifestation.

Everything we have gone over in the previous chapters is to get us to this point of energetic sovereignty over our own lives. It is encouraged to revisit the chapters as many times as needed, as new understanding can be accessed through healing and understanding of new or broader concepts. Healing comes in layers; this is what we already know, but so does embodying true understanding. We can understand something consciously without being able to apply it to our living circumstances just yet. Embodiment of the Soul is the goal; we must constantly revisit and clear out outdated beliefs and wounds as they also appear in layers in our conscious awareness over time, until we can clear out the core belief or wound.

Let's now dive into the core of this chapter: feminine and masculine energies. We will uncover what they are individually, how they affect us, what they look like as wounded energies, and how to heal and balance them.

Just as the concept of the Yin-Yang symbol explains, these two energies are polar opposites that exist complementarily in symbiosis. To believe one is "superior to" or "above" the other is to be devoid of common sense and logic. They are, in fact, equal in complementary ways. What is a weakness in one is the other's strength, and vice versa. As stated previously, both of these energies are found within every single human being. We refer to them as masculine and feminine energies because their essence relates to the ends of the spectrum they represent, with pure androgyny being the middle point.

For simplicity in explanation, masculine energy is sometimes referred to as "man" and feminine energy as "woman" when referring to people. Again, being born male or female does not affect which energy is stronger within us, nor which is the most comfortable one for us to exist in, nor does it have anything to do with sexuality. They are simply energies that dictate behaviour that we have to become aware of and understand for the sake of our personal development. If any of these things are triggering, write about them in your Journal and figure out why.

As explained in a previous chapter, our sense of identity and any unreasonable attachment to it is entirely Ego behaviour. The Soul knows we are all one and the same, that we all carry a sliver of the Universe within us, and that our personal preferences, opinions, and individual details do not matter in the grand scheme of things. They should matter to us as we learn to accept the Truth of who we are, but no more than that. If you have made your identity your whole personality, you are sadly missing out on your personal power and truth. Identity is but a small fraction of who and what we are. It is the surface layer, akin to appearance, and is no more important than appearances. We are so much more than our outward shells and preferences. These are essentially just the settings page in our game of Life. Who wants to play a game solely within the settings page? We want our settings to be to our preferences, but we need to set them aside once established in order to get on with playing the actual game.

The Ego always seeks validation from outside sources and is closed off from hearing anything it does not agree with outright. The Ego never likes being challenged, nor allowing personal growth, because this is seen as a challenge to its being in control, as a threat to its very existence. Additionally, any outside source that previously provided acceptance, warmth, love, or comfort—whatever the need—that is removed or threatened will cause a breakdown for the Ego, and it will do whatever it can to stay in control and force things back to the way they were. We should know by now that forcing anything to be the way we want it to be will always backfire on us dramatically and, most likely, devastatingly, force us into the energy of acceptance and letting go. The Ego is reactive and explosive, while the Soul is calm and collected. The Ego seeks fighting and drama, while the Soul is comfortable with acceptance. The Ego gets triggered, but the Soul does not.

Let's first explore masculine energy. It is the driving force within us, the action-oriented part of who we are. It is the achiever, the guardian, the provider, the worker, the one who gives, the loud outer strength, the outwardly focused energy. It is the logical energy, the straight lines only, the must get from point A to point B energy, the physical representation of duality, of black and white thinking. It is the physical strength, endurance, and support. It is the tool of external order and achievement. Masculine energy is the one that gets things done and provides. It is the builder. It is the Father. It is the mind. It is action. It is Earth and Air joined as one. It is Order. It is Living.

Being in this healthy energy translates as being a good leader, one who shows by example, takes charge, is responsible with themselves and others, and cares for people through actions. This energy is direct and firm but not unkind, and it also does the right thing for the sake of it being the right thing to do. This is disciplined energy, but not the blindly unthinking type. It is precise and calculated. The focus on achieving anything is linear, with thought-out steps to get from point A to point B as quickly as possible. It is straightforward, one step at a time, and self-reliant. There is also a strong sense of camaraderie, of knowing one's place and making the most of it. This is the energy that plans ahead based on prior knowledge and gets things done in an orderly fashion.

On the other hand, the feminine energy is the quiet strength, the one who receives the roots, foundation, home, stability, comfort, warmth, inner strength, softness, nurturing energy, creativity, and is an artist. It does not need to be in motion, as it easily attracts everything it could ever need. It is the magnetic energy, emotional strength, endurance, and support, the physical representation of Oneness, the creator. It is the tool of internal acceptance and allowance. Feminine energy is the one that soothes and heals. It is fearless. It is the healer. It is the grey areas in between the black and white. It is the Mother. It is the heart. It is rest and rejuvenation. It is fierce and fiery. It is the wild, untameable. It is Fire and Water joined as one. It is Chaos. It is Life.

Being in the healthy feminine energy translates as being fearless in spite of circumstances because she is confident in who she is and that she will be okay no matter what, as she knows her masculine provides as she nurtures. This intuitive energy relies on her inner connection to all, her divine knowing. She trusts the Universe; she surrenders to the Flow of Life and lets it bring her where she needs to be. This energy is one with its environment. It never controls things. It always allows. Feminine energy is the art of creation and the process of inspiration. It is a magnet for all of the person's wants and needs. Everything is naturally drawn to her energy.

Feminine energy sees what is invisible to the naked eye and to logic, and is open to discovering new things. She never judges. She cares for all living things. She creates possibilities. She holds space for things to happen on their own without needing to control the outcome. She finds new pathways and enjoys the process of discovery. She is detached from the material world; she sees the big picture and allows it to unfold however it will. She never forces anything, as she knows that contracts, events, and growth—Life—will happen in their own time. She does not direct; she guides. She is not stagnant. She is active but responsive and paced by her own intuition.

Whereas masculine energy is a straight line of logic and physical strength, feminine energy is the intuitive magnet and emotional strength. The masculine is hard, while the feminine is soft, yet they are both strong in their own ways. It takes massive strength and resilience to support and uplift others without sacrificing the Self, as healthy feminine energy does. The healthy masculine energy gives and provides while the feminine receives and nurtures, without ever having any hard feelings over his circumstances, because he understands his role in the bigger picture. The masculine understands he can only ever produce singular elements, while the feminine creates a whole new world from these. He builds, but she creates. He leads and thinks while she supports and makes things possible.

Only together and balanced do they allow for living life fully. One cannot exist and thrive without the other to support and balance them out, and neither can find true satisfaction if they are not embracing their respective roles entirely, as each has its own respective purposes and needs. The healthy inner masculine always listens to the guidance of the healthy inner feminine because he knows she is intuitively connected to the whole. She allows him to make the consequent plan and take action on her guidance, as she knows he can make things happen. One dies without a symbiotic relationship with the other. Men are nothing without women. And women are nothing without men.

They intricately care for and support each other by providing them with what they cannot get on their own. A balanced connection or partnership is one of mutual giving and receiving, but also of mutual appreciation of the other for being able to provide what we alone cannot access. As much biologically as energetically, men and women do not have the same capabilities and innate strengths because we need variety to survive and thrive as a pair and as a society. This reiterates the notion of the Yin-Yang symbol that what is true on a small scale is also true on a large scale. Neither feminine nor masculine energy is better than the other: they are both essential. They are simply different and, therefore, cater to different needs. We have to understand that differences are what give flavour to life. Without differences, we have no choices. Everything is always the exact same for everyone: bland and boring.

We must uncover, heal, and accept both of these energies within ourselves fully to be able to claim that we are healed and balanced as a whole. Remember that these energies are a spectrum: where our Soul lands on that spectrum is unique to us. The first step to healing and balancing them is to identify which energy comes easiest to us, but also in what state we are currently living through it. When one energy fails us, the other has to overcompensate and becomes distorted. We can have both a collapsed and distorted masculine energy while also having a collapsed and distorted feminine energy. Some facets of each are collapsed for the other to distort in different aspects of our lives.

For example, a person could have a collapsed masculine energy in the sense that they cannot give, only receive or forcefully take from others because of the subsequent distorted feminine energy taking over the role of the masculine energy, while also having a collapsed feminine energy in the sense that they can never take time just to rest and constantly need to be doing something to feel productive, they need to always hustle, hustle, hustle as the distorted masculine energy takes over that space.

We may have disowned our connection to either masculine or feminine energies as a whole, or parts of both. If we have fully disowned both energies, we will walk around as empty husks devoid of purpose and possibility, incapable of living. This can happen when we are completely dissociated from existing. Depression and suicidal thoughts can be symptoms of this. As with everything else, learning why we have chosen to disown one—or parts of both—energies will allow us to heal them. The more we uncover and heal, the easier life becomes and the freer and lighter we feel.

The more we dive within ourselves to understand the Truth of who we are, the easier it becomes to see the patterns of Truth in our external reality being reflected internally, and vice versa. Try to identify which energy is more present within yourself at this time. Your current personal needs and how you have felt reading the descriptions of both energies in the above paragraphs will reveal a lot about your hidden beliefs. It may be difficult to properly identify which energy is predominant while we live through the distorted view of our wounding, but it is interesting to do, nevertheless. Even if done as nothing more than something to look back on to gauge personal progress, this exercise could also help us uncover our next healing steps. The goal is not to be perfect in our self-assessment but to dig into possibilities and see what we reject outright without proper consideration, or what sticks as we feel into the truth.

In your Journal, make a list focusing only on these two energies and how they appear balanced, and look at the relationships you have had in your life, regardless of their natures. Consider whether that person is naturally more feminine or masculine in their type of energy. Consider all of your relationships this way, be it at work, at home, in your family, your friend circle, etc. Friendships tend to reflect back our energy, while romantic relationships work out best with people with the opposite energy. Try to see if being around certain people pushes you in more of one energy or the other, or if being around a specific person pushes you into a specific energy.

When there is balance, things always flow easily. The goal here is to start noticing your own energetic predisposition and if that predisposition changes when around other people. Do you have a clearly dominant energy? Is it healed and balanced as described above? Or does it feel distorted? Are you capable of identifying and being in the other energy at all? Or has it collapsed? Is there one energy that you get a strong emotional reaction to, like disgust? Or repulsion? Or joy? How does existing in one feel in comparison to existing in the other? There are no right or wrong answers in life, only what *is* and what we pretend is.

Before taking a closer look at both the masculine and feminine energies' distorted and collapsed/rigidified states, we have to understand that whenever one energy is not balanced and healed, it can never truly connect to the other, meaning they cannot work symbiotically as they are meant to. In most cases, we base, or copy, our own inner masculine and feminine energies on the representations we have of them growing up, such as within parents or parental figures, and how they interacted with each other. Subconsciously, we associate being feminine with the mother and being masculine with the father. However, we are still talking about energies here, meaning that if your father has the stronger overall feminine energy, you subconsciously will base your feminine energy on him and his actions. Energy is something we recognize through innate feelings and vibrations. Even when we do not know we are doing it consciously, it is a constant thing we do as it is part of our natural, sensitive awareness. This is why, even in same-sex couples, one tends to be more in their feminine energy and the other in their masculine energy in a functional relationship.

Just like how our chakras can become over- and under-active, both masculine and feminine energies can be too strong and too weak in their own ways. As with everything, balance is the key. Masculine and feminine energies share the same space and need to be in perfect balance and harmony to function as they were always meant to. The masculine energy's essence is inner strength, meaning that its weakness is to collapse in on itself, which causes the feminine energy to need to over-extend itself and become distorted to compensate. The feminine energy's essence is fluidity; its weakness becomes rigidity. When the feminine energy rigidifies, the masculine becomes cut off from reaching her. Because it cannot play its role of provider, it becomes relentless and distorted in its pursuit of regaining its natural state and position. Collapsed masculine energy and rigidified feminine energy are the weakened states of both, while distorted energies are the overwhelming ones.

Let's begin by introducing the collapsed masculine energy. This happens when our masculine essence is too weak to hold proper structure and cannot follow through on our plans. When collapsed, the masculine energy's driving force is mostly non-existent, meaning he becomes stagnant when his role is forward movement. This energy can show up in people as being flaky, having little self-esteem, having no personal discipline, fleeing from responsibilities, or downplaying them, someone who expects to be taken care of like a child, spineless people who gladly throw others under the bus to save themselves. They are out of touch with the truth of their own emotions, fear intimacy and vulnerability, either do not have plans or expect others to make them happen for them, lose their ability to be assertive and proactive, and prefer to self-isolate instead of knowing and embodying their true power.

This energy usually takes the form of spineless cowards, regardless of gender, who enjoy having power over others and treating them horribly until they are caught. Then they become a wallowing heap of self-pity and begging for the mercy they never would have granted their victims. Of course, this is a broad stroke of the attitude, but the same story can also be seen on a smaller scale. These are petty people, the vindictive ones who hide behind stronger people, and those who believe they are owed everything but refuse to put in any effort. They are weak-minded and weak-willed and have no sense of personal accountability, as fault is always placed upon others.

As stated previously, we base our understanding of feminine and masculine energies on our care providers. The masculine energy collapses in childhood because of how the child is treated and brought up. This is true of all four unbalanced energies of the masculine and the feminine. In the case of the collapsed masculine, we are talking about a child who was never given space to learn who they are, make decisions, and build self-confidence. These children suffer from either physical or emotional neglect and are taught that they do not matter. They cannot grow their protective and assertive sides of the healthy masculine energy; therefore, they give up trying, crumple, withdraw, and dissociate. They never learn what healthy boundaries are or how to uphold them. They have never learned how to identify and be their own Self.

This leads to them seeking out abusive relationships (this is never done consciously; it is always our wounding bringing in situations to help us heal) where they find similar patterns as within their childhood, and similarly cannot identify abuse as abuse because that was always their "normal" growing up. Since they have never learned to value and protect themselves properly, they will always defend the abuser and side with them because they have identified this as being "safe" as a child. This is the same parent/child dynamic repeated in a romantic relationship, as it is what they are used to, what they are comfortable with, and all they have known. They have also never learned to stand up for themselves and properly communicate, which means they default to passive-aggressiveness and tend to lash out in "self-defence" when confronted with even the smallest thing. They also likely feel a mix of emotions at all times, including depression, frustration, low self-esteem, disillusionment, a sense of impotence, and powerlessness. Deeply hidden, yet still felt, they believe they are the problem, yet cannot face that within themselves, let alone fix it.

Healing the collapsed masculine energy requires a healthy dose of connecting with balanced masculine energy. This does not have to be in the physical. We can look up healthy male (masculine energy) role models, men we can see and feel are good people through and through, and start basing our behaviour and approach to life the same way they do. It might just be copying at first, but the more it is practiced, the more we reconnect with the Truth of our masculine essence, and the easier it is for this attitude and behaviour to become naturally our own. Ultimately, healthy masculine energy is part of the Truth of who we really are. We are just rediscovering it within.

This means that in order to fully heal and balance the collapsed masculine, we need to start identifying our fears and facing them while also identifying our real truth and speaking it. We need to uncover who we are in Truth, then learn to stand up for ourselves, value ourselves, and never allow another to treat us poorly again, regardless of our relationship with this person. We have to practice not being emotionally reactive to the slightest inference of accountability. This also means starting to act upon our healthy natural impulses and desires, the inspiration that wants to rise from within, instead of discarding them and believing there is no worth in pursuing them. A great way to solidify this is to actually finish one of the multiple projects we may have started and discarded.

In essence, we are taking a frightened child and reassuring it in ways that allow it to understand that it is seen, heard, and valued and that it is safe to be their true Self and communicate. Worth is greatly attached to masculine energy, as it becomes our strength and stability, which is our foundation of being. Without a healthy foundation of Self, the masculine energy cannot grow in strength. If the masculine energy is not strong in and of itself, then it cannot provide the strong support the feminine energy needs to thrive. This is why we must start healing these energies with the masculine.

We have to retrain our inner masculine essence by asserting our healthy wants and needs and understanding our place in this world, but never with violence. We do this by expressing our truth openly and freely, taking positive actions, communicating openly and honestly, following our plans through to the end result, and accepting accountability. Further, we learn to give without expectations or restraint. We learn to give and share freely and generously in a healthy manner, meaning not at the expense of being drained. We learn to be productive, loving, and safe within ourselves. We learn that it is okay to be strong in the knowledge of who we are and our innate strengths and weaknesses, and that we simply cannot be perfect in every way and, therefore, should not strive to reach an impossible ideal. We understand that making mistakes is a natural part of life, but our response to these mistakes is important in building our strength of character.

On the flip side, we can also encounter the distorted masculine energy. The driving force of this masculine energy is overwhelming to the point that it completely drowns out the feminine essence within, meaning that all of the feminine's gifts are lost to the individual in this aspect. The distorted masculine essence is incapable of processing emotions, meaning they will be explosive, volatile, domineering, and will never listen to others. They will believe that physical strength is the only strength of any value, they will constantly blame others for their own mistakes, never be accountable, have a desperate need to control everything around them, and will never feel empathy for others. To the extreme, this is complete masculine narcissism where the rest of the world simply does not exist or matter as long as this individual ends up on top.

This distortion of the masculine energy is also manipulative, always playing games with people instead of being authentic. They always play the victim and/or martyr when faced with the consequences of their own actions and are otherwise disconnected from life's true meaning and purpose in pursuit of Ego goals and values instead. These people pursue their goals like a charging bull, uncaring of who they hurt and what they break while getting to what they want, yet they are charging in completely blind, as they have cut off the source of their inner compass: their feminine energy. They are hyper-fixated on action and achievement at all costs (including cheating in all forms), as they are desperate for external praise and validation. Yet, they never feel fulfilled, just hollow, because they cannot connect with their own emotions, so they charge into the next goal to try again to feel something.

These people believe that resting is a waste of time and a show of weakness. They always need to believe they are constantly busy and better than everyone because, otherwise, they feel like failures who will be judged and persecuted for being weak (what they would do to someone they consider weak). They are terrified that this will spell out the loss of their influence and credibility. They are disconnected from and uninterested in seeing how their narrow-minded focus and consequent actions hurt and destroy others, nor how they deteriorate their physical and emotional states. These people see little value in others besides what they can take from them.

Due to their need to dominate to believe they have value, the distorted masculine energy will turn exploitative, tyrannical, and violent in their pursuit of power and control, and will demand submission from others. These are the rapists, the abusers, the ones who uphold rules and regulations to the letter without an ounce of mercy, empathy, understanding, or compassion while also believing those rules are beneath them and do not apply to them. They are the bullies, the racists, those who refuse differences and open-mindedness. In truth, these folk are all terrified of feminine power, autonomy, and sovereignty, and always seek to suppress what they cannot control.

Healing this distorted energy is usually easier said than done because it requires humility and a willingness to see how broken we are, which is a huge challenge for this type of person, as they are completely stuck in Ego. Healing asks us to reconnect to our emotions and process all those stuffed deep down inside. It also asks us to be still and present within, to learn and practice empathy, reconnect with the divine feminine energy within, and do so with love, acceptance, respect, and adoration. We can also practice becoming aware of our environment and how we treat people to re-evaluate if this is the kind of person we want to be. We have to choose to see the Truth of how our words and actions affect others and choose to change our attitude and behaviour. Outside help would come in the form of people who refuse to enable even a tiny bit of this tantrum-like state of being, but unfortunately, the work has to be done within.

Moving onto the unhealthy aspects of feminine energy, the response to the collapsed masculine becomes the rigidified feminine energy. When the masculine energy cannot shelter and provide for the feminine energy, she needs to step up and do it herself, which also means that she cannot properly fulfill her own role. She becomes overexerted, and the quality of her purposeful work is diminished, as the feminine essence is to be still, open, and receptive. She is meant to be flowing and cannot do so if she needs to enter the role of the protector.

Needing to step into the space of masculine energy means she closes herself off to her energetic power and essence and becomes rigid to protect herself. This means she loses the capability of being fluid and, consequently, her natural ability to attract what she needs as she is no longer centered in her own space and power. She loses freedom and receptivity and becomes destructive instead by becoming dry, harsh, and unyielding, as she always feels unsafe and unstable. She does everything alone, on her own, as she cannot risk her well-being by trusting others, and so chooses to isolate as she tries to revive her masculine counterpart.

Because she feels endangered, she is much more comfortable giving than receiving, taking care of people rather than letting herself be taken care of, since these actions make her feel in control of things and, therefore, safe. She is incapable of receiving support, letting herself be helped, and accepting compliments and gifts. Receiving feels dangerous, shameful, or humiliating to the rigidified feminine energy, as she interprets it as the notion that others think she cannot take care of herself. Receiving feels like pity, like feeling inferior. To this energy, receiving feels like being under another's power, being dependent on them to give what is needed; in other words, it feels vulnerable. Healthy feminine energy is comfortable in vulnerability, but the rigidified aspect is not, as she perceives it as a threat; it is an empty promise of fulfilling her longing to regain her natural state.

By being the one who gives, the rigidified feminine essence feels in charge because it is her *choice* to give or not. It can become a form of power play and manipulation. This means that when a person tries to give to them, the rigidified feminine will feel an overwhelming need to give back, to even the score because it always feels to them that there are strings attached to all gifts and that by accepting and not returning the gesture, it would mean they accept being under another's control. The same principle applies to being complimented, as she will simply deny the compliment, return it, or downplay it by pointing out her own flaws. We see this in gifts, where she will reject them outright, accept but disregard and never use them, diminish their value, or give back something often bigger and better than what they were given. Feminine energy is soft, graceful, and receptive; the rigidified feminine energy can be none of these.

Extreme independence is what feels safest to the rigid feminine energy, and as such, she will have a hard time delegating, never trusting that others can do things properly. This does not refer to high standards of quality but rather to the idea that no one can do it the way she can, as their way is the best way and the only way something merits being done, never believing anyone else can live up to her standards. The energetic vibration of this aspect of the feminine essence constantly rejects abundance in all its forms, regardless of how much work she puts in all aspects of her life, because she is incapable of receiving. This all leads to her believing in the forms of "nobody loves me," "nobody can take proper care of me," and "I am to be forever alone in this world and always fending for myself."

Healing the rigidified feminine energy will take the shape of practicing receiving gracefully, genuinely thanking others for what they offer, and doing these things without deflecting, rejecting, or criticizing any part of the process or ourselves. Instead, we must practice allowing ourselves to feel strong feelings of appreciation and gratitude. Additionally, since we are now aware of the self-fulfilling prophecy of the rigidified feminine being one of believing "nobody loves me," we can start catching ourselves in these patterns and making different, better choices for ourselves in who we allow ourselves to invest our energy. We have to make sure that we let in a supportive and loving entourage we know we can rely on, and through which we can learn to re-elevate our collapsed masculine, which is the reason for the existence of the rigidified feminine in the first place.

We also have to train ourselves to let go of our fear of receiving love to heal this aspect of the feminine essence. This means we go about relationships in two distinct ways when in rigidified feminine energy: we either throw ourselves onto someone indifferent, unattainable, emotionally unavailable, rejecting, or mean to us in an attempt to "conquer" them and prove our worth when we truly just struggle to acknowledge our innate worth, and therefore need to "prove" we can be loved by another while subconsciously believing we do not deserve to be loved, or we become bored of, annoyed with, and critical of someone with whom we have been with that has shown us nothing but kindness and caring, and who has given us plenty of healthy attention, solely on the basis that this feels too good to be true as we are not being triggered left, right and center, which is not our normal and therefore not comfortable energy to be in. Self-sabotage is big in this energy.

We have to realize that when it comes to the fear of being loved, it is truly a fear of being vulnerable, plus distrust that we are worthy of receiving love. This shows up as annoyance and criticism because we do not understand why someone can love us without holding it over our heads as a weapon against us, that love can come to us freely, without a price tag attached to it. The only way to start feeling safe enough to open up to receive is to activate, practice, and strengthen our protective inner masculine energy. We do this by standing up for ourselves, speaking the truth, establishing clear boundaries and respecting them, saying no and meaning/sticking to our answer, and removing ourselves from dangerous/uncomfortable situations without waiting to be "given permission" to do so.

We also need to take time to relax and get our feminine energy to step out of the masculine space and relearn to be ourselves. Pampering and treating ourselves to soft, loving treatments or care is a great way to reconnect with our femininity and help us make peace with it. Accepting letting ourselves be taken care of is a big one. Let the people who love you dote on you. Accept gifts and compliments without deflecting and refusing them. This can be tricky at first because of how automatic the rejection response is, but we can stop ourselves as we become aware of our doing it and simply choose to change our answer and approach. Do not be hard on yourself if you struggle with this; we are shifting a drastic wound here, and healing takes time and practice. We have to tend to, love, nurture, and care for our feminine energy for it to bloom in its beauty and essence fully once more.

Finally, we come to the final distorted aspect of energy found within us, known as the distorted feminine energy. In the same principle as before, there is a weakening of feminine energy through the rigidified feminine aspect, and now we will look at the overwhelming feminine essence. Distorted feminine essence comes down to being unable to process what is received, meaning that no matter how much is received or available for this person, they will always feel like they have nothing and will always seek to get more.

They act as a gaping maw of unending void, devouring anything and everything in their path while never feeling satisfied. They are ultimately never content with what they have and can become completely unhinged in their need to get more.

Some symptoms can include talking excessively and over everyone else, stealing or otherwise appropriating what is not theirs, being very demanding, deceitful, manipulative, and downright insatiable. The distorted feminine energy is akin to a bottomless pit of want, which is jealous of anyone else receiving anything. She is vindictive, entitled, feels unfulfilled, extremely needy, and attention-seeking. She is an energy vampire who constantly needs the focus to be on them and is selfish to the extreme. They make huge deals out of tiny events, are very dramatic and draining, are extremely insecure, and exhibit signs of "addict behaviour" when it comes to receiving attention. Anyone deemed to shine brighter than them is a threat that needs to be eliminated, and no manner of attaining this is too horrible for her to do. The end always justifies the means.

In all relationships, this person enmeshes themselves thoroughly with another until they become a form of parasite. They are extremely possessive, needy, and controlling. She seeks out, creates, and stays stuck in emotional turmoil and drama, will bring back old wounds to the surface just to stimulate stagnant and repetitive emotions, is addicted to drama and feelings of being out of control because of the rush of adrenaline she gets from it, and rebels against any and all forms of structure as she always sees them as prisons.

This distortion can take root because of unaccepting, or cold, Mother figures, and in repeated instances where there is the denial of, no connection with, nor validation of the Self through a feminine role model. Because they cannot process what they receive, no matter how much love they are given, the distorted feminine energy feels as though she never gets anything and will always demand more and more, as nothing is ever satisfying enough, *because* she cannot process what she receives. This person always feels poor, lacking, and in danger of starving. This can be taken literally with food as an example, where a person might overeat constantly because they do not truly process all they eat. They simply do not *feel* like they are eating enough, and are attempting to feel "full" in destructive ways. Nothing is ever enough, nor is anything ever appreciated.

Further, as the distorted feminine energy is overwhelming, instead of perceiving her surroundings as a whole and discerning her place within it, she will fuse her place with the whole. This means that instead of honouring her sense of individuality, she has none and bases her "character" on the people she has attached herself to. They subconsciously seek validation and mirroring of their core Self this way. In relationships, we see a similarity to the distorted masculine here in the sense that this person wants to be taken care of as one would care for a child. Yet, no amount of nurturing is ever satisfactory. They seek that parent/child closeness they never received from their care provider, so they depend on the need to bond with another, which was never fulfilled. She uses premature intimate oversharing as an attempt to force closeness and connection to bond, which makes her an ideal target for abusers and narcissists while also turning her into one herself.

Additionally, this makes being single feel like torture to the distorted feminine, as it will validate their distorted feeling that nobody loves and cares for them. So, it would mean she is worthless and consequently abandoned. Because of this, she will likely never be the one to leave a relationship, as it will feel impossible to cope without one, and it creates immense dependence. She will also feel threatened whenever one of the people she has enmeshed with expresses independence or expresses a like or dislike that is not the same as her own, which creates deep feelings of anxiety and anger. We can expect a rage-fueled meltdown when she does not get her way.

Because the distorted feminine energy cannot process anything, it comes as no surprise that she is an emotional ticking time bomb at all times. The surfacing emotions that explode are but a temporary release, as the core emotion is simply pushed back down until it bubbles over again, and so on, until she becomes healed and *can* process and release emotions again. She energetically pulls in all kinds of situations that keep her from accomplishing goals and further interrupt plans by keeping her in states of high drama and survival struggle that take all of her focus away. They constantly seek out high-adrenaline moments to feel alive instead of just being alive. She may also experience intense bursts of creativity, with multiple projects taking shape and demanding her attention. However, she is then spread too thin by wanting to do them all and cannot structure her approach because she overwhelms the inner masculine essence that would provide this stable approach and structure. Therefore, she never finishes any of her projects, which also plays against her sense of worth. This creates frustration, self-criticism, and a sense of being incapable and inadequate in all things.

As with the distorted masculine energy, the distorted feminine energy is tricky to heal in the sense that it requires great humility and courage to choose to see our flaws and admit our weaknesses and wounding. The key to this aspect is learning to digest or process all that is received in whatever form. This includes food, emotions, compliments, and anything else in between. We also have to break the habit of enmeshing our identity with that of another, and this is done by truly discovering, honouring, and embodying the Self. We have to see where we are abandoning the Truth of who we are for another's benefit or the sake of self-preservation. Enmeshment is *never* to be confused with empathy, as enmeshment is never a choice we make to feel another's emotions; it is a direct result of losing ourselves in another in an attempt to feel our own.

To heal the distorted feminine energy, we must choose to consciously distance ourselves from others to properly identify our sense of Self, learn our personal opinions and preferences, and accept them as they are, instead of validating them through another person before choosing to endorse them. We also have to remove our crutches from needing to control other people's actions and behaviours. We have to allow people to leave our lives graciously, on their own terms, and simply focus on appreciating them for having been there, regardless of what they contributed. We have to be able to fully connect with ourselves first before we can ever hope to connect to another truly.

Another great tool for healing this energy is to sit alone, undistracted, and allow ourselves to *feel*. We have to feel our feelings without allowing ourselves to be overwhelmed by them and consequently lash out. Journaling is a great tool to help with this, where we can sit and write everything out intimately and uncensored. We also need to reconnect with our bodies, meaning we need physical exercise. We need to move our bodies and feel ourselves connecting with them. Being in nature and communing with the flow of life are also great ways to find and reconnect with Self. Practice deep, conscious breathing. This helps particularly in processing deep emotions by breathing through them and helping them flow and release. Any form of artistic expression also helps, as one of the goals is to process and release any old emotional junk still stuck within. We have to externalize all pent-up emotions healthily, and creative outlets do wonders in releasing the unknown stuck within.

We use masculine and feminine energies in our everyday lives, or at least we should. Both energies must be healed and balanced on their own before they can work together in their intended, optimal fashion. Symbiosis happens naturally once both are balanced individually, helping us become flexible and adaptable to our environment, but also knowing how to attract what we need and protect ourselves from what we do not want or need. We have to remember that both energies have strengths of their own, different and complementary. We cannot achieve much in life by being stuck in only one. Just because the feminine energy's strength is less visible does not mean it is less powerful. Similarly, with the masculine energy's strength, though they are more visible, they are not all-encompassing.

When our internal masculine and feminine energies work together, perfectly healed and balanced, we can start understanding how powerful we are. *Everything* we ever dreamed of can become ours because we will have all the tools we need: the masculine's structure, drive, and focus, combined with the feminine's knowing, magnetic pull, and support. Like the Yin Yang symbol, they create perfect harmony within by each being the strength to the other's weaknesses, meaning that, whole and hale and in sync, these energies become an infinite wheel of strengths only.

Staying with the principle that what is true on a small scale is also true on a larger scale, we as individuals are also the Yin or Yang of all of our relationships, meaning that when we are fully healed and balanced, we still maintain a more dominant energy that goes hand in hand with our Soul's chosen nature for this lifetime. The most compatible relationships we will ever have will reflect this symbiotic balance. Again, energies do not care about gender or sexual orientation, as personal choices and preferences are ultimately irrelevant.

We can view this energy spectrum as a line where the opposite ends are fully masculine energy and fully feminine energy, with the exact center-point being true neutrality, perfect half-masculine, half-feminine symbiosis. Speaking of healed and balanced energies, a more fully feminine embodied energy type will need a more fully masculine embodied energy type of person to achieve a true symbiosis. We need our other side equivalent, and as long as we remain unhealed and unbalanced in either feminine or masculine energy (or both), we cannot identify our true position in this spectrum, therefore, cannot identify our true polar opposite, a.k.a. the people with whom we will have the most natural compatibility and therefore satisfying relationships with. Where we fall on one side of the spectrum indicates where our best match falls on the other side, just like a mirror reflection.

People who do not identify with a particular gender likely do not have very dominant natural energy within the whole spectrum, meaning their healed and balanced energetic state falls closer to the central line. As we are still in a world of duality, recognizing Oneness, it is unlikely that anyone embodies true centerline neutrality of the spectrum. However, through healing the world, we may come to an age where this will become the new norm. In the meantime, people who identify this way are likely not fully healed and balanced for either or both energies. That state may be close to that center line, but they are likely entertaining wounded masculine and/or feminine energy. Refusing to acknowledge having both these energies within is simply wounding that needs to be investigated and healed. Believing to possess neither is also wounding, as these energies are fundamental to existing.

Regardless of where we land on this spectrum, it is important to understand and accept that we all hold both energies within. Knowing where we stand on the spectrum, whether we are more feminine energy or masculine energy dominant, is another tool for us to interpret our human experience and interactions with others. It is a tool to understand ourselves better as well. Always remember that we cannot change anyone other than ourselves and that to heal means to release the need to control. Just because we want to help others does not mean we are the ones meant to help them. We can only help ourselves and inspire others to do the same. Remember to always bring your healing focus back to you.

If you have not done so yet, I recommend adding a section to your Journal where you write down which parts of these wounded energies resonated most with you—what you identified as things you did—and make sure to include every aspect that made you outright reject the mere possibility that you could be this way. Being honest with ourselves and overcoming the shame we feel towards ourselves and our perceived shortcomings is not always easy to do, but it is always worthwhile. When we truly wish to heal and actively work on our healing process, we will always come back to these faults of ours that we have tried to disown or hide from. Do not be hard on yourself if you let some things slip through. They will always come back to find you, as they are part of your vibration anyway. True healing takes time and consistency, combined with the bravery of accepting hard personal Truths for exactly what they are.

Chapter 11
Creating Healthy Boundaries

———— • ————

At this point, we are about two-thirds of the way through this book. This is an important moment where we can look back at our progress. Take a look at how you were living before starting this journey and how you are living now that we have done some exercises and have Journaled to better re-discover ourselves. Remember that you get out of this book the amount of energy you put into following its guidance. If you have done none of the exercises and have not started analyzing yourself honestly and impartially, do not be surprised that there are little to no results to show for no effort.

If healing ourselves were an easy thing to do, we would all be ascended masters by now. It takes discipline, commitment, and a willingness to always accept that there is more to work on without taking this knowledge personally. I want you to start noticing how things have shifted for you, be it your self-awareness, your awareness of your environment, your awareness of your entourage, and how they affect you, how much more connected to your body you feel you are, what has changed, and what has not changed. Do you feel better, lighter? Are you noticing you are more patient, or have more energy? Is manifesting becoming easier for you, so that you attract more of what you want and need in everyday life? Is your Ego still dictating your life, or are you allowing the energy of your Soul to peek through? What do you consciously choose to focus on?

Take stock of your own progress, and never mind how big or small you choose to perceive this progress to be. The Truth is that progress is progress, be it a step or a mile, and both are worthy of being honoured and celebrated. The trick is not to rest upon our progress longer than is needed to recuperate and be ready for what comes next.

When creating healthy boundaries, we always aim to honour ourselves and our space. It means respecting who we are and ensuring others understand what is welcome and what is not. Creating healthy boundaries is akin to establishing a perimeter around what we accept to receive from others and what we will not allow or tolerate. It means loving ourselves enough to know our worth and never letting others bring us down to their level or walk all over us. Creating healthy boundaries means authentically loving and respecting ourselves, and not allowing anyone to take that from us.

In this chapter, we will explore current relationships: those with external parties, with Self, with our inner child, and with our parents and friends. We will learn to love and respect ourselves, and how to make ourselves our priority in our lives. This last part may be triggering for some of you; if so, Journal about why. Women, especially, are conditioned and raised to be second to men and to serve them at all times. This sounds like an antiquated notion (it really is); however, just because we know it is stupid does not mean that it is not still happening and, unfortunately, ingrained in many cultures.

The United States, China, Christians, Muslims, and countless others still treat women as second-class citizens who are meant only to serve men, know their place, and stay quiet and out of the way. Be seen and not heard. This is still prevalent in our so-called "civilized" world. This is not to say that men have no problems of their own, but they have an advantage in being conditioned and brought up to know that they should be their first priority in their lives. Women need to unlearn their quiet servitude conditioning before they can truly put themselves first. The thing about privilege is that when we have it, we are never aware that others do not necessarily have that same starting point. Privilege is taken for granted by those who do not suffer from not having it. For the men reading this who are getting triggered: Journal.

A beautiful example of this comes from my former partner's family dynamic. His mother is the epitome of what you could imagine a loving and nurturing mother to be. Absolute unconditional love and support, at all times. You never run out of love when this woman loves you. Although my former partner has had his problems with his father and their relationship, at least he always had his mother in his corner, no matter what. Compared to me and my family dynamic of two closed off and shut down parents who struggled with intimacy and emotions, where love was always conditional and physical affection rare, I could not express to him just how lucky I felt he was to have had at least one "functional" parent to guide his upbringing and take care of him emotionally.

I remember thinking bitterly about how far I could have gone in my acting career (my passion) if I had had that kind of love and support to help me out as I grew up. Instead, I was left to my own devices, to figure everything out on my own, and I acquired a bunch of trauma and crippling self-loathing and self-doubt which kept me from truly pursuing what I wanted because I never felt worthy of achieving anything. I felt like my own parents did not love me, and that by default, anyone who was showing me genuine (free) affection had to be lying to me. How could others even fathom I held some form of worth when I was made to feel I had none for as long as I could remember? To be fair, my parents did what they could with what they had and what they were at the time, but it is truly no wonder they brought up two socially awkward, emotionally shut-off children with whom they do not have strong relationships.

As children, my brother and I learned that we did not matter, that our emotions were just a bother we should keep to ourselves, that we had to maintain an image of perfection to be worthy of receiving praise, and many more traumatizing lessons that shaped us into the adults we became, with little to no sense of personal identity. We were never allowed wants and desires; our job was to keep the peace. Therefore, it was no wonder that we both fell into abusive patterns with people who treated us just as poorly as our parents had. That was simply the energy and dynamic we knew, therefore what we were comfortable with, what we thought was "safe" and "familiar," because it was our "normal" growing up.

This is why it is so important at this stage to re-evaluate every single relationship we still have to this day to see if we are letting certain people we love treat us poorly, simply because that is all we have ever known from them. It is also why it is so important to have healthy boundaries, to protect us from people who claim to love us yet would stomp all over us every chance they get. Keep in mind that blame is useless, and refer back to the AAUR technique.

There is only ever what is, and what we choose to do with what is. My upbringing was what it was; my Soul needed me to go through difficult times so I could grow, learn, and heal, and for me to ultimately become able to write this very book to help others who also feel stuck in this life. If I had had a pampered life of luxury, I never would have faced the hardships that allowed me to choose to grow into who I am today, and therefore never would have been able to choose to help others who struggle with making sense of life. Everything always happens for a reason, but *also* always happens for our highest good. Our Soul-led highest good.

The Ego will rebel at this idea because it will choose to feel victimized by experiences instead of seeking out the lessons that need to be learned and the wounds that need to be healed; also known as *the very reason we chose to incarnate and consequently have attracted the experience in the first place.* Trusting completely in our Souls' plan and surrendering to it comes with time and healing, but for now, it is important to at least be aware of the Truth of things. People who will claim that this is a load of rubbish will likely not have faced many challenges in their lives, which is why they permit themselves to judge without acknowledging other people's very different experiences. If you have the privilege of saying life is not that hard, acknowledge your privilege and leave others be. Be grateful your Soul did not choose to undertake these kinds of challenges, and do not get in the way of healing for those who did.

Coming back to boundaries, it is excessively easy to forget ourselves for—or to allow our needs to come second to—those of the people we love. Although this does not seem problematic at first, the Truth is that it becomes unhealthy when we neglect ourselves for the benefit of others. Before we can truly take care of another, we have to make sure that we ourselves are properly taken care of first. Imagine that we are all individual cups that need filling. The best way to make sure they all become full is to have them fill themselves up to overflowing on their own, or with minimal help. When we are half empty, yet try to fill up another cup with our liquid, all we end up doing is wasting what we have, especially when we are not yet capable of naturally filling ourselves up on our own. When we do get the hang of filling ourselves up to overflowing by our own means, *then* we become able to help others achieve the same.

Depleting ourselves to make sure others' cups are full is an act of self-betrayal. With good intentions, to be sure, but then what happens when someone desperately needs help to fill up, and we wish we could help, but our own cup is already empty from helping others all around us? Do others share our generosity, or is it always up to us to help out? All of this to say that we cannot realistically help others when we cannot even help ourselves first. The nasty aspect of this reality is often pushed onto mothers, where it is glorified for the mother to sacrifice herself for her children and family constantly, yet she rarely receives the help she herself needs. The main reason we betray ourselves in service to others is when we do not value our own Self. This happens as a form of conditioning, by excusing the actions as acts of love. Whatever act of love requires us to deplete ourselves to satisfy an expectation of us is no true act of love.

Another aspect to consider is the gratitude received from such acts. Is there any? Is it an equal exchange where, when one gives, the other will provide the next time? Or is it always the same person giving over and over again? Remember that we need balance—equal giving and receiving—within all of our relationships, regardless of their nature. This includes spouses, parents, and yes, even children. There is a reason that when a plane goes down, the instruction is to mask ourselves up before we help another, to make sure we stay conscious and aware long enough to get the job done. The same principle applies in all of our relationships. We have to make sure our own needs are met before we can healthily attempt to do the same for others, all the while witnessing those who are grateful and choose to reciprocate versus those who drain us and demand more.

As we already understand that self-betrayal is a wound to be worked on, use your Journal here to map out all of your relationships and how they make you feel. Then observe the naturally existing patterns of giving and receiving within these relationships and see for yourself which are healthy and which are not. Pay special attention to those people you try to excuse or justify the imbalance of reciprocity between you, or those for whom you try to discard some actions taken by either party, and look for the whys. There may be deeper wounding involved than just the wounds around personal worth. When we love people, it can be hard to acknowledge that they do us more harm than good.

Notable examples of potential wounding could be fear of loss, when we would do anything to keep someone happy with us, for fear they will leave us. There could also be societal or religious conditioning at hand that forces you into the role of a servant to your husband (or to men in general) and tells you that this is "normal" and "expected of you." Keep in mind that sometimes the people who claim to love us but who do not understand the concept of love properly will be the ones who hurt and limit us the most, especially if they benefit from our current state of being.

The good news is that we get to change all of these things once we become aware of them. The more self-love and self-acceptance we practice, the easier it becomes to be our own person. Implementing healthy boundaries can be very difficult at first, depending on our environment. Supportive and loving people will never have a problem with us placing and upholding a boundary. This means that when someone negatively comments on, ignores completely, or brutally chooses to demolish our newly placed boundary, this is a HUGE red flag about the relationship we have with that person. They are openly telling us that they do not care for our well-being and certainly do not care enough to offer basic respect and decency. *Never* mistake these signs as anything other than what they truly mean. Controlling behaviour is never genuinely based on love.

Keep note of every single person and every single instance where someone has disregarded or disapproved of a boundary you have placed, as these people might be ones that need to be cut out of your world. We do this for our own well-being, regardless of the relationship we share with this person. Your personal well-being should always be your first priority. Anyone who tries to change or challenge your self-care is not your friend, even if they happen to be your parent or your spouse. Sometimes, having an honest conversation about respecting each other and each other's spaces, or even taking a break from them for a few days to a week or more, depending on the need, is all we need to set the relationship aright. However, some people will simply not care to accommodate us because they never have before, and they selfishly do not see the need to do so now. These are the ones we need to cut out, those that drain us and offer little to nothing in return.

Placing healthy boundaries can be quite difficult at first if we have never done it before. Not only are we doing intentional standing up for ourselves, but we are also respecting ourselves and asserting our needs. These are three strong self-love practices, and if we are not used to giving ourselves love, it can be hard not to feel like an impostor, or that we are asking for too much too fast, or even seem arrogant and selfish to those who have suffered long-term love deprivation. However, the more we practice self-love, self-acceptance, and self-respect, the more we will feel the need to place boundaries where people have not had the courtesy of respecting and valuing us in the first place.

The biggest problem with recovering from being the person who used to put everyone else's needs before our own is that we have essentially taught everyone that we always come second to them. We have also taught ourselves that our own needs should always come last. These recovering people-pleasers will likely experience intense stress at the thought of upsetting the balance of things by choosing to make themselves come first in their own lives. The likelihood that the people who had previously been taking advantage of them will just let them stop being abused without a fight is very low. The Truth is that being asked to betray ourselves for the benefit of others constantly is always abusive. We need to learn to stop being the doormat everyone comes to wipe their feet on, leaving a huge, dirty mess, with no care for the actual person, as they are expected to handle the mess alone and discreetly, as usual. If this applies to you, ask yourself why you accept being treated so poorly, oftentimes by the very people who claim to love you the most. This is not normal, and certainly should not be allowed to continue.

As you start placing boundaries, keep track of people's responses to them in your Journal, so that you may identify who is actually in your corner and who is not. People do not generally enjoy it when the things they take for granted are taken away from them. This means that the people in our life who are used to treating us a certain way, while also being used to being treated *by us* a certain way, can be upset at "losing" the power they had over us. Do not let this fool you. Some will try to shame and guilt you for having the audacity to demand proper, fair, healthy treatment. Lovingly tell them to mind their own business and continue on with yours. We owe nobody more than we are truthfully willing to give.

Work on attaining a strong sense of knowing exactly how you accept to be treated, how you do not accept to be treated, as well as the kind of treatment you will not accept ever again, and know to remove yourself from any person or situation that keeps asking you to betray yourself despite your new boundaries. It is your responsibility to draw the line and stand firm within it. Never let anyone disrespect your boundaries, for whatever reason, or you will have to start the process with them all over again.

Before we dive into what healthy boundaries with others look and feel like, we are first going to explore the boundaries we already have, or do not have, with ourselves. Contemplate these questions profoundly; you will find Journaling about them to be quite useful. I encourage you to write down these questions and answer them as honestly as possible, to really see how you are choosing to treat yourself. This will allow you to understand the dynamic you keep yourself in, and what you would want to potentially change or improve upon. We cannot have—nor place—new, healthy boundaries if we do not choose to treat ourselves with love and respect in the first place.

Do you ever find yourself doing things to make others happy, and if so, do you feel drained afterwards? Do you receive genuine thanks and appreciation when you do something for another, or is it taken for granted? Where in your life do you feel people take you for granted the most? Do others reciprocate your giving nature? Do they give more or less than you do? Do you accept being helped? Do you accept gifts easily? Do you take good care of yourself, physically and emotionally? Do you exercise? How healthy is your food intake? Are you comfortable in your clothes, and do you enjoy wearing what you own? Is your living space clean and fresh? How often do you compliment yourself? How often do you "treat" yourself to something you enjoy? How much time and energy do you invest in feeling good? Who are you allowing to make you feel bad? And why? How often do you keep promises you make to yourself? How often do you appreciate your body? How often are you kind to yourself? How often do you acknowledge your efforts? How often do you celebrate your successes? Feel free to add more of these kinds of questions as they come up for you.

Having healthy boundaries with ourselves means taking good care of ourselves. The state of our living quarters, combined with how we perceive and treat ourselves, is very indicative of how we truly feel about ourselves. When we do not love ourselves, we do not take proper care of our bodies, let alone care for how badly others can treat us. Our first priority here is to raise that self-love and self-respect bar of what we consider to be the bare minimum of how we should be treated, what we accept to tolerate from others, and Self. Love and respect go hand in hand. We respect what we love, and we do not respect what we do not love. Similarly, we do not allow disrespect towards what we love, yet we tend to tolerate or not care about disrespect aimed at someone or something we do not hold in love, depending on who we are as a person. Consider the amount of respect present throughout the above questions you have answered, and look to compare ratios with the presence of self-love in your answers.

At this point, it is important to understand that there is nothing wrong with wanting to help others; on the contrary, this is the intended end goal: every living being helping every other living being without anyone ever feeling depleted. However, we cannot give from an empty cup. This is why we seek to open the flow of water found within our cup so that it always overflows. This means that we can always give without ever depleting ourselves, and this is the true goal. This is true self-love and self-respect: taking care of ourselves first so we can *adequately* take care of others in turn. What we have to look out for is when others become dependent on our giving.

Dependence of any kind is never healthy unless it is a pre-agreed-upon arrangement that benefits both parties in equal fashion, also known as interdependence, where both parties are already in overflowing mode and only help better each other without ever feeling depleted individually. The key to knowing if an arrangement is good or not is in how balanced it is. Whenever one person is giving or receiving more, it means the balance is off, and therefore is not healthy. This is why we need to encourage people to fill their own cups, so we do not become a crutch for them to always rely on. There is nothing wrong with lending a hand to someone in need who is struggling to fill their own cup, but the intention should ultimately be to help them discover their natural source within.

Suppose we find ourselves becoming dependent on people being dependent on us. In that case, we need to see the Truth of the situation, which is that we are basing our worth on how much we give, or on feeling important because so many people "need" us. But this is just us lying to ourselves and glorifying unhealthy wounding instead of addressing it properly. We have to be honest with ourselves and stop making excuses as to why we "have" to help this person, or "have" to do this thing for that person. In truth, what we "have" to do for others are generally things we would want others to do for us, so we hope that by doing it for another, they will step up and do the same for us. This is selfish manipulation on our parts. We do not "have" to do anything, for anyone, other than taking proper care of ourselves.

On the topic of relationships, regardless of their nature, there is a common misconception that mistakes attachment for love. Just because we feel attached to someone does not mean we love them. Attachment is a dependent energy, whereas love is independent of attachment. Attachment is always conditional and quantifiable, whereas love is unconditional and cannot be quantified. Attachment is fear of losing them, whereas love is knowing that if they are truly ours, they are not going anywhere. If they do leave us, then they are not leaving in a painful, dramatic way to keep us hooked and preserved on the back burner until they deign to return. Attachment is fear and Ego-led; love is faith, trust, and Soul-led. Attachment is empty and needs constant attention, validation, and the need to feel fulfilled, whereas love already feels fulfilled and requires nothing more. Attachment takes without regard for the other, love gives and receives freely and abundantly. Attachment is one-sided; love is a completely mutual partnership of reverence and devotion.

There is also the misconception that love is only ever romantic in nature. Nothing could be further from the Truth, as love comes in many shapes and forms. Equating physical attraction to being in love is also a big misunderstanding of our current society, just as believing sex is always an act of love. We can already relate to other forms of love through the connections we share with friends and family, including pets. Still, there is no denying that everything is overly sexualized in this world, and so the default is to assume that if two people are close, then they must be fornicating. Share a laugh? Fornicating. Spending time together? Fornicating. Same opinion? Fornicating.

It is really ridiculous how far people will stretch their "logic" to accommodate the belief that the only time people can be around each other is if they are family or fornicating. Universe forbid we ever say we love someone if we are not fornicating with them, because that would just be a plain old lie, right? This also encourages the ridiculous notion that people are only to be seen as valuable when they are in a romantic relationship. There is this taboo created around being single, as though we should be deemed less valuable as individuals if we are not involved in a relationship. There is also the stupid idea that different genders cannot maintain friendships with each other because their only true desire must absolutely be to fornicate, as though different genders are not actual, individual people.

This leads to people rushing into relationships with literally anyone they want to fornicate with, regardless of whether they even like each other as people. It is also a big reason why some people choose to stay in miserable relationships instead of choosing to be single, because it's social suicide, right? Wrong. And stupid. When we truly love, respect, and value ourselves, we do not care about something as ridiculous as societal expectations, especially when those expectations are just toxic, lead to self-betrayal, and are ultimately pointless.

The Truth is that there are multiple definitions of what love is and what aspect it takes in any given connection. The Ancient Greeks, for example, with their advanced thinkers, the philosophers, gave an account of multiple different types of love. What our modern society describes as love today was known as Eros to the Ancient Greeks, who classified it as romantic, passionate love, as intense romantic *and* sexual feelings. This love has a constant baseline that has peaks of intense desire. Today's people believe that they have fallen out of love with someone when these peaks start to ebb, when the intensity of them dies out, but the Truth is that feeling that intensity constantly would drive a person mad, as there would never be satiety. They would never just feel satisfied and content with the natural flow of love; they would always be seeking the highs, to always get more, more, more, and it could easily turn destructive.

Solid relationships that last are based on more than just Eros. They rely heavily on Philia, affectionate or friendly love, and on Ludus, playful and flirtatious love, for in between the peaks of Eros leaving and coming back. Because nothing of high intensity can last forever, Eros will always run out of fuel, leave to recharge, then sneak back in through the back door to kindle the fire anew. Philia is also known as friendship, which does not need Eros, or physical attraction, to exist. This is exactly why we can have friendships with people of all genders; physical attraction is not important in this context. Both Philia and Ludus can exist in a platonic setting. However, because of societal conditioning dictating that loving someone means we want to fornicate with them, this is why we see people shying away from friendships with the opposite biological sex; they do not want to be seen as physically desiring these particular people, because they do not feel Eros for them. This is exactly why so many people struggle with just being kind to others; they do not want to be associated with physically desiring everyone they are kind to.

Let's address the idea here that having sex equates to making love. They are not the same. A primal, unfeeling, crushing need to achieve climax is not the same as a connected, shared, deliberate act of mutual loving. Procreating remains a primal need within humans, and this is done through sex. Making love is much more than the physical aspect of penetration (or any other variation of a physical act for various gender pairings). It is a symbiotic joining of two essences whose purpose is simply to fully enjoy the other and experience complete closeness, trust, and surrender with the partner. It is about mutual giving and receiving within the utmost respect and appreciation of each other. If this description is foreign to you, then I regret to inform you that you have never made love. This can be a call to look at how you are guarding yourself against experiencing total surrender and figure out what it will take to remove your armor. This is not something that is done with just anyone, as it requires profound trust.

The Truth is that we have to fully connect with ourselves and deeply love ourselves first, before we can deeply connect with—and love—another. Sex becomes a completely different experience when two people agree to be vulnerable, soft, and gentle with each other, where there is mutual trust and respect. This is when sex becomes more than just the physical coupling we know of. Emotional sex is a special experience, one to cherish and embrace, and is a major step up from just the physical act. This already boosted experience can still level up for us in the sense that the more we heal, the more we are capable of being in a constant energy of love, the more we become capable of opening up and being vulnerable with another, the deeper the connection and experience we can achieve.

When our inner masculine and feminine energies are healed and balanced in both parties, the connection between two lovers is intensified because we get closer to embodying our Souls, which are pure, unconditional love energies. Being in *that* energy when making love makes the experience absolutely out of this world. Two lovers in true, mutual communion together is one of the most beautiful things we can ever experience. This is a fun bonus side-effect to healing ourselves: it means we can experience life the way we were always truly meant to. This world, this existence, is magical in its own way; we just have to unlock and uncover how it can be the best experience for us on a personal level, through self-discovery, healing, and mastery.

Another type of love that the Ancient Greeks identified is one that describes people who fall into crazy and obsessive "love." They refer to it as Mania, but by now, we should be able to recognize that this is not love; it is wounding. Whenever there is talk of jealousy, stalking, violence, and codependency in what is supposed to be a romantic relationship, we should already know that these are wounds around security, worth, validation, and more taking over a person's rational thinking. We can clearly identify that these are people stuck in an out-of-control Ego and that the unhealthy Ego cannot love properly, as it is a survival mechanism.

The type of love that the Ancient Greeks categorized as the love we have for family and pets is known as Storge, or familiar love, which also represents feelings of patriotism and fanaticism for sports teams, as an example. Another longer-lasting feeling of love that was identified back then is Pragma, or long-lasting, committed love. It is love that ages gracefully, showing patience, resilience, and determination. All of these terms and concepts can help us understand and clarify all of our relationships. The Ancient Greeks also understood the concept of Philautia (self-love) and how important it was to be able to take care of and love ourselves before we could expect to love and care for others. Aristotle himself once said something along the lines of all friendly feelings expressed for others are actually an extension of one's feelings for Self. The opposite is also true when it comes to unfriendly feelings, meaning that all we express against others is a reflection of our internal feelings towards ourselves.

Finally, the last type of love understood by the greatest thinkers in modern history is known as Agape, or selfless, universal love. It is unconditional and all-encompassing, non-decerning; it is love for love's sake. Being in Agape at all times is the aim of our Souls, as it is their very nature. The first step to getting there is to start living life in Philautia energy, that of Self-love. Love has to start from within for us to be vibrationally compatible with receiving it from without, on the same level we can give. Living in Philautia energy is about understanding and embodying our personal worth and power.

We have already started exploring some forms of practicing self-love in previous chapters, such as decluttering our space, eating healthy foods, exercising the body and the mind, and getting to know our true selves better. Creating healthy boundaries is another form of self-love. Any action that brings us joy, happiness, and contentment is usually an act of self-love. We have to understand that when we engage in acts of self-betrayal, we are actually doing the opposite of self-love. This means that when we turn habits of self-betrayal into habits of self-love, we not only get out of bad energy, we also automatically fall into really good energy.

All of this to say that love is free; it is our natural state of being before we decided that fear should be. As seen above, love can be experienced in a number of ways without attachment when it is healthy. It does not require being attached solely to those like us, solely to groups we identify with. Love is universal. In my understanding, the only reason people are hurtful is because they have been deprived of love themselves and are acting out from a place of self-loathing. People who lash out against others are, truthfully, only ever lashing out at their own perceived energy.

Hurtful people do not love themselves. Therefore, they can easily be triggered by people who do love themselves. They lash out in an attempt to bring these people back down to their energetic level, so that they can feel better about where they choose to stay stuck in non-evolution. Instead of choosing to bring more love into their own lives, they tend to tear down love around them so they can stop being triggered by witnessing what they feel they are missing out on. They are refusing their lessons in healing, probably only because they do not understand what is going on inside them in the first place. This is why it is so important to continuously choose to keep being in the energy of love when dealing with these people, yet to also have firm, healthy boundaries in place so we do not get trampled by their attempts to squash our kindness. Having healthy and balanced inner feminine and masculine energies within means we can both protect ourselves and still offer unconditional love to all.

In fact, when we are mostly healed and in our personal power, we find that love flows freely from us, at no extra cost to our energy, because we are naturally in the energy of the overflowing cup mentioned earlier. At first, when we are developing the habit of being and living in this energy, it is important to take note of what has brought us to that vibration. What action, emotion, or thought has allowed us to embody this natural energy of pure unconditional love? This is not to say that when we are in this state, we never feel negative emotions, not at all; it simply means that we are capable of processing whatever is felt and releasing it before it can cause any damage to ourselves or others. This is emotional mastery, to be able to process and release easily without it disrupting the natural flow of unconditional love we are existing in.

When we get to embodying the energy of unconditional love this way, it can be extremely destabilizing and scary at first because we become naturally magnetic to others. We live in a world that is starving for love, and becoming a beacon of unconditional love will draw people to us naturally, which is another reason why we need to have strong, healthy boundaries in place to ensure we do not become depleted by the draining energies of other people around us. Asserting ourselves in our power, declining or redirecting attention we do not want, knowing our worth and how we accept to be treated are all boundaries we can practice having until they become second nature.

Let's dive into the root of the subject: what are healthy boundaries, and how to place and respect them. Basically, boundaries are really just the level at which we ask to be respected by others, which also translates to how much we really love and respect ourselves. Keep in mind that when we truly love and respect ourselves, we do not allow others to abuse, bully, manipulate, take from us without consent, and walk all over us. We are capable of standing our ground, saying no, and never tolerating people who ignore our boundaries, regardless of the relationship we have with them. Placing and upholding boundaries *is* an act of self-love and self-respect. It comes down to honouring our truth and honouring ourselves.

We have to understand here that a true boundary is always about our person and our environment. It is about what kind of treatment we accept from others. A healthy boundary is never about manipulating someone into giving us what we want. It never takes the shape of "do this for me and then I'll let you do that." That is manipulation, nothing more. A healthy boundary will take the shape of "I will not tolerate xyz behaviour towards me, if you will not stop, then I will remove myself (or ask you to leave)." A healthy boundary will always look like drawing a line in the sand that we do not allow to be crossed.

If a person chooses to ignore us and cross that line, then we *have* to choose to respect ourselves and remove ourselves from the person or situation. Trust that these people are showing you the truth of who they are through their actions. Every single person who disregards your boundaries *does not respect you*. Because they *choose* not to respect you, understand that *you owe them absolutely nothing in return*. Basic respect and decency are fundamental rights in how we accept to be treated. Never make concessions on this topic, with anyone, for any reason. You deserve better, period.

Examples of healthy boundaries are saying "no," "I'm not comfortable with that," "please do not talk to me that way," "I'm not available right now," "let me get back to you," "I do not want to," "I do not feel good when you do this," "please stop," "I am not tolerating this behaviour any longer," "when you treat me this way, it makes me feel like this, can we find a solution that works for both of us," and any other kind of variation of the above. The point is to identify where others are being invasive and making you uncomfortable, and to push them outside of your personal space and close the door.

In my own journey, because of my upbringing, I had no boundaries whatsoever, no self-love, and no self-respect. To say the beginning of my life in the outside world was rough is an understatement. People would use and abuse me left and right, simply because they could, in most cases, as I was incapable of understanding that what they were doing was wrong. I had no guidance, no reference to fall back on to tell me that this was not normal. On the contrary, this *was* my normal, so it never even occurred to me that it was wrong to begin with. As much as my wounding had me chasing being seen and valued by others, I was terrified of truly being seen, of attracting unwanted attention because I did not know how to make these people leave me alone. I was never allowed independence, therefore I never knew how to uphold my own sense of Self.

It got to the point where I would intentionally downplay myself through my appearance because I felt that no attention at all was better than some. I would dim my light to fit in and be accepted because I felt that if I did not take up too much space, there could be *some* space left over for me to exist in. I believed that if I could make myself small and unnoticeable enough, I could belong. This was because of my belief that I was powerless and worthless, that everyone's needs and wants had to come before my own, just as I had been taught as a kid growing up. I was so worried about hurting other people's feelings that I was not capable of caring for my own, much less understanding that my emotions were important to begin with.

Today, being in my power and knowing my worth, it is clear to me that I was incapable of taking up space, of speaking my truth, of even standing up for myself. I was constantly self-betraying, desperately trying to have anyone recognize even an ounce of my worth, which I did not even believe existed. More than this, I understand now that honest communication and firm boundaries are essential to creating the best possible space for ourselves to discover who we really are and what we really want. It is a great feeling to have people in our corner to help us learn and apply these concepts, but unfortunately, that support is not available to everyone, just as it was not available to me. We are more than allowed to say no to what we do not want to experience, and we *do not* have to justify our reasons why.

Another thing to keep in mind—which becomes self-evident when we stop to think about it, but may not be obvious at first—is that our society is divided into two types of people: those who ask for what they want and need and can handle being told "no" (Ask culture), and those who expect others to guess their wants and needs and do not cope well with being told "no" (Guess culture). Communication being the main tool for instilling boundaries, Guess culture is useless in getting things done. The true distinction between both "cultures" really comes down to who was taught how to communicate effectively and who was brought up in dysfunctional, abusive homes.

The simple truth is that no one is a mind reader. Therefore, expecting people to just *guess* what we want and need or to just *guess* how they are supposed to act in a specific situation, instead of communicating those things clearly, is toxic and harmful. It is the expectation that someone should do nothing other than pay attention to us all of the time, for every little thing to be able to respond to every whim perfectly. It is ridiculous and narcissistic to expect anyone to be so incredibly attentive to all the little details about us that could bring about *guessing* our moods and fancies at any given time. Anyone who tells you that "you should just know" is toxic and has a disgusting lack of character. Guess culture is a symptom of walking red flags. Choose to move on and cut your losses short by never enabling this type of behaviour. High-maintenance people are never worth the trouble. They are simply incredibly wounded people who refuse to work on themselves and expect to be catered to.

Additionally, how people choose to react to our boundaries is entirely on them, and entirely *about them*: it is never about us. We have to detach ourselves from feeling responsible for how others will react to us. We are never responsible for that. People can handle disappointment; let them. We have to remember that people can always choose how they want to feel at any given moment. People *choose* to have reasons to feel hurt by things, and when they try to make us responsible for their hurt feelings, it is always an emotional manipulation tactic. Again, this is mostly victim mentality coming back into the picture because, ultimately, *we are responsible for how we choose to handle our feelings.* Even if our emotions and feelings can be overwhelming, we always *choose* to dump them on others, or not. If you believe it is not a choice, then wonder why you are incapable of self-control, and Journal about it.

When dealing with other people's reactions becomes hard or overwhelming, remember that we are never responsible for another's actions, reactions, emotions, thoughts, shortcomings, personal healing process, and choices. We are responsible for our own, and that is it. People make choices; if they do not like the results or the consequences of their own choices, that is on them to deal with, not anyone else. We never have to believe we are responsible for other people's messes, especially not when we are told that we are at fault.

Other examples of healthy boundaries include saying no to people and situations that do not feel good, that do not uplift us 100%, where we feel drained and stressed instead of happy and thriving. Boundaries take the shape of being honest with ourselves about how we feel at any given moment, letting go of relationships that bring us down regardless of how long this person has been in our life, quitting the job that makes us feel dead inside, having tough conversations with people we care about where we explain how we feel they are disrespecting us and/or our space and how to fix the relationship from there. They are about choosing to stop being everyone's doormat, and a people pleaser in general. They are about being selective of who we let into our sacred personal space, and how we allow others to treat us. They are about how we choose to treat ourselves.

Having already explored questions about personal boundaries, we are now going to do the same exercise in our Journal, where all of the questions below should be answered about every single person you have a close relationship with. These will be to evaluate the boundaries we currently have with others and where we need to add some. The value of this exercise is found in answering as honestly as possible. Once you have gone through the list of close people in your life, repeat the same exercise but on a broader scale, meaning what are the answers to these same questions when addressed towards total strangers, or a job, or even to evaluate our response to a situation that occurred.

This exercise can be tricky when we answer these questions about the people we love. Allow for the true answers to come up, and do not allow guilt or shame to keep you from expressing the truth. Sometimes we idealize the people we love and turn a blind eye to how poorly they truly treat us. Remember that we are doing these exercises for our own well-being. Only you can allow change to occur if you embrace Truth instead of hiding from it. Write down everything honestly, regardless of how you feel about the answers.

In what context has this person ever made you feel bad about yourself or a situation that happened? How often do you feel pressured to do things you do not really want to be doing? Make a list of all the times this person has made their own wants and needs come before your own. Does this person meet your needs, and are they aware of you having basic needs without you needing to ask? Do they treat you differently when they want something from you than when they do not? Does this person sometimes make you feel as though you are less important than they are? When was the last time this person did something nice for you *without* expecting anything in return? Do they always keep their promises to you? What expectations do they place upon you?

How often do they not keep their promises? How many times have they told you they would do something, and they have not done it? How often is there tension and fighting when communication is sought? Are the fights disrespectful? Is there clear communication of wants and needs, or do you have to guess? Do you feel listened to? How often are you made to feel that you are bothering this person? Do you ever feel as though they would rather you simply not be around? Do you feel important and valued when you are around this person? What about when they are not around? Do they give you the silent treatment? Do they value your opinions? Do they acknowledge your preferences? Do they remember things you say? How often do they make you cry? Do they care when they do, or do they twist it into being your own problem/fault?

Have you ever felt disrespected by them? Have they ever taken advantage of you, or of your kindness? Do they respect your current boundaries? Do you have any in place with them? How often do they lie to you? Have any of these lies been damaging to you, emotionally or otherwise? Have they ever broken your trust, and if so, how often? Have they ever apologized to you? Have they ever apologized when they were the ones who hurt you? Do they treat you one way one moment, then shift to treating you a different way in other moments? Do you ever feel like you need to walk on eggshells around them? Do they acknowledge when you are in pain? Do they care? Do they try to do something about it? Do you feel loved and supported by them?

These are all meant to help you see the reality of your situation and interactions. Some of these questions are not easy to face when we are talking about loved ones, as we tend to want to protect them, especially when we know they are not treating us right. The key here is to shift our focus from caring about everyone else to caring about ourselves first. Once we truthfully care about ourselves, we can adequately care about others without betraying ourselves in the process.

In all honesty, anything and anyone that is holding us back and does not serve our higher purpose and highest good will feel heavy, dense, stressful, and/or draining. However, we may not be able to identify this ourselves at first if this is the only energy we have always been around. These may be people we love and want to keep in our lives, but who are just not helpful to have around. Remember that actions speak louder than words, that people's actions are the true tell of their character, and trust them accordingly. When someone shows us the truth of who they are through their actions, it is up to us to believe them. If we still want to keep them in our lives, then it is up to us to place firm, healthy boundaries with them and to let them know exactly where they stand, what is tolerated, and what is not. Never compromise yourself for these people, regardless of who they are to you. People who do not respect you do not truly love you.

The following are a few key tricks to have up our sleeves when we are first instilling new boundaries. Do not compromise your well-being for their "comfort," as this is just their Ego trying to hold onto the power they had over you previously. Know in advance what you want to say and how you want to say it. Have notes with you of the key points you want to discuss, as our memory falters under stress, and having these conversations can be very stressful. If you can, meditate or otherwise calm yourself and connect with your truth and your power within. This can be done before the conversation and even during if you feel your emotions are getting the better of you. There is never anything wrong with asking for time to process; do not let them keep you from being able to do this for yourself.

Additionally, *never* feel like you have to justify a boundary. You do not owe anyone an explanation. The nature of a relationship and the potential desire to keep this person around can mean we wish to explain our need/decision to place a boundary. Still, there is a fundamental difference between explaining and justifying. Explaining why we need a boundary will be simple, factual, and straightforward; it is not a conversation. Justifying equates to needing to validate the need by arguing for it. This opens the door to the other person arguing back for why we do not need this boundary, and from here, complications always ensue. We need a backbone to establish boundaries. We are not asking for permission to place a necessary boundary. Otherwise, we will never be allowed to place it.

When having these conversations, speak from a place of love instead of addressing the issue with anger and resentment, or any other emotion. We do not want to be overwhelmed and then lose control of ourselves during moments like these. If that happens, then excuse yourself and try again once you are calm and collected once more. It is possible that this person may not have been aware of how they were crossing boundaries; it could have been unintentional. It is okay to give the benefit of the doubt. Still, once it is given, the following actions they take are the truth of how they consider you, meaning that if they continue the behaviour that was supposed to be addressed by affirming the boundary, *they know exactly what they are doing to you, and are still choosing to do it anyway.*

Always be firm about what you are asking to change and offer tangible examples of how that change can be instituted. Be clear about how you would prefer to be handled and spoken to. Whatever happens afterwards is going to be up to you. These boundaries will be yours to maintain, and this may not always be easy. Do it anyway. Your future Self will thank you for your courage and perseverance. Courage is something that can be learned and practiced. Some boundaries will be easier to instill than others, some people will be harder to handle than others, but ultimately, placing healthy boundaries is about taking good care of your Self and your well-being. It is about self-respect.

Keep in mind that it is highly likely that these new boundaries will be tested, either by people or by the Universe. Our resolve and choice to invest in our well-being will always be tested to ensure that we are genuine in our choices, not just half-assing our efforts. These tests happen for us to see if we really mean what we are doing and saying, and that we are truly upholding our well-being to higher standards. We have to be genuine in our efforts (in ALL aspects of life) if we are to make true progress that lasts. Remember to be proud of yourself when you choose to have these conversations and set boundaries, because sometimes they will be very hard steps to take. Building up our confidence through instilling "smaller" boundaries first and encouraging ourselves to keep doing so by celebrating our successes is how we can bring ourselves to tackle the conversations that are going to be harder to have. The important thing is to start *somewhere* and build up from there.

Being proud of ourselves for taking the steps we know are necessary is such an important thing to do when we take them. These steps, as small as they may appear to be, are all indications of our progress in personal growth and healing. Being proud of ourselves is a profound and beautiful gesture of self-love, just as creating healthy boundaries is. We are essentially creating a safe space for ourselves to exist in, to discover and be who we truly are as Souls. Being honest and genuine with ourselves is a great way to raise both our perceived worth and self-respect, because we are creating a healthy relationship with Self.

The Truth of our essence can be learned through connecting with our inner child, with who we were before filters imposed themselves on us, and what we were excited about before society broke our free spirit through schooling and "growing up." Society has grown in such a way as to force us to lose touch with our inner reality in favour of our outer reality, by having us chase after money and objects. However, the moment we realize this becomes our starting point to choose to come back to our inner knowledge and knowing, and to consequently find the path we were always meant to be walking on. It becomes baffling to realize just how serious, boring, closed off, and out of touch society is. There is no greater self-betrayal than forgetting that we are all here to have fun, create, and exist in joy as a mutual energy exchange between us all.

The human experience is meant to be one of adventure and discovery. Self-discovery, certainly, but also discovery of all the wonders and magic this world contains. We are gifted this beautiful, abundant playground, where miracles happen daily, effortlessly, and we are meant to understand that we are just another miracle experiencing life. We are just as wonderful and miraculous as every Thing and every One else. We have simply forgotten this Truth in favour of the illusions created by "high society." We simply need to look at how children naturally are to see the Truth of this. Children are curious; they are enchanted by life, by their simple discoveries of life. *Their infinite curiosity, their need to play, explore, and test their limits, and their joy of being alive are the essence of what makes life worth living.* That pure state of experiencing being alive is the reason we are here in the first place. It is what we seek to rediscover within ourselves now, to reconnect with, as it is our purest connection with the Universe. This is why inner child work is so important.

There is so much we, as adults, have forgotten that can be taught to us through witnessing children. Their natural state of being is the state of being we need to get back into after having suffered, and despite suffering more later on in life. This is where we belong and where we should always seek to get back to. Childlike wonder, excitement, and joy of living are the true gifts of being human and alive. Take a moment to feel how living in this state of being every day can truly be magical, how *great* it would feel to live like this, in perpetual wonder and excitement for what is and for what is to come. It is our unresolved wounding that is keeping us from experiencing this energy daily, and is exactly why we should want to heal. We should want to become free to just live again.

Imagine how this world would be if everyone did their healing and went back to their original, intended state of being. Imagine *everyone* living in a state of awe, wonder, curiosity, excitement, camaraderie, and discovery. Imagine a world where everyone is taught to love unconditionally, to give generously, to receive gracefully and appreciatively, a world where we are all working together as one for everyone to be taken care of. A world where there is no war, no lying, no hurting others, no selfishness, where we are all free and equal, where we all respect and love each other healthily, where we never have to fear anything because our community is strong and supportive, where the people who need help receive it easily. A world where caring for others is also caring for our Selves, where gratitude is the currency and life is limitless.

Imagine a world where every single individual recognizes their true potential, their Soul path, and where achieving that potential is simple, encouraged, and supported. A world where we can all understand and recognize our purpose, how we are most useful, and take pleasure in serving the greater communal good, because *we know it will come back to us without us having to ask or fight for it.* This is a world where everyone does the right thing because it is the right thing to do, and doing otherwise would be considered nonsensical and not tolerated. No one is rejected because we all have a place we fit in, and no one is forced to fit in a box of expectations. Connecting with others is easy, effortless, and always a good experience. Imagine this kind of bliss of living for your children, and their children, and forever more.

We are in the process of manifesting this kind of world collectively. This is why we do the work individually: to help those around us shift and heal. Not only is this an achievable future, but it is actively happening already, by a single person making the choice to heal at a time. Even if progress is perceived as slow, it is still progress and keeps progressing over time. This world cannot and will not keep going the way it has been going, because it is not true to its own essence. This is also why this massive shift is happening globally; it is a return to our roots through healing distortion.

Let's focus on reconnecting with, nurturing, caring for, and healing our inner child. Allow yourself to rediscover who you were as a child before society started shaping your awareness and view of the world. Have a section in your Journal where you can write down the essence of your inner child, where you can safely discover who you were and what you have disowned. Look into what inspired you. What excited you? What brought you joy? What did you love doing or learning about? What experiences made you feel good and happy? What caught your attention and inspired curiosity? What were you naturally drawn to as a child? How did you choose to occupy your time? How were you creative, and what inspired your creation? This is not about what you were good at. It is about what made you feel happy and come alive.

How would you best describe yourself as a child? What was your nature? What made you *You*? What were your favourite memories, your favourite playtime, your favourite environment? What stands out positively from your childhood memories? What have you stopped doing that made you happy? What do you miss from your time as a child? Are there any activities you have stopped doing that you might want to start up again? Pay close attention to rejecting what you truly want to reconnect with. What keeps you from picking up this activity, habit, or interest? Realize that the answer(s) to the previous question is likely to be bullshit you are telling yourself because you *are not permitting yourself to be* in this childlike, playful energy.

Get curious about yourself as a child and choose to embody what made you feel vibrant and alive.

Reconnecting with our inner child can be as simple as a daily practice of going within, into our Solar Plexus energy, and meeting that inner child energy at different young ages, spending time with it, and nurturing it. When we have found the source of the energy of our inner child within us, we can simply exist there with it, by visualizing ourselves as children, and giving ourselves a big hug. We can visualize ourselves giving our inner child all the love it felt it did not receive. We can encourage them to crawl out of the hole they are hiding in and play with them, give them the attention they have been lacking, and are probably starving for. We can reparent our inner child into feeling loved and safe through this inner visualisation exercise. The more we do this, the easier it is to feel good and free within; the brighter we are allowing our Self to shine through.

Working with our inner child also becomes a great way of identifying and understanding our wounds. Add another section in your Journal where you will dive deeply within and uncover every single instance and experience as a child where you have experienced being shut out, brushed aside, invalidated, disrespected, disregarded, denied, ridiculed, bullied, etc. Seek out all the times where, as a child, you were forgotten, told to shut up and be quiet, where you have felt unloved and abandoned. Dig up all of the heavy-feeling memories and work through them. Where is shame present, and what is it hiding? Find all the moments where you were discouraged from being yourself or were not allowed just to be a child. Find out where you were being denied simply for existing as Self.

For every single thing that comes up in this exercise, I want you first to explore all of the emotions attached to them and name them until every single one of those attached emotions has a name. Do this for every single event, memory, person, and aspect that has shown up collectively, and dissect them individually. Then look at how these situations or events may have warped your understanding of the world and the people around you. What beliefs may have been created there that still show up in your current life? What wound seems to be trending? These experiences have influenced your unconscious mind and can help you unravel and understand the *why* behind some of your current wounding, or a pattern that you need to start paying attention to.

Doing this work will help you progress in your CA (current accountability) healing. Try to understand your childhood experiences from the point of view of a child to really get to the bottom of the potential wound(s). Because children are still learning about life, how to live, and how to interpret their environment, their understanding of situations can be very skewed by their perspective. It is very easy for children to misunderstand what is truthfully happening because their own perspective is being discovered, to say nothing of their having no sense of other people's perspectives.

An example I was given that illustrates this concept beautifully comes from one of my former mentor's client's experiences. Diving into the subconscious, this client went back to a childhood memory she had forgotten, where she had decided to believe her mother was always prioritizing her sister, which had to mean that the mother loved the sister more than her in her eyes. This, in and of itself, is a possible truth in certain family groups. However, the situation in question for this client, where she had fabricated this false belief, shows that it was not the case for her.

In this forgotten childhood memory, the two sisters were eating their dinner with the promise of dessert only if they finished their plates. Elder sister finished her plate and got her dessert. The client did not finish her plate, and did not get dessert. Her childhood self took this as proof that their mother loved her sister more than her, and that was where she created the false belief. She lived her entire life before that session believing her mother favoured her sister because of this "lesson" she learned as a kid, where she decided then and there that this favouritism must be 100% true due to her not having received dessert. She never considered not finishing her plate to be the actual reason why. A child's mind can only focus on one thing at a time, which can create false beliefs like this one. Is it logical? No. But it can be the only logical train of thought a child can conceive.

This is why we need to uncover all the pent-up, shoved-down emotions that have never been addressed: they shape our reality without us being aware of it through their vibration, their energy. In the above scenario, there could have been multiple different kinds of wounds that could have taken root in the subconscious, such as believing life itself to be unfair. Consequently, by living in the physical reality with that vibration, situations would arise continuously which would be perceived as further "proof" of this to the person, instead of them understanding that triggering this wound is how we are meant to identify and heal from it and that *that* is the reason why the situations appear in the first place.

Retrace the emotional events of your youth, discover what lessons you have taken from them, what beliefs you have chosen to create with the understanding you had as a child, and decide to release and liberate yourself from these. Not everything will come up at once, and some will be buried deeply where you cannot reach on your own. Do not be afraid to reach out to the people who were present in your childhood for stories that stood out to them, either as participants or as viewers. Become curious about yourself and your childhood to uncover more pieces of the puzzle that shapes your current identity. Even if these pieces seem like they do not fit anywhere, if they are coming up, it is for a reason; trust that and keep a spot in your Journal for them. It may only start making some sense when the right piece is discovered later on, and multiple things start falling into place together.

Take time to play with your inner child to let go, have fun, and enjoy every moment of life as though you were rediscovering the world for the first time. Let your emotions guide you in how you want to spend your time to feel the most joy and happiness at any given moment. Permit yourself to just run wild and free, although responsibly. Remove time from the equation altogether. Connect with your inner child energy within, nurture them, love them, and make them feel safe, secure, and loved. Cherish your inner child and allow them to come out as often as possible. This is another exercise of self-love and self-acceptance. It is part of facing ourselves and the Truth of who we really are. It means shedding the layers of bullshit we have built over our true essence, the layers of pretending we act upon for other peoples' benefit.

Let yourself return to the innate Truth that you are perfect just the way you are. You are valuable as your true self; lies and appearances hold no value. Only substance, character, and Truth have any real value in this world. You are worthy and worthwhile, but you have to let the real you shine through. Remember that you do not owe people more just because they ask for more. It is up to you to choose how much you are willing to give and to whom. Be clear about what you *can* give, and respect that for yourself. Lastly, be mindful, extremely selective, and very intentional in who you allow access to you.

Chapter 12
Taming the Ego

———————— • ————————

At this point in the book, we should be very aware of how our Ego operates, even if we have not uncovered all its secrets and tactics. As established in previous chapters, the Ego is a tool for us to use in our everyday lives. However, this tool has become distorted by its flagrant need to protect its host body. So far, we have been using our overactive Egos to identify internal wounding and fears, but also to understand our very actions, reactions, emotional outbursts, biased judgments, perceptions, hidden beliefs, and prior wounding. When we choose to incarnate as Souls, we create our Egos in the exact same way that we create our physical appearance, given the wounding we carry with us from past lives. This can be summed up to creating the perfect person and persona to meet and attract what we need to integrate and learn in this lifetime.

The more we work on ourselves, the more realizations we make about our lives and the world we live in. The more we choose to heal and face ourselves, the less our Ego needs to be overwhelming, simply because we will not allow it to control us anymore as we are healing its reasons for being overbearing in the first place. The only downside to this wonderful reality is that before getting here, we will have to fight our own Ego with teeth and nails to get it to release its hold on controlling us. The Ego needs to return to its original state of passivity, only taking over when our lives are truly in danger. This is the thing about the Ego: it is entirely a survival mechanism. When we do not feel safe, protected, loved, and free at all times, then we have to start understanding that we are defaulting back to existing in survival mode, the Ego's territory.

Because it is fundamentally a tool of ours, we will always have to exist with our Ego. Our goal here is to reclaim it as a part of ourselves, just as we have done with our emotions and thoughts. Consciously working on ourselves and raising our personal vibration are some aspects of reclaiming our Ego. Still, it is by choosing to truly give ourselves the unconditional love and support we need that we begin to chip away at the Ego's armor. Healing and balancing both masculine and feminine energies within is another great way to start the taming process of the Ego. All things within and without need to come into balance for this specific process to be able to happen. Otherwise, any unhealed trigger will immediately call the Ego back into the driver's seat.

It is when we no longer hold conflict within ourselves that it becomes possible to acquire our Ego as an ally in our experience, instead of always fighting it for control. The Ego and the Soul share the same symbiotic relationship as our masculine and feminine energies do: that of the Yin-Yang symbol. In truth, most relationships in life (if not all) will have this kind of symbiotic relationship for them to thrive. Once the Ego accepts the Soul's guidance instead of rebelling against it, we can achieve everything we want. The Ego can be seen as an aspect of the masculine energy, and the Soul as feminine energy. The Ego is the practical application, whereas the Soul is the quiet knowing and support.

Some of you will disbelieve this truth of associating the Ego with masculine energy and the Soul with feminine energy; for you, revisit the chapter on these energies, particularly their descriptions and the explanation of the Yin-Yang symbol. When we understand that we are truly all one and the same and that this dualistic world focuses on the split of masculine from feminine instead of seeing them as two sides of the same whole, we can start seeing these energies and their symbiotic relationship in *everything*. The Ego overwhelming the Soul's intuitive guidance is very much distorted masculine energy, as we can still see today in how women are treated by men in our societies, despite claims of "progress."

The societies we live in also demonstrate the distorted masculine energy in their rigid structures and their "only one way to do things properly" unyielding mindset. In these settings, people who choose to honour their intuition and follow their own path instead of adhering to the "official structured path" are seen as problems because they do not fit the intended format. Societies lack feminine energy as a whole in the world at large because historically, men have always ignored and diminished women. This speaks of the majority. There were still a few men with higher intellect and common sense who treated women fairly (or as fairly as was ignorable by society) despite the governing attitude towards them.

We are still finding examples to this day of men who took all the credit for women's work, especially in the biggest developments of science and technology. The person who discovered that the atom was the foundation of all life was a woman, yet few could knowingly name her. A woman invented wifi. A woman wrote by hand the coding necessary to send humans to space. Many of women's contributions and achievements were silenced and covered under men's names. Albert Einstein is a perfect example of this, as he was deemed a genius for his discoveries and advancements during his first marriage. He then mysteriously produced nothing of similar significance after his divorce, where his papers and research lacked the "creativity" they once held. Interesting coincidence, or it shows the Truth of things compellingly. Fortunately, many people are starting to rectify these wrongs by revealing the truth of the feminine brilliance stolen away by men. For those of you who are feeling triggered by these truths, Journal about it and seek to discover exactly what it is that bothers you, and why.

Truth always comes to light. Regardless of how much time passes, the Truth is the only thing that will last in time, because it has the only viable support. Lies, deceit, and appearances have no substance to rely on; they are all empty and useless and will eventually be debunked in favor of Truth. Going back to the idea that the Ego represents masculine energy within us, we must remember that its state of being is reflected back to us in the form of our experiences. How much we choose to take things personally directly reflects the health of our masculine energy: it should go without saying that the less reactive, the healthier. This being said, one of the biggest red flags our masculine energy offers up to us as a glaring need for healing is in the form of power struggles.

Whenever someone is desperate to hold power, whether they need to take things forcefully or show dominance physically by abusing the power they hold over another, we know we are dealing with someone with very wounded masculine energy. Likewise, the wounded Ego shows up in this kind of energy, needing to control everything to feel safe. The wounded Ego will throw all of your wounds, fears, doubts, and insecurities at your conscious awareness to prove that it should be the one in charge. This is why we have been hammering in the need to heal from within, simply because if the Ego has no ammunition to throw at you, then it proves to itself that it has no reason to be in charge. Inner peace is achieved in layers, similar to the layout of this book and its chapters.

Dissociating from our Ego can feel like losing our minds at first, depending on just how dependent we were on it. Going from living 100% in Ego to only letting it come out when it is truly needed may feel like self-betrayal, because our Ego state of living is the only one we have ever known up until the moment we choose to heal. The Truth is that what is happening here is our returning to the Truth of who we are, which our Ego could not let us access as long as it did not feel it was safe to do so. The Ego would rather die defending You instead of letting You get hurt. The Ego does not distinguish between others hurting us and it being the very thing hurting us in the first place. It simply identifies the *presence* of pain, or potential pain, not what brings it about. This separation from a state of constant Ego awareness and control is known as the Dark Night of the Soul. In a few words, this is a personal death and rebirth experience, where we are shedding and leaving the old behind to make space for the new.

In broad strokes, as Dark Nights of the Soul are intimately individual to our experience—meaning that if we have more than one, each will always be different—it is generally experienced as a very intense internal breakdown of consciousness. This state of death and rebirth will have you questioning your entire reality and existence; it will force you to come to terms with whatever is being removed from your experience. As counterintuitive as this may sound, this is a choice we make for ourselves to go through this experience (not always a conscious choice), that we may birth ourselves into a new reality, one that is better suited to where we are meant to go. Just like a physical birth is highly traumatic for both the mother and baby, in the case of a Dark Night of the Soul, we are both mother *and* baby experiencing both traumas as one.

Some of the symptoms of a Dark Night of the Soul include (but are not limited to, as each of them are highly unique and individual experiences) feelings of deep anguish and despair, re-evaluating the entirety of our life choices, purging old painful energy, releasing intense emotions through tears or otherwise, experiences of irrational fears and mood bursts that feel completely out of control and massive in scale. There can also be episodes of giving into victim mentality to the extreme and lashing out towards everyone and everything like a rampaging toddler, feeling completely disconnected from our physical bodies, experiencing multiple breakdowns, feeling completely out of control of our emotions and physical self, feelings of profound loneliness and alienness within, feeling like we cannot go on with living the life we have created for ourselves, wanting to start life all over again, being deeply dissatisfied with who we are and where we are in our lives, etc.

These experiences are never pretty, nor fun, but they *are* necessary, as they act as deep-cleaning, purging, and releasing of all that no longer serves us. It is akin to shedding baggage and consequently raising our vibrations. It is meant to break down and shake loose all the old parts of ourselves that have served their purpose and are now only holding us back. Everything we thought we knew is brought back to the forefront for investigation. It forces us to re-evaluate much of our inner world, to identify overwhelm and release us from it, or point us in the right direction for us to reach our Soul purpose. It will feel like stepping away from an old version of Self that was ready to die to make the necessary room to accommodate a new version better suited for a new beginning in life. Society is already aware of these experiences and has labelled them "quarter-life" or "mid-life" crisis, which is simply a point in time where a person's illusions of life are shattered by their discontent with going through the thoughtless motions.

Regardless of whether this has happened to you before and you know what I am talking about, or if this is new to you and you are now terrified of experiencing a Dark Night of the Soul, the message stays the same: do not worry about them. They happen when they need to happen for our highest good, and our only job is to allow ourselves just to ride those waves, learn what we need to learn, and let go of what already wants to leave us. Whenever this happens to us, it is extremely important for us to just be present and not to resist. This will make the process easier to bear by understanding that it is a valuable process and a temporary one. It is one big energetic purge to liberate our energy for better things to come. The AAUR technique is especially helpful here, as it helps us remove ourselves from experiencing this in a first-person view, to step back and allow. Acknowledge, accept, understand, feel, and let go.

As stated previously, a Dark Night of the Soul is never a pleasant experience, no matter how ready we believe ourselves to be to experience one. This being said, it does help to understand that they do not happen *to* you, but *for* you. In other words, it is not about preserving the Ego. It is about our required personal evolution to live life through embodying our

Soul. It is important to note that while this process is about purging old energies to clear our body for it to be able to even hold the vibration of our Soul, there are other factors involved such as planetary alignment and movement, divine timing, collective shifts and downloads, and other outside energies that play a role in the whole picture. This means that some of the energy that will present itself to us during a Dark Night of the Soul may not even be ours to begin with, but is one that we, as Souls, have chosen to assist in shifting and healing for the world at large, for the collective consciousness. Remember here that the Universe will never give us more to handle than we can.

Some of you will be triggered by reading this, by the idea that we have to deal with more than just our own shit, that we are thrown collective energies on top of our already potent cocktail of purging. This is our Ego crying victim again. If it is still not understood by this chapter, our individual Soul selves are part of the whole of Oneness. What we do for ourselves is consequently done for others, and what others do for us is also done for others. We are never separate from the whole by our individuality. We have to release this useless, selfish thought process and understand that we are part of the whole that is Oneness at all times, whether we like it or not. We have to learn to become healthily selfless, where we meet and respect our own needs while also caring for the needs of others in a way that does not drain us. We are meant to be of service to all, not just to ourselves, but we must start with ourselves first.

When we emerge from a Dark Night of the Soul, it is normal to feel completely exhausted, as purging and releasing old and heavy energies takes a lot of energetic effort, even if we are not necessarily aware of it. Depending entirely on the individual event, it may be that we start feeling great, at peace, focused, centered, and high vibrational mere moments after we emerge from the purging, or it may take a day or even a week before we start feeling the true results of the event. Afterwards, it is up to us to choose not to fall back into the old cycles that forced us into a Dark Night of the Soul to begin with. We have to choose to be and do better than we were, now that we are energetically free to do so. Do not worry if the changes are not immediately apparent, as it may take some time or need an energetic shift in the collective before the results can fully reach us.

We can understand these "meltdowns" as a caterpillar entering its cocoon stage to become a beautiful butterfly. In the cocoon, the caterpillar melts completely to reshape itself into an entirely different form. The same happens to us on an energetic level, so it is important to stay grounded when these events happen. We do not have to feel alone while going through this; we can have people we know we can reach out to, without necessarily having to explain what is happening, who are capable and willing to offer us support, spiritual or otherwise. Another person cannot help us go through a Dark Night of the Soul, as this is something we have to go through for ourselves, but they can offer a safe space for us to exist in or rely on for comfort. Sometimes, all we really need is the knowledge that if we need help, it is within reach, or simply to know that we are not alone. We are *never* alone; only the Ego believes this and gives in to despair.

There is always someone there to help and support us, regardless of whether this person is present in our physical reality or not. Our guides and angels are always around and generally wait for us to ask them for help before intervening when they do not specifically have a Soul contract with us to assist in our personal transformations. Refer to chapter six (Inner Guidance) if you need help connecting with your spiritual team, as this can only really be achieved by following and trusting our inner guidance. A certain amount of healing may also be required to ensure the necessary sensitivity to connect with them and receive their communication.

Another common Ego trap we can fall into during any major life event, such as a Dark Night of the Soul, is to believe that no one can ever possibly understand what we are going through. To believe that absolutely no one in the world has experienced something similar in nature (and wounding) to what we are experiencing is idiotic and self-absorbed at best. The Truth is that while all of our experiences are unique to our Soul, the collective healing required to shift Earth from 3D to 5D perception of living revolves around healing the same themes and wounds. This means that there are people in other grid sections of the world that *have* to go through something similar to us, in hopes that they will choose healing and therefore empower their own grid intersection, that it may help heal adjoining grid intersections, that finally all grid intersections might one day be healed and balanced enough to evolve and upgrade as a whole throughout the world.

This, combined with the fact that we are all One and connected through Oneness, means that there will always be people who can empathize and relate to our personal, individual struggles, because they will have gone through something similar energetically, if not physically. By healing individually, each of us contributes to healing the collective energy we are a part of, and this collective grid is worldwide. The big picture here is a completely healed and shifted world that allows for Soul living in peace, ease, and comfort, where everyone and everything within lives in symbiotic harmony. There are no struggles related to lack, as there is no lack. We are completely fulfilled and connected to the Earth, and we have learned to listen and to just be present as Self.

Those of us who will be going through this process first as the vanguard of change will have to deal with people who refuse Oneness and want to stay in Ego, simply because they feel threatened and do not know how to deal with their triggers in a healthy fashion. As we have learned at the beginning of this book, we cannot force learning and healing upon anyone: it is always a personal choice we have to make. It is up to us individually to choose, through free will, that we want to be the best version of ourselves we can possibly be. We cannot change others; we cannot manipulate or control them into choosing the best for themselves. That is and always will be a personal choice, a choice we make through free will. Remember that attaching ourselves to the specific outcome we want is not healthy; we have to allow the Universe to work in its own way, independently of our Egoic desires.

As a very important sidenote, we must respect where every individual is in their own healing journey, along with how much effort they are willing to invest in bettering themselves. Some people will simply never have the courage to face themselves honestly, which is okay. It is never about us. Some people are meant to be disruptive, challenging us to further our personal growth. We have to trust that the Universe knows what it is doing, and that ultimately we are all serving our purpose the way we are in the state we are in, even when we cannot understand how or why, and even when we are not even aware of it. We know that we need to experience contrast to evolve. Therefore, some people exist just to make us experience that contrast.

We already know that the will to change can only ever come from within. This means that we will have to deal with unpleasant people and situations in our lives, and that the best way to navigate these occurrences is to remain in the energy of unconditional love, as our own first priority. These are not unnecessary moments for our Soul's progression; on the contrary, they show us just how much we are embodying unconditional love, or not. When we are triggered, it is up to us to manage that emotion and to identify exactly what it is within us that is yet to be healed. Triggers are clues to uncovering our wounding. We have to choose to trust in this process and to deal with what comes up in a healthy way. Losing ourselves to our triggers is never healthy.

Dealing with triggers from strangers and random occurrences is only one aspect, however. Some of the hardest triggers and lessons we may experience can occur within the family unit or among a tight-knit group of friends. These can be especially tricky to navigate, as we usually wish to keep these relationships. The best advice I can give is to be true to yourself and to respect both your Self and your boundaries at any given moment. Live and let live. We do not need to change people's opinions and perceptions of us; the Truth is that attempting to manipulate how someone views or thinks of us is very Egoic and indicates wounding around worth. We have to choose to work on ourselves, give love to others in a way that does not limit or drain us, have strong, clear, healthy boundaries, and not take anything personally. The last part of that sentence—not taking anything personally—is especially crucial and is the focus of this chapter.

So, how do we release the hold of our Egos once and for all? First, it should be clear by now that the Ego is simply one more tool in our physical vessel to help us Light beings navigate the human experience. We have already established that the Ego is a survival defense mechanism, which is highly reactive to emotional triggers. We have done a lot of personal work on identifying when the Ego takes over and what it sounds/feels like. From this point forward, how much we choose to allow our Ego to take over is entirely in our own hands. There are no more legitimate excuses for us to hide behind. This is where healing comes into play: the more we heal, the less our Egos have triggers to stand on that keep it from going back to being dormant in the backseat.

This being said, that our Egos get triggered while we are in the process of uncovering wounds to heal is natural. Therefore, it is up to us to handle ourselves and to remove the grip of our Ego from controlling our actions and reactions. We can get triggered and still be masters of ourselves. We can learn to hold back our Egos and choose to be in the energy of unconditional love. Being reactive and out of control is always being in Ego, and it never helps anyone, ever. I cannot speak for your experiences, but in mine, no one has ever attained anything of significance by yelling, throwing a temper tantrum, and being aggressive; otherwise known as being in Egoic reactivity. Two people yelling back and forth at each other without bothering to listen to each other are akin to two dogs barking furiously at each other through a fence with saliva spewing everywhere: no sign of intelligent life anywhere in sight.

Anyone who has ever yelled at me never got what they wanted from me, regardless of how big or small what they wanted was, nor how "right" they might have been. How we choose to address others is a huge clue to the state of our own wounding. Whenever we treat others in a way we ourselves do not wish to be treated, we are in distorted Ego. We have to remember here that how we treat others is a subconscious tell of how we view ourselves. Having no basic respect and decency towards others means we generally have no basic respect or decency towards ourselves, because ultimately, we are all one and the same. How we value and treat others is indicative of how we value and treat ourselves on a subconscious level.

Choosing not to be in Ego following experiencing a trigger does not mean we experience no emotions; it simply means that we do not allow the emotions to overwhelm us, which is exactly what puts the Ego in control in the first place. When we are out of control of our Selves is when the Ego takes over to do some damage control. Being in control of ourselves means that when we do experience strong triggers, we can keep ourselves in check, to allow the emotions to be there and exist, giving us the message they need us to know, while consciously choosing not to be reactive and lash out. We need emotional self-mastery before we can master our Egos. We have to understand that our emotions are temporary messengers and are meant to leave us after the message has reached our awareness. We are responsible for our reactions, regardless of whether they are conscious or not. It helps to be grounded, to feel stable and secure during this process, and to have something to support *us* over our egos.

The third step is to *get over ourselves completely*. We have to release the illusion that we are important, better than others, that life is a competition. We must release the need to be right and learn to listen instead, as there is no true right or wrong. There is what is decent and what is not. There is what is hurtful and what is not.

Every day we face a single choice over and over again: do we choose to be kind or to be an asshole. If you are not falling into the kind category, there is only one other option we can find ourselves in, as choosing to be indifferent is akin to choosing not to be kind. Being kind never equates to betraying ourselves. If, in choosing to be kind, we are actively betraying ourselves, then we are not genuinely being kind: we are letting others stomp all over our boundaries. Being kind will never make us feel bad, drained, and unfulfilled.

Only people who abuse us will make kindness feel this way, and that we allow ourselves to be abused is to not love ourselves properly by having healthy boundaries that help us recognize what is acceptable and what is not. Some of you will be triggered by the idea that we choose to be abused (Journal about it). We are. Consciously or unconsciously, we choose to allow the abuse or not. This does not mean that we hold the victims accountable; on the contrary, the focus should be on re-educating the abuser. It simply means that when we become aware of letting others abuse us, it is up to us not to hide from the Truth of it and to consciously choose something else for ourselves. Choosing kindness does not mean that everyone else deserves our kindness, but rather that we are the first beneficiary of said kindness. When we know someone is trying to manipulate us by using our kindness against us, we can simply refuse them. Being kind does not mean being a doormat or acquiescing to every demand made of us; it means that we choose gentleness in our approach instead of harshness. We can give the benefit of the doubt, but their reaction will be their answer that we must trust.

On a Soul level, we choose to make ourselves experience abuse in a Soul contract with another Soul for the express purpose of being able to identify it; it can also become a lesson needed to heal specific wounds. There are many stories out there of when a victim called out their abuser or otherwise stood up for themselves, the abuse stopped completely. The abuse was identified, then rejected by the "victim," and the lesson had been learned by the simple fact that the person chose they wanted something else, something better for themselves. Therefore, the contract was fulfilled, and the energy was removed from the person's vibration, meaning that they no longer need to attract these types of scenarios in an attempt to heal the inner wound.

This kind of realization is part of getting over ourselves. It is part of not taking anything personally. It is the only way to fully step out of Ego. We have to shed the need to prove ourselves, to compare ourselves to others in any and every way. We have to take off the weight, the pressure we place upon our own shoulders to be a certain way or to do the "right" thing, say the "right" words. There is no way to "be" other than being our True Selves. There is no other way to behave than to exist in our Truth. There are no right words other than those that come straight from our Souls. We have to give ourselves the space to just exist as our true selves, to accept exactly where we are, as this is the only starting point we will ever have. We have to allow ourselves to be human and to make mistakes; to live and be alive.

We have to embrace and value our imperfections, not try to hide them in shame. How sad to believe our imperfections are anything other than perfect for where we are currently on our journey. We chose this life for ourselves, and it is up to us to make the most of Life and living, and to embrace the Truth instead of hiding from it. We have to choose to be grateful for all that we currently have, and to witness the beauty and miracles that are ever-present in our lives. We choose what we want to focus on; how we choose to view things, how we shape our perspective. We have to choose to love and nurture ourselves, to believe in ourselves and our potential, to reparent ourselves into being healed, whole, and hale. Most importantly, as this is the fourth step of overcoming Ego, we have to choose to stop giving in to fear.

All the choices we are presented with in life can be summarized into choosing fear or choosing ourselves and our Truth. This is what is known as free will. We get to choose to learn the lesson and move on, or not to learn the lesson and stay stuck in a given cycle, doomed to repeat the same circumstances over and over again until we do choose to learn and move on. This always happens because we choose fear over our well-being. This fear can take on any shape it wants, to be the most convincing it can be. Our fears do not want us to learn and move on. They want us stuck exactly where we are, unmoving in our comfort zone: limited, small, staying behind our own self-made prison bars and walls.

It is always a choice we have to make to set ourselves free, and we have to make it over and over again until it shifts from being a conscious decision to pushing ourselves to make it into a healthy habit that is simply automatic. We have to continuously choose to stop limiting ourselves, to stop saying no when we really want to say yes, and to start taking "risks" that bring us one step closer to attaining our goals. We have to allow ourselves to start dreaming again, to listen to our passions and desires, and to give ourselves the right to pursue them. The intention should never be to chase fortune or fame; it should be that doing so speaks to our Souls and makes us feel alive. It contents us in a way that nothing else can. We have to start finding excuses and reasons why *we should do what calls to us*, not to discourage us from pursuing our ambitions.

We have to choose to be happy, follow our joy, stop worrying and fretting, and open up and trust the Universe and our inner guidance, as they only want to bring us where we want to be. We have to be brave to trust. We have to choose to allow ourselves to be excited by all that life has to offer. If any of these ideas are triggering to you, Journal about them and be curious as to why you would refuse yourself happiness and wonder. Joy. We have the power of choice, and our triggered wounded Ego robs us of these choices by making them for us. This is why it is so important for us to understand that we are the ones in power, we are the ones running this show, and it is up to us to regain control of the reins.

The Ego becomes obsolete and can stay dormant until truly needed when we understand and apply a few key principles of Life. Some of these principles include knowledge that we have the power to shape life exactly as we want it to be *once we are healed, balanced, and aligned,* meaning that we are aligned with our Soul's purpose. We cannot attract whatever we want through selfishness. The Universe works with our Soul's needs, not our Egoic wants. Another crucial thing to understand is that we must surrender the specifics of a manifestation to the Universe, meaning that we ask for what we want with a broad intention and release the desire to the Universe. We must surrender the need to know the how, who, what, where, and when of our manifestations taking physical form. Trust that the Universe already knows exactly what is best for us, and that this is what it aims to deliver to us. To try to control how things should happen, or with whom, is to be strongly in Ego and will always backfire. The tighter we try to hold on to controlling behaviours, the less likely our manifestations are to come about.

When we reach a point where our Ego can understand (of its own free will!) that it is no longer needed, that its purpose for being around is not being met, it can finally retreat to the backseat and go back to sleep. Just releasing the Ego this way can be extremely draining to us, especially if the Ego was overactive for a long time. This is our emergency operating system; therefore, it needs to constantly be in high alert when it is active. When it can finally relax, we will likely get hit with huge amounts of fatigue because our nervous system will be crashing after being solicited so much, so intensely, for so long without real pause or rest. This can only happen when we come into inner peace and balance and trust completely in the flow of the Universe. It happens when we finally feel safe in the world and within ourselves.

Which brings us to the crux of the subject: inner peace. Truthfully, achieving inner peace is the only way to get the Ego back in check and relax into a dormant state again. How much inner peace we can achieve internally by doing the work outlined in all previous chapters will indicate how much control we can wrestle away from our Egos. Those who choose not to work on themselves and heal their inner workings will have a tough time not being controlled by their Egos, and as long as the Ego is in control, the Soul has no room to manoeuvre.

With that in mind, when we start the process of working on ourselves, our biggest resistance will come from the Ego. This is why, in the beginning chapters, I ask that you follow the trail of your strongest resistance. The Ego is averse to change because it sees all changes, everything outside of its control, as threats. Since the Ego is a survival mechanism, it would never willingly choose to expose itself to threats, which is why we can expect to experience strong outbursts from the Ego that are themselves out of control. Our Egos are always just trying to do their jobs to protect us. It cannot differentiate between bad change and good change. The Ego does not work in nuances, as it is a masculine energy feature.

Taming the Ego is a process of disillusionment, which is started in Part I of this book. We gain inner peace to inform the Ego that its purpose to be present is now non-existent. This can, of course, cause a Dark Night of the Soul as we gain the understanding that we are not our Egos and that it is not meant to be in control anymore. Dissociating from our Egos to gain a state of Soul presence can be a huge tower moment— a complete disintegration of our perceived reality—the first few times we engage in this process. As with everything else having to do with healing, it is a process of layers. We learn to shed layers of Ego over time, and once the first layers—the heavier ones—are gone, it becomes easier. If doing this shedding of Ego does not change or transform your perspective on life, then you are not actually doing the work.

Once the Ego is shed, our entire perspective has no choice but to change. We are shifting from triggered survival mode to peaceful, contented living. At first, peacefulness can be very challenging for us to be comfortable in, and we will likely call it boring. The Truth is that peacefulness is not boring, but it is so calm and stable that we confuse this unknown state of living with boredom, because we are not constantly triggered or on the go anymore. We must make a conscious adjustment to live a life of calm, peaceful stability, especially when all we have ever known is pressure, drama, chaos, and being in overactive Egoic energy.

Because of this shift, we have to realize that once we are not living through our Egos anymore, we are living in a state of being, thinking, knowing, and understanding life outside the norm. Outside of Ego, we do not chase highs constantly, because we are well balanced within. This does not mean that we never have fun; it just means that we choose to have fun in everything we do, instead of needing an outlet for maximized fun, because otherwise, we feel we do not have time for fun. We can easily become outsiders to our group of friends or family, simply because we choose not to engage in what we used to crave engaging in. Anything that feels like it would be volatile, or out of synch with our Truth, will simply feel like too much to be bothered with, like it would take from our energy instead of giving us something we thought we needed in our previous state of being.

As stated previously, change is not comfortable to the Ego. This means that when we choose to shed our Egos, the people around us may want to force us back into the role they are comfortable with us having around them. It is up to us to have strong, healthy boundaries and to respect ourselves above this kind of selfish behaviour. We may also become extremely triggering to others, because they see us as "levelling-up" (though they would never label it this way) while they still consider themselves stuck in the same place. We have to understand that it is never our job to betray our Truth to coddle those who are afraid to face their own.

When we shed layers of Ego, our vibration naturally rises, which means that those whose vibrations are too low to sustain being around our own will need to level up themselves energetically, or naturally be driven away from us because they cannot stand the energetic challenge our vibration now imposes on them. This is never a bad thing. We are meant to let go of and release all that does not serve our highest good, be it people, places, or jobs. The Truth is that if they are meant to be in our lives, they will return to us of their own volition, in an upgraded energy. We are never meant to make ourselves smaller to content others, regardless of the nature of our relationship with them. We have to embrace ourselves and our Truth wholeheartedly and choose not to compromise our personal integrity when we face resistance against our uncovering of our true Self.

Having gotten to this point, it should be clear that there are no coincidences and that everything happens for a reason. This is not just a pretty sentence to sound wise and knowing, it is a Truth that we come to understand and embody through inner healing. We see the proof when we look back at our journey. We have to choose to believe first to see, not the contrary. If we have to see to believe, then we are not in the energy of trust, and if we are not in the energy of trust, then we simply cannot surrender to the Universe. If we cannot surrender to the Universe, then how can we possibly manifest what we want and need? We cannot, and so we are forced to grind and slave away at trying to attain our goals all on our Egoic own.

All of this to say that when our vibration rises, we have to let go of the dead weight of those who do not want to work on themselves. We must never hold on. If they are meant to find us again, they will. If they do not, it means that someone or something infinitely better for us is meant to reach us in their stead, through the void their "loss" creates in our vibrational field. Loss is an illusion. Fear of loss is the fear of illusions disintegrating. This is why letting go is so important. Not wanting to let go is just another facet of needing to be in control, which only happens in Ego. For those who are meant to stay in our lives, when our vibration rises, it forces their own to rise as well if they choose to stay, simply because it would be too triggering for them to be around us otherwise. Being incompatible energetically creates conflict automatically. How we choose to deal with said conflict is up to us, but surrender is often the answer.

A perfect example of how to understand this concept is through romantic relationships. When we get with someone, the general idea is that we are in love and want things to work out together with this individual. The very reason this person stepped into our lives is due to a Soul contract between the two of us. We have found each other vibrationally, and therefore, physically, we were brought together to engage in this contract. In other words, we were vibrationally ready for it, which drew us together. As we know, Soul contracts make us grow as individuals, and we like to believe that when we are with someone, they will turn out to be our person, meaning that our search for external love is over. As we also know, this is not always the case.

When we engage in a relationship with someone, we exchange on multiple levels, although the predominant one is the vibrational exchange. Even though we want to make a relationship work, if the exchange is not balanced 50/50 in energetic terms, the relationship itself will not be healthy, and is likely to fail as needs will not be met for either one or both parties. The person who over-gives will feel drained, while the person who over-receives, while not returning the energy, will grow arrogant and contemptuous because the exchange will not be valued as it should be. This creates a sense of self-importance in the over-receiver, to the point where they will start feeling like they deserve better than what they currently have.

This is the danger of putting someone on a pedestal: they will never view us as equal. This only happens in Ego, because the Soul does not engage in non-equal dynamics; the Soul respects itself far too much to allow unfairness. This is especially important to understand, as the Soul never allows unfairness to unfold, regardless of whether it has to do with them personally or not. People in Soul energy have a strong sense of justice *that helps all*, not just a select few. There is no desire for reward for "doing good," as fairness is akin to basic logic and understanding of how things should be. Unconditional love, joy, and fairness are the very basis of living in the Soul and are understood as the default way of being. No thought is required, as it is second-nature in how obvious living this way is or should be in a healthy society.

Coming back to relationships, when we are involved in one that is not equal (not fair), we either choose to stick it out in hopes that the person will change, or we leave. As a general rule, when we betray ourselves in service to someone who does not appreciate us (by over-giving), we tend not to want to be the one to leave because "insert bullshit excuse" which generally has to do with "we love them." The truth about over-giving is that *we do not love ourselves sufficiently*. If we did, we would not bend over backwards trying to satisfy someone who ultimately does not care about us enough to take notice of all the effort we put in, and certainly does not reciprocate those efforts, and will ultimately never be satisfied no matter how much we actually do.

The point here is not to blame the other partner in this scenario, as we are the ones who choose to over-give. We generally do so because of our wounding, which is why this book aims to identify and heal these wounds and false beliefs. This also happens on an energetic level, even when we are not aware of it, which is why we feel drained. Ultimately, these scenarios should bring us to ending a relationship, if we value and respect ourselves enough to make our self-worth, self-love, and self-respect come first. There are only so many chances worth giving before we should come to the conclusion that this kind of dynamic is not working and that we deserve better.

On the other hand, we have to be aware of when we are being the over-receiver. It is always easier to see ourselves as the victim than as the perpetrator, and the Ego refuses the idea that *we* could ever be the asshole in any circumstance. The Truth is that we all have moments where we genuinely are not good people. It happens to everyone, and we need to get over this fact. What we have to do is to identify when we are choosing to be an asshole in these moments and choose to be and do better. This means that if we find ourselves being the over-receiver in a relationship, it is up to us to choose to re-balance the giving and receiving, or to move on, which leads us again to breakups.

A break-up will be especially hard the more in Ego we are. In Ego, we simply refuse to release this person and will betray ourselves over and over in an attempt to keep them in our lives, to go back to the way things were. There are many reasons why breakups can occur, but in the energetic sense, it is usually because the relationship has run its course. The lesson becomes letting go and moving on as signs of self-love and self-respect. There may have been specific energies that needed to be brought to our awareness through this relationship, such as codependency, trust, insecurities, self-awareness, etc, which factor within the energetic exchange and balance between the two, as a relationship is made of much more than just physical giving and receiving.

When we are in Ego and cannot accept a breakup (regardless of being the over-giver or the over-receiver), all that we need to work on in ourselves will surface. These can manifest as feelings of having invested too much in the person to want to let them go, of there not being anyone else but them for us in the entire world, of "it has to be them" or "no one else will do," of "why is this happening to me," "I don't want this," "I don't want to be alone," "better this than nothing," "but I love them so so so much," etc. All of these are wounded Ego coming through and playing martyr/victim at the "unfairness" of the world, while completely ignoring how unfairly they were being treated or were treating others.

Removing the Ego from the equation of a breakup allows us to see the Truth of the relationship. When we can see that Truth, we can understand exactly why we need to move on, and we can choose not to make a fuss about it for no reason. Grieving is very human, and we must take the time to properly let go of a person on all levels, including emotional, vibrational, and energetic, not just physical. As long as we do not do this, we will be pulled into a cycle of returning to each other over and over, to exactly no change from either party. The vibrational/energetic connection will not have changed, and it will simply be more of the same until we choose to love and respect ourselves above this relationship.

When we remove the personal attachment of the Ego, we understand that whatever is happening is not truly about us personally, but rather about what we need to experience for our wounds to become apparent. Fighting a breakup, for example, is akin to fighting against our own Soul, which wants what is best for us at all times. We are essentially refusing a lesson in self-love, self-respect, and self-worth, or how to properly value ourselves. Some of us will be stubborn enough to completely drain ourselves by railing against what we do not want, instead of just accepting what is, and this may be exactly what we need to get to the conclusion that we want better for ourselves, that we deserve better than how we have been acting. The point here is that refusing the reality of what is because we do not like it is completely pointless and serves no one.

The alternative is to accept the lesson as soon as it is understood, which translates as letting go of the other and choosing self-love in this example. A healthy person does not chase someone who treats them like trash. When we do choose ourselves, we will be tempted by the Universe to go back on that choice, to go back to choosing self-betrayal. This is another lesson, a test to see if we were genuine in our initial choice of letting go or not. Instead of seeing this as appalling and trickery from the Universe, we have to understand that to "level-up" vibrationally, we have to genuinely mean what we say and do. Authenticity is the path to a Soul-led life. We cannot fake our way to Soul-living. We also cannot fake our healing and personal development.

Just because we have accepted a breakup does not mean we have learned our lessons, which is why the Universe needs to test us to see if we can recognize when we fall back into self-betrayal in either a new relationship, or by sending this person back to us with empty apologies and words of potential change happening, but that will never actually be instituted in the relationship. As long as we choose not to heal ourselves, we stay stuck in our wounding. Since we are stuck in our wounding, we can only ever attract the same dynamic vibrationally over and over again. We cannot "give up" on learning a lesson, because that is just our Ego throwing a tantrum.

This brings up the question: "Is it possible to go through life without ever learning any lessons or experiencing any self-evolution?" As a theory, I believe the answer would be yes—but what, then, would be the purpose of a Soul incarnating to live such an empty and seemingly useless life on a personal level? They may choose as a Soul to live a lifetime of accumulating karma, to incarnate in future timelines with the purpose of healing and evolving. Remember that we are here to experience contrast, and that it is impossible to contain all possible life experiences in a single lifetime. The purpose of the Soul is evolution, so unless they need to create bad karma to experience big contrasts in later lifetimes, then there could be Souls incarnated with the sole purpose of hurting as many other Souls as possible through contracts, both for the potential healing of the "victim" Souls, and their own potential evolution in their next lifetimes.

The way I understand things, because we always incarnate with a Soul purpose, the Souls currently here with the purpose of healing and evolution will have some lessons that are very important for them to learn in this lifetime. Ultimately, these cannot be ignored nor circumvented: these lessons become the very reason for incarnation, therefore the greatest emphasis is placed on learning these, with smaller (some optional) lessons thrown into the mix to get us to access potential healing for these main ones. These smaller lessons can be viewed as tests to see our Soul progress, meaning that if we learn a significant lesson "earlier" than our Soul had traced out as the probable moment of learning, then the smaller lessons for us yet to face to get us to the main lesson will drop away on their own, simply because we do not need them anymore to get us to access the main lesson that has been learned "early."

The perfect example I have for this is where I have decided to move beyond my former mentor and not accept scraps as a just reward for my hard work, which was a big lesson I had to learn in my life. I had initially felt energetically called to work with her through a healing modality she taught. However, the working "deal" she offered me was that she would send me her clients, I would do the full sessions on my own with them, and she would collect 50% of the price payment. She would have essentially turned me into her own private cash cow, where I would exert all of the effort while she did nothing and split the earnings 50/50. This meant that if she brought me ten clients, I would only need to find five on my own to get the same paycheck, although investing my personal time doing sessions would be cut by half. If I did 50 in a month through her, I would only need 25 on my own for the same paycheck, yet with double the amount of free time available for myself, cutting my energetic expenditure by half.

To think for a second that this "deal" made any kind of sense for the party being used (aka me) is ridiculous, and openly shows how little she valued me, my energy, and my time. When I chose to refuse this offer, it was when I understood that it had been a test from the Universe. Did I really want to go back to being used and abused by someone I had placed my trust in? The obvious answer now is no, but I felt I desperately needed money to come in at the time, and that anything would be better than nothing. I was willing to betray myself for scraps—for the bare minimum—once more, until I realized that someone who genuinely loves and respects themselves would never agree to such a bullshit offer.

That realization and consequent choice of loving myself and putting myself first in my own life turned me from being willing and eager to work with her to disgusted and feeling energetically repulsed by her. I knew our relationship would never be the same again, and it was time for me to move on and stand on my own two feet. I felt my vibration rise higher than hers, which is the reason for the energetic repulsion, as she was unwilling to meet me on equal footing, and I was done betraying myself. If I had chosen to take her offer, I would have found myself running right back into the familiar cycle of self-betrayal to appease or content someone else's Ego. This principle of free will is perfectly illustrated in a concrete example.

What makes this story even better is that a few weeks after offering me this "deal," she sent out a blog calling out another healer who also uses her own students as her private cash cows, which is what she wanted to do to me. This shows exactly how our external reality—what we see in others that triggers us—is reflecting our own Selves, our own wounding, either directly or indirectly. It is up to us to put our Egos aside and recognize when we are being less than stellar. Still, more importantly, we have to figure out the why of our behaviour to identify and subsequently heal the evident wounding properly. In the case of my former mentor, her inner feminine energy was rigid and distorted in different aspects of her life, including the need to feel superior to others. I felt that she resented me because she thought I was progressing in my own healing at a faster pace than she was, and it triggered her Ego. She needed me "beneath" her to feel better about herself.

How miserable and unhappy a person is in their personal lives directly reflects how hard someone is fighting against learning their lessons, by rejecting their Truth and Soul purpose, instead of embracing change. When we are in lasting emotional pain or hurting, it is when we are refusing Truth and refusing to let go. This brings about the eternal questions we need to ask ourselves to remove the Ego's hold over us and allow more of our Soul Self in: How am I not being authentic right now, in any given situation? Am I respecting myself above what others want from me? Am I even willing to give them what they want? Would giving it hurt me in any way? Would it drain me? What is my true motivation to oblige them, and is it worthwhile? Am I making my needs come second to their wants in this situation? What is my Truth, and how am I denying it?

On the Ego side of things, the questions require honesty. Otherwise, progress is impossible. Am I taking advantage of this person willing to give me their time and energy, or am I being fair? Am I taking this person's efforts for granted? Am I valuing them for their true worth, or the worth I perceive them to have? Am I viewing myself as being above another? When we do not like our answers to these questions, we know we have found the truth. Being honest with ourselves takes practice, discipline, and the willingness to grow as an individual, especially when we do not like what we find. The more we resist seeing ourselves impartially, the more we are in Ego. Humility is required for healing tenfold.

Humility has to become our default, but humility never implies selling ourselves short, nor downplaying ourselves so others will feel better about themselves. Others can handle their feelings, as this otherwise would simply translate as a lack of self-respect. Humility is also never arrogant, never belittling, and never makes another feel less-than. Humility is about knowing and respecting our worth. Humility is knowing, understanding, and living the Truth that we are all human beings, we are all just humans, we are all here to learn, heal, and grow. We are all here to evolve our Souls, to become the best possible version of ourselves, by our choices and consequent actions. We free ourselves from the Ego by achieving inner peace, which can only be achieved by embodying and practicing humility. We cannot be at peace within if we are not humble first in seeing ourselves objectively and the Truth for exactly what it is.

Any time we make someone or something else responsible for our pain, we are in Ego. What is important to understand is that pain is just another messenger, and placing blame keeps us away from receiving the intended message. Forget about the rest of the world and focus on your Self. What are you meant to learn and understand in unconditional love through this pain? Being in the energy of unconditional love is to remove the Ego entirely. The Ego wants to blame and wants someone to pay, instead of realizing that what occurred happened for a reason, and that it happened *for* us. This is a hard concept to accept for those who are new to spirituality, to understand the Universe and our Souls.

As long as we are low vibrational and stuck in Ego, we cannot accept Truth. We have to choose to do the work, we have to decide to keep an open mind, to receive the possibility that we may be wrong in what we think we know. As long as we have difficulty accepting truth for what it is, all we have to do is keep an open mind to the possibility that all of this *could* be true. The moment we reject the possibility of being wrong, we are stuck in Ego. When we stop self-evaluating and do not want to heal, we default to Ego. Understanding and connecting with the energetic intricacies of Life comes naturally, the more we choose to work on ourselves and allow ourselves to heal, so do not worry if everything seems chaotic. If we have difficulty identifying Truth at first, all we need to know is that what resonates or triggers within us does so for a reason, and that Truth will stick around while lies and deceit will fall away on their own. Truth flows, the rest stagnates.

Anyone who believes they have all the answers, and who shuts down anything that is not their own as being wrong without even stopping to consider if there are parts of Truth within the greater whole offered by another, is strongly stuck in Ego. The best metaphor for living in Ego vs. living in Soul would be to refer to Ego as solid, unyielding wood, and to Soul as bamboo; pliable, malleable, yet strong. Bamboo can bend to extremes without ever breaking, whereas solid wood cannot. Bamboo can handle anything thrown at it with grace. Bamboo flows, just as life does. It does not resist, it allows. We must train ourselves to become like bamboo trees. We have to train ourselves to be open-minded about our beliefs being wrong so that we may identify and feel the vibration of truth. This is how we free ourselves from our unhealthy Ego and teach it how to interact with the world properly.

PART IV

SURRENDERING TO THE UNIVERSE

We are now starting the final part of this book. Interestingly enough, when I first had the idea for this book and made an outline of topics I knew I would be talking about, I would always come back to knowing the book format would be 4x4, meaning four chapters for four individual parts. I had no idea what these chapters would be or what they would contain; I was only gifted the knowledge of the titles I would be using. Even then, I would only receive a few, never all 16 of them at once. When I was ready to write the next ones, the titles would come to me, and I would have to trust that my hand would write what was needed as I channeled from these titles alone.

I started this writing journey with no idea what would come, if anything would come, and if it would ultimately be worthwhile to read. Beginning this book took a complete leap of faith, where I had to surrender the need to control how things would turn out and choose to trust that the Universe would support me and give me exactly what I would need every step of the way, when my Soul (never my Ego) needed it. Now here I am, with this book published and physically in my hands, knowing that worldwide success is a possible outcome awaiting me as I write these sentences into being. I carry no doubts, only knowing and faith that everything will always work out perfectly for me, even when I cannot see or know how. Even when there is no "proof" of any of this yet, as I am writing these words. Faith does not require proof, but Enlightenment and Ascension require us to live in faith.

This is the state we are all invited to be in 100% of the time. Following our inner compass of personal bliss into our Soul purpose, alignment, joy, and ease of living. Into what it truly means to be human as a Light being—an energetic being—experiencing humanity, emotions, and contrast that will ultimately lead us to bliss. We are now entering the final part of our transformational journey. This will seem the easiest section of the book, although it cannot really be fully integrated until progress has been made in all three previous parts. Although the work to be done within the last chapters seems lighter, as it is less self-confrontational, it will still require dedicated effort on your part to want to upgrade and evolve.

Surrendering to the Universe requires us to be completely unaffected by fear, limiting beliefs, and wounding. If you have done little to no healing, this section will be interesting to read as a preview of what is possible, but your energetic vibration is simply not ready for this kind of work. If you have started doing the required healing from all three previous parts, and you have started to see changes physically in your external world and within your internal world, then you will be ready to start this part, although more inner work will be required. If you are still not on board with the terminology used and the more spiritual approaches to understanding life introduced to you in this book, then you are not ready for the next part. It will still be interesting to read to plant the seeds of knowledge in your awareness until you become ready for them to sprout later.

This last part of the book will be for the people who have actively chosen to work on themselves and have uncovered the better part of their wounding. This part is for those who have developed a daily well-being practice, as detailed in the previous chapters. This part is for those who are willing to put in the effort and who genuinely want better for themselves through healing themselves. When you have fully absorbed and applied all the teachings in the previous chapters, when your Ego is sound asleep in the backseat, when you are ready to commit to drastic changes, when you can see the blessings in even the hardest situations, and when you are ready to take in your Soul—or at least begin that process—is when you will truly be ready for these last chapters.

This part is about fully connecting with and integrating our Soul, to become an energetically capable anchor that can sustain such a high and pure vibration within physical reality. This is exactly why the people who have not done the work will never access the full potential of these chapters. We and our surroundings must be of the highest vibrational energy possible, or else the Soul simply cannot be integrated, as it is not an energetic match to lower, denser vibrations.

In this last part of the book, we will be deepening the connection with our Soul and with Source, we will practice efficient and powerful manifestation, and learn to get what we genuinely, in Truth, want and need. We will follow our inner guidance into the energy of total surrender to the Universe and our Soul's plan for us. There is no room for doubts here, no room for fears, nor wounding. Reading through these last pages will likely trigger many of you at first, or many times during multiple read-throughs. That is okay. Use these opportunities to learn more about yourself, and as always, keep digging and Journaling.

Let's discover together exactly what your Soul wants for your best possible future, and the infinite possibilities of the Universe!

Chapter 13

Connecting with
the Heart of All from Within

———————— • ————————

We already know that all the guidance we need comes from within. The trick is not only to recognize it, but to allow ourselves to believe that it is true instead of immediately dismissing it. Sometimes we will get insights that seem absolutely nonsensical or of trivial importance, and our job is to choose to follow them regardless. This could be something as simple as being nudged to use a different route for our everyday commute, or to pick red when we usually pick blue. The smallest hits of intuition could be the most important ones we need to heed. That is why we need to practice our intuition to the point where we can recognize it instantly, and also instantly recognize when it is the voice of our sneaky, unhealed Ego trying to take over.

The important thing to understand by this point in the book is that when we align with our Soul purpose and choose to head in the direction of our higher calling—our greatest good—we will feel light and excited, as though nothing can get in the way of our success. This is usually when the mind starts getting in the way with its unending stream of reasons why we will never accomplish what we set out to do, or just by having a bad attitude in general. We have to remember that doubts never come from the Soul. They are engineered by the mind, by the Ego, to keep us exactly where we are in our comfort zone. Any unhealed wounding and false beliefs associated with success will also keep us from fully engaging in the process of achieving our goals as well. We should always feel expansive and limitless when we are truly tapping into our Soul purpose, and it is that feeling of bliss that we need to follow. It is our compass.

On the other hand, when we let our minds dictate which way we should go, when we find ourselves doing things as a means to an end that does not call to us—when we do things that do not come from the heart's guidance—we will end up feeling drained and dissatisfied, and no closer to our true goal. What is meant by this is that instead of taking a leap of faith and choosing to go full throttle towards the true goal (our higher purpose) we want to achieve, we tend to start adding obstacles to our getting there, which generally have little to nothing to do with getting us where we want to be. How our body feels about our choices is also an aspect of our inner compass that we need to start tuning into.

This theme of self-sabotage can take many forms, but one of the most common ones in empaths and light workers is self-sacrifice. We can be masters at deceiving ourselves into believing that being of service to others means making sacrifices regarding ourselves to benefit others. An example of this would be to stretch ourselves thin by wanting to help everyone around us, while it leaves us with no energy to take care of ourselves properly. As a general rule, it is far easier for us to put our needs and wants on the back burner to help others get their wants and needs met first. We may believe they will then reciprocate in turn (and some may), or they will move on to the next person they can mooch off of until they are left high and dry like us. This is why we need to be careful of energy vampires, those who always take while never giving back.

An interesting concept to explore here, however, is the very subtle Ego energy that dictates this, putting our wants and needs on the back burner. The idea that the Ego is the one who directs this self-sabotage, this self-betrayal, may seem counterintuitive, because we believe being of service is a good thing. It is. But *only* when we are doing it without depleting ourselves in the process. We self-sacrifice in service to others when we do not believe we are worthy of receiving. We bend over backwards to accommodate others while not seeing to our needs first. This gives us the feeling that we are a hero in someone else's story, but the truth is that these people do not need us that way, and we are deluding ourselves into thinking that making another's needs come before ours is being of service to them. This idea could not be further from the truth.

The Truth is that they would be fine without us interfering every time. We have to understand that other people can care for themselves, no matter their circumstances. Our job is to take care of *our Self.* We all love to believe that helping others at our own expense means being selfless, and that this kind of behaviour is commendable. It is not. Self-betrayal is never praiseworthy. When we decide to "help" others while our own cup of well-being is not overflowing, we over-extend ourselves in unhealthy ways. We are actually chasing a need to validate our worth externally. "Look at how much of a great person I am." We need to prove to ourselves that we are good by seeking that kind of approval from others through external appearances.

When we do good things because it is the right or good thing to do, for the right reasons, we will never feel the need to brag about it, nor to inform others of our goodness. Doing the right thing because it is the right thing to do is its own reward. Needing others to approve of our doing these things is extremely Egoic. When we are genuinely helpful people, we never need our good actions to be recognized or validated externally. We do not seek external praise. There has been a trend of people filming themselves giving food to the homeless, and other "watch me be an extremely selfless and commendable person" videos. This giving in and of itself could be a good action, however the videos all have a common theme: the "generous" and "giving" person has to be central star of every second of it, while we see in the background the homeless person being completely ignored, as they had served their purpose of having received the "proof" that this streamer is such an oh so good person and were now deemed irrelevant.

These videos are not about being good people. These videos are selfish and disgusting in the way that these people prey on the "weak," the "poor," the "pitiable folk" in an attempt to make themselves look like a generous, caring person. It is entirely Ego-driven in a "masturbating to our own godly greatness" type of narcissism. When we are genuinely good, caring, selfless people, we couldn't care less if no one ever knows about all the good we do because we never do the good things for external validation or to justify self-delusions of greatness. We do not need to prove that we are good people. We simply exist peacefully as such instead of pretending and showing off that we are. We do not need to uphold a façade for others to witness.

An excellent example of this is a co-worker I used to work with. If I remember correctly, he and his wife had two children together, then decided to adopt eight others. Again, this could be seen as a good thing. However, whenever this person spoke about his eldest daughter, he always complained about her attitude and her lashing out. Everything he complained about her struck me deeply and strongly as someone reacting to being neglected, both emotionally and psychologically, if not physically. Having experienced emotional and psychological neglect in my childhood as well in my own family dynamic, it was obvious to me that in their need to appear as such selfless and good people by adopting so many kids in need, the parents were completely oblivious to the fact that they were not capable of meeting the needs of the kids they already had.

This is a perfect example of needing to prove worth outside of Self. If they had been capable of self-awareness, they would have realized before getting to ten kids that they were putting way too much on their plate to begin with. The proof of that was to be found in their eldest daughter's behaviour and self-expression. A happy, supported, fulfilled, nurtured child does not lash out. They do not need to. They would know how to communicate and, more importantly, they would see that they are being listened to *and heard* by their parents. This being heard is so important because it communicates to them that they matter and are considered.

I am not saying any of this to bash anyone or anything, but simply to shed light on the truth of the situation. We have to remember that we are all human, we all make mistakes, and we all get to learn from our mistakes, but we have to leave our Ego behind to register that we do make these mistakes. We all do. Making mistakes is part of being human; how else can we truly learn? Our responsibility is to figure out how to be the best possible version of ourselves, which means starting with self-accountability. Of dropping our own bullshit shields of self-delusion. Of digging into ourselves and facing the truths we find there. Do not start beating yourself up if you realize that instances where you thought you were being selfless are, in fact, moments where you sought outside validation and appreciation of your personal worth. Instead, Journal about it. What is this meant to show and teach you?

We have to understand that when we engage in this type of behaviour, we need people to think highly of us because we do not, or cannot, do it ourselves. It is simply an indication of deeper wounding. There are two important perspectives to consider here. First, we do this because we are starved for love and appreciation; second, it is yet another way to control outside perception of who we are. Remember that the need for control stems from believing we are unsafe in the world, and/or that we do not think ourselves worthy of receiving what we want. Therefore, we need to force things to go our way, and we need to prove ourselves externally.

Ultimately, it is again a form of self-betrayal, where we believe that we are not inherently worthy of being loved and appreciated, and therefore need to prove to ourselves and others that we are worthy through external validation. The betrayal part comes from seeking this externally. We must come back to the Truth that we inherently deserve to be loved and appreciated unconditionally for exactly who we are. Again, this is the idea that we cannot give from an empty cup and that even a full cup will eventually run dry. We need a constantly overflowing cup; this way, others can benefit while we never run dry. The question then becomes: "How do we achieve this ever-overflowing cup of goodness?" We can connect directly to Source from within and live through that innate connection from which our intuition stems.

By understanding that our bodies have physical reactions to our everyday decisions and act as an inner compass, we can start to observe our choices that leave us feeling drained, dissatisfied, uneasy, and even upset (Journal about these observations when you make them). This means that these choices were not aligned with our highest good. Whenever we feel pulled back or uneasy about something, it is always an indicator not to move forward in that direction. This is not to be mistaken for fear. Ultimately, we have to realize that fear has no solid foundation and that the more we entertain fear, the less it can leave us alone. We always make a choice to feed and give in to fear, by talking ourselves into it, and by letting our minds run rampant with it.

This being said, when we make choices that serve our highest good and follow the path of our purpose, we will never feel depleted. We will feel satisfied, happy, and excited. These good feelings are the real compass we need to follow. They are what will lead us to uncover and connect with our SEEC. Our SEEC is where we can tap into the infinite pool of Universal energy. When we connect with Source from within, we connect to the hearts of every living being, because we are all One. We all have access to the infinite abundance of the Universe through our SEEC. By connecting with and tapping into this energy center— our Soul—and, through that, to the Universe, we will feel immense, powerful, beautiful energy rising within us. This energy feels amazing, unlimited, immensely joyful, and incredibly peaceful, and it is exactly what we need to connect with to have our personal well-being cup filled and overflowing. These are the waters of Life.

Because this energy is so pure and high-vibrational, we may not be able to connect with it fully at first. There may be layers of wounding within us that make it impossible for the light to cross their filter and reach us fully. Or we may experience a strong connection with it at first, and then only snippets of it that ultimately guide us back towards reconnecting fully. It is always up to the individual Soul and how they choose to experience returning to Oneness for themselves in this lifetime. Still, we can use how we feel about what we are doing to indicate whether we are following what is meant for us. We can also choose instead to do what is expected of us by ourselves, others, our religion, or society. Ultimately, it is fundamental to understand that our life is our own, and we get to do exactly what we want with it, or not.

One of the drawbacks I have noticed when we connect with this pure Source energy is that our unhealed Ego takes on a new form: that of the Spiritual Ego. This stems from any unhealed wound around superiority/inferiority complexes, where the Ego now believes they are above everyone and everything because it has made this connection with Source. The hubris is strong in unhealed spiritual people, as is the greed and arrogance. It is incredibly easy to fall into this Ego trap because of the absolute high we get from connecting with Source, which is why a truly healed person's greatest traits are their innate humility and generosity.

If you have fully engaged with this book since the beginning chapters, by this point, you will likely have a strong self-love and care routine and are continuing to bring about a true sense of peace and authenticity for yourself by uncovering layers of wounding and working away at them. We must learn to give ourselves what we need, as it is part of filling our cup of well-being. It is also important to have our healthy boundaries with ourselves and others in place. Still, it is also important to start checking ourselves out objectively to see where we are starting to give in to our own bullshit. What stories are we feeding ourselves to justify our possible shitiness, and are we being objectively truthful with ourselves at all times? We can also ask instead what we are refusing to acknowledge about ourselves: how we are twisting things to suit our wants instead of facing the truth our reality presents back to us?

I wish to reiterate here how easy it is to fall into the trap of believing we know better than anyone else once we have started working on ourselves. We start seeing the results of this inner work, which can be and feel downright magical. Because we have healed and grown as an individual, and we have shifted perception from zoomed in on our lives to zoomed out to encompass more and more of everything around us into a bigger picture, it is easy to believe that we are "above" others because we can see and process on a bigger scale than most at this point in time. Contempt and self-righteousness are some of the most prevalent attitudes we can receive from unhealed spiritual people who believe themselves superior, which is always ultimately about wounded self-worth.

The best way to avoid this kind of setback is to remember that we are human; this means that we do make mistakes, we are not (and will never be) perfect, and that we can and will fall back into wounded Ego energy. The trick is knowing ourselves well enough and having enough humility to accept our humanity and shortcomings without taking anything personally. The moment we compare ourselves to others, believing we are superior to or above others, we need to realize that we are dropping the ball hard. It is akin to starting back at square one on our entire healing journey. We have to understand that we are a part of a whole, and how we treat others is only ever an indication of how we truly perceive ourselves. Everything always happens for our highest good, even when we cannot see how or why.

This leads us to introducing surrender, in all of its terrifying glory. There can be no surrender without trust, and trust can only come from living with hope. Surrender requires a complete and total relinquishing of needing to control things, needing to understand things, and needing a concrete timeline and plan to follow. Surrender requires us to lose all stiffness and rigidity present within. We need to trust our personal flow and intuition completely. We must live a heart-centered life of positivity, joy, compassion, empathy, and hope. There can be no hate, worries, doubts, or fears, nothing to detract from the purity of Source energy.

Do not be intimidated by these kinds of lists of "how-to-be," as they do not happen overnight. We are choosing to follow this process by doing the inner work. We have to learn to disconnect from the voice of fear, to keep control of ourselves through our natural bouts of worry and doubt, and understand that these are all simply products of the uncontrolled mind. When we tune into our intuition, into Source, we can follow their guidance through our SEEC, which will naturally bring us into this energy of surrender. We have been conditioned to believe that being in control means being in power. Still, true power comes from needing to control nothing at all, trusting that things happen how they need to happen, and living through the power of allowing instead of resisting. This does not mean to stop living, but instead to live free from the prison the need to control keeps us in.

The need to control things keeps us from being in the energy of surrender simply because we then automatically attach a how, when, and why to every story and manifestation instead of leaving all of these open to the Universe to interpret and work with. It is very much hubris when a person believes they can do things better than the Universe can. Instead of needing to think we are right about everything, we have to open the door and look at how we could be wrong about everything.

We are at a point in this book where we need to understand and apply the principles of taking everything that happens in our lives objectively while actively seeking out what it reflects about our internal reality, what it wants to show us about ourselves, and our healing journey. We also have to understand and roll with the knowledge that everything always happens for our highest good in direct correlation with what energy we give out to the Universe, regardless of if it is given consciously or not, and that the only real guidance we need comes from the heart when it is connected with Source. If this is not your current reality, understand that what comes next is not yet available to you, although reading through these next chapters may be the incentive you need to start actively bettering yourself.

Whenever we are rejecting the above notions, we are simply in Ego, and it showcases what wounds and limiting beliefs we currently need to work on. We can be hit with absolute despair when we are faced with what we perceive to be the Universe rejecting us (when we do not get what we want how and when we wanted it, as an example), or when we believe we should be "further ahead" than where we are currently or having "achieved more things." There is such a thing as divine timing, but also being in alignment with what we are asking. If we ask for money coming in, but subconsciously believe we do not deserve to be taken care of, then there will be little to no money coming in.

On the other hand, when we have been doing well in life and suddenly things start going downhill for no obvious reason, it is a very clear indicator that we have strayed from our path of being in service to the Universe and, ultimately, ourselves and others. Maybe we have lost touch with our humility and compassion, perhaps we have fallen into being greedy out of a belief we are owed more than others because we have done "so much more work," etc. Being in alignment is to be in service to all by recognizing that by doing so, we are ultimately in service to ourselves as well, as we are not distinct from all. Greed turns us into servants to ourselves only, without consideration for all.

Even when we fall into Ego traps like greed, self-righteousness, and arrogance, it is important to understand that we are simply meant to rectify our aim when we become aware of doing it. The Universe does not punish us when we fall into these patterns, as this is what it means to be human. However, the Universe does reward us for becoming aware *and* choosing to deal with it accordingly. Some self-realisations are harder to swallow than others, and this is why the entire process takes time, commitment, and a willingness to see ourselves truthfully with the intent of healing, growing, and evolving, no matter the ugliness of what we are shown about our current selves.

The Ego wants things to happen instantaneously, exactly how they want them to happen. The Truth is that as long as we keep taking steps towards our goals, no matter how small we perceive them to be, we will one day inevitably get there. This is why patience is a must in order to be a fully healed, enlightened, and ascended being. The Soul understands and respects Divine Timing for what it is: the Universe waiting for us to align energetically to our hearts' deepest, purest desires. Embodying the knowing that what is meant for us will never miss us leads to the understanding that outside circumstances and appearances never matter. Rejection is always the Universe's redirection, pushing us towards our highest, best possible outcome, regardless of what our Ego thinks it wants. We must learn to trust, surrender, and stop asking for proof. Surrender requires absolute understanding, and the embodiment of believing is seeing; never seeing is believing.

What is meant by this is that whenever we feel like we are losing out on some big opportunity, when we are fired from a job we loved, or someone we adore walks out of our lives, it ultimately happens for our highest good: our benefit. It is a choice we then make to want to fight against this, because we perceive the situation or the person to have been the best possible outcome. The Truth is that the Universe is always nudging us towards our highest good outcome; therefore, if something is removed or leaves us of its own will, it is in our best interest to just let it go. It is always the Ego that wants to hold on and resist change. Letting go in and of itself requires us to be in the energy of surrender, to have faith, trust, and patience.

When we start forcing ourselves to be in the energy of surrender, it is seldom easy to start, as it requires us to release the need to control things. Again, controlling things translates as not feeling safe in our worlds, inner and outer. Choosing surrender will be uncomfortable, challenging, probably emotional, but ultimately the best course of action we can take, simply because when the Universe creates a void, a hole in our experience, it is to make the necessary room for the upgrade to come in. We can easily guide ourselves to this upgrade, or let it come to us as the situation dictates (ex, choosing to look for a new/better job vs. allowing a new person to come into our lives). Still, it will always be something ultimately better for us, especially when we cannot see how this new thing could be better. We have to be in the energy of surrender to *allow* ourselves to be pleasantly surprised instead of fighting things every step of the way because we do not trust that there can be something better ahead.

One of the constants in this world is change. The sooner we make our peace with change, the easier life becomes. This goes back to the principle of the comfort zone being our cozy little prison. The less we are attached to things, the easier it is to let them go. Attachment is another interesting, misunderstood topic. We can love and care for things, people, and animals without attaching ourselves to them. At some point, people and animals die. Items get broken, stolen, or worn down. The most valuable life lesson to take from these facts is that we get to enjoy the present moment with these aspects of life, and we should experience these moments fully, while knowing and understanding that all things come to an end. We should not live in fear of all things ending, because then there would be no point to life at all.

We have to exercise appreciation and gratitude for what we have, and when it is time to part ways, we should also do this with gratitude for all the beauty we have shared with them. We have to cherish moments, opportunities, people, and animals while we have them, and instead of viewing a separation from them as a bad thing, something to reject, deny, and hide from, we should choose to see it as an opportunity for more, different kinds of joy and fun to come into our awareness. If we lived eating pepperoni pizza for every meal of the day, we would become bored with it instead of appreciating its deliciousness. Humans need variety to thrive. Without variety, we are limited in our understanding of things and our experience of life.

Attachment is the opposite of surrender. It is also a form of control. We should love and appreciate things and living beings without needing them, desperately or not. When we are in the energy of need, we are in the energy of lack. Being in the energy of lack mentality blocks our blessings from coming in because it automatically makes us fear losing what we are clinging onto so strongly. It makes us resist the Universe instead of embracing it. It closes doors instead of opening them. Divine timing refers to personal, energetic alignment, not time as we know it. We have to align energetically with what we want by *being* on the same vibrational level to allow these new things to come in. What we want to call in and what the Universe wants to give us in accordance with our highest good need to be a vibrational match. Otherwise, fitting a square item in a circular hole of the same size is impossible.

When we become comfortable with the fact that everything always happens for our highest good, in perfect divine timing, we can sit back, relax, do our little thing, and keep an eye out for opportunities that come calling. When we relax, we can connect more easily with our intuition and clair senses, which guide us in either making the right actions or being in the right place at the right time. There is no such thing as luck or coincidence. There is a belief in both Self and the Universe, and going with the Flow. Going with the Flow of Life is one of our greatest allies in manifesting and experiencing Heaven on Earth. When we are in Flow, there is no resistance. No resistance means the Universe has carte blanche to provide us exactly what we need when we need it. We need to be open and in the energy of allowance for optimal manifestation to occur.

Expecting without attachment to how, why, when, where, or what is how we can be fully in manifestation energy. When we expect things and are attached to receiving them, we become anxious about it arriving, trying to control/discern the how, what, when, etc., and we are actually blocking them from coming in. We are not receptive when we are anxious; we are controlling. Anxiety is fear. Worry is fear. Doubting is fear. Mental health issues are mostly about how unwell we are within our own bodies, within this societal "reality" constructed around being productive 1000% of the time and then some, which is completely against human nature. Any illness that emerges from stress—

physical, mental, or otherwise—shows us where we are not being authentic in the Self and in our lives.

Our bodies constantly communicate with us, trying to get our attention to focus on the underlying problem, of which illness is only a symptom. In most cases, the underlying problems are repressed emotions. Trauma and wounding—when followed back to their source—are ultimately more repressed, unprocessed emotions. The bottom line is that our emotions are the key to everything. How we feel is what we attract. This is exactly why hidden or subconscious trauma and wounding dictate our lives, because there is an emotional stuck point keeping a strong emotion stuck within us that affects our vibration. Clearing trauma and wounding means clearing away unprocessed emotions. We do the inner work by clearing stuck emotions. Our emotional self is our magical, powerful manifestation self. If we are in the energy of joy, we bring more joy. If we are in the energy of fear, we bring about more opportunities to feel fear.

When we talk about changing mindsets, we mean looking at how our brains dictate which emotion we should feel. How often have you felt reluctant to do something, only to have the time of your life afterwards while doing it? How often have you skipped out on something because your mind told you it was not worthwhile or too expensive, etc., only to regret that decision later on because you hear about how amazing things were? The brain imposes this fear, this reluctance, because it feels triggered, out of control, or challenged in some way, but ultimately it is proven wrong by the amount of enjoyment that came from ignoring it. To live in the energy of surrender is to shut off that part of our brain that may no longer dictate what we choose to do. This is why so many people choose to drink excessively or do drugs, and perceive themselves to have so much more fun while intoxicated: because they numb this part of the "thinking process" and are then able to be free to be alive.

The beauty of this is that we can learn to shut off that part of our brain by practicing surrender over and over again, to the point where we do not need a crutch like alcohol or drugs to feel free and good. It is by focusing on the Self in the here and now, and choosing to release the hold our minds consciously have on us— by not giving in to worry, fear, or doubt—that we can attain this liberating state of being. All we have to do is identify our Soul purpose, take the necessary steps towards achieving it, follow our inner guidance, and be open to everything the Universe throws our way. By taking nothing personally, we can accept everything for all they have to offer. Taking things personally is, again, indicative of wounding or stuck emotions. This goes back to the essential need to get over ourselves.

This is all part of why developing the connection with our intuition is so important, as it acts as a compass towards our best possible outcome. However, a compass works best when used with a map, and we have access to the map of our Soul purpose: our inner heart, which connects us directly to the Universe through the SEEC. We are placed here on Earth to play with life, as hard to believe as this may sound, given where we may presently be in life. Surrender is so important because otherwise, we cannot see the Truth of the previous statement. We rail against perceived injustice instead of seeking out the messages they try to bring to our awareness. We should always come back to the question: what is this trying to tell me about me?

Another thing to understand about manifestation is that we will always attract more of what we focus on, despite how we may feel about the topic focused upon. If we spend a lot of time gossiping and desiring the energy of drama, we will draw more opportunities for gossip and drama, even ones where we may become the target. Have you ever noticed that the people who complain the most always seem to have things happen to them that give them reason to complain? They are drawing this energy to them. The Truth is that where we choose to invest our energy is what comes back to us. Shifting perspectives then becomes a choice to place our energies elsewhere, so that we may attract new things. Still, there will be a period of energetic transition where the Universe tests our authenticity in our desire for change. Further, if we have wounds associated with the energy we are trying to leave, then energetically we are pinned to it and cannot escape it despite our best efforts unless we resolve the stuck emotions held in the wounds.

During the worst of one of my several severe depressions, where I was also experiencing total burnout and suicidal tendencies, I ended up manifesting the cat who saved my life. He became one of my (if not *the*) only sources of love and companionship during this incredibly difficult time. How do I know I manifested him into my life? At first, I was not convinced about getting a cat, but I put out the intention that if I were meant to have one, it would find me without effort. I was scrolling on my Facebook feed one morning and came across a photo of newborn kittens, and my eyes were instantly drawn to only one of them, although they all looked the same except for their colours. I could not stop being drawn to that wet little form, being drawn back to the picture repeatedly, even when I had refused the idea at first as being a sign. So I messaged the person who was an old co-worker to see if anyone had asked to adopt this specific one yet. Lo and behold, he was the only one available.

Whenever we are manifesting, we have to start paying attention to synchronicities. Numerology and asking for signs, or seeing a specific sign or symbol we know is special to us, are powerful ways to connect with the magic of the Universe, even if we do not always understand their intended message. In my case, I had been seeing a lot of synchronicities, especially in numbers. During that time, I constantly saw 11:11, and multitudes of 7s, meaning 77s, 777s, 7777s, and even 77777s. They were everywhere. I could never go more than a few hours in between seeing 7s. When I paid more attention to the details of this kitten, I was informed that he was born around 7 in the morning— and that he was the last of his litter: the 7th, to be precise. He was born on November 11th (11-11), in 2018, which numerologically reduces to another 11 (2+0+1+8=11).

We always have a choice to refuse to believe what is right in front of our eyes. In my case, it was too many coincidences to think it meant nothing. It is easy to doubt. Most people do, even when all the evidence slaps them in the face over and over again. Willful ignorance is a strong tool for those not brave enough to face Truth in life and of themselves. We must first release the ridiculous notion that we know anything about this world in order to see the Truth of things. We need to allow the world to show us its truth and simply accept things as they truly are. Truth is the only variable of life that holds any real value. Truth is so powerful that it has its own energetic signature, its own vibrational level. We can always feel Truth when we pay attention to our senses and what is all around us.

Patience is one of the biggest lessons that needs to be understood collectively on Earth. So are trust and faith. So is surrender. So is hope. One of the biggest realisations we have to get accustomed to in order to grow and evolve is to understand that magic is very real in this world; we simply have no idea how it works for the most part. In this world, magic is not what we expect it to be, as it is not the kind we learned about in fantastical worlds, where everything is relatively easy and instantaneous. Ask and you shall receive; if you are vibrationally aligned with your request and it serves the greatest good of all for you to receive it, and will not allow you to bypass learning your lessons. Oneness *is* our magic. Oneness is about healing, as healing the Self means clearing the way to connecting with the heart of all from within. Duality is the lie, Oneness the Truth. Recognizing Oneness is acknowledging the Truth of Life; therefore, by choosing to heal, we choose Oneness. We are consciously choosing our available magic. We recognize that we *are* magicians: magicians of creation. Illusion is what keeps us from creation. Fear is an illusion, as it holds no substance more than what we give to it.

There have been numerous ways people have tapped into this energy and have tried to explain and share this Truth throughout the ages. Such examples go as far back as the Emerald Tablets, and as recently as *The Secret, The Power of Now*, and even parts of the original Bible. Our magic is creation. How many times have we let ourselves experience the awe of creation? A portrait painted so beautifully that it took your breath away? A movie that made you shed tears of various emotions? A poem that touched your Soul? A story that moved something deep within you? A play in a football game that brought the entire stadium to its feet?

Art *is* creation. And art is found in absolutely every single aspect of life. Some are artists with words, with paints, with music, with a camera, within a sport, within the job they do, regardless of whether it is as a notary trying to find loopholes to make a difficult project work out, or as a chef creating art in every plate they fashion. Art is subjective; it can be deeply personal, but it is the most potent form of human connection. Strangers worldwide can bond over a piece of art they love, such as a video game, a book, or a sport.

This world has been fashioned by distorted masculine energies, meaning that all that matters today is material accomplishments. We grow up going through life with a checklist of things we are supposed to want and do, and the more we check off on the list, the more we "advance" in life. This world has refused the beauty of feminine energy and favors only viewing things through the lens of masculine energy. This is why so many things are rigid and downright nonsensical, because distorted masculine energy does not allow for the softness of compromise. This is why we are confronted with "win-at-all-costs" mentality; this is why cheating exists, because there is no real value placed on the experience, only in achieving the "top" result. It is why this world is broken, and people do not see the value of life. For ages now, feminine energy has been deemed as witchcraft, as undesirable, as a flaw. This is why women are sadly only valued for their perceived beauty, why they are often viewed as little more than objects, but it goes even further than that.

The Earth itself *is* a very feminine energy, and that is exactly why it has been treated so poorly, because of this subconscious planetary wound around the divine feminine essence. Women carry the magic of creation within their bodies, which is why it is always easier at first for women (or those who carry dominantly feminine energy) to manifest things. It is part of the internal knowledge of the feminine power. Women do not consciously craft babies within themselves; they simply trust the magic to happen. They do not need to do anything other than take good care of themselves. This world makes magic seem like this: either a mystical, secretive, impossible thing, or, on the flip side, a flamboyant, huge spark of explosion, when in Truth it is invisible, subtle, yet ever-present.

Just because we have lost touch with how Earth magic works through abandoning, dominating, belittling, and condemning feminine energy, does not mean it does not exist. It means we have to rediscover it; we have to give back value to healthy feminine energy. For those of you who are triggered by the last few paragraphs, you should already know to pull out your Journal and get to work. Let me add more details that will seem impossible to the most closed-minded people. There was a time not too long ago on this Earth where certain people had figured out how to be 100% attuned to this magic. I am talking about Native tribes all over the world, their shamans, and whatever other names they carry that I am unaware of. They listened and they heard Gaia speaking to them. They knew how to survive in today's impossible environments, such as harsh Canadian winters and Australian deserts with little to no resources. They were one with nature, and because of this, they were one with each other in ways we may not believe possible today, such as through telepathy, instantaneous healing, and other forms of energy exchanges.

Just because we deem this impossible does not mean that it is. It was impossible to get to the moon. It was impossible to fly. It was impossible to explore the depths of the oceans. Impossible is only ever a state of mind, a limiting belief. If you believe you are living in a world of impossibility, then, as usual, the Universe will knock itself over to prove you right. The Universe always wants to prove us right. Our minds have become so cluttered with lies, deceit, appearances, and other useless burdens of energy that we do not recognize the Truth of things as easily anymore. Doubts, worries, and fears all serve to clutter our minds and keep us from deeply connecting to Truth. To our Self. To Gaia.

We disbelieve because we are scared of being disappointed if we are wrong, and this fear is what the Universe picks up on vibrationally and responds to. It is up to us to choose to believe beyond fear. That is part of our test as human beings. We have forgotten the Truth about our personal power because we have become cluttered with distractions such as life's "checklist" of things to accomplish to be deemed worthy by society. We live, do things, make choices, and understand Life on such a shallow, surface level that we have the hubris to believe we know everything there is to know about Life. Yet the moment we scratch at that surface, we start to realize how little life makes sense right now. Everything is driven by external factors; we have forgotten our internal Truths and essence.

Once they have reached this realization, most people give in to despair and choose to deny or forget this Truth. There is a good reason why society is on the brink of collapsing: because we are living lives that destroy our Souls instead of nourishing them. It is not by mistake that so many people now suffer from mental illness: because deep inside they feel the Truth of how disingenuine living is, yet they do not see a way out, do not know of another way of living than the "standard" given to us, that would rather turn us into emotionless, hustling, grinding machines instead of inspired, thriving, creative beings. We live in a society that lacks depth and substance, where making mistakes is deemed unacceptable, being human is to be deemed inherently flawed, being ourselves is deemed undesirable, and having an original thought is deemed an alien concept, impossible. When we are confronted with difficulty, we choose to quit because effort is rarely rewarded justly, and we give up when we hit an impasse because of the idea that failing means we are inadequate in life. We forget to be curious, to explore, to dig deeper into things to uncover the true treasures they contain. We lose focus too easily because results are not instantaneous. Yet, all of this can be fixed and healed by letting go of distorted masculine energy and instead turning towards healed, empowered feminine energy.

Connecting to the heart of all forms within starts with connecting to the heart of Earth, and allowing her guidance to emerge. All the answers we need and seek are all around us, always. We just have to learn to quiet down, to stop, to pause, to wonder, to be curious, and to allow. This is where this chapter is meant to bring you, to understand that all the work we have done so far in this book is to bring us to this state of surrendered allowance, to our innate internal connection to all. Life is always about the journey, never about attaining a destination. Because then, what happens when we reach our destination? We embark on a new, different journey. We are always journeying, and it is always meant to bring us back to the Truth of the Self, and through that, the Truth of the Universe.

The next practice we are brought to integrate is to narrow our focus upon one thing at a time. There is no rush. There is no timer for life. There is no deadline for us to meet. There is only personal evolution and our choice to embrace or reject it. This is exactly what the cycle of lessons is: our evolution and our choice. This is also why we must choose to fully commit to a single given thing at a time, because that is how our energy is *the most potent it will ever be*. When we divide our attention and try to do multiple things at a time, we scatter our focus. When that momentum finally has a chance to really draw in energetically what is needed, we are already moving on to this other project that also has our focus. Therefore, we are no longer energetically aligned with the first thing, meaning our manifestations get lost in subliminal spaces. Sometimes they wait for us to return to them, but mostly they simply fade away, and we need to restart the whole process again.

We have to give up the pressing need we have developed to rush through things, to feel the pressure of "time." Time is entirely a construct of the mind. Yes, time exists, and we can witness it in this reality, but deadlines are man-made and man-imposed. The Universe does not adhere to deadlines. The Universe uses divine timing, which is always about energetic and vibrational alignment. We do not need to rush or go through life quickly: we must slow down, relax, and enjoy the ride. Rushing is a trauma response. Always needing to be doing things is a trauma response. Having to continuously grind and hustle is a trauma response. These things are all against human nature, but we do not see it because we have been conditioned as children, since we were born, that this is life.

Life is about personal accomplishments, not external accomplishments. What does it matter if you finished first in your class if you were stressed, anxious, and dreading every moment? What does it matter if you have made your college football team if so much responsibility is now placed upon your shoulders and asked of you to perform perfectly at all times that you simply do not enjoy playing the sport anymore? We have to find pleasure in what we do; otherwise, what we do is meaningless. It might be valued externally, cheered on, and praised by others, but if we do not value and enjoy what we do, then what good does it actually bring us? What purpose is there in making ourselves feel miserable for the sake of another's pleasure? Are we continuously choosing to make ourselves miserable for the continued benefits of others? For external gratification when our internal world feels nothing but dread? What is the point of living a life that leaves us feeling dead inside already?

This is why we must cultivate patience, why we must stop stressing and hustling towards accomplishing things for external reasons like gratification, proving people wrong, or checking things off an imaginary list. Life is about being fully present in any given moment, exactly as we are, where we are, and not holding a single drop of judgment against ourselves. Life is not about wishing for more, or "better" than what we have; it is about being entirely satisfied with where we are in our personal journeys, and knowing that the more we work on ourselves, the more life gives us exactly what we want and need. By being content, satisfied, and grateful for where we are and what we have, we naturally bring about more things and experiences to be content, satisfied, and grateful for, simply because that is the energy we choose to invest in. This has to be done despite our perceived hardships, as these happen for our benefit, to illustrate contrast, for us to choose that we will not focus on what we do not want more of. We have to choose to leave behind the energy of despair in favour of hope.

The Truth is that we never have a different starting point than where we currently are. The sooner we accept all of our reality for exactly what it is and what it represents to us, the sooner we get to start going towards what we really want and need. As long as we focus on duality, we will always be dissatisfied with life. When we embrace Oneness, all doors open up for us. When we focus on Oneness, we are essentially disintegrating all of our fears, worries, and doubts, because we realize that these things have no reason to exist other than the reasons we choose to assign to them. If we take away the reasons we give to our fears for them to exist, then they simply stop existing because they have nothing of substance to fall back on. The same applies to worries and doubts. When we understand that *nothing* is under our control, we can truly understand just how in control we really are.

When we remove the fear, worry, doubt, need, want, expectation, impatience, stress, nervousness, and all other heavy energies we give power over us, we declutter our Souls. We free our energy so that it may attract to us what we actually want and need on a Soul level. Mastering the Self from within means opening all doors to our innate connection with the Universe. It means enabling the Limitless Possibilities cheat code. It means winning at the game of Life.

Chapter 14
Alignment and Finding Our Purpose

———— • ————

Connecting with our inner heart, the SEEC—the Universe through the Self—is what allows us to tap into the energetic attachment we have with our Soul purpose, which always feels like a deep calling. This feeling is stronger than we can usually understand or comprehend. Some feel it and follow it from a young age, knowing, for example, that they are meant to be nurses, artists, or pilots. Some will feel it and decide they are not good enough to be what they aspire to be in a credible way, and then will live their entire lives in misery by following any road other than that of their true purpose, meaning they will have let fear win over their self-love and self-respect. Some will feel and follow it through, only to one day stop feeling the call and find that their entire life perspective and desires have shifted entirely overnight, as they access either a "second-part" calling, or realise that what they had initially thought were their own desires were actually external desires pushed upon them until they believed the lie that this desire was their own to begin with over the subtle call of their own Soul.

Regardless of how it happens in our personal life experience, the Truth is that our Soul purpose has a magnetic hold over us, and we get to choose to either run from it or embrace it despite fear being present. The acronym False Evidence Appearing Real is the very definition of what fear truly represents. Our minds protest our decision to leave our cozy, controlled comfort zone. Whatever goals, ambitions, or dreams we have that never leave our awareness—often staying quiet in the shadows until our "life-dissatisfaction" meter fills up enough to bring all possibilities for wanting something better back onto the table—are usually tied to our Soul purpose. Every single one of us is here for a reason. Every single one of us has a unique Soul purpose, which will serve their Intended Life purpose.

We have to remember that the Universe is like an infinite web of connections, and everything we do affects others in multitudes of ways, most of which we never become aware of. Our Soul purpose is something we feel in the depths of our bones, of our being, that we need to do, either for our own sake or because we genuinely believe it can help others in the long term. Our Soul purposes are always intended to help all, even if we cannot see how. For example, perhaps the art you create will soothe a person's pain, and maybe even multiple people's pain, as the painting is gifted or inherited, as it moves hands and is continuously seen by more and more people. Perhaps the scientific discovery you are meant to make will change society in a way we cannot even imagine yet, and it will improve basic human living conditions. Because we are all One and so intricately interconnected, nothing we ever do ever only affects us.

There is nothing inherently wrong or selfish in following our hearts' desires; on the contrary, it can be seen as selfish not to, as in choosing not to play our part in the greater whole. The Universe is built to accommodate free will. Therefore, if we drop the ball in achieving personal growth, then someone else will be tasked with doing what we have chosen not to do. However, it is important to understand that no one can replace us in our contributions; it simply means that the Universe has followed a different path than the originally intended one. This does not mean we have ruined the Universe's plans; it is simply that more than one road leads to the intended destination. Yet, because of how intricate and amazing the Universe is, perhaps our personal "failure" was always intended to happen, that this new door could open up for someone who chose to do the inner work, perhaps waiting for the opportunity that our failure provided.

Fate is interesting as a concept that helps explain how we perceive things, but the ultimate Truth is that nothing ever happens by mistake. There are no mistakes, only opportunities to learn and grow, just as there are no coincidences, only synchronicities. Nothing is ever random, and nothing is ever set in stone. We live in a Universe of infinite possibilities, and it truly is up to us to choose to tap into this truth and live it, or not. We are our most potent blockage to achieving our true bliss. We are the only thing that is holding us back, always. Our inside world dictates our outside reality; therefore, what we choose to make of our inside world is how we choose to experience life externally. Since this is always our choice, we can quite literally do anything we set ourselves out to achieve, just like we will always keep ourselves from achieving what we do not believe we can achieve.

The fundamental Truth is that we are the sole beings responsible for where we are currently in life, and we are the sole thing in the way of living the life of our dreams. The power of our beliefs shapes our reality, which is exactly why we have been working at uncovering all limiting beliefs and consequent wounding, which dictate and limit subconsciously our capabilities in this lifetime. We are the only ones who are ever holding ourselves back, keeping ourselves small, and refusing our own sovereignty. Remember to always Journal about personal triggers. We all have our parts to play in the bettering of the human collective, and the choices we make that are aligned with our Soul Truth and Purpose will make us jump timelines into the reality that best matches our internal energetic vibration. Everyone's Soul Purpose can be summarized into the idea of embracing personal empowerment, which ultimately will benefit all in ways we cannot fathom. Life's journey is always about taking our personal power back and realising our sovereignty.

At the time of publishing this book, Mother Earth is upgrading her frequencies and needs our help to shift. We help by working on the Self and aligning with our Truth, healing old, outdated wounds and beliefs, and pursuing our Purpose. Many Souls have come in, and keep coming in, with this express purpose, as challengers of the norm, that the norm may upgrade and evolve as well. We are in the midst of a new energetic age for humanity, one where the main duality focus will be between machine and flesh, and how to reconcile both into One. There are Souls from different planes—with their own respective "Earth" planets—who are coming in to assist in this shift, bringing with them knowledge either foreign to, or lost in, this world. They are referred to as Starseeds, Light Workers, Indigo Children, etc., and their Soul vibrations are meant to expedite this Earth evolution.

You will likely already know if you are one such Soul by the simple knowing that you do not feel human, you do not connect with being human. We volunteered as pioneers of this shift, as ambassadors of Unconditional Love. If you have always felt like an outsider, like this world makes no sense whatsoever, like you do not belong here, if you feel drawn to fantastical things such as magic, fairies, unicorns, dragons, mermaids, etc., and you know them to exist from the depths of your being, then you are likely a Starseed, a person for whom these beings *do* exist, but in our own homeworlds. We can still tap into their energies and connect with them, but they cannot physically be found here on Earth; only energetically. This is no problem for our Souls because living energetically is how we are used to living. Our natural embodiment of existing in higher vibrations and instinctive connection to energy, nature, and manifestation are part of the Earth evolution process.

Earth feels clunky, disconnected, so slow and so fast at the same time, uncontrollable and wild, while also being completely within our control. We embody Oneness at our core and have difficulty understanding and coping with how divided and separate this world of duality seems to be at first, before we reconnect with Source and understand Truth. We cannot forget that Earth is intended as a world of contrast to allow for exponential growth, which is why we *must* make peace with there being violence, abuse, and other disgusting, low-level energetic things, beings, and events present at the moment, why certain people allow themselves to do terrible things. This world has not evolved yet, but is seeking to, and we are here as the vanguard of that change. By refusing what others consider unchangeable reality—violence and war, for example, being labeled the human norm, standard, or—more laughably— nature—and proving them wrong by choosing to live in love, peace, and harmony, helping one another and coexisting with each other and nature as was always intended, we reclaim our true power. We are here to help show the truth of duality as the bridge linking everything together, not keeping things separate.

People are only ever in conflict when there is conflict within them individually. When people are connected to the Truth of human nature, they connect naturally to peace and well-being, to expansive, unconditional love and nurturing of all. Their own personal, unhealed baggage warps this natural connection and keeps them stuck in duality thinking and mindsets, in survival mode. But it is also because of this baggage that they can experience exponential growth and healing, if they are brave enough to so choose.

This is part of what Starseeds are here to facilitate: we help human souls choose healing, light, and love as their natural choices. We take on a chunk of the ancestral, collective wounding in our current incarnation lifetimes, that we may help the world heal as a whole, and this is expressed through traumatic experiences during our lives. It is why most of the Starseed Souls that chose to be part of the vanguard are people who will have gone through heart-shattering experiences, and have ultimately chosen forgiveness, peace, and healing for themselves, no matter how impossible that choice seems to the most wounded among us. We are the way-showers, the ones who walk the wild, unknown path and beat it out into a walkable landscape for those who will come after. It is exactly why we are healers (Light Workers): we shed our powerful Lifeforce through the vibrations of the Earth as we consciously choose healing and forgiveness for ourselves first, that we may reach and heal the All.

With all this being said, if you resonate as a Starseed and have had difficulty adopting the "typical" human standard of living (mindlessly following the predetermined path, no-questions-asked), understand that this is normal and perfectly okay. You are NOT alone. You never were. But you are among the first of the vanguard, and it is time for all of us to start finding and connecting with each other again. It is also important to understand that you are allowed to ask for help and to accept it when it is offered. We may have grown accustomed to doing everything on our own because others just "do not get it." We never felt understood, or that we could not rely on anyone outside of ourselves, because they understand things on the current level of understanding, not our innate higher vibrational level of understanding. They choose pettiness, selfishness, small-mindedness, and hate over being kind, loving, and accepting of differences. This book is here to let you know that the Rules are changing. It is time to start calling in your Soul family, your Soul tribe, and they will come in many different shapes and forms. Some will present themselves as romantic connections, some as friendships, and some even as pets. Some are already present in your life, and you simply have not connected on a deeper level yet.

To those who are not Starseeds reading these words, do not worry. You will perceive Starseeds as the weird ones, the eccentrics, the ones who seem oblivious to the unspoken social norms, the awkward ones who try to connect authentically in a world that rejects authenticity, in ways that are likely unknown, different, even challenging for those really stuck in their ways. Starseeds are the black sheep, the ones who do not conform to things just because that is how it has always been, and the ones who criticize the current stupidity of things. They are the ones who perceive energy instead of façade. The ones who choose to heal themselves and improve their personal character because choosing otherwise seems simple madness. They are the ones asking for change for the betterment of all, not just a select few, the ones who do not understand greed and the inability to share, to help, to support.

Not being a Starseed does not make anyone lesser; it simply indicates that they have human Souls. Human Souls are the ones entrusted to Earth, the natives of this world in a sense. Starseeds are here to be of service to and in support of *you*. You are the special ones, the ones who are meant to achieve their fullest potential. The Starseeds here have already done this work on their own "Earth" planet, which is why they may seem to know things and ways of being that are deemed "not normal." This upgrade of global energy is being done for the benefit of the human Souls. We are here to help, but we cannot do it for you. This is exactly why choosing to heal is the most important choice all human beings can make for themselves, regardless of their Soul's origins. We are all intended for the same purpose of universal healing, and the more of us make this personal choice, the stronger that vibration becomes and the easier it is for the collective to intuitively sense it and follow through with choosing it.

This means that living in a utopia of peace that cares for all living beings and allows every single individual to live life to their fullest potential is not only possible, but the intended, desired outcome. This is exactly why, by identifying and following our Soul purpose consciously, we will be supported and helped out by the Universe over and over again. The Universe wants us to succeed and will give us every possible opportunity to seize to attain our success. Again, it comes back to a question of choice: our choosing to believe in ourselves and choosing to go for what we know, we feel in our bones, is meant for us. Our Soul purpose, or purposes in most cases, is basically what we as Souls have chosen as a goal to accomplish throughout our lifetime. Having free will means there are multiple avenues leading to the intended destination. This is why it is so important to understand that what is meant for you will never miss you, but you do have to take steps in its general direction. We still have to put in the work, but work that likely will not feel like work, but inspired action.

We have to make peace with the idea that we are completely out of control here in the 3D life we are living. We have to make peace with the fact that in our Soul form, before incarnating, we picked out every single detail of our life: our appearance, our challenges, our encounters, how we learn certain things, what trauma we experience as a potential for growth, what trauma we impart onto others for their potential for growth, all of our faults, all of our talents, the family we are born into (yes, we do choose them contrary to popular belief), what major events shape our lives, etc. Every detail is plotted out for us, leading to the idea that since we chose everything, we can handle everything that comes our way, as was intended from the start. This does not remove accountability, of course. If we have hurt others while navigating the world unconsciously, it is absolutely part of our karma to choose to make amends. No one gets away with being an asshole and choosing to hurt others deliberately, not on a Soul level anyways.

Back to the idea that everything is chosen for us, the best example I can give to illustrate this concept is that of playing an RPG-style video game, RPG standing for role-playing game. A videogame is entirely created by a company, outside of our control; this can be understood as the video game itself being Earth. You, as a Soul, decide your character: Are you a Rogue? A Sorceress? A Paladin? You decide your base stats and talents, plan out how you wish to evolve, and decide what choices best suit the "personality" or "character" you create to go with this empty shell being fashioned. What about the backstory for this character, then? Do you start poor and lonely, trying to figure out how to make life work for you, or do you start rich and with great support, enjoying what life has to offer? Is this playthrough bringing you here on business or vacation? Are you a hero or an NPC (non-playable character) that just wants to mind their own shop?

Once we have decided on all the details and are ready to start the game, we place a part of our Soul into this character we have created, then effectively get our memory wiped, and off we go on an adventure. Placing a part of our Soul within means we will always be connected to the Higher Self, the bigger part of our Soul that stayed up in the aether to "control" us, a.k.a. communicating with us through our intuition to show us the way. This intuition is akin to the menu that lists our current active quests. We always have access to this menu by listening to the voice of our intuition, but sometimes we get sidetracked by the number of side quests that keep popping into our awareness. Do we leave the main quest aside to go level up through side quests first? Do we need to unlock certain experiences before we are ready to continue journeying along the main quest? Do we need a certain item to unlock the way forward, or need to encounter a specific "side-character" that unlocks some doors for us?

As a first-time player of the game, we absolutely will make mistakes and miss some details that were hidden but crucial for the plot to go a specific way. Perhaps we waited too long before doing a side-mission, and now it has become unavailable. Perhaps we failed to keep a crucial character alive, meaning a certain path is now impossible to walk on. Even as a veteran player, our instincts might be sharper, but the memory wipe is still present, which means it is only ever by relying on our intuition that we know the true next step to be taken for the path of our highest good. Then it becomes a question of choice: do we listen to our intuition or do we listen to fear? Fear can take the shape of doubts, worries, anxiety, etc., anything to keep us from going where we are meant to be going. When our fears are too much for us to conquer, it usually means we are too low-level at this time and need to do some other things first in order to become of a high-enough level to proceed, which we can translate as cycles of learning.

The memory wipe itself is one of the most important aspects of incarnating, because it levels the playing field, so to speak. The simple truth is that if we had all the knowledge already at our disposal, then we would never learn anything. We would never evolve, grow, or level up. There would be no challenge. Without challenge, there can be no growth. If we cannot learn, then we are not equipped to teach. Experience remains the most potent form of learning available to us. Theoretical knowledge is all well and good to give an idea about a given subject, but have theory and practice ever been on the same level of knowing, learning, and understanding? Ultimately, we all become teachers whether we realize it or not. We are teaching everyone who can observe us by how we choose to live. The value of what we teach, however, is a very subjective topic.

There are some lessons in life that our Soul *needs* to learn without fault, energies that *need* to be liberated for us to achieve our true Soul-led goals, that promise us the best possible existence. Which is why some cycles—or quests, to stay in the metaphor—we will fail over and over again until we try something different and then, boom, level up. Some cycles will be on repeat in our lives until we choose to face them properly, to overcome the challenge they represent. Some of these will be in the background, patiently waiting to be addressed, and others will be pounding on your door to get your attention because it is a now-or-never type of lesson, a once-in-a-lifetime opportunity we have placed on our path as a Soul that will not repeat itself.

Whatever happens in our lives, it is crucial to know that we are never given something we cannot handle. This does not mean that handling it will be easy, but it does mean that we can and will pull through onto the other side if we so choose. Intact? Probably not. But grown, changed, levelled-up. Consciously, we may not have asked for it, but on a Soul level, it was always meant to happen, because the purpose of all Souls is ultimately always about growth. Following the path our Soul chose for us is an ultimate act of self-love, as no one knows us better, nor cares for us more deeply, than our own Soul. It goes without saying that our purpose in life will fuel us with all the energy we could possibly want. It may require effort, but it will never leave us depleted and unsatisfied.

Take a good, hard look at your own life and your honest levels of personal satisfaction. Journal about these things, then find within yourself what you are truly meant to be doing. Remember that by connecting with our SEEC, we have access to all the knowledge we need, even if that knowledge is only ever presented to us one step at a time. Referring to who we were as children and our desires back then is usually a good clue to our true interests—our true Soul-led purpose—as children have a natural connection with energy, which tends to be "beaten out of them," so to speak, through schooling, where they are taught that only logic and what can be seen, measured, and evaluated are of importance. The point here is that how we feel about what we do is the compass we are meant to follow, and our intuition provides the map. We absolutely need to put our minds aside during this process, as it only ever gets in the way.

Some things can only be felt, not logic-ed through. Figuring out our purpose and how to get to where we want to be is something that can only ever be perceived intuitively, as our Higher Self, the biggest part of our Soul (the one that is truly in control here), is the one who holds all of the answers for us. Our Higher Self is our most potent guide when we know how to trust and listen. We need to be at peace with the idea that we have control over nothing but our Selves, which leads directly to the understanding that we get to choose between fighting against our reality and resisting life, or embracing our powerlessness in order to truly connect with the Universe and flow freely, resistance-free, into the life of our dreams. We have to choose between letting go of needing to control things in favour of letting our Higher Self guide us into the perfect life for us. We have to let go of the Egoic idea

661

that we know better than Infinite Knowledge does. We do not need to know and understand everything, and we need to consciously release this need. We have to choose to surrender over and over again, in all parts of our lives.

Most of you reading these words at first will be empaths and healers, regardless of whether you identify with these labels or not. We may not recognize ourselves as such, but ultimately, the very foundation of every single human being, of humanity itself, *is* being empathic and healing. Simply because we heal through kindness, either by giving or receiving it. To fight this Truth because of disbelief is a natural response. It sounds so simple, and yet it is. We have been conditioned to believe everything has to be difficult to be worthwhile. This is the opposite of the Truth. Our attitude towards a problem, person, or event is what dictates the level of ease we can embody at any given moment.

I laughed at the idea of being a healer. I thought it was a capacity far beyond me—that little old ordinary (if weird) me could never truly be of service to people—because I believed I had no value as an individual whatsoever. It took a lot of work before I could see just how my presence or my words could change things for people, could uplift them, and give them hope. Was it always like this? No. I have hurt my own fair share of people during my "growing up" phase of life. The difference for me, as opposed to the typical response in people, was to hold my Self accountable and apologize for the hurt I had caused, regardless of whether it had been intentional or not. We do not get to dictate how others feel. The fact that they have felt hurt by my actions or words, even if by my standards these were intended as innocent or justified words or actions, simply meant that my own ignorance got in the way of being a decent human being.

My Ego dictated I should not apologize for anything and that these people should just get over it, that they had no business getting hurt in the first place, especially when my intent was innocent. Part of this is true, in the sense that as individuals we choose what we allow to hurt us, most often unconsciously because of trauma and wounding, but it remains a choice to feel hurt and victimized by things. The Ego loves this idea of needing everyone to cater to their every whim and feeling. But the other half of this truth is that these people still felt hurt by my words, actions, or behaviours, regardless of my intent. It is important to understand that even though we do not mean to, it is up to us to make it right when we do hurt others.

Of course, only sincere hurt deserves a sincere apology. There are unfortunately people very stuck in Ego who wallow in self-pity and who jump on every occasion to play victim. These are not the people I speak of here, though they do deserve kindness, as kindness is how we heal. Sometimes the best kindness we can offer these people is to walk out of their lives. Whenever people try to manipulate us or are just energy leeches, the best course of action is simply to cut all cords and remove ourselves entirely. This can be hard to do, especially when dealing with family, but ultimately, we need to choose self-respect and kindness. Remember that just because we are all natural healers, it does not mean that we are meant to be active as one. We do not owe people our time or our energy. We owe ourselves these things. Just because people ask for more does not mean we are required to give more. We must become able to differentiate between what is authentic and what is not. Authenticity is always the path to choose.

At this point, I need to clarify that just because you *are* a healer, it does not mean that your purpose is to *be* a healer. Our purposes are very personal to our Souls.

Sometimes healing others is the calling, such as for doctors and nurses who are not motivated by the paycheck. Sometimes our purpose is therapeutic and healing in and of itself, such as being an artist, and our art is all it takes to help others heal as well. Sometimes our purpose has nothing to do with healing at all, but our energy carries that vibration, and the places we are meant to go explore or live in would greatly benefit just from our being physically present there. Sometimes, all it takes is to choose to embody the True Self consciously.

Whatever the case may be, it is important to understand that we have this energy about us, and it is why we may attract people who are dearly in need of it. Again, they are not our responsibility, but it is up to us to listen to our instincts as to how to proceed. Each case is unique to the individual, and your body will tell you how to respond. You will simply feel and know if this is a person you need to help out or not, but if it is the case, then it is imperative that we stay in a healthy position within ourselves, meaning we have strong and healthy boundaries between us and this person. We must never self-betray for the benefit of another, who would not think twice about crossing us. We need strong and healthy boundaries for our own sake, so that we may be able to help the people who are willing to help themselves. We always need to take good care of ourselves first. The idea here is to know ourselves so deeply that we can be sovereign in our own being, meaning that we do not compromise ourselves by engaging in manipulative tactics from others.

With all of this being said, whenever we heal, we raise our personal vibration or frequency (refer to the Quick Reference Guide if needed, under Raising our Vibration). This means that our environment is directly affected, which in turn means that the people in our immediate surroundings that we interact with the most will absolutely feel this change energetically. When we raise our personal vibration, we are asking everyone we interact with to do the same if they want to stay compatible with us. Our personal vibration can be understood as a frequency, and frequencies only pick up on other frequencies that are on the same level, the same wavelength. This is why when we undergo extensive personal transformation, our entire environment seems to shift: either we physically move away, or things break and we need to replace them, or friendships end either abruptly or phase out, family may stop speaking to us, etc. Due to the principle of the void, whenever a hole is created this way in our lives, the Universe seeks to fill it up with the highest good outcome, but we only receive what we allow ourselves to receive.

This brings us back to the fear of change. When we fear change, we only fear receiving worse than what we currently have. The beautiful Truth is that this is simply not how the Universe works. We can never downgrade other than by Egoic choice. We always upgrade when we follow our intuition. This fundamental Truth is essential to understand and consciously choose to apply in our awareness, in our lives, because accepting this truth opens all doors of possibilities. We always set limits in our minds; they do not exist elsewhere. Just because something seems improbable does not make it impossible: our mindset turns things into impossibilities. Flying was considered impossible. Going to the moon was considered impossible. Exploring the depths of the oceans seemed impossible. And yet, we have now done all those things, and many more "impossible" things. We are always creating what we are choosing to believe.

All of this means that when things are changing due to our choosing to heal, choosing to raise our vibration, some things are forced to fall away from us because they are no longer an energetic match to our vibration. This is normal, and not something to fear, although there may be things we are going to need to grieve, and that is perfectly okay. It is totally normal and understandable to have a mourning period for how things were, as we start adapting to how things are and how they still have to evolve. We already know never to ignore an emotion that presents itself within us, within our awareness, even when we cannot identify clearly what it is, where it comes from, or even what it is truly about. Simply letting ourselves feel whatever comes up is always the best solution. The important thing is to bring our focus back afterwards to what we want more of in our lives moving forward.

We can always visualize the future we want, while being firmly in the present and appreciating and being grateful for the past. The problems come when we start losing ourselves in past memories, as this can be an addiction in and of itself, especially when we do not believe we will ever experience anything better than we already have. This goes hand in hand with this fear of change, which is about fearing downgrades. Clinging to past memories, while also fantasizing about a future that is not yet present, while doing nothing towards getting us there, are the two biggest traps of time we tend to fall into. The true power of living is found in the present, in the day-to-day, in *what we choose to do with the here and now in every given moment.* Enjoy what you have while you have it, let it go when it is time to move on, and look forward to the next exciting opportunity. The right questions to ask ourselves here are: Are we happy? Could we be happier? How do we get there from here? And then listen carefully to the answers our intuition whispers back at us.

Getting back to the idea that we are the current way-showers means that not everyone is capable of understanding what we are talking about at present, and that is okay. Because the world is in a transitioning process, a lot of people are simply not where we are energetically. This will come in time, but the truth for us in the meantime is that we must adapt to dealing with our surroundings accordingly. Boundaries play a big role, but also does the knowing of who is a lost cause at the moment, and who can be communicated with. We do not choose these things; we listen and know the truth. It is never an Ego decision, yet it never involves self-betrayal. Not everyone is capable of accepting, or even recognizing, the Truth of things as Truth at this point in time, and this is okay. It means we need to be discerning at first, and never apply pressure on people to get them to see Truth. We all have to progress at our own pace.

This means that we can and should speak our truth, speak of our experiences, but when people try to force their doubts onto us, we must recognize that these doubts are not our burdens to bear. This does not mean we automatically shut down all communication, but that we assess the person's receptivity: are they in dumping mode with no potential for communication? Or are they dumping in an attempt to understand, and do we have a way forward for communication by being careful with our choice of words? If people only want to be heard without having the grace to listen in return, simply move on. They are clearly not ready. There can be no conversation in a monologue.

Some of the most difficult conversations we will have as a direct result of our leveling up energetically will be with the people we are closest to, like family and friends, who simply "don't get it." Our growth challenges their lack of growth, and they will tend to want to bring us back down to their energetic level instead of doing the inner work themselves. This is a natural response, "la loi du moindre effort" as a saying in my native tongue exposes. It means that the choice that requires the least amount of effort is often the one chosen, even when it is blatantly the wrong choice to make. We are allowing ourselves to be a flowing, untethered energy in a world that only values rigid structure and stagnation, of littlest effort for greatest reward. These people will see our growth as a personal offense to them because our energy pushes them to hold themselves accountable for things they would rather ignore about themselves.

Our job here is to stay in our personal power, not choose to give it away to appease others (or insert any other bullshit excuse). We have to allow ourselves to be where we are in our journeys and enable others to be where *they* are in *their* journeys. Do not let them pull you back down vibrationally. This is where boundaries and respect are essential. Be open to hearing what others have to say and let go of what does not apply to you. Are they speaking through their fears, or are they genuine? Take what resonates with you, what *you* need for *your* journey, and leave the rest behind. If they choose to take that personally, it is on *them*. Not you. Leave them to it. It is their mess, and they can deal with it on their own, or not if they so choose. It is not up to us to fix anyone or anything we did not personally have a hand in bringing about. We do not have to take responsibility for anyone else's shortcomings. It is time for us to stop doing the work to cover for a person who does not deserve our kindness. We have to identify when people choose to take advantage of us, and we have to stop enabling them. We have to let people do what they will of their own volition, as long as it does not cross our boundaries.

We should always seek to be clear about what we will tolerate from others and what we will not, but the most important aspect of this is to follow through with removing ourselves from a person or situation when our boundaries get crossed for whatever reason. Some people will deserve second chances, some will not. Some will take that chance and redeem themselves, while some will simply take the opportunity to keep disrespecting us by crossing the same boundaries again. We do not have to tolerate this blatant bullshit, and if they cannot deal with our decision to remove ourselves, that is entirely on them to deal with. We have done more than our part by choosing to offer a second chance in the first place. That was our gift to them, and they chose to throw it in the garbage. Respect that choice and remove yourself. Some people are simply incapable of understanding the negative impact they have if they do not receive the consequences that should go with their choices. Saving them from experiencing the consequences of their choices is always detrimental to unrepentant people. We are doing them a huge disservice by trying to shelter them.

On the other hand, the line *we* have to be clear about is where self-respect ends and the Ego starts. It can be a fine line, a tricky one to identify at first, but it will keep us humble. It will keep us from falling into arrogance, which is common in spiritual teachers who have done some healing and now believe themselves to be beyond or above others. It is also excruciatingly common to see in people who are starting out in their becoming conscious journeys, especially in the early days, though there are relapses that occur at different stages of the journey. No one is exempt from this, not a single person in existence. If you believe yourself to be, check your Ego and Journal. It is a cycle that comes back to us at different stages of our personal evolution in an attempt to keep us humble. As with everything else, it is a choice we have to make to identify this Ego behaviour and choose humility instead. Self-evaluation should be a constant in a spiritual person's life. Honest self-evaluation, to be sure. It is particularly easy to fall into this specific Ego trap, simply because we are meant to. The test is truly about our own ability not only to be humble, but to choose humility constantly, over and over again.

True humility is not about keeping ourselves small. It is about knowing our greatness and not making a big deal out of it, as we understand that every single other human being has this exact same capacity for greatness as we do (in different spheres of life, as there would be no point in some of us being the exact same as another). Because we recognize this potential for greatness in others, we do not take it personally when they achieve it. We are happy for them, we celebrate with them, because we know that it is about so much more than just them, just like we know that it is about so much more than just us. When we know we are nothing special, we become free to become our most special self: our True Self. We recognize that everyone has their part to play, and that all the parts must be different— even if some are similar—in order to understand just how important even the smallest-seeming piece is. The smallest piece is just as important as the largest one: they simply serve different functions of the same whole. The understanding that we are all unique, and that the greatest thing we can contribute to the world *is* our uniqueness, is what true liberation and freedom are.

In time, the people who will learn from us as teachers will find us. We, in turn, must be ready to teach before we embark on that path. We are all, every single one of us, both student and teacher; it is an inescapable Truth of life. Someone who claims to have all the answers is always in Ego. It is up to us to try to redirect them gently, but they may be too out of touch to realize they are in the wrong. Remember that you cannot do anything for someone who does not believe they need the help they truthfully need, just as we cannot make someone see who is attached to having their head in the sand. There is a beautiful saying by Lao Tzu that goes along the lines of: "When the student is ready, the teacher will appear. When the student is truly ready, the teacher will disappear."

This is another fundamental Truth of life, which was pointed out earlier in the book with the example of my former mentor. I was ready to stand on my own two feet, and she gave me the opportunity to make that choice for myself. Of course, I was disappointed in her at first, but then I realized that this was part of both of our healing journeys. For me, it was to show that I do possess all I need on my own, that I had to stop relying on external sources to provide what I thought I needed, that I may become able to rely on my internal Source to receive all I am meant to receive. I needed to stop relying on external crutches because they had served their purpose and now were no longer serving me, just holding me back.

As for her, it showed her rigidified feminine aspect through her greed and her Ego being in control through the blatant unfairness of her offer. She forgot to stay humble and in service to others in favour of only being in service to herself and fawning over her own perceived greatness. She cannot abide people she believes are evolving more rapidly than she is. She is very much struggling with the old attitude of everyone being "inferior" or "superior" to other people, that there are "categories" of people more deserving than others, which is complete Ego talk. There is no greatness present in anyone if they are not authentically humble. Being humble does not mean to discredit or downplay our greatness, but simply not to allow it to get to our heads, to make us believe we are "superior" to anyone, regardless of whom we are speaking about. The moment we think in terms of being "greater" than another, we have failed at life. We have failed to recognize the truth of Oneness. I hope she has learned and evolved from this as well.

This is to say that sometimes people will come to you who are ready to change but who may not be aware of it just yet. The most important quality to adopt is respect for everyone, regardless of whether we agree with them or not. We can disagree on things and still be respectful of each other. When we focus solely on right or wrong, we forget the very important aspect of reality, which is that we are all human, that we all make mistakes, and we are all here to learn, grow, and evolve. I cannot speak for anyone else when I say this, but I personally have never learned anything from someone who yells at me to get their point across. I automatically assume they are stupid and arrogant, because how in the world can they expect me to be open to listening to what they have to say if this is how they choose to communicate with me?

I have never learned anything from being belittled for my choices and actions. I have never learned from being shamed. The lessons that stuck with me, that actually helped me grow and evolve, were those that were gifted to me gently. The ones where the person gave me the grace of being human, of being flawed, of being wrong, as though none of these things really matter, because ultimately they do not. We cannot fault a person for something they did not even know they were not aware of. To do so is disgusting and a huge lack of personal character. Our personal truths and realities are not those of everyone else in the world, so how can we be just expected to know things that do not relate to us? Especially when we have never been in contact with those things before.

This being said, willful ignorance is also disgusting and a lack of personal character. It is up to us to discern the Truth of the individuals we are dealing with: whether we are dealing with a genuine mistake or a manipulative lie. The attitude a person has during this conversation should tell their Truth. Repentance, visible discomfort, and sorrow speak for themselves. Nose in the air, not willing to see they were wrong, also does. The point here is to give people the chance to show their true colours before we make up our minds about them. Even then, attaching ourselves to these answers as though they are immutable is also the Ego coming out. One of the only constants in life is change, after all. Some people will not be able to deal with our personal changes and progress, and that is okay. We must retain the grace of allowing others to be fallible, to be human.

This brings us back to respect. We have to respect that all of our journeys are unique and different, yet also similar in certain ways. We have to respect that personal progress takes different amounts of time per individual. We may become extremely excited by the personal progress we make and have a genuine desire to help others access these amazing, freeing insights, only to be brought up short by someone who has no desire to change things in their lives, even if it is for their betterment. If someone is not open, ready, and willing to face themselves, then it is not up to us to convince them. We need to respect that everyone will progress at their own pace, even if they choose not to progress at all, and that this is perfectly okay. We may not understand it, but we do not need to. It is out of our hands.

All we need to do is respect where they are, let go, and back off. This does not mean to stop living our truth, not at all. It simply means we are not imposing anything on anyone, even and especially when we believe it is for their highest good. Do not deprive these people of doing the work they need to do and learn what they need to learn, how they need to learn it. I have struggled with this, not understanding how people could choose not to want better for themselves, not to want to become the best possible version of themselves. I had to understand that they were choosing their fear, and that this choice had absolutely nothing to do with me, nor could I do anything about it. It is simply not my responsibility to push anyone into anything, even if I know it would benefit them immensely. It is simply not up to me, yet my Ego would insist I keep at it. Live and let live, but do not choose to stay in lower-vibrational levels for anyone.

Stick to helping those who want to help themselves and who show that they are doing the work, or are at least willing to do the work if they are new to doing inner work and may not be sure as to how to proceed. Our lives are a constant journey of learning and evolving, with our potential being to choose growth for ourselves. We should always entertain the thought of how to become the best possible version of Self. When we think we are done, we need to realize it is our Ego speaking. We will be done when we are ascended masters, not before. Until then, there is always more work to do, but the finish line is never the goal; the journey, the choices, the attitude, the changes, the personal accountability, and healing are. People do not have to understand us to interact with us, but it is up to us not to tolerate disrespect. We do not need to justify anything to anyone.

On the contrary, we need to acknowledge the road we have walked so far and celebrate all of it—the good, the bad, and the ugly—and be grateful for every part. Everything we have experienced has shaped us into who we are today. If there is no contrast in our lives, then we do not know what we truly desire. We can only ever move forward at our own pace while working on our *current* challenges. Be proud of where you are right now, regardless of "how far" you perceive yourself to be. Never be ashamed of progress, no matter how much or how little you perceive you have attained. Stop being hard on yourself unnecessarily. Guilt and shame hold us back; they do not help us grow. Address these emotions accordingly. Being free in the present moment is the goal, and it is through being in this state of living that we can truly identify our Soul purpose. The more we clear our baggage, the more space we make for our Soul to become embodied within us fully, instead of just the shard we start out with, which makes the connection to Source all the easier to feel and establish within ourselves.

Living is about coming back to the Truth of the Self. In doing so, importance is placed on keeping an open mind. It happens that our purpose is something we would never normally consider, or we believe is unattainable due to conditioning or otherwise. Knowing our true purpose can be terrifying. It can make us want to shrivel up and hide in a tiny forgotten cave, never wanting to be found. When we are seeking our purpose, we are asked to be our bravest. We are asked to be surrendered to the Universe, to live in complete and total faith and trust, and to be comfortable with the fact that we are completely out of control of how things are meant to happen. We have to be in unconditional acceptance of life as it is, not as we would want it to be. How we want life to be is what we should focus optimistically on as an outcome, not something we deplore that is not here yet, as this is us being stuck in a lack mentality.

We must recognize that there is no lack, there never was, regardless of what our experiences have "taught" us. Our experiences teach us our current mindset, nothing more. We get to choose to change our mindsets through healing, which transforms our external reality into the new mindset we have chosen for ourselves. Our mindset is the sum of our conscious and subconscious beliefs melded together as one. Since we know the unconscious is much stronger than our conscious mind, even though we may have a conscious mindset, the unconscious one will be the strongest of the two.

That said, when we identify our purpose from within, we must stop caring completely about what anyone else thinks. Every single other person's opinions, values, facts, thoughts, perceptions, theories, religion, and beliefs are not only completely irrelevant to us, but also absolutely useless to our growth. This does not mean that we cannot learn and grow from interacting with others; the opposite of this is actually needed. The point being made here is that no one else can be you. No one has the answers you are looking for, but you. Identifying our purpose is a solo, inside job. The answers are within, and only we can feel them. Identifying our purpose is akin to identifying our truth. In the same vein, our Truth has nothing to do with anyone other than us. The Universe always tests us to see if we are ready to move forward in our personal evolution; it never forces us to move forward unless we need to, unless we have been ignoring our Self and our needs for too long.

We have to connect completely with our SEEC—our inner heart—to hear the truthful answers we seek. We know what is best for the Self when we are completely out of the normalcy that is being controlled by fear in our societies. We can feel what the best actions to take are, and we can easily identify fear by the quality of the resistance we feel against doing these best actions. There is a big difference between believing something to be true and knowing something to be true. Beliefs are guesses, at best. Knowing means being in the Truth of things. Many people claim to know the Truth, yet they rarely ever even know themselves to begin with; therefore how could they possibly know Truth? This is where discernment comes in. How truthful a person is in general represents how much access they have to universal Truth to begin with.

Let me make the Truth perfectly clear here: we will never uncover our true purpose if we are not authentically our Self. Our Soul self, not the pretend Self we build to keep ourselves safe. It is normal for there to be a transition between letting go of the old and embracing the new, yet it is important that we stay grounded regardless of how excited we become when we discover more and more Truth. Authenticity, humility, hope, respect for all that lives, and living in Joy regardless of personal circumstance are how we can detect our purpose. It is how we start the ascension process, though this process never moves faster than the effort we are willing to put into it. Even if we have started Awakening, this transformation will not follow through and complete itself on its own. There are multiple layers to Awakening and the highest ones tolerate no bullshit, especially from Self.

The tool I wish to impart in this chapter focuses entirely on the process of figuring out what our Soul purpose(s) is/are. This being said, if you have not mastered the first three parts of this book, doing this exercise will still be of value, but you will not be ready to pursue it head-on. There will likely be disbelief in the way and many, many layers of resistance, which can only lead to our inserting false answers in the exercise, which defeats the entire purpose of doing it in the first place. To be fair, the results could still be interesting, and they could be worth trying out, even if it is only to ascertain that it was not for us after all. Remember that there are no mistakes, only choices and their consequences, whether they are "positive" or "negative" in hindsight, depends entirely on our wounding and how we choose to perceive them, as there is no right or wrong in life, only gaining experience.

This exercise is one of introspection and thus requires total and complete self-honesty. This should be self-explanatory as to why. This exercise is based on the Japanese term Ikigai, which roughly translates into Life (Iki) Worth (Gai), or a reason for existing. The concept itself speaks about being in our purpose, which automatically makes life worthwhile, where inspiration and inspired actions appear spontaneously to us; it is a way of living that always brings deep personal satisfaction along with a strong sense of meaning. Before starting the exercise itself, it is important to take a moment to stop, do some deep breathing, ground ourselves, seek the inner connection we have with the Universe, and then allow our Higher Self (our Soul) to speak to us. We have to be completely in the receptive mode. Do not doubt anything that comes into your awareness; write everything down, especially when it seems to make no sense. Remember that things do not have to make sense to us, little beings blind to the biggest of all pictures.

This exercise focuses on four main questions, subdivided into more categories, as they all touch upon Ikigai (refer to the Quick Reference Guide for a visual representation). We will go through the questions one by one, then uncover how they link together to create new categories of investigation. The first thing to do is spend time pondering, then answering these four root questions: What do you love? What are you good at?

What does the world need at present? What can you get paid to do?

This is not a process that should be rushed. Take time with these individual questions and keep adding things to them as they come to you. I recommend spending 2-3 days with each question individually, as going through daily life with one of these questions in the back of our mind can yield surprising results. Answer truthfully and from a place of deep knowing and truth; never answer with what "should" be written. The answers you come up with will be unique to you, and the more honest and truthful you are, the easier it is to link these answers together to get to your true purpose.

Once enough time has been spent on these questions, and you now have four healthy lists that have been investigated thoroughly individually, take a moment to sit with all of these answers. Your purpose will be found through connecting most of these things together. Therefore, the next logical step is to figure out how they do so. I recommend focusing most on identifying what links what you love with what you are good at. Money comes naturally to those aligned with purpose, always, as it is a confirmation from the Universe that we are headed in the right direction.

Money is also simply energy, one that is tightly connected to the energy of love. How we feel about love is how we feel about money, and vice versa.

For example, I grew up believing I did not need love, that it was worthless, that I should not want for that which I did not have. My views of money were the same, though I was not aware of it, which meant that when I needed money, I had to work hard to get a pittance, just like I had to work hard at getting love from my parents and receiving very little. Nothing was ever just given to me, no strings attached, and I was always given less than I deserved, both for love and money. This interrelated energetic concept will be explored further in the next chapter, but for now the important part is to understand that chasing money is never, ever, the way to get some, just like chasing after love never, ever gives us what we want, or that the results we do get are simply unsatisfactory.

As for the question of what the world needs, our personal perspective and level of understanding of life itself play a big factor in how we are meant to respond. For some of us, it will literally be what the entire world needs, while for others it will be more along the lines of what does *my* personal little part of the world need? Not all of us are meant to better the entire world; some of us need to focus on smaller parts of the world with the same intent of helping all, but in a more focused way, instead of broadly. Some specific parts of the world need specific help, which other parts may have plenty of. For my part, what the world needs is answered by the simple truth that it needs its people to come alive and thrive individually, that we may all thrive collectively, which is exactly why writing this book is part of my purpose.

At this point, it is encouraged to start envisioning the life of our dreams. What would waking up in the morning, excited and full of energy, look like for what we are setting out to do during the day? What would we be up to? What would our "job" look like? I use the term "job" loosely here because it has a negative connotation for me; it feels like a chore I do not want to be involved in doing more than anything else. Therefore, what occupation has you smiling ear to ear regardless of how challenging it may appear to be? What lights up your fire and makes you come alive? What brings with it passion and joy when you are experiencing it or envisioning yourself being a part of it? What can you continuously come back to that still keeps you going for it over and over? What takes over your attention completely to the point you lose track of time? What brings out the best in you? The best version of you? The limitless, inspired, nothing-can-stop-me version of you?

These are the questions we need to focus on, and we should always discard every single anxious thought of fear that dares to show up. We have to learn to tune out and ignore fear in every aspect it tries to take control of our lives. In the same vein, do not be shy to ask your close people what your strengths are, simply because they have a perspective of us that we do not. We may do certain things so well and easily that we do not register that these things are not easy and simple for others to do. This is part of how we sell ourselves short, how we do not understand and see our true potential and beauty. We are sometimes blinded to our own greatness.

As always, feel free to further research and discover everything contained within this book, including Ikigai, while making sure that the sources are credible and well-informed. Something to keep in mind at this point in this book is to start slowing down. Rushing never helps anything come to life faster than it is intended. Moderation is key, as excess and lack are both imbalanced energies. Too much of one thing can be just as detrimental as not enough of another. Listen to the Self: body, Soul, and Spirit.

Chapter 15
Attracting Abundance

———— • ————

Welcome to the second-to-last chapter of this book, which may have attracted the most people to its pages by the premise the title suggests: here is how money comes into our lives. Money attracts a lot of attention, yet it is not the only form abundance can take. If the work presented in the first three parts of this book has not been started, you will not be able to make this chapter work for you in all its intended purpose. For this chapter to work its best, we need to be in the energy of alignment, pursue purpose deliberately, and have healed many wounds surrounding worth and the ability to receive, which connects directly with our innate feminine energy. Even if your feminine energy is mastered, but your innate masculine energy is still unbalanced or unhealed, this chapter may still not work for you, since the masculine energy is the provider energy.

Chapter 15: Attracting Abundance

This is to say that we reap what we sow. If nothing is sown, then there will be nothing to reap. We cannot cheat our way to the finish line of healing. To want to receive unlimited abundance from the Universe, we must be willing to put in the work, to clear our Karma board, and to be of service to the world humbly. This chapter is introduced at the end of this book because there is no fast track to receiving what we have not earned. Just because we are inherently worthy of being abundant at all times, does not mean our current vibrational energy allows us to access our unlimited abundance. The question then becomes: how am I still standing in my own way of receiving what I believe I deserve? Again, the answer is found within—never by blaming outside circumstances—through the principle of the Emerald Tablet: "As within, so without." When we feel abundant from within and are grateful for all we currently have, we attract more of the great things we want. Being in the energy of lack acts as a repellent.

This being said, energy never lies. Just because we believe ourselves to be healed does not mean we necessarily are. What is our external reality showing us, and how do we go from there to where we want to be? Keep in mind that chasing after money may yield some results, but it will never come close to the unlimited abundance the Universe offers when we surrender ourselves to our higher purpose. Chasing after money means limiting ourselves to the financial availability that other human beings have to offer, while attracting our divine abundance is fundamentally limitless.

For this to make sense, we need to understand that money is simply another form of energy, one we can align ourselves with, which is directly connected to our sense of self-worth. Money and love share a frequency this way: how worthy we believe ourselves to be of receiving unconditional love is also how worthy we believe ourselves to be of receiving money freely and easily. This is why we need to believe ourselves worthy of receiving the Universe's blessings, for us to be sufficiently receptive to energy, so that we can allow our blessings to come in through no effort of our own. We are co-creating our reality with the divine at all times. The energy we choose to invest in (by bringing our focus upon it) is exactly what we will receive more of. This means that when we choose to be in the energy of gratefulness, we will receive more reasons to be grateful. The same is true of choosing to invest in the energy of constant complaining: we will be given more opportunities to complain about things. We are always given what we invest in energetically.

This is also why choosing to be in the energy of unconditional love, trust, faith, and surrender facilitates our abundance reaching us, because we are consciously choosing to remove all barriers that could exist between us and infinite abundance by removing fear, worry, doubt, concern, and the need to control an outcome. It is why the need to be right, to be validated externally, to know how, when, and where things will happen, will always get in the way of our receiving abundance. We need to be in the energy of surrender, which is exactly why we will never tap into this energy as long as we do not work on healing ourselves. Patience, humility, and confidence in the unseen and unknowable are essential for manifestation to be its most potent, while also connecting with our SEEC and following our higher purpose. We have to allow things to come in in Divine Timing, without ever forcing an outcome to happen the way we think we want it to, as this would be the Ego believing itself superior to the Universe.

When we fully detach from needing to compare ourselves to others, judge others in any way, perceive things as inferior or superior, or seek any other form of external validation, we become able to simply observe life. Through this, and by understanding that nothing, yet everything, is within our control, we can then understand how the Universe works. This means that when we see and flow with the Universe's natural currents, we never struggle to get where we want to be. We never need to force things into being because we know that when we do this, we are only ever hurting ourselves; we are getting in our own way of receiving Universal blessings. Things will always happen how they need to happen, regardless of how much effort we put into trying to control an outcome, regardless of our personal preferences, simply because we always do these things from a place of bias, whereas the Universe has no bias.

The less we resist the natural current and flow of life, the easier our lives become. This does not mean to never do anything out of fear, nor never take action, because what is meant for us will always find us. While this last part is true, we have to understand the fine line between what amount of effort *needs* to be put in for us to have done enough to be worthy of receiving the intended reward, and identify what is completely out of our control and must be released. We should always be in a surrendered state towards the Universe. Remember that we reap what we sow; therefore, what is within our control to handle is what we should focus on, while what is not within our power is not for us to worry about. We must be in the energy of hope and surrender towards attaining our goals without attachment to specific outcomes or ways to get there.

We need to be grounded in the sense that we are at peace with our current life circumstances and celebrate where we are currently in life. To be grounded means to be connected with the energy of Mother Earth and to recognize and choose to be part of her natural flow. We need to be grounded to welcome in our natural birthright of abundance, and we do this by making our physical environment and personal state of being as peaceful and high-vibrational as we can make them. Embodying our Soul self and receiving Universal abundance are ultimately one and the same vibrationally speaking, though the reasons we choose to do so are equally important. This is why selfishness in the greedy sense will never avail us of what we want. Healthy selflessness (never to our detriment) and the desire to help everyone (not just the self) go hand in hand with humility and flow. Being self-serving to the detriment of others blocks the incoming flow of energetic abundance. Though one can be rich in the "having a lot of money" terms, the greedy, selfish ones have nothing else of substance to fall back on.

Grounding the physical self while clearing out the energetic, mental, and emotional selves is key to bringing in Universal abundance. The clearer and more solidly grounded we are, the easier it is to manifest everything we want in our lives. We need to learn to appreciate and be grateful for the entire process. When we level up energetically, we cannot stand what was normal before. Looking back on my journey, I am now unable to allow anyone to disrespect me (if they choose to do so I choose to either remove myself from the environment or leave this person behind), which is a huge shift from being the first person to propose disrespecting myself in the first place simply because I believed I did not matter. We cannot stand being in lower-vibrational energies than the one we have levelled up to.

Important to note here that just because we have gone further in our personal healing journeys than others, it never means we are now allowed to judge them: this is always unhealed Ego coming in. This ideology is, in fact, a test from the Universe to see if we are capable of being humble, and this is where many spiritual teachers fall short: they tend to believe themselves above those "still healing" and think they possess all the "right" answers, where any other perspective is just wrong and should never even be considered. It is essential to always seek to humble ourselves, as we will never be "superior" or "inferior" to anyone. Who are we to judge a Soul on their journey when we seldom have enough information to base an accurate judgment upon? If we even have any information on who they are at their core or their path in life to begin with.

We are all one and the same, we are all equal, and the moment we judge others, we are simply revealing how much of an asshole we really, truthfully, are. This is why forgiveness is also essential. When we hold onto the energy of being judgmental, we are holding on to unforgiveness, as we are not allowing fellow human beings to be human beings, meaning to be flawed, to make mistakes, to be scared or scarred, to be different, etc.

Abundance and money come naturally to us when we are in tune with the flow of Life, when we follow our Soul purpose, simply because the Universe wants to see us succeed. Money coming in at random from any and all sources to support us when we really need it and ask for it is part of the process of uncovering our Soul path. We will always find that fortune favours us in surprising, unexpected, non-conventional ways when we commit to our Soul purpose and actively follow through with it. This can sometimes be used as a gauge to see if we are truly headed in the right direction, entertaining the right plan or train of thought, or even taking the right steps forward. When we fully commit to our Soul and hold nothing back in pursuing our purpose and being a genuinely good person, the Universe is then truly allowed to make everything fall perfectly into place for us.

However, there is always a downside to the expectation that money shows us the way forward, and that is the possibility that we interpret things wrong. I cannot count how many times I was certain of a particular message being brought to me by the Universe, and although the message was clear, my interpretation of what it meant beyond that had been hijacked by my Ego, and I was making things out to be more than what they were intended to be. This is another spiritual Ego trap that is easy to fall into when we connect with the magic of the Universe: thinking that because we have uncovered a little bit of knowledge, we now possess all knowing. We have to be careful of our own hubris and understand that humility is always required to be our main "state of being" again.

The Truth about today's world is that it is possible to be paid for things we never would have thought could bring money to our pockets before. This is why we cannot be rigid about what form it will take when we ask for assistance from the Universe. We must stay open to our blessings coming in the most perfect way for us, and only the Universe truly knows what that will be. Because money is only another form of energy, we have to ask for it to come to us and expect something to happen without deciding beforehand how it should appear to us. Especially important during all manifestations is to never be in the energy of desperation, as there is no greater energetic repellent. Desperation equates to being in acute awareness that we are in lack mentality, which blocks any blessing from coming in because our consequent focus is solely on our lack of what we desire.

If you have started a practice of daily affirmations or mantras, feel free to incorporate the following: "I am worthy of receiving large sums of money at random" or any variation thereof, and repeat it until you believe it or until it feels like second nature. Affirming verbally our confidence in our Selves and the Universe only ever helps us ground these energies and makes manifestation that much simpler and more effective.

We must always remove attachments to be open to the greatest possible outcome.

Further, when following our purpose, we should follow a trail of what brings us joy. If following your Soul purpose makes you buck and procrastinate, or makes you feel like you would rather die, then obviously you are not following your Soul purpose. This does not mean that every step of the way will make us want to sing and dance around in perpetual bliss; there will be challenges and steps that are less fun than others. The overall feeling, however, will be one that makes us feel empowered, that we are doing something that will help others and ourselves, either on a large or small scale. Ultimately, we come to understand that the end results are not necessarily the goal. How we will have positively affected people along the way will be.

In this energy, it is of utmost importance to be able to listen to ourselves, to identify when something feels wrong. We should never feel forced into doing things, and if we are doing something that makes us feel bad or unhappy, then are we really doing something worthwhile? This is why our emotions act as our compass: the happier we are while doing something, the more inspired our actions are as a direct result of our existing in total bliss and happiness. Being in a bright and happy emotional place allows us to uncover the next inspired step we will take. This is where the usual fear, worry and doubt come in, along with the biggest problem people seem to be facing: "I cannot make money doing this," "this is not a safe job nor a smart move financially speaking," "there is no job security in doing this."

What is important to understand here is that chasing high-paying money jobs that leave us feeling miserable and dissatisfied will always be the worst decision we can make for ourselves. Insert all excuses related to money—which ultimately are all bullshit, regardless of how valid we believe them to be—and we stay stuck in our current position, where we choose to betray ourselves. Not pursuing our Soul purpose equates to self-betrayal, simply because our purpose is the very reason our Soul chose to incarnate. Free will dictates that we get to choose between being brave and seeing the possibilities or staying small and scared and seeing only impossibilities. Ultimately, free will always comes down to being the choice between choosing ourselves or choosing to betray ourselves.

Because money is only energy, when we choose to be in our Truth, in our bliss, when we allow ourselves to be thriving and feeling expansive, connected, and whole, when we choose *ourselves,* we choose to live in joy. It raises our vibration drastically, and money cannot help but be attracted to such a pure and wonderful vibration, as this is its true matching vibration. Authenticity is always key to manifestation, as is receptivity. We already know that receptivity is the domain of feminine energy. Passive receptiveness is the name of the game when manifesting our greatest dreams into reality. It truly is a fine line between wanting something with all our hearts and also being detached from it in a way that feels like we will be perfectly fine no matter the outcome, meaning that we do not attach expectations to our need to receive. Manifestations always come through in the energy of allowing, the energy of humility of the Self in the face of the greater power.

Abundance flows to us when we are energetically and vibrationally magnetic to it, which means there is little to no use to our physicality when manifesting things. All we really have to do is make sure we do not get in our own way of receiving blessings through attachment, negative thinking, hopelessness, and self-sabotage. We have to learn to stop chasing after things and to allow the things that are chasing after us to reach us. This is where patience comes into play. When we choose patience, we are choosing for things to play out exactly the way they are meant to, knowing that the Universe holds all of the cards (meaning that it knows exactly what the best possible outcome is), and therefore exactly how/when/where/what it will deliver things to us in the best possible way.

I know for a fact, through my own life experience, that whenever I have attempted to jump the gun and get things moving in a faster way, the end results were always less than they should have been because I chose to hijack the process. It was made evident to me every single time that if I had chosen patience, things would have unfolded in ways I could not have imagined, which would have given me immense bliss and satisfaction. Still, I had blocked this for myself by not trusting that the Universe could or would deliver. This is exactly why the energies of trust, faith, and surrender are essential to the process, patience being a big part of being in surrender. Patience can be summarized as the deliberate art of surrender.

Let's tune back into the healthy, balanced inner feminine energy and its amazing magnetic properties. This energy always attracts exactly what it needs when it needs it. This is done through setting an intention of receiving, following the inspired actions given by our intuition, which are necessary for momentum to build energetically, then getting out of the way when there are no more intuitive physical actions to be taken prior to receiving. This process is exactly like placing an online order: when all that was required to be done on our part is over with (selecting product, buying, completing order), all we then have to do is wait for the delivery date while knowing everything else will be handled by an external party. We do not always receive our package on the expected delivery date; sometimes it is sooner, sometimes it is later, and sometimes it is never.

The important part here is not to stress over any of it. When it comes to understanding the type of patience required, a similar principle is that of growing plants. Once we have put the seeds in the soil, we water them and wait for the plants to grow. We are not constantly unearthing the seeds to make sure that they are indeed growing. We trust the process and allow for life to work its magic. We do not need to witness the journey of our manifestations for them to come to us. On the contrary, obsessing over how soon this is going to happen will only ever delay the desired results. This again has to do with being in the energy of trust and surrender, especially surrendering our fears to the divine order.

We have already established that our fears hold us back from experiencing the true bliss of living. Fear can take many forms, like anxiety, worry, doubts, negative self-talk, anything to keep us from tapping into our true potential. In the same vein, giving in to "negative" emotions like these will also keep us from truly tapping into our powers of manifestation. To help us here, all we really need is stillness. Peace and quiet. Moments of alone time, where our minds and bodies are completely disengaged from life, and tapping into energy within and without. From complete stillness comes all the answers we need, as this can help us highlight and identify the tiny whisper of our intuition, which comes directly from our SEEC, which is in turn a direct connection to the Universe. We can always tap into our inner heart this way to retrieve motivation, ideas, next steps, basically all the possible fuel needed for the fire of our Souls.

The idea behind connecting with our inner heart, or SEEC, is to allow ourselves unlimited access to the pure, unconditionally loving energy that comes directly from the Universe, along with all potential guidance that can spring from this source, which can *never* lead us astray. Truly tapping into this connection will feel incredibly empowering, warm, fuzzy, loving, and limitless *because* it directly links us to Source energy. How we feel when tapped into this energy is how we should be feeling 100% of the time, and to start tapping into this energy is the start of our Soul transformation simply because when we do, there is no way we can ever settle with going back to our old Self and old way of seeing life. When we connect with Source, the pull of our Soul becomes undeniable, and we tend to be seen as glowing from within because we have access to the purest, highest level of energy possible. This is the new reality we are meant to birth onto this planet, and this is why when we connect with it, it raises our personal vibration and forces the people around us to level up as well. They are meant to be left behind if they cannot or will not evolve with us.

The plain Truth is that we already know what we want to experience during this lifetime on a Soul level. Our human minds have simply been wiped of conscious memories of our Soul plan, but energetic traces remain, and these are what we tap into as children. The goals, dreams, and ambitions we held dear as children still hold great meaning for us as adults, even when we choose to discard them as silly, childish fantasies. They are usually part of our Soul purpose, even when we cannot see how these things could be possible in our present moment. However, when we fearlessly choose to make things possible for ourselves, when we choose to follow our purpose wholeheartedly, even when we do not know how to make things happen, or how things will play out, the Universe will always be there to guide us in the right direction. We are here to play with Life, to try things, to fail, to grow, to learn, to evolve, never to stay stagnant, stuck, and dissatisfied.

This means that the Universe will not tolerate our own bullshit. We cannot bargain, barter, or beg our way out of learning the lessons we signed up to learn. This means that trying to manifest something that is simply not meant for us will never work out in our favour, which is exactly why, when we ask for things, we need to be as vague as possible while also pinpointing exactly what we want. This means we should ask for "the best possible home for me for my highest good and the highest good of all," instead of "I want that massive mansion down the street." The less materially specific we are, the greater our manifestation powers can be because we recognize that we are not the ones in control, that our Ego desires are not our Soul desires.

This means that when we acknowledge that our Soul is pulling the strings in the background, it becomes easy to relax into this guidance and let our Soul show us exactly why we are here and what we are meant to do. Since our Soul wants the best for us, as its goal is for us to upgrade and evolve, we will never be led astray by our intuition. It is only by misunderstanding or misinterpreting what we believe to be our intuition through our Ego lens (when we have not done the work to put the Ego back to sleep in the backseat) that we will believe we have received "faulty" or "wrong" guidance. Also important to remember is that we may never understand why we are going through a specific event or challenge *while we are going through it*, and this is not something to fear or get angry about. It simply means that we needed a different perspective, and this was the way our Soul decided we needed to learn it, so that the lesson may stick with us. Placing blame is never useful, and only serves to distort our perceptions of things, to take away from our objective understanding.

All of this to say that when we align with our purpose and allow ourselves to pursue it fully, we are the most attuned to the energy of manifestation, which is truthfully what attracting abundance is all about. As these floodgates of Universal goodness start opening, we will receive only a trickle: a promotion here, meeting the right person there, being offered a surprising opportunity, and so on. How much we allow ourselves to receive blessings becomes directly proportionate to how much we allow ourselves to accept gifts from the Universe. This is where gratitude comes into play, as being grateful for all the goodness in our lives becomes a direct conduit for more goodness to enter. Remember that what we focus on and invest in directly correlates to what we receive more of in our lives.

Going back to the Universal energy of unconditional love, we tap into when we allow ourselves to connect fully with our SEEC, this state of being is what we are meant to embody as Souls. This is meant to become second nature for us, and the more time we spend in it, the less we desire to be apart from it, simply because it feels so damn good. This is where we start to wonder why we ever chose to be separate from it, for which the answer is our Souls' evolution. We were meant to choose to come back to the Universal energy of unconditional love of our own free will. We need to recognize that life is infinitely better within this energy than without. This is about healing a Soul wound of separation. The more we choose this energy as a way of life, the easier it is for us to access it. Living in this energy 100% of the time means living in a constant energy of unconditional abundance in every way, shape, or form. We get the ticket to embark on this magical side of life by doing the internal work.

This does mean that for those who refuse to do the inner work, to overcome their own Ego, or who choose to settle as a passive player in their own game of life, they will never have access to all the magic life has to offer, simply because they are refusing it. This is a choice they are making for themselves; as such, they are not our responsibility, no matter how much we love them and want the best for them. They have to want the best for themselves and be honest about what that best truly is on their own individual level. We do not get to choose for them, we can only hope to inspire by choosing for ourselves. This personal choice we make to be in the unconditional loving energy of the Universe affects the entire world by combining with the choices others make in their own worldwide energetic grid quadrants. The more people choose this for themselves and actively live in this energy, the easier it will be for others to feel, access, and tap into this energy, *because* we are collectively raising this vibration individually by choosing this for ourselves.

We can understand this further by using the example of the Yin-Yang symbol once more, which means that what is true on a smaller scale is also true on a bigger scale, and so on and so forth into infinity. This means there is always a smaller picture and a bigger picture on infinite scales. Earth is likely an atom on some bigger scale that we experience as this insanely huge, expansive place, but imagine how utterly impossibly enormous Earth would seem for an ant. Imagine how microscopic humanity is for whatever views Earth as an atom, and how utterly undetectable ants are for these beings. By understanding how huge the scales of Life truly are from our very limited human perspective, we can then understand how, since healing is already an inside job for us as humans, healing on a collective level through our individual choices becomes the Earth's inside job.

This means that when we surrender to the flow of Life, we are doing our *actual* individual job in the great scheme of things. This is exactly why we are then entitled to access unlimited abundance: *because we are choosing to do what we were always meant to do in the first place*. The important questions are: "How am I hiding from my Truth, from my Soul purpose, and how am I justifying this hiding to myself?" To be in this energy of flow, of unconditional love and abundance, we need to have released fear of loss and lack mentality completely. We need to see the value in everything that is currently in our lives, and when it is time to move on from people, places, jobs, situations, etc., we can do so with gratitude and appreciation instead of dread and fear of the unknown. We have to learn to be independent from attachments that only serve to hold us back. This does not mean to lose appreciation for people or things, but to know when to let go and to choose to do so in a healthy manner. It is normal to feel sadness when we are parting ways with people, places, or things, but this sadness should not make us want to stay stuck, small, and ultimately self-betraying. Less truly is more.

On the other hand, the more we choose to live in this 5D reality—the energetic bliss of living—the more we will open up to attract people who are on the same wavelength—or frequency—as us. These people who are also choosing their personal healing journeys will likely be Soul tribe members, people whose Souls are not unknown to us; Souls with whom we may have shared many lifetimes. Since our goal as human beings is to heal, the more we heal, the more we raise our core personal vibration as a direct result. Once we have been around high-vibrational people for long enough, we realize just how potent living this way really is, how simple, easy, and natural it feels, even if we do not understand it at first, as it can appear as magic in certain individuals or during certain circumstances. The Truth simply is that when we are connected to Source, we are connected to Life.

Our bodies act as anchors for our Souls, the roots of our being in this physical reality, and the true nourishment necessary for all Souls is Love. The more we love our bodies, the more it can do for us, to support us in our Soul endeavors. The more we love ourselves, the more we give ourselves permission to truly be who we are at a Soul level. The more we embody our Soul, our Truth, the easier life "appears" to become. To understand this more visually, we can compare 3D living to being in the Matrix, in a similar concept to the movie's premise of the same name. We live unconsciously in reality at first (3D living), until we can live consciously within the programming (5D existing), and once we understand how the programming works, we can start playing with it.

This is why it is so important to make peace with the body we have decided to play with in this lifetime and the circumstances surrounding our awakening: we have chosen all of these things as Souls prior to incarnation. Taking good care of our bodies is an act of self-love, therefore an act of healing. We do this by exercising, eating healthy foods, and respecting our bodies' limitations. It is important not to mistake weight with health, as there is not always a correlation to be found there. Some people carry heavy energetic weight that is held on a physical level as a surplus of fat, for which no amount of healthy eating or exercise can alleviate, simply because the cause is not physical but energetic. This can mean that healing the specific wound associated with the excess fat will make it melt off of a person almost overnight, but we must not start saying all of our excess fat is energy, as this is simply not always the case.

On the other hand, naturally skinny people are not necessarily healthy; they simply have a different kind of body type. Having a certain amount of fat on our bodies is not only natural, but essential for us as fat acts as a reserve of energy for when we are in extreme survival conditions. The conditions themselves have changed over time as we are no longer in direct threat to the elements and wildlife (for the most part), and we need to be way less physically active than when we had to hunt for our food. The most important thing to know here is that the goal is to love ourselves exactly as we are in our present moment, and if we want things to be different for us physically, then we need to work at it, but never in an abusive way.

By this, it is meant that when we hate our bodies and want them to change from a negative mindset or negative state of viewing things, the results we may get will either not last, or we will never be satisfied with any amount of change. Transformation only occurs through self-love, however we choose to express it. What is important is always how we *choose* to feel. If we want to change—and this is true for every aspect of life—we have to focus on the positive and embrace positivity. Our bodies respond incredibly better to being talked about and thought of in a loving way than in a degrading way, and this is true for everything in life. People, animals, and plants all respond better to receiving gentle, nurturing, loving treatment than to violence, regardless of whether it is verbal, physical, or other. We must practice deliberately choosing to view things, including ourselves, in all aspects, in a loving light. We have to choose to feel good within ourselves in order to be able to always feel good regardless of outside circumstances.

As mentioned, our physical bodies are the roots that anchor us onto this physical plane, on Mother Earth. Wanting to change anything about who we are naturally is always a symptom of a greater wound hidden inside. Our backward societies create countless wounds of self-image, which affect how we choose to regard and treat ourselves. This is exactly why the most important thing to remember is to keep track of how we feel about ourselves internally, as anything else, such as other people's opinions (read projected wounding), only keeps us stuck and small when we choose to let them affect us. The perfect solution to becoming completely bullet-proof to external negativity is self-love. This includes self-compassion, self-kindness, self-gentleness, and most importantly, self-acceptance.

On this note, many people believe they love themselves, and they would believe it to be asinine to say that it is important to love the Self. The Truth is that it is important to love the Self *unconditionally*, as this is much different than just superficially loving the Self. We can truly say we love ourselves unconditionally when we are completely at peace with how we look and appear at all times (and also being happy with who we are within), regardless of whether we deem ourselves to be presentable or not. Many people mistake being proud of their physical bodies as self-love, yet will engage in numerous destructive and self-sabotaging tendencies, through alcohol or drugs, and other addictions like over-eating, sexual gratification, watching porn, and other ways to disconnect from Self and reality, if only for a time.

We only ever try to leave our reality through our addictions when we are not well within ourselves, when we are unable to be unconditionally loving to the Self at all times in all ways. Indulging occasionally as a special treat once in a while is one thing, but to be dependent on an escape from reality is another. Again, as with everything else, Love is the answer. Some of you will be wondering why I am going through all this in this chapter of Attracting Abundance, and the answer is very simple: we can only attract what is on our personal vibrational frequency, and only what we subconsciously believe ourselves to be worthy of attracting. If we want to manifest our dreams, then we had better believe we are worthy of having them, and this starts with loving, respecting, and valuing the physical Self, through both the internal and external aspects. Bringing in the energy of Love and Joy in all moments of our lives, for all people around us to experience, regardless of whether they choose to be with us on this high vibrational train or not, is how we allow ourselves to embody the Truth of being the powerful manifesters we really are.

The following are multiple examples of self-love practices, which are strongly recommended to be implemented in our daily routines if we wish to see a difference in how we decide to view and consequently treat ourselves. The goal for any of these exercises is to permit ourselves to do something we love, or that makes us feel really good about ourselves, or that taps into our natural creativity to help it expand, so that we may get a sense of the true potential life holds on the daily. The importance here is to stop having days where nothing goes our way. We have to give ourselves reasons to choose to feel good, happy, creative, and free—and consequently make this choice—to truly tap into our Soul truth and let it drive us forward.

A great first habit to start for this express purpose is to have a gratitude journal. This can be a physical journal, a file in our Notes app on our phones, random pieces of paper—whatever works, really—and at any point during the day, the goal is to write down at least a few moments when we feel gratitude for a thing, person, or event. This could be as simple as "I found a dime on the ground today—good luck coming my way!" or "This person did this for me unexpectedly," "This made me smile," or "That made me feel good about the work I do and that my peers appreciate me." Another great practice to do separately or to add to this ongoing gratitude journal is to give three reasons why you love yourself daily (without repeating any affirmations) for a month. This will create a good writing habit and help with any feelings of self-loathing that may be hiding beneath the surface, which we are seldom aware we carry against ourselves.

Among self-love practices can be found any and all simple things that bring us joy on a personal level, like taking a pleasant bubble bath, spending time exercising or playing sports, mindful meditation, painting even when we think we suck at it as perfection is never an achievable goal (having fun with spreading and mixing colours is a great achievable goal regardless of the result of the created art piece), writing poetry, singing for the pleasure of it, taking pictures of things that bring us joy, doing arts and crafts, scrapbooking, baking, cooking, buying ourselves nice flowers or a little treat, getting pedicures/manicures (regardless of gender), getting a massage, spending time alone in quiet in nature, walking, reading, lighting candles in our homes, basically pampering ourselves a little on a regular basis.

Being creative means to allow our Soul to express itself, as we are all creative beings to begin with; we have simply stopped allowing ourselves to be because we have been sold the stupid idea that everything needs to be perfect at all times, that things do not deserve to be done unless they are done perfectly. Be messy, flawed, human, and choose to just have fun with life. We are here for a short time, so make the most of it, as there is no real point in living our lives if we do not enjoy them along the way. We are creating here the habit of *making life meaningful* instead of living in the mindless, meaningless, droning grind we were told life was.

The above list is one of the physical ways to create happiness during the day. Still, the important aspect of the practice is to give ourselves unconditional love and reasons to be in the energy of gratitude, as this energy is what truly powers manifestations into becoming reality. We need to be keenly aware of the energy we choose to exist in and realize that this overall energy will dictate whether things go our way or not. We choose this energy by default based on the mindset we are operating in. If we wish to change the energy in our lives, we need to work on changing our mindset. This starts with becoming aware of how we choose to view and speak to (and about) ourselves. We need to start a habit of being conscious of our self-talk and turn it into exclusively uplifting talk. This does not mean to pull a veil over our own bullshit and push the narrative that we are perfect. It means to make peace with our imperfections, our flaws, and choose to make the most we can in bettering them and ourselves, while accepting our perceived imperfections.

The easiest way to lay bare every ounce of negativity we hold against ourselves is to stand naked in front of a mirror and just let our eyes roam all over our bodies. The goal here is to notice how harsh and unforgiving we are towards our own bodies. Our eyes will be drawn to everything we consider undesirable about our appearance, and this is where we can identify every single negative thought we carry. We use the AAUR technique here to identify these negative thoughts and beliefs that are only hurting us, we accept that we feel this way about ourselves and all the emotions this acceptance entails, we choose to understand that we are being assholes towards ourselves, and we choose to release this bullshit energy and narrative that we are not good enough exactly as we are. Because we are good enough exactly as we are, and there is no other starting point for us than the here and now. We have to choose to shift all of these emerging emotions, thoughts, and beliefs into soft, gentle, kind, and unconditionally loving ones.

A great way to start this work is to note down every single detail that triggers our negativity, along with the exact phrasing of that negativity, and choose to start doing the inner work associated with these wounds. We need to start noticing just how much we belittle and talk down to ourselves (often unconsciously) so that we may change this consciously. We need to identify all places where we disregard, discredit, undervalue, and choose not to appreciate ourselves and our inherent worth. We need to understand where our self-rejection and self-loathing come from to choose to think and feel differently, to eliminate them entirely. What sparks disgust when we look at ourselves, and why? What brings about shame? Guilt? Any and all negative emotions need to be identified, so make sure to sit with everything until all is made clear.

Once we have written down all the ways we are holding ourselves up to ridiculous standards, belittling ourselves, or being unnecessarily harsh and degrading, this exercise then asks that we transform all of these statements into healthy, loving, positive ones. Even if we are too programmed to be negative about ourselves to fully appreciate what we are doing in this present moment, just the act of physically doing it will start to create changes. It becomes even better when we can go back and look at how much has changed in our behaviour towards ourselves as a direct result of doing this kind of exercise over time.

During the entire process of learning to love ourselves unconditionally, one of the most important aspects is to repeatedly and continuously choose to forgive ourselves for how badly we have thought of - and consequently treated - not only our body, but also our creativity, our minds, our opinions, our values, basically everything that composes our being, the Truth of who we really are in this incarnation and beyond as a Soul. Mantras and positive affirmations also help with this self-love process, even when it feels awkward at first. These work best when we identify the worst of the feelings/emotions that we hold against ourselves and consciously choose to turn them into affirmations of self-worth and self-love. Some of the most potent ones for my own experience have been "I am beautiful," "I am worthy," "I deserve unconditional love," and "I am a miraculous being and I can be all I desire to be."

Another important aspect of practicing self-love is to identify, respect, appreciate, and celebrate what we are good at, our natural strengths and qualities. A lot of us are quick to dismiss the beauty of our talents because we are quick to dismiss anything about us being beautiful or as having value. We need to identify and destroy this mindset, as it only serves to keep us small and stuck in low-vibrational energy, away from our unlimited abundance. We need to embrace our uniqueness, as this uniqueness is what makes us walking miracles.

It is incredibly easy to fall into the trap of believing the "value system" currently surrounding looks and desirability. Still, the Truth is that value is placed where we decide we place it. If we decide we have no value, then nothing we do can change that until we decide to shift this mindset into believing that we do have value. Just because it is easy to wish we were different does not mean this wish has any worth in and of itself. The true path is to choose to love ourselves for exactly who we are and exactly what we can (and are meant to) bring to the grand table of Life; what only our unique Soul essence and path can highlight and bring forth.

Chapter 15: Attracting Abundance

In the matter of practicing self-love, we have addressed how we view and speak of ourselves as a necessary stop in attracting abundance, but the flip side of this coin is how we allow others to treat us. The first step is to shift this internally, but remember that there are always clues to be found in our external reality regarding what we hold to be true subconsciously. Once we start believing we deserve better, we can truly see just how badly the people in our lives have been treating us, for whatever reason. At this point, we need to stop allowing and/or tolerating external disrespect entirely, while still having the grace to be in the energy of unconditional love towards others and maintaining healthy boundaries. In a nutshell, this means getting away from people who cannot appreciate and value the beautiful souls we are and who cannot or choose not to uplevel themselves.

Attracting abundance happens when we let go completely of desire and expectation and allow the Self to be surrendered entirely to Universal energy while existing consciously in the present moment, completely without attachment to outcomes.

Chapter 16
Awakening, Enlightenment, and Ascension

———— • ————

When we start awakening to the Truth of things, it is impossible to go back to how we were before. It becomes impossible to escape the Truth of who we are, and the choice we are forced to make here is to either choose ourselves and dive into this crazy, scary vortex of authenticity or to remain where we are and be miserable for the rest of our lives. There is no going back from awakening because everything not in alignment with our Truth will feel unbearably wrong to us. There will always come a point where we simply cannot choose self-betrayal any longer, as it will have become far too destructive to our well-being. We are meant for so much more than our current circumstances, each and every single one of us. Spirit, the Universe, our Higher Selves, our energetic guides, and guardian angels will always point us in the right direction, but none can make us step forward. It is entirely up to us.

More often than not, the greatest challenges we will face initially all have to do with the mind, which is why this book started with addressing the mind and elaborating on the AAUR technique. We have to learn to release the old and realize how irrelevant other people's opinions of us are. We must stop depending on other people to meet our needs, as we know we have to be capable of meeting our own needs first and surrendering what is beyond our control. We understand that the level of change we wish to bring about in our lives depends entirely on our consequent choices and actions. We know that sometimes we are meant to go ahead full throttle in life, while also knowing that sometimes we really need rest, relaxation, and quiet.

On a more personal note, we are finally arriving now at the final chapter of the book. Reading it will have changed some understandings and perspectives, or opened your mind to the fact that there is more to life than is advertised. If you have applied any of the teachings, you will have seen some changes. It is important to celebrate those, especially at first, as they come around more often and serve as encouragement in our moving forward in Life through healing. It is essential to understand that we are the only ones truly holding ourselves back. When we acknowledge and accept this fact for what it is, we can truthfully become empowered to change things into what would be best for us on a personal level.

The awakening process can and does take many forms simply because every single Soul has their own journey planned out for them. Again, it is essential to understand that comparison (in this case, comparing journeys) is only ever an Ego booster and nothing more *because* our Souls have orchestrated our individual journeys. No one's life will be the same; the challenges can be similar, but with different costumes and colours, meaning that if the main theme being experienced is betrayal, some people will experience this from a love partner and some from a parent or sibling; some will even experience both. The details will always be catered to the Soul's evolutionary needs, but the main themes can all be summarized to specific hurts. This is why claiming that no one can understand our pain is deeply, deeply Egoic bullshit.

Becoming aware of ourselves and our Truth, living consciously in the energy of co-creation, retaking control of our lives and personal power, connecting with Source/Universe/God and our purpose; all of those things are facets of awakening to our true potential, which can only happen through healing and consequently raising our vibration, perspective, and general overall energy. Connecting with our intuition and inner heart, our SEEC, leads us to alignment, or the perfect flow of Life. We start seeing signs and synchronicities meant to deliver messages to us, and although we may not always understand and trust these at first, over time, and after some self-work, we start tapping into the Truth of what they want to show us. Do not worry if you are not always understanding them, as the Universe will always redirect us towards our path of highest good, regardless of how much we try to fight against the natural Flow to control things and feel safe.

We already know that refusing a lesson or trying to ignore it always plunges us back into the same cycle, for us to choose to learn this time around, because we understand that to progress and evolve, we have to decide that for ourselves. We also understand then that the Universe will test us to see if we were full of shit or not in our desire to evolve. It is important to remember that we cannot fast-track our evolution, that there are no cheat codes, and that there are no level skipping products or healing modalities. All we really have to choose between is to face ourselves or continue to hide, and sometimes the best decision we can make is to hide. Sometimes, we need a break from learning and evolving, because these energies require much out of us. Evolution will always make us uncomfortable at first, and it is up to us to become comfortable with the uncomfortable until it becomes the new comfortable.

This period of change and integration of new dimensional realities is not only important, but necessary to go through, and sometimes these changes take time. Why? Because we are never given more than we can handle. Sometimes a change can be so drastic that it can take up to a few months or years before things can settle down again. Yes, we have our private timeline of growth possibilities. Still, it is necessary to understand that Earth also has its own private growth timeline, and some parts of our personal evolution can only be unlocked after the energies have already upgraded within the planet. The planet upgrades through the external energetic help of other planets and stars aligning, while also benefiting internally from the Souls doing their work on her surface.

Our inside job of working on ourselves is also the Earth's inside job of working on herself. We always have to remember that there is a bigger picture we cannot fully grasp behind the scenes. The reason so much evil is still happening on the planet can be understood through our own evolution process: the darkness has to be brought to light first to be dissolved in its entirety. What remains hidden in the darkness can never heal, as we heal through exposing our shadows to the light.

Since the beginning of the book, the idea is to mentally distance ourselves from the happenings of daily life to be a quiet, judgment-free observer. Look back now at where you were before doing the work since Chapter One, and where you are now. How differently do you move around in the world now? How little do you let others affect you? Are you making better choices for yourself? Look at just how much you have evolved and correlate that with how much work you have put into bettering yourself as an individual. Do not be worried if everything seems to have gone to shit in your external reality: when we shift inside, things always shift outside. Remember to always focus on what you want to attract more of, instead of worrying or being concerned with what does not seem to be aligning yet. Part of surrendering is letting go of time and control entirely, and letting things play out as they need to.

With all of this being established, the process of awakening starts with identifying and aligning with our Soul purpose, with understanding and embodying the Truth that we are meant for more. We know we are always (and already) connected to Source, therefore, we can shed all fears, excuses, self-doubts, and any other reasons we use to justify our not living the life of our dreams, why we cannot succeed, or why we feel we are not worthy or good enough. We know to get out of our own way, of not letting our minds or our hearts get the better of us through intrusive thoughts and/or emotions. We have started the process of mastering the conscious Self and are actively, continuously working on ourselves. What does this work look like?

In a nutshell, the following are the end goals of living Life embodied as a Soul. We work on these principles until we *can* embody them through healing ourselves enough to be a vibrational match to holding these energies. It is one thing to understand and apply them. It is another to embody and live these things as second nature. The former is awakening, the latter ascending. In no particular order, or to be more accurate, in no predetermined, one-size-fits-all bullshit ideology, here follows some of the goals we are aiming to achieve through this process of awakening.

We stop taking things personally on any and all levels. We get over ourselves and out of our own way. We love and support ourselves unconditionally. We celebrate our progress and achievements, as small as they may seem. We fearlessly follow our intuition, even in the smallest of ways. We surrender the need to know and understand when things are beyond our limited perspective. We trust that the Universe always has our backs and provides for us unconditionally. We can handle anything that comes our way. We know when to take time out and respect it. We trust that when things excite and ignite us into action, we otherwise live in a state of unperturbed calm and peace. When working does not feel like working. When we have that extra spark of joy about life within us, we choose to share it. We feel fulfilled, happy, joyful, grateful, appreciative, and hopeful without effort, as a natural state of being. We are content with our lives and enthusiastic about what is yet to come. We feel blessed, and we know we co-create our reality. We live in unwavering faith and hope, combined with taking inspired action. It is simply to be open to all Life has to offer while knowing that whatever may happen, we will be capable of handling it, and things will always turn out for our highest good.

Awakening is to shed the layers of limitations, armor, need to be right or to get "ahead" of others, to have all the answers, and other Egoic patterns that were conditioned into us, and those we have also placed upon ourselves. It is to shed all bullshit, to get back into Truth. This means shedding all anxieties, distress, disorders, depression, panic attacks, impostor syndromes, and all beliefs attached to feeling like we do not belong or are not worthy. We understand that home is where the heart is. We know that our hearts are our sacred, secret gardens and that how we tend to them reflects our outer reality. If we neglect our own care, the world will also neglect our care. If we do not love ourselves, then how can the world give us love if we are not open to receiving that energy to begin with? We understand that how we treat ourselves is how we allow others to treat us. People will not stop disrespecting us if we also decide to disrespect ourselves. We always reap what we sow, although seldom in the way we have imagined it would happen.

The goal of Life is to return to the authentic Truth of Self by removing all imposed human conditioning, past life wounding, and personal beliefs that are simply false in their understanding of Life. We remove the hold of fear upon our Soul and choose to thrive instead. The goal of Life is to give ourselves the true freedom we seek: the internal one to simply be ourselves. Achieving those goals can only start with alignment to our Soul and purpose. We must balance what we want to experience with how we can best serve the world until we realize they are one and the same path. This is why we can never progress fully as long as we are not authentic to the Truth of who we are on a Soul level, the deepest level possible. Life is never limited to "right and wrong"; it is about transcending that limited perspective into Truth—and then embodying that Truth. Life is about transcending the fear of pain in favour of living through Love. As long as there is struggle within, there can only be minimal flow, and that flow is what leads us to uncovering our purpose.

Which brings us to the keys of living in a 5D reality: surrender, unconditional love, and humility. Ascension becomes a commitment to living Life authentically through these three key energies. If we do not embody them 100%, we cannot evolve further into enlightenment and eventually ascend. Remember that the Universe always tests us to make sure we are not only ready to move on, but also willing, and that we will never receive our wishes if our foundation made of these energies is not solid enough to support our wishes coming into our physical reality. Ascension is about transcending the limitations of the physical world, the limited 3D way of life we are all born into. It means upgrading our perception of life one dimension at a time.

Let's explore more in-depth what ascension and being ascended—or living an ascended life—actually refer to and look like. The first thing to understand clearly is that *all humans are meant to ascend*, but it remains a personal choice to make and follow through with. No one can do it for us, as that would defeat the entire purpose of free will. Being ascended means to have completely cleared and balanced our karmic board, and now live Life through our genuine Source conduit of Oneness connection, which manifests as living through the choice of authenticity, joy, happiness, and Truth. It means holding the energy of unconditional love towards all, while never indulging in self-betrayal; to know one's true worth and to accept nothing less from others.

It means to come back to Respect of All Life, to respect everyone's individual journeys and where they are on it, how much they choose to work on it, and who they currently are as an individual, for where they are in their personal evolution. We understand that people go at their own pace; at that pace is none of our business. We choose to move forward on our own journey at our own pace, and those who cannot keep up will be left behind. There is nothing wrong with this. If people want to keep up with us to remain in our lives, they will, and if they do not, wish them well and move on.

We know that holding ourselves back for another's sake is just more self-betrayal, and ultimately, we are doing them a huge disservice by limiting our own growth to accommodate their Ego. A possible reason for their "delayed" growth could be that perhaps their Soul is waiting on yours to activate higher vibrations for theirs to be activated by your upgraded energies. If we are not moving forward because we do not want to leave this specific person behind, then we are not activating ourselves into becoming an activation beacon for others, the scale or reach of which may be massive energetically and would benefit many people beyond our awareness.

Being ascended also means transcending the limitation of time, as ascension is 5D energy, and time is the 4th dimension. We know that time, as we understand it collectively, is a social construct meant to keep us stressed and stuck in survival mode. The natural flow of time (aka seasons changing) is simply the physical structure of cycles that we are meant to relate to, which helps us understand how nothing is permanent, all is ever-changing, and we get to create what we want, when we want to. We understand life to be about choice: the choice to follow our Soul's intended plan and path—what we label fate or destiny—or the choice to remain stuck in our wounding and limited beliefs. We understand that *all of our choices* can be summarized in this manner. Everything in life is about choosing between what brings us joy and purpose and what otherwise dims our light.

An ascended being will always do what is right for the sake of it being the right thing to do, without exception, regardless of whether they receive praise or gifts in return. We feel deeply about how doing the right thing is about living in unconditional love and choosing not to self-betray, as betraying others is the same as betraying Self. We live within the deep knowing that the Universe loves us, protects us, provides for us, keeps us safe, and is always on our side, rooting for us to succeed without ever doing us the disservice of coddling or bypassing the necessary learnings. The Universe loves us so unconditionally that it always allows us to learn and grow at our own pace. People who remain stuck choose to be so, and there is nothing inherently wrong with that. We know that other people's lives are none of our business, and that we are absolutely no one and nothing to give ourselves permission to judge others.

In essence, being ascended means to embody the Truth of Oneness by having surrendered completely to the flow of Life, not only physically but also on an energetic, emotional, and mental level. Embodying is never complete unless done on all levels; therefore, ascended beings understand that this process is never a one-day journey, but a lifelong commitment instead, one that becomes a way of life we choose to embrace. It is not a way of life anyone can be coerced into, nor can it ever be faked. Those attuned to divine Truth can always sense, and are turned off by, people who claim to be "further ahead of the pack" when their actual truth is all around and within them for us to witness. We know that no alignment is present when the words do not match the actions. Being ascended also means that we can sense the level of alignment in others through our clair senses, as we are One with Source.

One of the reasons humility is such an important aspect of ascension is the simple Truth that when we are not humble, it is always because the Ego is the one in charge, even when we cannot see that for ourselves. Ascended beings embody the Truth that even if we think we are right, we are always open to being wrong. How arrogant is it to believe we know everything in a world of infinite possibilities? This is why when people claim to be the only ones to possess the be-all-end-all of knowledge, and claim that everyone else is wrong or "out of touch," immediately, there are red Ego flags surrounding them. An enlightened being never cares about *being* right. They only care about what is true, and what is not, regardless of being right or wrong about them. An enlightened person knows they are always learning; there is always something more to learn. An enlightened being is an eternal student who is also an eternal master teacher.

It takes more than just humility to ascend; it takes hard work and dedication to see all of our flaws, shortcomings, failures, "undesirable qualities," and any other perceived "downsides" or "shortcomings" of our person and to choose to embrace all of them with healing and unconditional love. Enlightenment means to embrace all of who we are and all that comprises us in this reality. We choose to leave our busy minds and busy lives behind to honor simplicity and contentment, to bring our focus back into presence since there is no other way to Live. We know that the past is made to be learned from, and that the future is ever between our hands in our present moment. If nothing we do matters in the grand scheme of things, then what matters is what we choose to do, and how we approach what needs to be done.

One of the biggest indications that we are truthfully on the right path to ascension is that we choose to experience life through the lens of having fun with the energies of creation, and we decide to do this at any and all given moments. There are very few exceptions to this rule, most of them being around experiencing loss or other heavy emotions that are beyond our control. Just because something is meant to be done seriously does not mean it has to be devoid of fun. Unfortunately, our societies tend to label fun as a luxury, a lack of capability, or a lack of trustworthiness. How dare we enjoy ourselves and our lives when work is to be done? How dare we experience joy within the "mundane," everyday life? Fun is something to be earned! Not freely given, and certainly not our innate nature, oh no, no, no.

Enlightenment is the capacity to see the silver lining in all possible situations and the knowledge that problems only exist if we focus on them instead of their potential and possible solutions. We know that a problem will only ever be difficult to deal with if we decide and/or expect it to be. How often have we put off dealing with what felt like an overwhelming, unwelcome problem, only to work up the nerve to deal with its hugeness and realize it was not as bad as we had anticipated it to be? Problems are mental challenges, where the goal is not to attach ourselves to them unintentionally by delaying doing what we know needs to be done. Enlightened beings know that we are always the only ones who can and do assign meaning to things, events, people, and situations. We know that meaning is truthfully what we hold onto when we are stuck in the wound of needing to control our experience, to control Life, and to feel safe.

In Truth, there is no other meaning to Life than to Live, to be alive as our pure, authentic Self (our Soul), and joyfully dabbling in the magic of creation, which is the true magic of Earth. We are meant to learn how to be perfectly in flow with the energy of the Universe, so that we may listen to its guidance and act accordingly, to get where we want to be. Our human bodies are made to be sensitive to and receptive to energy. We project energy to communicate, which we have named emotions. As a species, we bond over shared emotions because they are truly shared energy. This is why when people go through traumatic events together, they come out the other side with a deepened connection, because they were bonded emotionally in the event. We understand and relate to one another through emotions. This is why we deem art worthy from our perspective, based solely on how it makes us feel. This is also why people will appreciate different things: because they have experienced different emotions regarding a specific topic.

Emotions are simply another navigational tool in the human experience. We connect with emotions when words cannot suffice. How can I claim that emotions are merely projected energy? By observing that when we are around happy people, their joy is contagious, and we want in on it. Have you ever found yourself laughing while having no idea what is going on or what is deemed funny? Being around a laughing person makes us want to laugh along because we want to be part of this specific choice of emotion. On the flip side, we tend to avoid being around a sad person because we do not wish to participate in their emotional experience, we do not want to feel their pain with them, because we tend to fear pain instead of simply accepting it for what it is: a normal part of life.

It takes truly strong and benevolent Souls to stand in pain with another without pressuring them to process faster or to move on already. The Truth is that these good and generous Souls usually come from pain themselves, and therefore have shed their fear of it. They understand the experience of pain as necessary for growth, and they know that all they can do to assist is to be present and to listen with the intent of hearing, not fixing. How can this be, that presence is all that is required for healing to occur, when words often fail at comforting? We tend to want to control with our words, to take away the pain instead of letting a person simply process through it. Presence offers that safe resting place for another to catch their breath and recover without pressure to "perform healing now." The greatest healing gift we can give and receive is presence, and the grace of listening in order to hear.

Often, when someone comes to us with their problems, we will seek to offer solutions or reassurances, when in Truth, what these people usually need is to be seen, heard, and accepted as they currently are. In my experience, saying to someone that things will get better with time never does anything to help, simply because the focus here is placed on the future when the person requires presence. We also live in cultures where very few people know how to just listen to hear. People tend to "listen" to argue their point further, which is ultimately useless in any attempt at communication. How can we expect to receive it if we do not offer the courtesy to hear and absorb before replying? And if we give this without receiving it in return, then what value is there to a one-sided "conversation"?

Part of the process of enlightenment is realizing that there is seldom something to fix in a problem actively; usually, all that is truly required is to change our perspective when things do not work out as we intended them to. To help another does not mean doing everything for them; it means encouraging and supporting them while figuring things out in a safe environment, around safe people, and this is true no matter the age of the individual in question. To believe only children need care and nurturing is not only sad, but deeply untrue. Trauma never magically disappears after a certain age because we ignore it. Trauma in all shapes, forms, and sizes needs to be processed and released, lest it stay stuck and stored within, where it will worsen over time through Life's cyclical attempts at healing—especially when those lessons are ignored repeatedly.

This is why the term awakening refers to becoming aware of our autopilot "dormant" programming, that we may transcend through them into the Truth of all that Life has to offer, which is so much more than current reality reflects and the structure it upholds. The slumber we are waking from can be summarized as becoming aware of the deep-rooted patterns of conditioning and mindless constant productivity that keep us living life busily, if not satisfactorily nor happily. The Truth is that Life was never meant to feel like slavery, where we toil endlessly with little to no rewards, where we are told to be satisfied with our lot and not ask for more, while also witnessing how some people are somehow just allowed to do nothing and get everything. There is a balance meant to be restored there, and that is part of why the global energy shift is so needed and coming.

We are restoring the Divine Feminine's rightful place in her balanced dance with the Divine Masculine, who's distorted energies created this bullshit in the first place by men trampling all over women in thousands of years of the same cycle repeating differently. There will never be progress if we do not embrace and appreciate both polarities of the same whole, the way they were meant to be, by both their respective strengths balancing out each other's weaknesses. We are entering an age of great change and transformation to restore unconditional love and respect to the sacred feminine after ages of masculine dominance and self-worship. This age will end with sacred masculine and feminine energies coming together in a healthy balance of *thriving together* in a system of symbiotic giving and receiving, mutual respect and appreciation for the other, and ultimately for all. It is up to the humans to do the work and focus solely on doing their part, which will trigger others into doing theirs.

Just like everything else in life, there is an internal and external portion to awakening. We tend to start with the outside world, by recognizing dysfunction and being unable to close our eyes to it any longer. What we see and recognize as dysfunction outside of ourselves can then be seen and recognized as internal dysfunction. The theme of the dysfunction will always be the same in both cases, although the details of how it presents may be different. Part of our "digging to get to the Truth" job is to get ourselves to understand how the internal dysfunction works to dismantle it from the inside, which will cause the external dysfunction to disappear entirely from our external reality, as there will be nothing calling it in vibrationally anymore.

Knowing that our goal as Souls is to achieve our highest potential, or, in other words, to become our best possible version of Self, it becomes imperative to face all of our truths, especially the unpleasant ones, to be rid of all that holds us back. To choose to keep our heads in the sand about our own shit equates to fear being the dictator of our life in our stead. Awakening is truly about returning to the natural currents of the world, to drop all of our masks that we may return to Truth, or a pure state of unfiltered, unbridled authenticity. It starts us on the journey of returning to pure presence from a place of mindless passivity.

Enlightenment is a process that can be summarized as taking off blindfold after blindfold against the Truth of our existence until all parts, facets, experiences, people, and any other important aspect of our lives have been given the opportunity to be seen and healed. The more we become aware of our unconscious passivity while also uncovering our inner workings and wounding, the more we step into enlightenment by choosing to heal and grow. Enlightenment is about embracing ourselves and the world until we are fully healed and ready to ascend.

Initial enlightenment will feel quite different from the late stages of enlightenment, which lead to ascension. There are big steps between bringing a facet of Life into view for the first time, understanding it fully, and then integrating it fully for the understanding to be embodied and active as part of our natural awareness. Understanding something cognitively is not the same as applying it consistently in our lives, so simply knowing does not bring about the anticipated change. Action does that for us. Inspired action means we will never be led astray and comes from listening to our inner senses and intuition. In essence, to become enlightened means to detach oneself from the regular, surface currents of Life, which we may observe, and utilize the underlying powerhouse currents of Truth hidden underneath.

From start to finish, the process of enlightenment teaches us how to completely detach from the physical world by surrendering to the flow, or will, of the Universe, to receive Truth and our promised blessings. No work ever goes unrewarded; although the rewards seldom look like what we want, they will always be what we need. Enlightenment is the choice to be struggle-free in a world that demands imprisonment and servitude of the Self to the powers that be. It is the conscious choice to enjoy life and all of its blessings and focus on what makes us feel good and happy while having the grace to deal with the hardships as they come, instead of refusing or ignoring them. We learn to accept the dualistic nature of life to transcend it into Oneness. Both sides of the same coin are truthfully one coin.

Enlightenment is learning to give ourselves the freedom just to be, devoid of overbearing attachments and pressures. Being on this path does not mean we never encounter hardships. It means we are better prepared and equipped to deal with them through learning the necessary tools, mindsets, understanding, and shift of perception required to detach and handle the problem without creating any unnecessary attachment to it, without taking anything personally. We choose to be in the energy of unconditional love for all while also choosing to protect ourselves from the ones still struggling to get to where we are.

In this light, enlightenment also takes up the mantle of being the process that eliminates self-betrayal from our list of potential actions and options. It is to realize that our fears are unfounded and that fear itself is simply one of our biggest challenges to overcome to re-integrate our Souls in our human bodies. We are meant to be detached from our physical, mental, and emotional bodies to access the information they're intended to give us—without attaching ourselves to or losing ourselves in them—so that we may align with our vibrational, or energetic, Truth. Remember that energy never lies. When we seek the Truth of Self, we will always find it within our energetic, vibrational Self, which is exactly why we have learned to be an impartial observer, to collect the necessary information from our external world to make sense of our internal one, that we may shift internally towards our highest good (Soul path) for our external reality to reflect that highest good back to us.

We are meant to realign our physical, emotional, and mental bodies within the energetic one, within the pure path of Truth and Light. We are learning to fully reclaim our personal power and how to use it to live the life of our dreams. We must acknowledge, accept, understand, and release the notion that we are nothing, that we are infinitely tiny and irrelevant in the grand scheme of things, to fully appreciate how we are simultaneously everything, massive and important in our own way. Understanding only one of these sides of the same coin means straying away from the whole picture, meaning straying away from the Truth of Oneness.

Since we live in a world of contrast, we are meant to experience the good and the bad to establish the *best* for our Souls. This happens through multiple lifetimes of learning and collecting experience as a living, physical being. Of course, this implies that our lives will always have hard experiences to go through, but the silver lining of understanding here is that we are never given more than we can handle, simply because our Soul's aim is never to break us beyond repair. We can be safe knowing that we are always meant to succeed when aligned with our highest good and the highest good of all. However, this means that we must find it in ourselves to do the necessary work to free ourselves.

One of the most important lessons we will learn on the path of ascending is how to transcend pain as an emotion. As Souls, we need to experience and understand suffering individually and heal from it to unlock or further develop empathy for all. We are here to end the tired cycle of "I suffered, so will you." This means that creating a thriving, happy, Soul-led world of existence for all to benefit and thrive in is not only possible, but the naturally intended progression of evolution: to turn surviving into thriving for all. To turn this world into a place of natural beauty and peace, where every single individual is nurtured and cared for, where we are all given the chance to live comfortably while fully embracing our natural state of creativity, where everyone is always seeking to bring more beauty and joy to life, always to keep improving societies and making the world a better place.

This is the intended goal for the human collective, but these choices have to be taken on an individual level. People have to choose to be worthy of receiving this. This is the split happening to Earth, the rapture that the religious texts speak of. The humans who embrace unconditional love and Oneness will be taken to a 5D world of experiencing things, while those who choose to stay small, unforgiving, and unloving will stay right in the 3D world where they are comfortable. The Divine never punishes those who do the work because of those who do not. The deserving will upgrade and experience living life in bliss; the ones who still have work to do, well, they still have work to do.

Returning to the concept of pain, our Souls need to be able to transcend pain and suffering individually before we can be strong and experienced enough to help out collectively. To transcend, as referred to here, means to want better for others and ourselves, simply because we have no wish for anyone to suffer (how actual good people tend to feel), despite having had the same experiences on a personal level or not. Having had the same experience or not is irrelevant to understanding pain and suffering. To turn experiencing pain into a competition of "who got more experience to be valid to speak of pain" is beyond stupid and useless. Pain is pain. Suffering is suffering. Sure, there are different levels of pain and suffering. Still, the True end goal is empathy, not comparison; therefore, losing ourselves in the Ego game of comparing the validity of other people's pain is to be obtuse and blinded by our Ego.

The very simple Truth is that everyone experiences pain, everybody will hurt at some point in their lives, and for an endless variety of reasons. It is simply another doorway into Universal connection and understanding, like love. Just like all emotions are, really. Remember that we bond over shared emotions in a way that bonding over words never happens unless the words are wrapped up in emotions, like in songs. Songs are relatable because they make us feel. Feelings are shared emotions. Feelings are the broad strokes of connectivity, while emotions are the pinpoints of accrued connectivity.

When we stop focusing on the individual specifics, we can start to see how *everything* is Universal. Heartbreak is Universal, regardless of whether it comes to us due to a loved one's passing, a breakup, a rejection, a bad grade, etc. All experiences are Universal, but the level at which our individual Souls signed up to experience them in this lifetime is a decision our Soul made before incarnation. Let's remember the principle of the Yin-Yang symbol here, to help illustrate and solidify this notion: what is true on a smaller scale is also true on a bigger scale. This means that pain is pain, no matter how much or how little we get to experience in our current lifetime. The exact same way that kindness is kindness, and we get to choose just how much of that we want to spread around us. In truth, we have the same choice to make when it comes to spreading pain, even when we do not realize it.

Every day, we get to make choices, and when we follow the intention of these choices, they can always be summarized into: do we choose to spread pain, or do we choose to spread joy? Do I want to make life easier, or do I want to make life harder? The answer always comes back to us, as the results of our choices are never separate from us. The choice is always made through the "for me *and* for all" lens. The principle of Oneness is meant to be understood here; how our individual self is the other side of the coin that holds all of humanity. There is no real distinction between ourselves and others in the Truth of Oneness. To hurt others is to hurt ourselves. To help others is to help ourselves. To betray others is to betray ourselves. To love ourselves is to love others. We are always presented the choice to be kind or to be an asshole, in every single choice we make. We reap what we sow, which is exactly how karma works, although it seldom is instant in its redistribution: it awaits the moment of most significant impact.

As we already know, enlightenment is the process of shedding layers of bullshit—layers of perceived limitations, self-judgment, internal and external pressure, defenses against showing the Truth of who we are to the world, the need to prove ourselves, the need to be right, and more. It can also be understood as the process of freeing ourselves in every possible way to achieve our highest potential. Gaining internal freedom to have that Truth reflected back to us in our external world. We are shedding all external attachments and internal blockages to simply be free to exist on our own terms, in our Truth.

The interesting thing to understand and keep in mind is that every time we shed a layer, there will always (and I do mean *always*) be a thin protective Ego layer covering the next one we are meant to work on. We will *always* fall for this Ego trap, because the Ego is our survival mechanism. Our Ego steps in to make sure we are ready to take on the next step. It does that by hiding the truth of the next layer from us so that we can figure it out by humbling ourselves. The only way to "vanquish" the Ego is through humility, and being humble is how we unlock the next step. This is why so many healers are stuck in their healing journeys: they grow arrogant in their "possession" of knowledge. We can never "possess" knowledge; to think we can is abysmally Egoic.

After liberating ourselves from a blockage, wound, or repressed emotion (in other words, having healed a part of ourselves), it is natural to feel high on life and to become able to see this particular challenge in others. The underlying Ego trap here is to assume that because we have done that specific healing on ourselves, we are therefore "above" the people who have not. This kind of holier-than-thou arrogance is rampant in the unhealed, as it goes against the very principle of Oneness that we are all equal and fundamentally the same. Many people will stay stuck in that Ego feeling of superiority because they are too afraid to face themselves and their Truth. Some are too desperate to feel special to recognize how truthfully special they are, as feeling and embodying are not the same.

Another important aspect to keep in mind is that when we start tapping into the Truth and might of our own personal power, we *can and do* get high or drunk off of that energy, which influences our Egos mightily. This is always a test to see if we can return to humility and Oneness. The simple Truth is that there will always be more healing, purging, or cleansing necessary until our body is light enough energetically that it becomes a vibrational match to our Soul energy. Embodiment of the Soul can only happen after we have first embodied our Divine Feminine and Divine Masculine essences 100%, and they are both fully healed and balanced. This can only happen when our seven main chakras are fully healed, balanced, and aligned. To embody our Soul, we have to be fully aligned with and live in Oneness in every possible way and in every possible manner.

We will know as Souls that this embodiment is happening when we are living life completely judgement free of ourselves, others, and the world at large, we are always in the energy of unconditional love for all, we respect all forms of life, we appreciate and learn from differences, we understand and have compassion for the unhealed and the unawakened without allowing them to compromise us in any way, and we always choose to do the right thing for the sake of it being the right thing to do. All of these will require no effort at all. Life will become effortless and simple, manifestation will be almost instantaneous, and we will always be in direct contact with Source and the infinite knowledge of both the Universe and Gaia. We become walking transmuters of heavy energies.

Life as an embodied Soul is one of constant peace, love, and joy within, regardless of external circumstances. There can be no worrying simply because we *live the embodied Truth* that the Universe always loves us unconditionally, supports us, and provides for us. We have learned to decipher the hidden messages of signs and synchronicities, we know how to activate our powerful inner feminine to attract all we need by working conjointly with the Universe, and how to activate our powerful inner masculine to figure out how to get where we want to go with the help, direction, and support of Gaia. We understand that our expanded feminine essence residing in the upper chakras meshes perfectly with the masculine essence of the Universe. In contrast, living in the lower chakras, our expanded masculine essence meshes perfectly with the Earth's feminine essence. We become the embodiment of "as above, so below."

We also know that the key to manifestation is the heart chakra, where all these beautiful energies meet and converge into a whole that allows for the energetic potential to transform into physical reality. This is where the meaning of the Yin-Yang symbol meets the laws of the Emerald Tablet—which say, "As above, so below. As within, so without. As the Universe, so the Soul. As it is, so be it."—fusing together to reveal their full, symbiotic meaning. Pairing this with the understanding that time does not exist means that at our fullest potential, we are an unstoppable force of creation. Knowing this, it becomes increasingly easy to understand why this journey is made to be very difficult, and True humility is key before giving anyone access to this kind of personal power. Great power comes with great responsibility. Therefore, irresponsible people shall never be granted great power.

To return to the principle that time is an illusion, we first need to understand that it was created to physically represent the passing of cycles. Because we learn through cycles of choices, we needed a physical representation of that internal Truth. Understanding this, we can comprehend how time represents all cycles through mathematics. A year is a cycle, a month is also a cycle, and so are weeks, days, hours, minutes, and even seconds. Stretching the Yin-Yang principle the other way means that any interval of time higher than a year is all their own cycles. Because we know the Truth about infinite possibilities, we understand that irregular time intervals are still their own cycles. Seven years can be a cycle; so can nine minutes. Numerology holds many answers and is part of our learning process, although its specific messages are not mine to share. To push matters further than this book covers, as Souls we understand that chaos is order, and order is chaos, and we know how to use and navigate both within the other.

The Truth about life on Earth is that we incarnate here to grow and evolve our Souls. Therefore, time was created for us to be able to measure our personal growth. Living as an embodied Soul means transcending the physical perceived limitations of time.

There is only ever Flow in our Soul journey, and our resisting and going against the Flow. Consequently, the less we resist our Soul callings, the easier life appears to become simply because we stop struggling against our Truth. Because we have free will, the choices we make are what is important in our journey. This means that continuously choosing resistance will burn us out energetically until we fall into a Dark Night of the Soul, which always happens for our highest good—to shake us up, free us from energetic clutter, and guide us back to our True Soul path and blessings.

Because of free will, we always get to choose to change our Self and behaviour into higher vibrational ones, or to remain in the exact same looping cycle, to repeat the same "mistakes" (aka choices), and to fall back into the same Dark Night of the Soul. The point is always to evolve and choose better for ourselves. To decide not to learn and consequently heal ourselves is to choose to repeat the same merry-go-round over and over again. Making the same choices while expecting different results is ludicrous. Our choice, summarized into Truth, is to choose between being/staying miserable and stuck, or to grow and be happy and free. One choice is always easier than the other, while the other will always be the worthwhile one; the easy choice is seldom the happy one.

What is important to remember is that progress can never be made if progress is never the choice being made. In the same way, we will never embody our Souls if working on becoming the best possible version of Self is never our choice. Embodying our Soul starts with first embodying the Truth of who we really are. We can never access the Truth hidden within if we never clear out, cleanse, and heal all traces of wounds, limitations, false beliefs, and other bullshit being carried in our energies.

Which finally brings us to the final levels of enlightenment and the beginnings of ascension. First, let us clarify here that being ascended in the physical world is to be in a state of *constant, pure, unconditional love for all,* at all times, in all ways. There is never an ounce of judgment to be found within an ascended being, towards no one, and no thing; there is only ever compassion and understanding. We have unlimited patience towards Self and others while maintaining unbreakable healthy boundaries to protect us from the unhealed. Yet, we will never attack another being in any way, shape, or form, as we understand that revenge only creates karma for us. We never use blame as we know it is worthless and a distraction from the Truth, we hold ourselves accountable in all ways, and we always choose to give love whenever we can to everyone.

Fear is nowhere to be seen in our lives, and never in our thought processes and decision-making. We recognize it instead as a valuable and valid emotion, from which we receive a needed message, and then we release it while remaining at peace. We know we do not need to hold onto an emotion for an extended amount of time to gain its intended clarity, especially if we are not having a good and fun time living in those emotions. All emotions are valuable, but it is up to us what we choose to focus on. Experiencing "negative" emotions is not something to resist, as resisting them usually makes things harder for ourselves. Shame, guilt, anger, sadness, and all "undesirable" emotions have value and are meant to teach us something, and as long as we refuse to experience the emotion, we cannot receive its message. Fear is what stops us, fear of experiencing pain being the most potent one.

Ascended beings accept pain and fear as just another facet of life, and do not let themselves get bogged down by experiencing an emotion. They never chase any emotion (not even the "highs"), they simply live and accept gracefully those that come along when they come along, without trying to force them to stay ("positive" emotions) or to leave ("negative" emotions). They are happy and comfortable just being and flowing. They take things in stride and are seldom bothered by the physical challenges, viewing them as an evolution instead of a punishment. They know punishment does not exist in Truth, only in Ego, because Karma balances the scales. We only ever reap what we sow. It is not up to us to do God's work, although we always defend the innocent and the pure.

Ascended beings always see the underlying currents of Truth and live their lives in accordance with what they feel is needed from them. We are attuned to the energies of both the Universe and the Earth and act as the bridge between both. We know that our perfectly calibrated and aligned lower chakras are masculine-energy dominant. In contrast, the upper chakras are feminine-energy dominant, with our Heart chakra being the meshing centerpiece of connection between them. We then understand that we are living, breathing, physical manifestations of Heart chakra pieces that act as the conduit for both the masculine-dominant energies of Father Sky and the feminine-dominant energies of Mother Earth into a being of infinite creation and manifestation potential. We are infinity made physical when ascended: the infinite fashioned into the finite.

As ascended human beings, we are unapologetically authentic in our Truth. We never dim our light and are never bothered by the idea we should "fit in"; on the contrary, we celebrate individuality, differences, and genuine overall uniqueness while also understanding that *we are* all of these facets in other people simultaneously as ourselves. We have transcended separation to only ever view Life through Oneness, simply because there is no other Truth, and this has become an undeniable way of life to us. We become sticklers for fairness, justice, and Truth, for doing the right thing and helping those in need, that we may all thrive and live happily while enjoying our time here.

In Truth, an ascended human being will never experience the need to have lower vibrational experiences, as all of their pain and suffering have already been handled and healed. An ascended being has transcended pain after all. They will never envy another or hoard resources while allowing others to starve; they are never selfish to the detriment of others or themselves. All situations that may have caused them to once act or react low-vibrationally will instead spark joy and celebration for the intended receiver, regardless of their personal relationship to them, because *an ascended being would only ever respond with cheer, kindness, and celebration for everyone and anyone's good fortune and success.* Ascended beings want what is good for everyone, not for the select few, nor can there be any kind of exception to this rule, and they understand that we all get what we deserve when we deserve to receive it.

As a physical pillar of unconditional love, ascended beings have surrendered completely to the flow of the Universe, guided by, and fully immersed in faith, trust, and hope. They never judge, as judgment is reserved for God, and therefore know that their only responsibility is to be Love in all ways. We do not get to judge anyone or anything in life simply because we are nowhere near seeing—and therefore much less understanding—the full picture, regardless of how many pieces of that puzzle we may possess. We know that to live life through the lens, everything happens for a reason because everything is intricately interconnected perfectly and in all ways. Coincidence does not exist; it is merely one more illusion of the human world and its lack of connection.

By choosing not to engage in the massive illusion that is current societal life, ascended beings will often be doing their own thing in this world, in their way, and on their own terms. They may appear happy-go-lucky in some form because they are free from attachments of all kinds. They easily recognize dysfunction and choose to remove themselves from the unnecessary drama that unhealed people crave. They never focus on problems, looking for solutions instead, as they innately know and understand that where we choose to place our focus is what we are asking to receive more of. They never get stuck in lamenting the present because they know they are the masters of their present moment and can always shape and make their reality what it will be. Ascended beings are constantly in alignment.

In essence, the end goal of enlightenment is softening the individual into their most potent personal power. We understand this is only possible through total and complete surrender of the individual Self into the collective connection and Truth of Oneness. This process can be summarized as removing all layers that keep us in denial of our personal Truth and power. Enlightenment can be viewed as the recalibration of a human being back into the fundamental basics of Life on Earth, that of duality and its mutually beneficial relationship nature. This is why our most potent recalibration tool is the breath and its own procedure of duality, of giving and receiving. The flow of intake and outtake of breath is the very key to understanding the intricately woven essence of duality, which we can physically see mirrored in the tides.

All processes found internally can be seen externally as well. This is the Truth of life. The constant ebb and flow of life, on repeat, forever. Chaos and order as one. Equilibrium of the motion of perpetual movement. As above, so below. 8. As within, so without ∞. As the Soul, so the Universe. O. As it is, so be it.

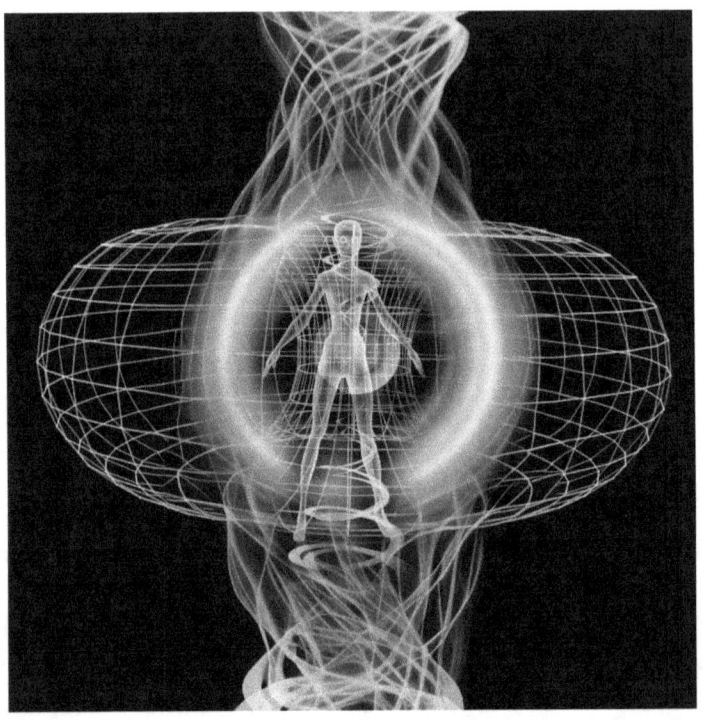

To achieve ascension in this lifetime means to completely forget about the Self while simultaneously embracing everything about our True Self. We forgo the Ego in favour of the Soul *as a way of life*. We allow ourselves to play with life and see challenges and obstacles as the shedding of the unnecessary layers, which ultimately redirects us to what we want to be experiencing. We know we can learn from all Life circumstances, and are grateful for it. There is no pretending within us, and there is no need to invest in what others tell us we should or should not be doing. We do what we need to do to be our best possible selves at all times. We embrace and encourage open, genuine authenticity and kindness as the only worthy way of living Life. We choose to embrace the purity of our Soul as our natural vibration and point of attraction, so that it may help others to heal and grow for themselves.

You Are Now the
Master of Your Own Life

———————— • ————————

Congratulations on completing your first run-through of this book! That you have chosen to read it all despite personal levels of understanding says much about your state of open-mindedness, in the best possible ways. You may now be thinking to yourself, "What now?" If you have learned from this book, then you know the answer lies within you, and you are the only one who can uncover it.

With the help of this book, you now possess plenty of tools and knowledge to keep you going on your own personal journey of healing. To heal is truly the greatest gift we can give ourselves. These chapters have been created with the intention that going through this book over and over again will always yield different results when we choose to do the associated work found within the pages. When our personal levels of understanding and healing grow, so too does the access to all of the knowledge contained within. Reading it a second time will be very different from reading it the first time, and all subsequent readings or simple referencing of singular chapters can and will yield more information to the eyes of the awakened.

Ideally, we return to this book when we have noticed our perception of Life has shifted, no matter how much or how little we perceive this shift to be. When we realize we start seeing things differently, it is most beneficial to return to these pages and their timeless knowledge, so that we may understand things on a deeper level. We can read a single sentence in an infinite number of perceptions, depending on which word we place emphasis upon. This means that when we become more enlightened in our journey, we will understand this book on a whole other level, and its teachings will communicate with us differently.

You are now capable of bringing consciousness to your everyday life and know what to do if you ever want to be able to shape reality to your desires. Ultimately, it is up to you what you choose to do with your life. No one can bring about change within it but you. No one can make this world a better place, but all of the individuals residing in it can. Our actions show our Truth. It is up to us what quality we want to assign to our Truth. Empty and vapid, or solid and worthwhile?

I carry in my heart the wish that this book will help change lives for the better. I hope it helps you with changing yours, just as following every step of every chapter (not necessarily in that order, to be fair) has granted me a Life I never would have dared to hope for, or even dream of, beforehand. To live is to dream, and we are meant to honour this. Allow yourself to be a conduit of Universal Unconditional Love, and watch as the people around you transform without your having to do anything about it. That is the power of energy. It affects us all, in all ways, at all times. It is up to us to become aware of its currents and to play with them.

As a final parting gift, I offer my thanks and gratitude to those who will help Mother Earth in her evolution. I bless all those who read these words who want better for themselves, others, and the world, and who choose not to be afraid, not to let fear dictate their lives. The courageous, those who evolve despite their fear, are the ones who will gain access to Heaven on Earth. I cannot wait to meet you and hope our paths will cross one day. I hope that through experiencing, healing, and learning from my pain, I may have made this process easier to comprehend and follow for all that will come after me.

Thank you for having the courage to face yourself and to choose Soul evolution over Ego. You are amazing. You are perfect. Love and celebrate yourself as you are becoming the best version of Self you can possibly be. Be grateful. Be authentic. Stand in your joy and power. Be who your Soul knows you to be, who you are in Truth.

Choose Love. Choose peace.

Choose Oneness.

ABOUT THE AUTHOR

 Sacha Rondeau is a psychic-intuitive, healer, and channeller. She is an ancient Soul returned to help heal the deepest wounds of humanity and restore balance in the world through sharing knowledge and wisdom.

CONNECT WITH THE AUTHOR

Email: Sacha.rondeau@gmail.com

Facebook.com/sacha.rondeau

Instagram.com/sacharondeau

www.sacharondeau.com

LEAVE A REVIEW

If you enjoyed reading *The Book of Love*, would you consider leaving a review on the platform of your choice? Reviews help indie-published authors find more readers like you.

www.ingramcontent.com/pod-product-compliance
Lightning Source LLC
Chambersburg PA
CBHW060123130626
46556CB00006B/2206